T0197980

Get the eBooks FREE!

(PDF, ePub, Kindle, and liveBook all included)

We believe that once you buy a book from us, you should be able to read it in any format we have available. To get electronic versions of this book at no additional cost to you, purchase and then register this book at the Manning website.

Go to https://www.manning.com/freebook and follow the instructions to complete your pBook registration.

That's it!
Thanks from Manning!

Microservices Patterns

Microservices Patterns

WITH EXAMPLES IN JAVA

CHRIS RICHARDSON

MANNING

SHELTER ISLAND

For online information and ordering of this and other Manning books, please visit
www.manning.com. The publisher offers discounts on this book when ordered in quantity.
For more information, please contact

> Special Sales Department
> Manning Publications Co.
> 20 Baldwin Road
> PO Box 761
> Shelter Island, NY 11964
> Email: orders@manning.com

Manning Publications Co.
20 Baldwin Road
PO Box 761
Shelter Island, NY 11964

Development editor:	Marina Michaels
Technical development editor:	Christian Mennerich
Review editor:	Aleksandar Dragosavljević
Project editor:	Lori Weidert
Copy editor:	Corbin Collins
Proofreader:	Alyson Brener
Technical proofreader:	Andy Miles
Typesetter:	Dennis Dalinnik
Cover designer:	Marija Tudor

ISBN: 9781617294549
Printed in the United States of America

Where you see wrong or inequality or injustice, speak out, because this is your country. This is your democracy. Make it. Protect it. Pass it on.

— Thurgood Marshall, Justice of the Supreme Court

brief contents

contents

preface

One of my favorite quotes is

The future is already here—it's just not very evenly distributed.

—William Gibson, science fiction author

The essence of that quote is that new ideas and technology take a while to diffuse through a community and become widely adopted. A good example of the slow diffusion of ideas is the story of how I discovered microservices. It began in 2006, when, after being inspired by a talk given by an AWS evangelist, I started down a path that ultimately led to my creating the original Cloud Foundry. (The only thing in common with today's Cloud Foundry is the name.) Cloud Foundry was a Platform-as-a-Service (PaaS) for automating the deployment of Java applications on EC2. Like every other enterprise Java application that I'd built, my Cloud Foundry had a monolith architecture consisting of a single Java Web Application Archive (WAR) file.

Bundling a diverse and complex set of functions such as provisioning, configuration, monitoring, and management into a monolith created both development and operations challenges. You couldn't, for example, change the UI without testing and redeploying the entire application. And because the monitoring and management component relied on a Complex Event Processing (CEP) engine which maintained in-memory state we couldn't run multiple instances of the application! That's embarrassing to admit, but all I can say is that I am a software developer, and, "let he who is without sin cast the first stone."

Clearly, the application had quickly outgrown its monolith architecture, but what was the alternative? The answer had been out in the software community for some time at companies such as eBay and Amazon. Amazon had, for example, started to migrate away from the monolith around 2002 (https://plus.google.com/110981030061712822816/posts/AaygmbzVeRq). The new architecture replaced the monolith with a collection of loosely coupled services. Services are owned by what Amazon calls two-pizza teams—teams small enough to be fed by two pizzas.

Amazon had adopted this architecture to accelerate the rate of software development so that the company could innovate faster and compete more effectively. The results are impressive: Amazon reportedly deploys changes into production every 11.6 seconds!

In early 2010, after I'd moved on to other projects, the future of software architecture finally caught up with me. That's when I read the book *The Art of Scalability: Scalable Web Architecture, Processes, and Organizations for the Modern Enterprise* (Addison-Wesley Professional, 2009) by Michael T. Fisher and Martin L. Abbott. A key idea in that book is the scale cube, which, as described in chapter 2, is a three-dimensional model for scaling an application. The Y-axis scaling defined by the scale cube functionally decomposes an application into services. In hindsight, this was quite obvious, but for me at the time, it was an a-ha moment! I could have solved the challenges I was facing two years earlier by architecting Cloud Foundry as a set of services!

In April 2012, I gave my first talk on this architectural approach, called "Decomposing Applications of Deployability and Scalability" (www.slideshare.net/chris.e.richardson/decomposing-applications-for-scalability-and-deployability-april-2012). At the time, there wasn't a generally accepted term for this kind of architecture. I sometimes called it modular, polyglot architecture, because the services could be written in different languages.

But in another example of how the future is unevenly distributed, the term *microservice* was used at a software architecture workshop in 2011 to describe this kind of architecture (https://en.wikipedia.org/wiki/Microservices). I first encountered the term when I heard Fred George give a talk at Oredev 2013, and I liked it!

In January 2014, I created the https://microservices.io website to document architecture and design patterns that I had encountered. Then in March 2014, James Lewis and Martin Fowler published a blog post about microservices (https://martinfowler.com/articles/microservices.html). By popularizing the term microservices, the blog post caused the software community to consolidate around the concept.

The idea of small, loosely coupled teams, rapidly and reliably developing and delivering microservices is slowly diffusing through the software community. But it's likely that this vision of the future is quite different from your daily reality. Today, business-critical enterprise applications are typically large monoliths developed by large teams. Software releases occur infrequently and are often painful for everyone involved. IT often struggles to keep up with the needs of the business. You're wondering how on earth you can adopt the microservice architecture.

The goal of this book is to answer that question. It will give you a good understanding of the microservice architecture, its benefits and drawbacks, and when to use it. The book describes how to solve the numerous design challenges you'll face, including how to manage distributed data. It also covers how to refactor a monolithic application to a microservice architecture. But this book is not a microservices manifesto. Instead, it's organized around a collection of patterns. A pattern is a reusable solution to a problem that occurs in a particular context. The beauty of a pattern is that besides describing the benefits of the solution, it also describes the drawbacks and the issues you must address in order to successfully implement a solution. In my experience, this kind of objectivity when thinking about solutions leads to much better decision making. I hope you'll enjoy reading this book and that it teaches you how to successfully develop microservices.

acknowledgments

Although writing is a solitary activity, it takes a large number of people to turn rough drafts into a finished book.

First, I want to thank Erin Twohey and Michael Stevens from Manning for their persistent encouragement to write another book. I would also like to thank my development editors, Cynthia Kane and Marina Michaels. Cynthia Kane got me started and worked with me on the first few chapters. Marina Michaels took over from Cynthia and worked with me to the end. I'll be forever grateful for Marina's meticulous and constructive critiques of my chapters. And I want to thank the rest of the Manning team who's been involved in getting this book published.

I'd like to thank my technical development editor, Christian Mennerich, my technical proofreader, Andy Miles, and all my external reviewers: Andy Kirsch, Antonio Pessolano, Areg Melik-Adamyan, Cage Slagel, Carlos Curotto, Dror Helper, Eros Pedrini, Hugo Cruz, Irina Romanenko, Jesse Rosalia, Joe Justesen, John Guthrie, Keerthi Shetty, Michele Mauro, Paul Grebenc, Pethuru Raj, Potito Coluccelli, Shobha Iyer, Simeon Leyzerzon, Srihari Sridharan, Tim Moore, Tony Sweets, Trent Whiteley, Wes Shaddix, William E. Wheeler, and Zoltan Hamori.

I also want to thank everyone who purchased the MEAP and provided feedback in the forum or to me directly.

I want to thank the organizers and attendees of all of the conferences and meetups at which I've spoken for the chance to present and revise my ideas. And I want to thank my consulting and training clients around the world for giving me the opportunity to help them put my ideas into practice.

I want to thank my colleagues Andrew, Valentin, Artem, and Stanislav at Eventuate, Inc., for their contributions to the Eventuate product and open source projects.

Finally, I'd like to thank my wife, Laura, and my children, Ellie, Thomas, and Janet for their support and understanding over the last 18 months. While I've been glued to my laptop, I've missed out on going to Ellie's soccer games, watching Thomas learning to fly on his flight simulator, and trying new restaurants with Janet.

Thank you all!

about this book

The goal of this book is to teach you how to successfully develop applications using the microservice architecture.

Not only does it discuss the benefits of the microservice architecture, it also describes the drawbacks. You'll learn when you should consider using the monolithic architecture and when it makes sense to use microservices.

Who should read this book

The focus of this book is on architecture and development. It's meant for anyone responsible for developing and delivering software, such as developers, architects, CTOs, or VPs of engineering.

The book focuses on explaining the microservice architecture patterns and other concepts. My goal is for you to find this material accessible, regardless of the technology stack you use. You only need to be familiar with the basics of enterprise application architecture and design. In particular, you need to understand concepts like three-tier architecture, web application design, relational databases, interprocess communication using messaging and REST, and the basics of application security. The code examples, though, use Java and the Spring framework. In order to get the most out of them, you should be familiar with the Spring framework.

Roadmap

This book consists of 13 chapters:

- Chapter 1 describes the symptoms of monolithic hell, which occurs when a monolithic application outgrows its architecture, and advises on how to escape by adopting the microservice architecture. It also provides an overview of the microservice architecture pattern language, which is the organizing theme for most of the book.

- Chapter 2 explains why software architecture is important and describes the patterns you can use to decompose an application into a collection of services. It also explains how to overcome the various obstacles you typically encounter along the way.

- Chapter 3 describes the different patterns for robust, interprocess communication in a microservice architecture. It explains why asynchronous, message-based communication is often the best choice.

- Chapter 4 explains how to maintain data consistency across services by using the Saga pattern. A saga is a sequence of local transactions coordinated using asynchronous messaging.

- Chapter 5 describes how to design the business logic for a service using the domain-driven design (DDD) Aggregate and Domain event patterns.

- Chapter 6 builds on chapter 5 and explains how to develop business logic using the Event sourcing pattern, an event-centric way to structure the business logic and persist domain objects.

- Chapter 7 describes how to implement queries that retrieve data scattered across multiple services by using either the API composition pattern or the Command query responsibility segregation (CQRS) pattern.

- Chapter 8 covers the external API patterns for handling requests from a diverse collection of external clients, such as mobile applications, browser-based Java-Script applications, and third-party applications.

- Chapter 9 is the first of two chapters on automated testing techniques for micro-services. It introduces important testing concepts such as the test pyramid, which describes the relative proportions of each type of test in your test suite. It also shows how to write unit tests, which form the base of the testing pyramid.

- Chapter 10 builds on chapter 9 and describes how to write other types of tests in the test pyramid, including integration tests, consumer contract tests, and component tests.

- Chapter 11 covers various aspects of developing production-ready services, including security, the Externalized configuration pattern, and the service observability patterns. The service observability patterns include Log aggregation, Application metrics, and Distributed tracing.

- Chapter 12 describes the various deployment patterns that you can use to deploy services, including virtual machines, containers, and serverless. It also discusses the benefits of using a service mesh, a layer of networking software that mediates communication in a microservice architecture.

- Chapter 13 explains how to incrementally refactor a monolithic architecture to a microservice architecture by applying the Strangler application pattern: implementing new features as services and extracting modules out of the monolith and converting them to services.

As you progress through these chapters, you'll learn about different aspects of the microservice architecture.

About the code

This book contains many examples of source code both in numbered listings and inline with normal text. In both cases, source code is formatted in a `fixed-width font like this` to separate it from ordinary text. Sometimes code is also **in bold** to highlight code that has changed from previous steps in the chapter, such as when a new feature adds to an existing line of code. In many cases, the original source code has been reformatted; the publisher has added line breaks and reworked indentation to accommodate the available page space in the book. In rare cases, even this was not enough, and listings include line-continuation markers (➥). Additionally, comments in the source code have often been removed from the listings when the code is described in the text. Code annotations accompany many of the listings, highlighting important concepts.

Every chapter, except chapters 1, 2, and 13, contains code from the companion example application. You can find the code for this application in a GitHub repository: https://github.com/microservices-patterns/ftgo-application.

Book forum

The purchase of Microservices Patterns includes free access to a private web forum run by Manning Publications where you can make comments about the book, ask technical questions, share your solutions to exercises, and receive help from the author and from other users. To access the forum and subscribe to it, point your web browser to https://forums.manning.com/forums/microservices-patterns. You can also learn more about Manning's forums and the rules of conduct at https://forums.manning.com/forums/about.

Manning's commitment to our readers is to provide a venue where a meaningful dialogue between individual readers and between readers and the author can take place. It's not a commitment to any specific amount of participation on the part of the author, whose contribution to the forum remains voluntary (and unpaid). We suggest you try asking the author some challenging questions lest his interest stray! The forum and the archives of previous discussions will be accessible from the publisher's website as long as the book is in print.

Other online resources

Another great resource for learning the microservice architecture is my website http:// microservices.io.

Not only does it contain the complete pattern language, it also has links to other resources such as articles, presentations, and example code.

About the author

Chris Richardson is a developer and architect. He is a Java Champion, a JavaOne rock star, and the author of *POJOs in Action* (Manning, 2006), which describes how to build enterprise Java applications with frameworks such as Spring and Hibernate.

Chris was also the founder of the original CloudFoundry.com, an early Java PaaS for Amazon EC2.

Today, he is a recognized thought leader in microservices and speaks regularly at international conferences. Chris is the creator of Microservices.io, a pattern language for microservices. He provides microservices consulting and training to organizations around the world that are adopting the microservice architecture. Chris is working on his third startup: Eventuate.io, an application platform for developing transactional microservices.

about the cover illustration

Jefferys

The figure on the cover of Microservices Patterns is captioned "Habit of a Morisco Slave in 1568." The illustration is taken from Thomas Jefferys' *A Collection of the Dresses of Different Nations, Ancient and Modern* (four volumes), London, published between 1757 and 1772. The title page states that these are hand-colored copperplate engravings, heightened with gum arabic.

Thomas Jefferys (1719–1771) was called "Geographer to King George III." He was an English cartographer who was the leading map supplier of his day. He engraved and printed maps for government and other official bodies and produced a wide range of commercial maps and atlases, especially of North America. His work as a map maker sparked an interest in local dress customs of the lands he surveyed and mapped, which are brilliantly displayed in this collection. Fascination with faraway lands and travel for pleasure were relatively new phenomena in the late 18th century, and collections such as this one were popular, introducing both the tourist as well as the armchair traveler to the inhabitants of other countries.

The diversity of the drawings in Jefferys' volumes speaks vividly of the uniqueness and individuality of the world's nations some 200 years ago. Dress codes have changed since then, and the diversity by region and country, so rich at the time, has faded away. It's now often hard to tell the inhabitants of one continent from another. Perhaps, trying to view it optimistically, we've traded a cultural and visual diversity for a more varied personal life—or a more varied and interesting intellectual and technical life.

At a time when it's difficult to tell one computer book from another, Manning cel-
ebrates the inventiveness and initiative of the computer business with book covers
based on the rich diversity of regional life of two centuries ago, brought back to life by
Jeffreys' pictures.

Escaping monolithic hell

This chapter covers

- The symptoms of monolithic hell and how to escape it by adopting the microservice architecture
- The essential characteristics of the microservice architecture and its benefits and drawbacks
- How microservices enable the DevOps style of development of large, complex applications
- The microservice architecture pattern language and why you should use it

It was only Monday lunchtime, but Mary, the CTO of Food to Go, Inc. (FTGO), was already feeling frustrated. Her day had started off really well. She had spent the previous week with other software architects and developers at an excellent conference learning about the latest software development techniques, including continuous deployment and the microservice architecture. Mary had also met up with her former computer science classmates from North Carolina A&T State and shared technology leadership war stories. The conference had left her feeling empowered and eager to improve how FTGO develops software.

1

Unfortunately, that feeling had quickly evaporated. She had just spent the first morning back in the office in yet another painful meeting with senior engineering and business people. They had spent two hours discussing why the development team was going to miss another critical release date. Sadly, this kind of meeting had become increasingly common over the past few years. Despite adopting agile, the pace of development was slowing down, making it next to impossible to meet the business's goals. And, to make matters worse, there didn't seem to be a simple solution.

The conference had made Mary realize that FTGO was suffering from a case of *monolithic hell* and that the cure was to adopt the microservice architecture. But the microservice architecture and the associated state-of-the-art software development practices described at the conference felt like an elusive dream. It was unclear to Mary how she could fight today's fires while simultaneously improving the way software was developed at FTGO.

Fortunately, as you will learn in this book, there is a way. But first, let's look at the problems that FTGO is facing and how they got there.

1.1 *The slow march toward monolithic hell*

Since its launch in late 2005, FTGO had grown by leaps and bounds. Today, it's one of the leading online food delivery companies in the United States. The business even plans to expand overseas, although those plans are in jeopardy because of delays in implementing the necessary features.

At its core, the FTGO application is quite simple. Consumers use the FTGO website or mobile application to place food orders at local restaurants. FTGO coordinates a network of couriers who deliver the orders. It's also responsible for paying couriers and restaurants. Restaurants use the FTGO website to edit their menus and manage orders. The application uses various web services, including Stripe for payments, Twilio for messaging, and Amazon Simple Email Service (SES) for email.

Like many other aging enterprise applications, the FTGO application is a monolith, consisting of a single Java Web Application Archive (WAR) file. Over the years, it has become a large, complex application. Despite the best efforts of the FTGO development team, it's become an example of the Big Ball of Mud pattern (www.laputan .org/mud/). To quote Foote and Yoder, the authors of that pattern, it's a "haphazardly structured, sprawling, sloppy, duct-tape and bailing wire, spaghetti code jungle." The pace of software delivery has slowed. To make matters worse, the FTGO application has been written using some increasingly obsolete frameworks. The FTGO application is exhibiting all the symptoms of monolithic hell.

The next section describes the architecture of the FTGO application. Then it talks about why the monolithic architecture worked well initially. We'll get into how the FTGO application has outgrown its architecture and how that has resulted in monolithic hell.

1.1.1 The architecture of the FTGO application

FTGO is a typical enterprise Java application. Figure 1.1 shows its architecture. The FTGO application has a hexagonal architecture, which is an architectural style described in more detail in chapter 2. In a hexagonal architecture, the core of the application consists of the business logic. Surrounding the business logic are various adapters that implement UIs and integrate with external systems.

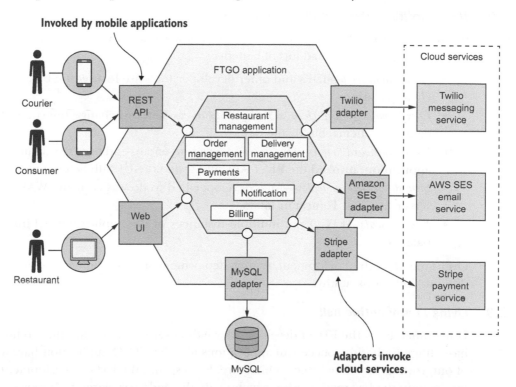

Figure 1.1   The FTGO application has a hexagonal architecture. It consists of business logic surrounded by adapters that implement UIs and interface with external systems, such as mobile applications and cloud services for payments, messaging, and email.

The business logic consists of modules, each of which is a collection of domain objects. Examples of the modules include `Order Management`, `Delivery Management`, `Billing`, and `Payments`. There are several adapters that interface with the external systems. Some are *inbound* adapters, which handle requests by invoking the business logic, including the `REST API` and `Web UI` adapters. Others are *outbound* adapters, which enable the business logic to access the MySQL database and invoke cloud services such as Twilio and Stripe.

Despite having a logically modular architecture, the FTGO application is packaged as a single WAR file. The application is an example of the widely used *monolithic* style of software architecture, which structures a system as a single executable or deployable component. If the FTGO application were written in the Go language (GoLang), it would be a single executable. A Ruby or NodeJS version of the application would be a single directory hierarchy of source code. The monolithic architecture isn't inherently bad. The FTGO developers made a good decision when they picked monolithic architecture for their application.

1.1.2   The benefits of the monolithic architecture

In the early days of FTGO, when the application was relatively small, the application's monolithic architecture had lots of benefits:

- *Simple to develop*—IDEs and other developer tools are focused on building a single application.
- *Easy to make radical changes to the application*—You can change the code and the database schema, build, and deploy.
- *Straightforward to test*—The developers wrote end-to-end tests that launched the application, invoked the REST API, and tested the UI with Selenium.
- *Straightforward to deploy*—All a developer had to do was copy the WAR file to a server that had Tomcat installed.
- *Easy to scale*—FTGO ran multiple instances of the application behind a load balancer.

Over time, though, development, testing, deployment, and scaling became much more difficult. Let's look at why.

1.1.3   Living in monolithic hell

Unfortunately, as the FTGO developers have discovered, the monolithic architecture has a huge limitation. Successful applications like the FTGO application have a habit of outgrowing the monolithic architecture. Each sprint, the FTGO development team implemented a few more stories, which made the code base larger. Moreover, as the company became more successful, the size of the development team steadily grew. Not only did this increase the growth rate of the code base, it also increased the management overhead.

As figure 1.2 shows, the once small, simple FTGO application has grown over the years into a monstrous monolith. Similarly, the small development team has now become multiple Scrum teams, each of which works on a particular functional area. As a result of outgrowing its architecture, FTGO is in monolithic hell. Development is slow and painful. Agile development and deployment is impossible. Let's look at why this has happened.

COMPLEXITY INTIMIDATES DEVELOPERS

A major problem with the FTGO application is that it's too complex. It's too large for any developer to fully understand. As a result, fixing bugs and correctly implementing new features have become difficult and time consuming. Deadlines are missed.

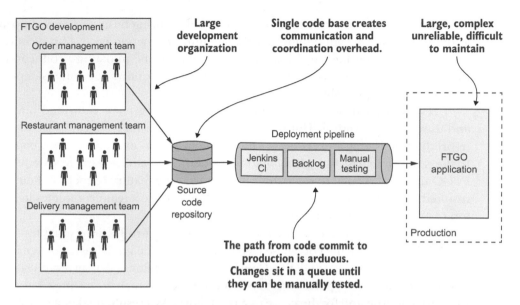

Figure 1.2   A case of monolithic hell. The large FTGO developer team commits their changes to a single source code repository. The path from code commit to production is long and arduous and involves manual testing. The FTGO application is large, complex, unreliable, and difficult to maintain.

To make matters worse, this overwhelming complexity tends to be a downward spiral. If the code base is difficult to understand, a developer won't make changes correctly. Each change makes the code base incrementally more complex and harder to understand. The clean, modular architecture shown earlier in figure 1.1 docsn't reflect reality. FTGO is gradually becoming a monstrous, incomprehensible, big ball of mud.

Mary remembers recently attending a conference where she met a developer who was writing a tool to analyze the dependencies between the thousands of JARs in their multimillion lines-of-code (LOC) application. At the time, that tool seemed like something FTGO could use. Now she's not so sure. Mary suspects a better approach is to migrate to an architecture that is better suited to a complex application: microservices.

DEVELOPMENT IS SLOW
As well as having to fight overwhelming complexity, FTGO developers find day-to-day development tasks slow. The large application overloads and slows down a developer's IDE. Building the FTGO application takes a long time. Moreover, because it's so large, the application takes a long time to start up. As a result, the edit-build-run-test loop takes a long time, which badly impacts productivity.

PATH FROM COMMIT TO DEPLOYMENT IS LONG AND ARDUOUS
Another problem with the FTGO application is that deploying changes into production is a long and painful process. The team typically deploys updates to production once a month, usually late on a Friday or Saturday night. Mary keeps reading that the state-of-the-art for Software-as-a-Service (SaaS) applications is *continuous deployment*:

deploying changes to production many times a day during business hours. Apparently, as of 2011, Amazon.com deployed a change into production every 11.6 seconds without ever impacting the user! For the FTGO developers, updating production more than once a month seems like a distant dream. And adopting continuous deployment seems next to impossible.

FTGO has partially adopted agile. The engineering team is divided into squads and uses two-week sprints. Unfortunately, the journey from code complete to running in production is long and arduous. One problem with so many developers committing to the same code base is that the build is frequently in an unreleasable state. When the FTGO developers tried to solve this problem by using feature branches, their attempt resulted in lengthy, painful merges. Consequently, once a team completes its sprint, a long period of testing and code stabilization follows.

Another reason it takes so long to get changes into production is that testing takes a long time. Because the code base is so complex and the impact of a change isn't well understood, developers and the Continuous Integration (CI) server must run the entire test suite. Some parts of the system even require manual testing. It also takes a while to diagnose and fix the cause of a test failure. As a result, it takes a couple of days to complete a testing cycle.

SCALING IS DIFFICULT

The FTGO team also has problems scaling its application. That's because different application modules have conflicting resource requirements. The restaurant data, for example, is stored in a large, in-memory database, which is ideally deployed on servers with lots of memory. In contrast, the image processing module is CPU intensive and best deployed on servers with lots of CPU. Because these modules are part of the same application, FTGO must compromise on the server configuration.

DELIVERING A RELIABLE MONOLITH IS CHALLENGING

Another problem with the FTGO application is the lack of reliability. As a result, there are frequent production outages. One reason it's unreliable is that testing the application thoroughly is difficult, due to its large size. This lack of testability means bugs make their way into production. To make matters worse, the application lacks *fault isolation*, because all modules are running within the same process. Every so often, a bug in one module—for example, a memory leak—crashes all instances of the application, one by one. The FTGO developers don't enjoy being paged in the middle of the night because of a production outage. The business people like the loss of revenue and trust even less.

LOCKED INTO INCREASINGLY OBSOLETE TECHNOLOGY STACK

The final aspect of monolithic hell experienced by the FTGO team is that the architecture forces them to use a technology stack that's becoming increasingly obsolete. The monolithic architecture makes it difficult to adopt new frameworks and languages. It would be extremely expensive and risky to rewrite the entire monolithic application so that it would use a new and presumably better technology. Consequently, developers are stuck with the technology choices they made at the start of the project. Quite often, they must maintain an application written using an increasingly obsolete technology stack.

The Spring framework has continued to evolve while being backward compatible, so in theory FTGO might have been able to upgrade. Unfortunately, the FTGO application uses versions of frameworks that are incompatible with newer versions of Spring. The development team has never found the time to upgrade those frameworks. As a result, major parts of the application are written using increasingly out-of-date frameworks. What's more, the FTGO developers would like to experiment with non-JVM languages such as GoLang and NodeJS. Sadly, that's not possible with a monolithic application.

1.2 Why this book is relevant to you

It's likely that you're a developer, architect, CTO, or VP of engineering. You're responsible for an application that has outgrown its monolithic architecture. Like Mary at FTGO, you're struggling with software delivery and want to know how to escape monolith hell. Or perhaps you fear that your organization is on the path to monolithic hell and you want to know how to change direction before it's too late. If you need to escape or avoid monolithic hell, this is the book for you.

This book spends a lot of time explaining microservice architecture concepts. My goal is for you to find this material accessible, regardless of the technology stack you use. All you need is to be familiar with the basics of enterprise application architecture and design. In particular, you need to know the following:

- Three-tier architecture
- Web application design
- How to develop business logic using object-oriented design
- How to use an RDBMS: SQL and ACID transactions
- How to use interprocess communication using a message broker and REST APIs
- Security, including authentication and authorization

The code examples in this book are written using Java and the Spring framework. That means in order to get the most out of the examples, you need to be familiar with the Spring framework too.

1.3 What you'll learn in this book

By the time you finish reading this book you'll understand the following:

- The essential characteristics of the microservice architecture, its benefits and drawbacks, and when to use it
- Distributed data management patterns
- Effective microservice testing strategies
- Deployment options for microservices
- Strategies for refactoring a monolithic application into a microservice architecture

You'll also be able to do the following:

- Architect an application using the microservice architecture pattern
- Develop the business logic for a service
- Use sagas to maintain data consistency across services
- Implement queries that span services
- Effectively test microservices
- Develop production-ready services that are secure, configurable, and observable
- Refactor an existing monolithic application to services

1.4   *Microservice architecture to the rescue*

Mary has come to the conclusion that FTGO must migrate to the microservice architecture.

Interestingly, software architecture has very little to do with functional requirements. You can implement a set of *use cases*—an application's functional requirements—with any architecture. In fact, it's common for successful applications, such as the FTGO application, to be big balls of mud.

Architecture matters, however, because of how it affects the so-called *quality of service* requirements, also called *nonfunctional requirements*, *quality attributes*, or *ilities*. As the FTGO application has grown, various quality attributes have suffered, most notably those that impact the velocity of software delivery: maintainability, extensibility, and testability.

On the one hand, a disciplined team can slow down the pace of its descent toward monolithic hell. Team members can work hard to maintain the modularity of their application. They can write comprehensive automated tests. On the other hand, they can't avoid the issues of a large team working on a single monolithic application. Nor can they solve the problem of an increasingly obsolete technology stack. The best a team can do is delay the inevitable. To escape monolithic hell, they must migrate to a new architecture: the Microservice architecture.

Today, the growing consensus is that if you're building a large, complex application, you should consider using the microservice architecture. But what are *microservices* exactly? Unfortunately, the name doesn't help because it overemphasizes size. There are numerous definitions of the microservice architecture. Some take the name too literally and claim that a service should be tiny—for example, 100 LOC. Others claim that a service should only take two weeks to develop. Adrian Cockcroft, formerly of Netflix, defines a microservice architecture as a service-oriented architecture composed of loosely coupled elements that have bounded contexts. That's not a bad definition, but it is a little dense. Let's see if we can do better.

1.4.1   *Scale cube and microservices*

My definition of the microservice architecture is inspired by Martin Abbott and Michael Fisher's excellent book, *The Art of Scalability* (Addison-Wesley, 2015). This book describes a useful, three-dimensional scalability model: the *scale cube*, shown in figure 1.3.

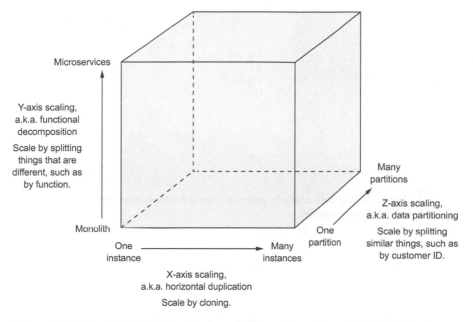

Figure 1.3 **The scale cube defines three separate ways to scale an application: X-axis scaling load balances requests across multiple, identical instances; Z-axis scaling routes requests based on an attribute of the request; Y-axis functionally decomposes an application into services.**

The model defines three ways to scale an application: X, Y, and Z.

X-AXIS SCALING LOAD BALANCES REQUESTS ACROSS MULTIPLE INSTANCES

X-axis scaling is a common way to scale a monolithic application. Figure 1.4 shows how X-axis scaling works. You run multiple instances of the application behind a load balancer. The load balancer distributes requests among the *N* identical instances of the application. This is a great way of improving the capacity and availability of an application.

Z-AXIS SCALING ROUTES REQUESTS BASED ON AN ATTRIBUTE OF THE REQUEST

Z-axis scaling also runs multiple instances of the monolith application, but unlike X-axis scaling, each instance is responsible for only a subset of the data. Figure 1.5 shows how Z-axis scaling works. The router in front of the instances uses a request attribute to route it to the appropriate instance. An application might, for example, route requests using userId.

In this example, each application instance is responsible for a subset of users. The router uses the userId specified by the request Authorization header to select one of

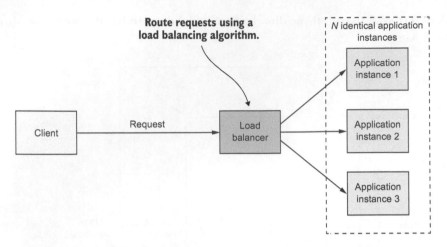

Figure 1.4   X-axis scaling runs multiple, identical instances of the monolithic application behind a load balancer.

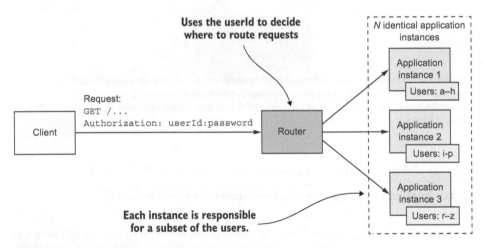

Figure 1.5   Z-axis scaling runs multiple identical instances of the monolithic application behind a router, which routes based on a `request` attribute . Each instance is responsible for a subset of the data.

the *N* identical instances of the application. Z-axis scaling is a great way to scale an application to handle increasing transaction and data volumes.

Y-AXIS SCALING FUNCTIONALLY DECOMPOSES AN APPLICATION INTO SERVICES

X- and Z-axis scaling improve the application's capacity and availability. But neither approach solves the problem of increasing development and application complexity. To solve those, you need to apply *Y-axis* scaling, or *functional decomposition*. Figure 1.6 shows how Y-axis scaling works: by splitting a monolithic application into a set of services.

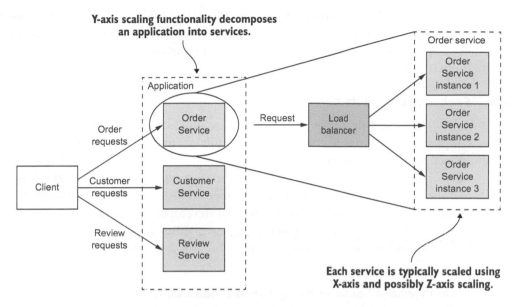

Figure 1.6 **Y-axis scaling splits the application into a set of services. Each service is responsible for a particular function. A service is scaled using X-axis scaling and, possibly, Z-axis scaling.**

A *service* is a mini application that implements narrowly focused functionality, such as order management, customer management, and so on. A service is scaled using X-axis scaling, though some services may also use Z-axis scaling. For example, the Order service consists of a set of load-balanced service instances.

The high-level definition of microservice architecture (microservices) is an architectural style that functionally decomposes an application into a set of services. Note that this definition doesn't say anything about size. Instead, what matters is that each service has a focused, cohesive set of responsibilities. Later in the book I discuss what that means.

Now let's look at how the microservice architecture is a form of modularity.

1.4.2 *Microservices as a form of modularity*

Modularity is essential when developing large, complex applications. A modern application like FTGO is too large to be developed by an individual. It's also too complex to be understood by a single person. Applications must be decomposed into modules that are developed and understood by different people. In a monolithic application, modules are defined using a combination of programming language constructs (such as Java packages) and build artifacts (such as Java JAR files). However, as the FTGO developers have discovered, this approach tends not to work well in practice. Long-lived, monolithic applications usually degenerate into big balls of mud.

The microservice architecture uses services as the unit of modularity. A service has an API, which is an impermeable boundary that is difficult to violate. You can't bypass the API and access an internal class as you can with a Java package. As a result, it's much easier to preserve the modularity of the application over time. There are other benefits of using services as building blocks, including the ability to deploy and scale them independently.

1.4.3   *Each service has its own database*

A key characteristic of the microservice architecture is that the services are loosely coupled and communicate only via APIs. One way to achieve loose coupling is by each service having its own datastore. In the online store, for example, `Order Service` has a database that includes the `ORDERS` table, and `Customer Service` has its database, which includes the `CUSTOMERS` table. At development time, developers can change a service's schema without having to coordinate with developers working on other services. At runtime, the services are isolated from each other—for example, one service will never be blocked because another service holds a database lock.

> **Don't worry: Loose coupling doesn't make Larry Ellison richer**
>
> The requirement for each service to have its own database doesn't mean it has its own database server. You don't, for example, have to spend 10 times more on Oracle RDBMS licenses. Chapter 2 explores this topic in depth.

Now that we've defined the microservice architecture and described some of its essential characteristics, let's look at how this applies to the FTGO application.

1.4.4   *The FTGO microservice architecture*

The rest of this book discusses the FTGO application's microservice architecture in depth. But first let's quickly look at what it means to apply Y-axis scaling to this application. If we apply Y-axis decomposition to the FTGO application, we get the architecture shown in figure 1.7. The decomposed application consists of numerous frontend and backend services. We would also apply X-axis and, possibly Z-axis scaling, so that at runtime there would be multiple instances of each service.

The frontend services include an API gateway and the Restaurant Web UI. The API gateway, which plays the role of a facade and is described in detail in chapter 8, provides the REST APIs that are used by the consumers' and couriers' mobile applications. The Restaurant Web UI implements the web interface that's used by the restaurants to manage menus and process orders.

The FTGO application's business logic consists of numerous backend services. Each backend service has a REST API and its own private datastore. The backend services include the following:

- `Order Service`—Manages orders
- `Delivery Service`—Manages delivery of orders from restaurants to consumers

- `Restaurant Service`—Maintains information about restaurants
- `Kitchen Service`—Manages the preparation of orders
- `Accounting Service`—Handles billing and payments

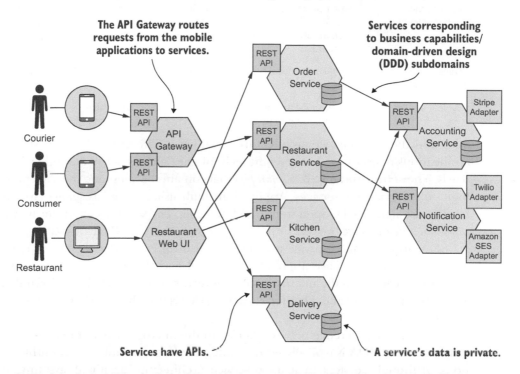

Figure 1.7   Some of the services of the microservice architecture-based version of the FTGO application. An API Gateway routes requests from the mobile applications to services. The services collaborate via APIs.

Many services correspond to the modules described earlier in this chapter. What's different is that each service and its API are very clearly defined. Each one can be independently developed, tested, deployed, and scaled. Also, this architecture does a good job of preserving modularity. A developer can't bypass a service's API and access its internal components. Chapter 13 describes how to transform an existing monolithic application into microservices.

1.4.5   *Comparing the microservice architecture and SOA*

Some critics of the microservice architecture claim it's nothing new—it's service-oriented architecture (SOA). At a very high level, there are some similarities. SOA and the microservice architecture are architectural styles that structure a system as a set of services. But as table 1.1 shows, once you dig deep, you encounter significant differences.

Table 1.1 Comparing SOA with microservices

	SOA	Microservices
Inter-service communication	Smart pipes, such as Enterprise Service Bus, using heavyweight protocols, such as SOAP and the other WS* standards.	Dumb pipes, such as a message broker, or direct service-to-service communication, using lightweight protocols such as REST or gRPC
Data	Global data model and shared databases	Data model and database per service
Typical service	Larger monolithic application	Smaller service

SOA and the microservice architecture usually use different technology stacks. SOA applications typically use heavyweight technologies such as SOAP and other WS* standards. They often use an ESB, a *smart pipe* that contains business and message-processing logic to integrate the services. Applications built using the microservice architecture tend to use lightweight, open source technologies. The services communicate via *dumb pipes*, such as message brokers or lightweight protocols like REST or gRPC.

SOA and the microservice architecture also differ in how they treat data. SOA applications typically have a global data model and share databases. In contrast, as mentioned earlier, in the microservice architecture each service has its own database. Moreover, as described in chapter 2, each service is usually considered to have its own domain model.

Another key difference between SOA and the microservice architecture is the size of the services. SOA is typically used to integrate large, complex, monolithic applications. Although services in a microservice architecture aren't always tiny, they're almost always much smaller. As a result, a SOA application usually consists of a few large services, whereas a microservices-based application typically consists of dozens or hundreds of smaller services.

1.5 Benefits and drawbacks of the microservice architecture

Let's first consider the benefits and then we'll look at the drawbacks.

1.5.1 Benefits of the microservice architecture

The microservice architecture has the following benefits:

- It enables the continuous delivery and deployment of large, complex applications.
- Services are small and easily maintained.
- Services are independently deployable.
- Services are independently scalable.
- The microservice architecture enables teams to be autonomous.
- It allows easy experimenting and adoption of new technologies.
- It has better fault isolation.

Let's look at each benefit.

ENABLES THE CONTINUOUS DELIVERY AND DEPLOYMENT OF LARGE, COMPLEX APPLICATIONS

The most important benefit of the microservice architecture is that it enables continuous delivery and deployment of large, complex applications. As described later in section 1.7, continuous delivery/deployment is part of *DevOps*, a set of practices for the rapid, frequent, and reliable delivery of software. High-performing DevOps organizations typically deploy changes into production with very few production issues.

There are three ways that the microservice architecture enables continuous delivery/deployment:

- *It has the testability required by continuous delivery/deployment*—Automated testing is a key practice of continuous delivery/deployment. Because each service in a microservice architecture is relatively small, automated tests are much easier to write and faster to execute. As a result, the application will have fewer bugs.
- *It has the deployability required by continuous delivery/deployment*—Each service can be deployed independently of other services. If the developers responsible for a service need to deploy a change that's local to that service, they don't need to coordinate with other developers. They can deploy their changes. As a result, it's much easier to deploy changes frequently into production.
- *It enables development teams to be autonomous and loosely coupled*—You can structure the engineering organization as a collection of small (for example, two-pizza) teams. Each team is solely responsible for the development and deployment of one or more related services. As figure 1.8 shows, each team can develop, deploy, and scale their services independently of all the other teams. As a result, the development velocity is much higher.

The ability to do continuous delivery and deployment has several business benefits:

- It reduces the time to market, which enables the business to rapidly react to feedback from customers.
- It enables the business to provide the kind of reliable service today's customers have come to expect.
- Employee satisfaction is higher because more time is spent delivering valuable features instead of fighting fires.

As a result, the microservice architecture has become the table stakes of any business that depends upon software technology.

EACH SERVICE IS SMALL AND EASILY MAINTAINED

Another benefit of the microservice architecture is that each service is relatively small. The code is easier for a developer to understand. The small code base doesn't slow down the IDE, making developers more productive. And each service typically starts a lot faster than a large monolith does, which also makes developers more productive and speeds up deployments.

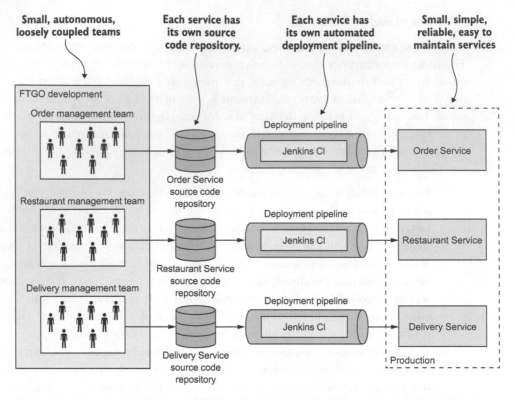

Figure 1.8   The microservices-based FTGO application consists of a set of loosely coupled services. Each team develops, tests, and deploys their services independently.

SERVICES ARE INDEPENDENTLY SCALABLE

Each service in a microservice architecture can be scaled independently of other services using X-axis cloning and Z-axis partitioning. Moreover, each service can be deployed on hardware that's best suited to its resource requirements. This is quite different than when using a monolithic architecture, where components with wildly different resource requirements—for example, CPU-intensive vs. memory-intensive—must be deployed together.

BETTER FAULT ISOLATION

The microservice architecture has better fault isolation. For example, a memory leak in one service only affects that service. Other services will continue to handle requests normally. In comparison, one misbehaving component of a monolithic architecture will bring down the entire system.

EASILY EXPERIMENT WITH AND ADOPT NEW TECHNOLOGIES

Last but not least, the microservice architecture eliminates any long-term commitment to a technology stack. In principle, when developing a new service, the developers are free to pick whatever language and frameworks are best suited for that service.

In many organizations, it makes sense to restrict the choices, but the key point is that you aren't constrained by past decisions.

Moreover, because the services are small, rewriting them using better languages and technologies becomes practical. If the trial of a new technology fails, you can throw away that work without risking the entire project. This is quite different than when using a monolithic architecture, where your initial technology choices severely constrain your ability to use different languages and frameworks in the future.

1.5.2 *Drawbacks of the microservice architecture*

Certainly, no technology is a silver bullet, and the microservice architecture has a number of significant drawbacks and issues. Indeed most of this book is about how to address these drawbacks and issues. As you read about the challenges, don't worry. Later in this book I describe ways to address them.

Here are the major drawbacks and issues of the microservice architecture:

- Finding the right set of services is challenging.
- Distributed systems are complex, which makes development, testing, and deployment difficult.
- Deploying features that span multiple services requires careful coordination.
- Deciding when to adopt the microservice architecture is difficult.

Let's look at each one in turn.

FINDING THE RIGHT SERVICES IS CHALLENGING

One challenge with using the microservice architecture is that there isn't a concrete, well-defined algorithm for decomposing a system into services. As with much of software development, it's something of an art. To make matters worse, if you decompose a system incorrectly, you'll build a *distributed monolith*, a system consisting of coupled services that must be deployed together. A distributed monolith has the drawbacks of both the monolithic architecture and the microservice architecture.

DISTRIBUTED SYSTEMS ARE COMPLEX

Another issue with using the microservice architecture is that developers must deal with the additional complexity of creating a distributed system. Services must use an interprocess communication mechanism. This is more complex than a simple method call. Moreover, a service must be designed to handle partial failure and deal with the remote service either being unavailable or exhibiting high latency.

Implementing use cases that span multiple services requires the use of unfamiliar techniques. Each service has its own database, which makes it a challenge to implement transactions and queries that span services. As described in chapter 4, a microservices-based application must use what are known as *sagas* to maintain data consistency across services. Chapter 7 explains that a microservices-based application can't retrieve data from multiple services using simple queries. Instead, it must implement queries using either API composition or CQRS views.

IDEs and other development tools are focused on building monolithic applications and don't provide explicit support for developing distributed applications. Writing automated tests that involve multiple services is challenging. These are all issues that are specific to the microservice architecture. Consequently, your organization's developers must have sophisticated software development and delivery skills in order to successfully use microservices.

The microservice architecture also introduces significant operational complexity. Many more moving parts—multiple instances of different types of service—must be managed in production. To successfully deploy microservices, you need a high level of automation. You must use technologies such as the following:

- Automated deployment tooling, like Netflix Spinnaker
- An off-the-shelf PaaS, like Pivotal Cloud Foundry or Red Hat OpenShift
- A Docker orchestration platform, like Docker Swarm or Kubernetes

I describe the deployment options in more detail in chapter 12.

DEPLOYING FEATURES SPANNING MULTIPLE SERVICES NEEDS CAREFUL COORDINATION

Another challenge with using the microservice architecture is that deploying features that span multiple services requires careful coordination between the various development teams. You have to create a rollout plan that orders service deployments based on the dependencies between services. That's quite different than a monolithic architecture, where you can easily deploy updates to multiple components atomically.

DECIDING WHEN TO ADOPT IS DIFFICULT

Another issue with using the microservice architecture is deciding at what point during the lifecycle of the application you should use this architecture. When developing the first version of an application, you often don't have the problems that this architecture solves. Moreover, using an elaborate, distributed architecture will slow down development. That can be a major dilemma for startups, where the biggest problem is usually how to rapidly evolve the business model and accompanying application. Using the microservice architecture makes it much more difficult to iterate rapidly. A startup should almost certainly begin with a monolithic application.

Later on, though, when the problem is how to handle complexity, that's when it makes sense to functionally decompose the application into a set of microservices. You may find refactoring difficult because of tangled dependencies. Chapter 13 goes over strategies for refactoring a monolithic application into microservices.

As you can see, the microservice architecture offer many benefits, but also has some significant drawbacks. Because of these issues, adopting a microservice architecture should not be undertaken lightly. But for complex applications, such as a consumer-facing web application or SaaS application, it's usually the right choice. Well-known sites like eBay (www.slideshare.net/RandyShoup/the-ebay-architecture-striking-a-balance-between-site-stability-feature-velocity-performance-and-cost), Amazon.com, Groupon, and Gilt have all evolved from a monolithic architecture to a microservice architecture.

You must address numerous design and architectural issues when using the micro-service architecture. What's more, many of these issues have multiple solutions, each with a different set of trade-offs. There is no one single perfect solution. To help guide your decision making, I've created the Microservice architecture pattern language. I reference this pattern language throughout the rest of the book as I teach you about the microservice architecture. Let's look at what a pattern language is and why it's helpful.

1.6 The Microservice architecture pattern language

Architecture and design are all about making decisions. You need to decide whether the monolithic or microservice architecture is the best fit for your application. When making these decisions you have lots of trade-offs to consider. If you pick the microservice architecture, you'll need to address lots of issues.

A good way to describe the various architectural and design options and improve decision making is to use a pattern language. Let's first look at why we need patterns and a pattern language, and then we'll take a tour of the Microservice architecture pattern language.

1.6.1 Microservice architecture is not a silver bullet

Back in 1986, Fred Brooks, author of *The Mythical Man-Month* (Addison-Wesley Professional, 1995), said that in software engineering, there are no silver bullets. That means there are no techniques or technologies that if adopted would give you a tenfold boost in productivity. Yet decades years later, developers are still arguing passionately about their favorite silver bullets, absolutely convinced that their favorite technology will give them a massive boost in productivity.

A lot of arguments follow the *suck/rock dichotomy* (http://nealford.com/memeagora/ 2009/08/05/suck-rock-dichotomy.html), a term coined by Neal Ford that describes how everything in the software world either sucks or rocks, with no middle ground. These arguments have this structure: if you do X, then a puppy will die, so therefore you must do Y. For example, synchronous versus reactive programming, object-oriented versus functional, Java versus JavaScript, REST versus messaging. Of course, reality is much more nuanced. Every technology has drawbacks and limitations that are often overlooked by its advocates. As a result, the adoption of a technology usually follows the *Gartner hype cycle* (https://en.wikipedia.org/wiki/Hype_cycle), in which an emerging technology goes through five phases, including the *peak of inflated expectations* (it rocks), followed by the *trough of disillusionment* (it sucks), and ending with the *plateau of productivity* (we now understand the trade-offs and when to use it).

Microservices are not immune to the silver bullet phenomenon. Whether this architecture is appropriate for your application depends on many factors. Consequently, it's bad advice to advise always using the microservice architecture, but it's equally bad advice to advise never using it. As with many things, it depends.

The underlying reason for these polarized and hyped arguments about technology is that humans are primarily driven by their emotions. Jonathan Haidt, in his excellent book *The Righteous Mind: Why Good People Are Divided by Politics and Religion* (Vintage, 2013), uses the metaphor of an elephant and its rider to describe how the human mind works. The elephant represents the emotion part of the human brain. It makes most of the decisions. The rider represents the rational part of the brain. It can sometimes influence the elephant, but it mostly provides justifications for the elephant's decisions.

We—the software development community—need to overcome our emotional nature and find a better way of discussing and applying technology. A great way to discuss and describe technology is to use the *pattern* format, because it's objective. When describing a technology in the pattern format, you must, for example, describe the drawbacks. Let's take a look at the pattern format.

1.6.2   *Patterns and pattern languages*

A *pattern* is a reusable solution to a problem that occurs in a particular context. It's an idea that has its origins in real-world architecture and that has proven to be useful in software architecture and design. The concept of a pattern was created by Christopher Alexander, a real-world architect. He also created the concept of a *pattern language*, a collection of related patterns that solve problems within a particular domain. His book *A Pattern Language: Towns, Buildings, Construction* (Oxford University Press, 1977) describes a pattern language for architecture that consists of 253 patterns. The patterns range from solutions to high-level problems, such as where to locate a city ("Access to water"), to low-level problems, such as how to design a room ("Light on two sides of every room"). Each of these patterns solves a problem by arranging physical objects that range in scope from cities to windows.

Christopher Alexander's writings inspired the software community to adopt the concept of patterns and pattern languages. The book *Design Patterns: Elements of Reusable Object-Oriented Software* (Addison-Wesley Professional, 1994), by Erich Gamma, Richard Helm, Ralph Johnson, and John Vlissides is a collection of object-oriented design patterns. The book popularized patterns among software developers. Since the mid-1990s, software developers have documented numerous software patterns. A *software pattern* solves a software architecture or design problem by defining a set of collaborating software elements.

Let's imagine, for example, that you're building a banking application that must support a variety of overdraft policies. Each policy defines limits on the balance of an account and the fees charged for an overdrawn account. You can solve this problem using the Strategy pattern, which is a well-known pattern from the classic *Design Patterns* book. The solution defined by the Strategy pattern consists of three parts:

- A strategy interface called `Overdraft` that encapsulates the overdraft algorithm
- One or more concrete strategy classes, one for each particular context
- The `Account` class that uses the algorithm

The Strategy pattern is an *object-oriented* design pattern, so the elements of the solution are classes. Later in this section, I describe *high-level* design patterns, where the solution consists of collaborating services.

One reason why patterns are valuable is because a pattern must describe the context within which it applies. The idea that a solution is specific to a particular context and might not work well in other contexts is an improvement over how technology used to typically be discussed. For example, a solution that solves the problem at the scale of Netflix might not be the best approach for an application with fewer users.

The value of a pattern, however, goes far beyond requiring you to consider the context of a problem. It forces you to describe other critical yet frequently overlooked aspects of a solution. A commonly used pattern structure includes three especially valuable sections:

- Forces
- Resulting context
- Related patterns

Let's look at each of these, starting with forces.

FORCES: THE ISSUES THAT YOU MUST ADDRESS WHEN SOLVING A PROBLEM

The *forces* section of a pattern describes the forces (issues) that you must address when solving a problem in a given context. Forces can conflict, so it might not be possible to solve all of them. Which forces are more important depends on the context. You have to prioritize solving some forces over others. For example, code must be easy to understand and have good performance. Code written in a reactive style has better performance than synchronous code, yet is often more difficult to understand. Explicitly listing the forces is useful because it makes clear which issues need to be solved.

RESULTING CONTEXT: THE CONSEQUENCES OF APPLYING A PATTERN

The *resulting context* section of a pattern describes the consequences of applying the pattern. It consists of three parts:

- *Benefits*—The benefits of the pattern, including the forces that have been resolved
- *Drawbacks*—The drawbacks of the pattern, including the unresolved forces
- *Issues*—The new problems that have been introduced by applying the pattern

The resulting context provides a more complete and less biased view of the solution, which enables better design decisions.

RELATED PATTERNS: THE FIVE DIFFERENT TYPES OF RELATIONSHIPS

The *related patterns* section of a pattern describes the relationship between the pattern and other patterns. There are five types of relationships between patterns:

- *Predecessor*—A predecessor pattern is a pattern that motivates the need for this pattern. For example, the Microservice architecture pattern is the predecessor to the rest of the patterns in the pattern language, except the monolithic architecture pattern.
- *Successor*—A pattern that solves an issue that has been introduced by this pattern. For example, if you apply the Microservice architecture pattern, you must

then apply numerous successor patterns, including service discovery patterns and the Circuit breaker pattern.

- *Alternative*—A pattern that provides an alternative solution to this pattern. For example, the Monolithic architecture pattern and the Microservice architecture pattern are alternative ways of architecting an application. You pick one or the other.

- *Generalization*—A pattern that is a general solution to a problem. For example, in chapter 12 you'll learn about the different implementations of the Single service per host pattern.

- *Specialization*—A specialized form of a particular pattern. For example, in chapter 12 you'll learn that the Deploy a service as a container pattern is a specialization of Single service per host.

In addition, you can organize patterns that tackle issues in a particular problem area into groups. The explicit description of related patterns provides valuable guidance on how to effectively solve a particular problem. Figure 1.9 shows how the relationships between patterns is visually represented.

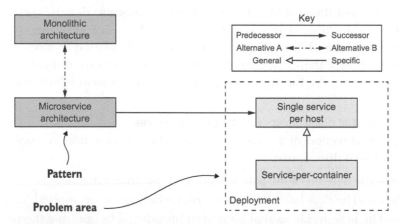

Figure 1.9   The visual representation of different types of relationships between the patterns: a *successor* pattern solves a problem created by applying the *predecessor* pattern; two or more patterns can be *alternative* solutions to the same problem; one pattern can be a *specialization* of another pattern; and patterns that solve problems in the same area can be grouped, or *generalized*.

The different kinds of relationships between patterns shown in figure 1.9 are represented as follows:

- Represents the predecessor-successor relationship
- Patterns that are alternative solutions to the same problem
- Indicates that one pattern is a specialization of another pattern
- Patterns that apply to a particular problem area

A collection of patterns related through these relationships sometimes form what is known as a pattern language. The patterns in a pattern language work together to solve problems in a particular domain. In particular, I've created the Microservice architecture pattern language. It's a collection of interrelated software architecture and design patterns for microservices. Let's take a look at this pattern language.

1.6.3 *Overview of the Microservice architecture pattern language*

The Microservice architecture pattern language is a collection of patterns that help you architect an application using the microservice architecture. Figure 1.10 shows the high-level structure of the pattern language. The pattern language first helps you decide whether to use the microservice architecture. It describes the monolithic architecture and the microservice architecture, along with their benefits and drawbacks. Then, if the microservice architecture is a good fit for your application, the pattern language helps you use it effectively by solving various architecture and design issues.

The pattern language consists of several groups of patterns. On the left in figure 1.10 is the application architecture patterns group, the Monolithic architecture pattern and the Microservice architecture pattern. Those are the patterns we've been discussing

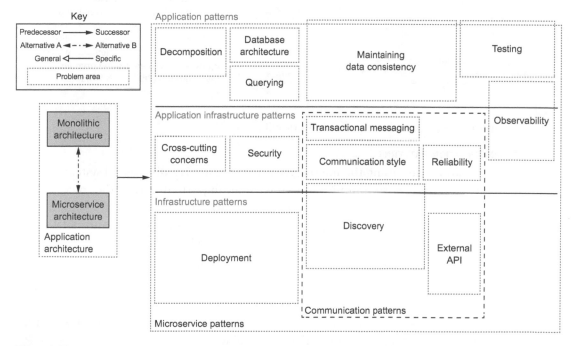

Figure 1.10 A high-level view of the Microservice architecture pattern language showing the different problem areas that the patterns solve. On the left are the application architecture patterns: Monolithic architecture and Microservice architecture. All the other groups of patterns solve problems that result from choosing the Microservice architecture pattern.

in this chapter. The rest of the pattern language consists of groups of patterns that are solutions to issues that are introduced by using the Microservice architecture pattern.

The patterns are also divided into three layers:

- *Infrastructure patterns*—These solve problems that are mostly infrastructure issues outside of development.
- *Application infrastructure*—These are for infrastructure issues that also impact development.
- *Application patterns*—These solve problems faced by developers.

These patterns are grouped together based on the kind of problem they solve. Let's look at the main groups of patterns.

PATTERNS FOR DECOMPOSING AN APPLICATION INTO SERVICES

Deciding how to decompose a system into a set of services is very much an art, but there are a number of strategies that can help. The two decomposition patterns shown in figure 1.11 are different strategies you can use to define your application's architecture.

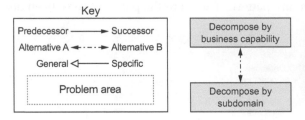

Figure 1.11 There are two decomposition patterns: Decompose by business capability, which organizes services around business capabilities, and Decompose by subdomain, which organizes services around domain-driven design (DDD) subdomains.

Chapter 2 describes these patterns in detail.

COMMUNICATION PATTERNS

An application built using the microservice architecture is a distributed system. Consequently, interprocess communication (IPC) is an important part of the microservice architecture. You must make a variety of architectural and design decisions about how your services communicate with one another and the outside world. Figure 1.12 shows the communication patterns, which are organized into five groups:

- *Communication style*—What kind of IPC mechanism should you use?
- *Discovery*—How does a client of a service determine the IP address of a service instance so that, for example, it makes an HTTP request?
- *Reliability*—How can you ensure that communication between services is reliable even though services can be unavailable?
- *Transactional messaging*—How should you integrate the sending of messages and publishing of events with database transactions that update business data?
- *External API*—How do clients of your application communicate with the services?

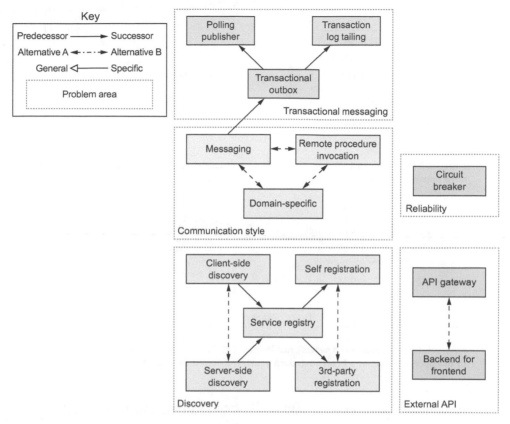

Figure 1.12　The five groups of communication patterns

Chapter 3 looks at the first four groups of patterns: communication style, discovery, reliability, and transaction messaging. Chapter 8 looks at the external API patterns.

DATA CONSISTENCY PATTERNS FOR IMPLEMENTING TRANSACTION MANAGEMENT

As mentioned earlier, in order to ensure loose coupling, each service has its own database. Unfortunately, having a database per service introduces some significant issues. I describe in chapter 4 that the traditional approach of using distributed transactions (2PC) isn't a viable option for a modern application. Instead, an application needs to maintain data consistency by using the Saga pattern. Figure 1.13 shows data-related patterns.

Chapters 4, 5, and 6 describe these patterns in more detail.

PATTERNS FOR QUERYING DATA IN A MICROSERVICE ARCHITECTURE

The other issue with using a database per service is that some queries need to join data that's owned by multiple services. A service's data is only accessible via its API, so you can't use distributed queries against its database. Figure 1.14 shows a couple of patterns you can use to implement queries.

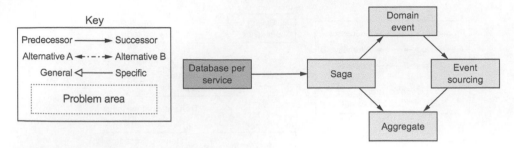

Figure 1.13   Because each service has its own database, you must use the Saga pattern to maintain data consistency across services.

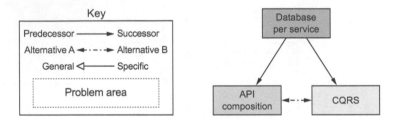

Figure 1.14   Because each service has its own database, you must use one of the querying patterns to retrieve data scattered across multiple services.

Sometimes you can use the API composition pattern, which invokes the APIs of one or more services and aggregates results. Other times, you must use the Command query responsibility segregation (CQRS) pattern, which maintains one or more easily queried replicas of the data. Chapter 7 looks at the different ways of implementing queries.

SERVICE DEPLOYMENT PATTERNS

Deploying a monolithic application isn't always easy, but it is straightforward in the sense that there is a single application to deploy. You have to run multiple instances of the application behind a load balancer.

In comparison, deploying a microservices-based application is much more complex. There may be tens or hundreds of services that are written in a variety of languages and frameworks. There are many more moving parts that need to be managed. Figure 1.15 shows the deployment patterns.

The traditional, and often manual, way of deploying applications in a language-specific packaging format, for example WAR files, doesn't scale to support a microservice architecture. You need a highly automated deployment infrastructure. Ideally, you should use a deployment platform that provides the developer with a simple UI (command-line or GUI) for deploying and managing their services. The deployment platform will typically be based on virtual machines (VMs), containers, or serverless technology. Chapter 12 looks at the different deployment options.

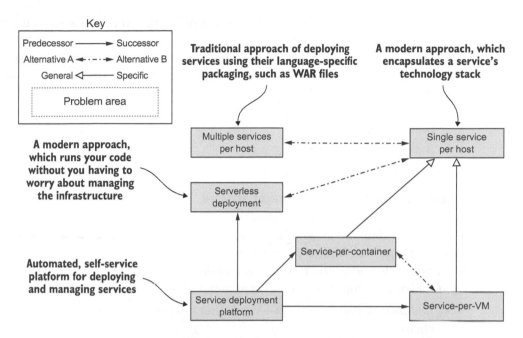

Figure 1.15 **Several patterns for deploying microservices. The traditional approach is to deploy services in a language-specific packaging format. There are two modern approaches to deploying services. The first deploys services as VM or containers. The second is the serverless approach. You simply upload the service's code and the serverless platform runs it. You should use a service deployment platform, which is an automated, self-service platform for deploying and managing services.**

OBSERVABILITY PATTERNS PROVIDE INSIGHT INTO APPLICATION BEHAVIOR

A key part of operating an application is understanding its runtime behavior and troubleshooting problems such as failed requests and high latency. Though understanding and troubleshooting a monolithic application isn't always easy, it helps that requests are handled in a simple, straightforward way. Each incoming request is load balanced to a particular application instance, which makes a few calls to the database and returns a response. For example, if you need to understand how a particular request was handled, you look at the log file of the application instance that handled the request.

In contrast, understanding and diagnosing problems in a microservice architecture is much more complicated. A request can bounce around between multiple services before a response is finally returned to a client. Consequently, there isn't one log file to examine. Similarly, problems with latency are more difficult to diagnose because there are multiple suspects.

You can use the following patterns to design observable services:

- *Health check API*—Expose an endpoint that returns the health of the service.
- *Log aggregation*—Log service activity and write logs into a centralized logging server, which provides searching and alerting.

- *Distributed tracing*—Assign each external request a unique ID and trace requests as they flow between services.
- *Exception tracking*—Report exceptions to an exception tracking service, which deduplicates exceptions, alerts developers, and tracks the resolution of each exception.
- *Application metrics*—Maintain metrics, such as counters and gauges, and expose them to a metrics server.
- *Audit logging*—Log user actions.

Chapter 11 describes these patterns in more detail.

PATTERNS FOR THE AUTOMATED TESTING OF SERVICES

The microservice architecture makes individual services easier to test because they're much smaller than the monolithic application. At the same time, though, it's important to test that the different services work together while avoiding using complex, slow, and brittle end-to-end tests that test multiple services together. Here are patterns for simplifying testing by testing services in isolation:

- *Consumer-driven contract test*—Verify that a service meets the expectations of its clients.
- *Consumer-side contract test*—Verify that the client of a service can communicate with the service.
- *Service component test*—Test a service in isolation.

Chapters 9 and 10 describe these testing patterns in more detail.

PATTERNS FOR HANDLING CROSS-CUTTING CONCERNS

In a microservice architecture, there are numerous concerns that every service must implement, including the observability patterns and discovery patterns. It must also implement the Externalized Configuration pattern, which supplies configuration parameters such as database credentials to a service at runtime. When developing a new service, it would be too time consuming to reimplement these concerns from scratch. A much better approach is to apply the Microservice Chassis pattern and build services on top of a framework that handles these concerns. Chapter 11 describes these patterns in more detail.

SECURITY PATTERNS

In a microservice architecture, users are typically authenticated by the API gateway. It must then pass information about the user, such as identity and roles, to the services it invokes. A common solution is to apply the Access token pattern. The API gateway passes an access token, such as JWT (JSON Web Token), to the services, which can validate the token and obtain information about the user. Chapter 11 discusses the Access token pattern in more detail.

Not surprisingly, the patterns in the Microservice architecture pattern language are focused on solving architect and design problems. You certainly need the right architecture in order to successfully develop software, but it's not the only concern. You must also consider process and organization.

1.7 Beyond microservices: Process and organization

For a large, complex application, the microservice architecture is usually the best choice. But in addition to having the right architecture, successful software development requires you to also have organization, and development and delivery processes. Figure 1.16 shows the relationships between process, organization, and architecture.

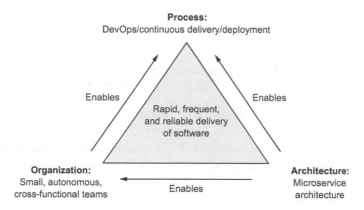

Figure 1.16 The rapid, frequent, and reliable delivery of large, complex applications requires a combination of DevOps, which includes continuous delivery/deployment, small, autonomous teams, and the microservice architecture.

I've already described the microservice architecture. Let's look at organization and process.

1.7.1 Software development and delivery organization

Success inevitably means that the engineering team will grow. On the one hand, that's a good thing because more developers can get more done. The trouble with large teams is, as Fred Brooks wrote in *The Mythical Man-Month*, the communication overhead of a team of size N is $O(N^2)$. If the team gets too large, it will become inefficient, due to the communication overhead. Imagine, for example, trying to do a daily standup with 20 people.

The solution is to refactor a large single team into a team of teams. Each team is small, consisting of no more than 8–12 people. It has a clearly defined business-oriented mission: developing and possibly operating one or more services that implement a feature or a business capability. The team is cross-functional and can develop, test, and deploy its services without having to frequently communicate or coordinate with other teams.

The reverse Conway maneuver

In order to effectively deliver software when using the microservice architecture, you need to take into account Conway's law (https://en.wikipedia.org/wiki/Conway%27s _law), which states the following:

Organizations which design systems ... are constrained to produce designs which are copies of the communication structures of these organizations.

Melvin Conway

In other words, your application's architecture mirrors the structure of the organization that developed it. It's important, therefore, to apply Conway's law in reverse (www.thoughtworks.com/radar/techniques/inverse-conway-maneuver) and design your organization so that its structure mirrors your microservice architecture. By doing so, you ensure that your development teams are as loosely coupled as the services.

The velocity of the team of teams is significantly higher than that of a single large team. As described earlier in section 1.5.1, the microservice architecture plays a key role in enabling the teams to be autonomous. Each team can develop, deploy, and scale their services without coordinating with other teams. Moreover, it's very clear who to contact when a service isn't meeting its SLA.

What's more, the development organization is much more scalable. You grow the organization by adding teams. If a single team becomes too large, you split it and its associated service or services. Because the teams are loosely coupled, you avoid the communication overhead of a large team. As a result, you can add people without impacting productivity.

1.7.2 *Software development and delivery process*

Using the microservice architecture with a waterfall development process is like driving a horse-drawn Ferrari—you squander most of the benefit of using microservices. If you want to develop an application with the microservice architecture, it's essential that you adopt agile development and deployment practices such as Scrum or Kanban. Better yet, you should practice continuous delivery/deployment, which is a part of DevOps.

Jez Humble (https://continuousdelivery.com/) defines continuous delivery as follows:

Continuous Delivery is the ability to get changes of all types—including new features, configuration changes, bug fixes and experiments—into production, or into the hands of users, safely and quickly in a sustainable way.

A key characteristic of continuous delivery is that software is always releasable. It relies on a high level of automation, including automated testing. Continuous deployment takes continuous delivery one step further in the practice of automatically deploying releasable code into production. High-performing organizations that practice continuous deployment deploy multiple times per day into production, have far fewer production outages, and recover quickly from any that do occur (https://puppet.com/ resources/whitepaper/state-of-devops-report). As described earlier in section 1.5.1, the microservice architecture directly supports continuous delivery/deployment.

> **Move fast without breaking things**
>
> The goal of continuous delivery/deployment (and, more generally, DevOps) is to rapidly yet reliably deliver software. Four useful metrics for assessing software development are as follows:
>
> - *Deployment frequency*—How often software is deployed into production
> - *Lead time*—Time from a developer checking in a change to that change being deployed
> - *Mean time to recover*—Time to recover from a production problem
> - *Change failure rate*—Percentage of changes that result in a production problem
>
> In a traditional organization, the deployment frequency is low, and the lead time is high. Stressed-out developers and operations people typically stay up late into the night fixing last-minute issues during the maintenance window. In contrast, a DevOps organization releases software frequently, often multiple times per day, with far fewer production issues. Amazon, for example, deployed changes into production every 11.6 seconds in 2014 (www.youtube.com/watch?v=dxk8b9rSKOo), and Netflix had a lead time of 16 minutes for one software component (https://medium.com/netflix-techblog/how-we-build-code-at-netflix-c5d9bd727f15).

1.7.3 The human side of adopting microservices

Adopting the microservice architecture changes your architecture, your organization, and your development processes. Ultimately, though, it changes the working environment of people, who are, as mentioned earlier, emotional creatures. If ignored, their emotions can make the adoption of microservices a bumpy ride. Mary and the other FTGO leaders will struggle to change how FTGO develops software.

The best-selling book *Managing Transitions* (Da Capo Lifelong Books, 2017, https://wmbridges.com/books) by William and Susan Bridges introduces the concept of a *transition*, which refers to the process of how people respond emotionally to a change. It describes a three-stage Transition Model:

1 *Ending, Losing, and Letting Go*—The period of emotional upheaval and resistance when people are presented with a change that forces them out of their comfort zone. They often mourn the loss of the old way of doing things. For example, when people reorganize into cross-functional teams, they miss their former teammates. Similarly, a data modeling group that owns the global data model will be threatened by the idea of each service having its own data model.

2 *The Neutral Zone*—The intermediate stage between the old and new ways of doing things, where people are often confused. They are often struggling to learn the new way of doing things.

3 *The New Beginning*—The final stage where people have enthusiastically embraced the new way of doing things and are starting to experience the benefits.

The book describes how best to manage each stage of the transition and increase the likelihood of successfully implementing the change. FTGO is certainly suffering from monolithic hell and needs to migrate to a microservice architecture. It must also change its organization and development processes. In order for FTGO to successfully accomplish this, however, it must take into account the transition model and consider people's emotions.

In the next chapter, you'll learn about the goal of software architecture and how to decompose an application into services.

Summary

- The Monolithic architecture pattern structures the application as a single deployable unit.
- The Microservice architecture pattern decomposes a system into a set of independently deployable services, each with its own database.
- The monolithic architecture is a good choice for simple applications, but microservice architecture is usually a better choice for large, complex applications.
- The microservice architecture accelerates the velocity of software development by enabling small, autonomous teams to work in parallel.
- The microservice architecture isn't a silver bullet—there are significant drawbacks, including complexity.
- The Microservice architecture pattern language is a collection of patterns that help you architect an application using the microservice architecture. It helps you decide whether to use the microservice architecture, and if you pick the microservice architecture, the pattern language helps you apply it effectively.
- You need more than just the microservice architecture to accelerate software delivery. Successful software development also requires DevOps and small, autonomous teams.
- Don't forget about the human side of adopting microservices. You need to consider employees' emotions in order to successfully transition to a microservice architecture.

Decomposition strategies

2

This chapter covers

- Understanding software architecture and why it's important
- Decomposing an application into services by applying the decomposition patterns Decompose by business capability and Decompose by subdomain
- Using the bounded context concept from domain-driven design (DDD) to untangle data and make decomposition easier

Sometimes you have to be careful what you wish for. After an intense lobbying effort, Mary had finally convinced the business that migrating to a microservice architecture was the right thing to do. Feeling a mixture of excitement and some trepidation, Mary had a morning-long meeting with her architects to discuss where to begin. During the discussion, it became apparent that some aspects of the Microservice architecture pattern language, such as deployment and service discovery, were new and unfamiliar, yet straightforward. The key challenge, which is the essence of the microservice architecture, is the functional decomposition of the application into services. The first and most important aspect of the architecture is, therefore, the definition of the services. As they stood around the whiteboard, the FTGO team wondered exactly how to do that!

In this chapter, you'll learn how to define a microservice architecture for an application. I describe strategies for decomposing an application into services. You'll learn that services are organized around business concerns rather than technical concerns. I also show how to use ideas from domain-driven design (DDD) to eliminate god classes, which are classes that are used throughout an application and cause tangled dependencies that prevent decomposition.

I begin this chapter by defining the microservice architecture in terms of software architecture concepts. After that, I describe a process for defining a microservice architecture for an application starting from its requirements. I discuss strategies for decomposing an application into a collection of services, obstacles to it, and how to overcome them. Let's start by examining the concept of software architecture.

2.1   *What is the microservice architecture exactly?*

Chapter 1 describes how the key idea of the microservice architecture is functional decomposition. Instead of developing one large application, you structure the application as a set of services. On one hand, describing the microservice architecture as a kind of functional decomposition is useful. But on the other hand, it leaves several questions unanswered, including how does the microservice architecture relate to the broader concepts of software architecture? What's a service? And how important is the size of a service?

In order to answer those questions, we need to take a step back and look at what is meant by *software architecture*. The architecture of a software application is its high-level structure, which consists of constituent parts and the dependencies between those parts. As you'll see in this section, an application's architecture is multidimensional, so there are multiple ways to describe it. The reason architecture is important is because it determines the application's software quality attributes or *-ilities*. Traditionally, the goal of architecture has been scalability, reliability, and security. But today it's important that the architecture also enables the rapid and safe delivery of software. You'll learn that the microservice architecture is an architecture style that gives an application high maintainability, testability, and deployability.

I begin this section by describing the concept of *software architecture* and why it's important. Next, I discuss the idea of an architectural style. Then I define the microservice architecture as a particular architectural style. Let's start by looking at the concept of software architecture.

2.1.1   *What is software architecture and why does it matter?*

Architecture is clearly important. There are at least two conferences dedicated to the topic: O'Reilly Software Architecture Conference (https://conferences.oreilly.com/software-architecture) and the SATURN conference (https://resources.sei.cmu.edu/news-events/events/saturn/). Many developers have the goal of becoming an architect. But what is architecture and why does it matter?

To answer that question, I first define what is meant by the term *software architecture*. After that, I discuss how an application's architecture is multidimensional and is best described using a collection of views or blueprints. I then describe that software architecture matters because of its impact on the application's software quality attributes.

A DEFINITION OF SOFTWARE ARCHITECTURE

There are numerous definitions of software architecture. For example, see https://en.wikiquote.org/wiki/Software_architecture to read some of them. My favorite definition comes from Len Bass and colleagues at the Software Engineering Institute (www.sei.cmu.edu), who played a key role in establishing software architecture as a discipline. They define software architecture as follows:

> *The software architecture of a computing system is the set of structures needed to reason about the system, which comprise software elements, relations among them, and properties of both.*

Documenting Software Architectures by Bass et al.

That's obviously a quite abstract definition. But its essence is that an application's architecture is its decomposition into parts (the elements) and the relationships (the relations) between those parts. Decomposition is important for a couple of reasons:

- It facilitates the division of labor and knowledge. It enables multiple people (or multiple teams) with possibly specialized knowledge to work productively together on an application.
- It defines how the software elements interact.

It's the decomposition into parts and the relationships between those parts that determine the application's *-ilities*.

THE 4+1 VIEW MODEL OF SOFTWARE ARCHITECTURE

More concretely, an application's architecture can be viewed from multiple perspectives, in the same way that a building's architecture can be viewed from structural, plumbing, electrical, and other perspectives. Phillip Krutchen wrote a classic paper describing the 4+1 view model of software architecture, "Architectural Blueprints— The '4+1' View Model of Software Architecture" (www.cs.ubc.ca/~gregor/teaching/papers/4+1view-architecture.pdf). The 4+1 model, shown in Figure 2.1, defines four different views of a software architecture. Each describes a particular aspect of the architecture and consists of a particular set of software elements and relationships between them.

The purpose of each view is as follows:

- *Logical view*—The software elements that are created by developers. In object-oriented languages, these elements are classes and packages. The relations between them are the relationships between classes and packages, including inheritance, associations, and depends-on.
- *Implementation view*—The output of the build system. This view consists of modules, which represent packaged code, and components, which are executable

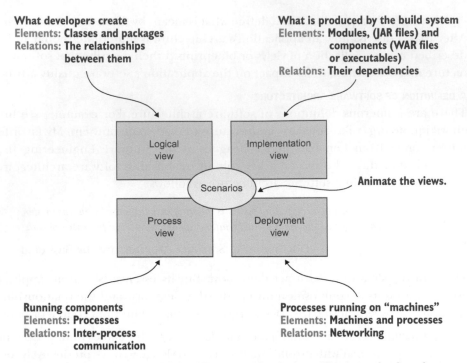

What developers create
Elements: **Classes and packages**
Relations: **The relationships between them**

What is produced by the build system
Elements: **Modules, (JAR files) and components (WAR files or executables)**
Relations: **Their dependencies**

Logical view

Implementation view

Scenarios

Animate the views.

Process view

Deployment view

Running components
Elements: **Processes**
Relations: **Inter-process communication**

Processes running on "machines"
Elements: **Machines and processes**
Relations: **Networking**

Figure 2.1   The 4+1 view model describes an application's architecture using four views, along with scenarios that show how the elements within each view collaborate to handle requests.

or deployable units consisting of one or more modules. In Java, a module is a JAR file, and a component is typically a WAR file or an executable JAR file. The relations between them include dependency relationships between modules and composition relationships between components and modules.

- *Process view*—The components at runtime. Each element is a process, and the relations between processes represent interprocess communication.

- *Deployment*—How the processes are mapped to machines. The elements in this view consist of (physical or virtual) machines and the processes. The relations between machines represent networking. This view also describes the relationship between processes and machines.

In addition to these four views, there are the scenarios—the +1 in the 4+1 model—that animate views. Each scenario describes how the various architectural components within a particular view collaborate in order to handle a request. A scenario in the logical view, for example, shows how the classes collaborate. Similarly, a scenario in the process view shows how the processes collaborate.

The 4+1 view model is an excellent way to describe an applications's architecture. Each view describes an important aspect of the architecture, and the scenarios illustrate how the elements of a view collaborate. Let's now look at why architecture is important.

WHY ARCHITECTURE MATTERS

An application has two categories of requirements. The first category includes the *functional* requirements, which define what the application must do. They're usually in the form of use cases or user stories. Architecture has very little to do with the functional requirements. You can implement functional requirements with almost any architecture, even a big ball of mud.

Architecture is important because it enables an application to satisfy the second category of requirements: its *quality of service* requirements. These are also known as *quality attributes* and are the so-called *-ilities*. The quality of service requirements define the runtime qualities such as scalability and reliability. They also define development time qualities including maintainability, testability, and deployability. The architecture you choose for your application determines how well it meets these quality requirements.

2.1.2　*Overview of architectural styles*

In the physical world, a building's architecture often follows a particular style, such as Victorian, American Craftsman, or Art Deco. Each style is a package of design decisions that constrains a building's features and building materials. The concept of architectural style also applies to software. David Garlan and Mary Shaw (An Introduction to Software Architecture, January 1994, https://www.cs.cmu.edu/afs/cs/project/able/ftp/intro_softarch/intro_softarch.pdf), pioneers in the discipline of software architecture, define an architectural style as follows:

> *An architectural style, then, defines a family of such systems in terms of a pattern of structural organization. More specifically, an architectural style determines the vocabulary of components and connectors that can be used in instances of that style, together with a set of constraints on how they can be combined.*

A particular architectural style provides a limited palette of elements (components) and relations (connectors) from which you can define a view of your application's architecture. An application typically uses a combination of architectural styles. For example, later in this section I describe how the monolithic architecture is an architectural style that structures the implementation view as a single (executable/deployable) component. The microservice architecture structures an application as a set of loosely coupled services.

THE LAYERED ARCHITECTURAL STYLE

The classic example of an architectural style is the layered architecture. A *layered architecture* organizes software elements into layers. Each layer has a well-defined set of responsibilities. A layered architecture also constraints the dependencies between the layers. A layer can only depend on either the layer immediately below it (if strict layering) or any of the layers below it.

You can apply the layered architecture to any of the four views discussed earlier. The popular three-tier architecture is the layered architecture applied to the logical view. It organizes the application's classes into the following tiers or layers:

- *Presentation layer*—Contains code that implements the user interface or external APIs
- *Business logic layer*—Contains the business logic
- *Persistence layer*—Implements the logic of interacting with the database

The layered architecture is a great example of an architectural style, but it does have some significant drawbacks:

- *Single presentation layer*—It doesn't represent the fact that an application is likely to be invoked by more than just a single system.
- *Single persistence layer*—It doesn't represent the fact that an application is likely to interact with more than just a single database.
- *Defines the business logic layer as depending on the persistence layer*—In theory, this dependency prevents you from testing the business logic without the database.

Also, the layered architecture misrepresents the dependencies in a well-designed application. The business logic typically defines an interface or a repository of interfaces that define data access methods. The persistence tier defines DAO classes that implement the repository interfaces. In other words, the dependencies are the reverse of what's depicted by a layered architecture.

Let's look at an alternative architecture that overcomes these drawbacks: the hexagonal architecture.

ABOUT THE HEXAGONAL ARCHITECTURE STYLE

Hexagonal architecture is an alternative to the layered architectural style. As figure 2.2 shows, the hexagonal architecture style organizes the logical view in a way that places the business logic at the center. Instead of the presentation layer, the application has one or more *inbound adapters* that handle requests from the outside by invoking the business logic. Similarly, instead of a data persistence tier, the application has one or more *outbound adapters* that are invoked by the business logic and invoke external applications. A key characteristic and benefit of this architecture is that the business logic doesn't depend on the adapters. Instead, they depend upon it.

The business logic has one or more ports. A *port* defines a set of operations and is how the business logic interacts with what's outside of it. In Java, for example, a port is often a Java interface. There are two kinds of ports: inbound and outbound ports. An inbound port is an API exposed by the business logic, which enables it to be invoked by external applications. An example of an inbound port is a service interface, which defines a service's public methods. An outbound port is how the business logic invokes external systems. An example of an output port is a repository interface, which defines a collection of data access operations.

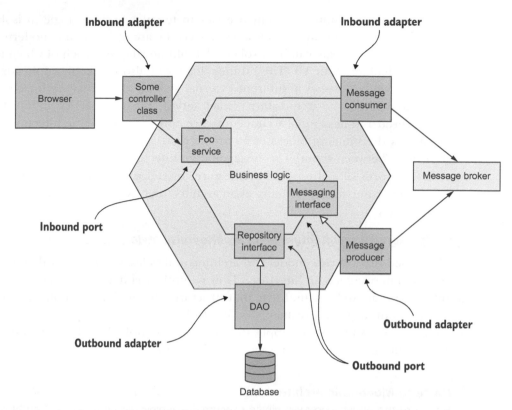

Figure 2.2   **An example of a hexagonal architecture, which consists of the business logic and one or more adapters that communicate with external systems. The business logic has one or more ports. Inbound adapters, which handled requests from external systems, invoke an inbound port. An outbound adapter implements an outbound port, and invokes an external system.**

Surrounding the business logic are adapters. As with ports, there are two types of adapters: inbound and outbound. An inbound adapter handles requests from the outside world by invoking an inbound port. An example of an inbound adapter is a Spring MVC Controller that implements either a set of REST endpoints or a set of web pages. Another example is a message broker client that subscribes to messages. Multiple inbound adapters can invoke the same inbound port.

An outbound adapter implements an outbound port and handles requests from the business logic by invoking an external application or service. An example of an outbound adapter is a *data access object* (DAO) class that implements operations for accessing a database. Another example would be a proxy class that invokes a remote service. Outbound adapters can also publish events.

An important benefit of the hexagonal architectural style is that it decouples the business logic from the presentation and data access logic in the adapters. The business logic doesn't depend on either the presentation logic or the data access logic.

Because of this decoupling, it's much easier to test the business logic in isolation. Another benefit is that it more accurately reflects the architecture of a modern application. The business logic can be invoked via multiple adapters, each of which implements a particular API or UI. The business logic can also invoke multiple adapters, each one of which invokes a different external system. Hexagonal architecture is a great way to describe the architecture of each service in a microservice architecture.

The layered and hexagonal architectures are both examples of architectural styles. Each defines the building blocks of an architecture and imposes constraints on the relationships between them. The hexagonal architecture and the layered architecture, in the form of a three-tier architecture, organize the logical view. Let's now define the microservice architecture as an architectural style that organizes the implementation view.

2.1.3 *The microservice architecture is an architectural style*

I've discussed the 4+1 view model and architectural styles, so I can now define monolithic and microservice architecture. They're both architectural styles. Monolithic architecture is an architectural style that structures the implementation view as a single component: a single executable or WAR file. This definition says nothing about the other views. A monolithic application can, for example, have a logical view that's organized along the lines of a hexagonal architecture.

> **Pattern: Monolithic architecture**
> Structure the application as a single executable/deployable component. See http://microservices.io/patterns/ monolithic.html.

The microservice architecture is also an architectural style. It structures the implementation view as a set of multiple components: executables or WAR files. The components are services, and the connectors are the communication protocols that enable those services to collaborate. Each service has its own logical view architecture, which is typically a hexagonal architecture. Figure 2.3 shows a possible microservice architecture for the FTGO application. The services in this architecture correspond to business capabilities, such as Order management and Restaurant management.

> **Pattern: Microservice architecture**
> Structure the application as a collection of loosely coupled, independently deployable services. See http://microservices.io/patterns/microservices.html.

Later in this chapter, I describe what is meant by *business capability* . The connectors between services are implemented using interprocess communication mechanisms such as REST APIs and asynchronous messaging. Chapter 3 discusses interprocess communication in more detail.

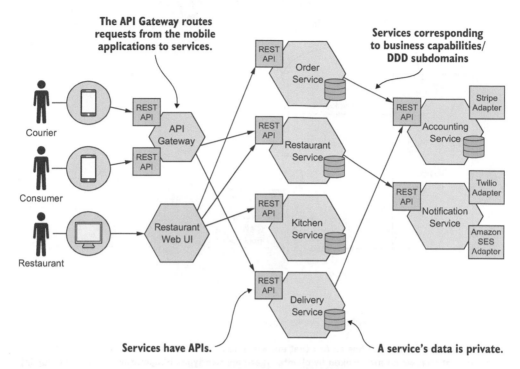

Figure 2.3 A possible microservice architecture for the FTGO application. It consists of numerous services.

A key constraint imposed by the microservice architecture is that the services are loosely coupled. Consequently, there are restrictions on how the services collaborate. In order to explain those restrictions, I'll attempt to define the term *service*, describe what it means to be loosely coupled, and tell you why this matters.

WHAT IS A SERVICE?

A *service* is a standalone, independently deployable software component that implements some useful functionality. Figure 2.4 shows the external view of a service, which in this example is the Order Service. A service has an API that provides its clients access to its functionality. There are two types of operations: commands and queries. The API consists of commands, queries, and events. A command, such as createOrder(), performs actions and updates data. A query, such as findOrderById(), retrieves data. A service also publishes events, such as OrderCreated, which are consumed by its clients.

A service's API encapsulates its internal implementation. Unlike in a monolith, a developer can't write code that bypasses its API. As a result, the microservice architecture enforces the application's modularity.

Each service in a microservice architecture has its own architecture and, potentially, technology stack. But a typical service has a hexagonal architecture. Its API is implemented by adapters that interact with the service's business logic. The operations

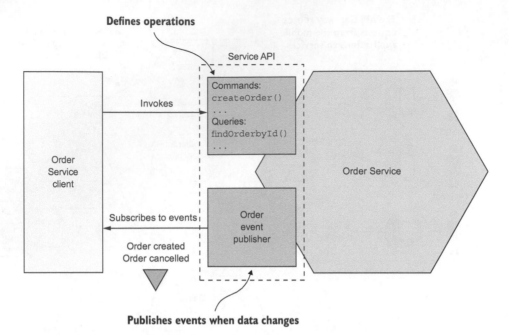

Figure 2.4   A service has an API that encapsulates the implementation. The API defines operations, which are invoked by clients. There are two types of operations: commands update data, and queries retrieve data. When its data changes, a service publishes events that clients can subscribe to.

adapter invokes the business logic, and the events adapter publishes events emitted by the business logic.

Later in chapter 12, when I discuss deployment technologies, you'll see that the implementation view of a service can take many forms. The component might be a standalone process, a web application or OSGI bundle running in a container, or a serverless cloud function. An essential requirement, however, is that a service has an API and is independently deployable.

WHAT IS LOOSE COUPLING?

An important characteristic of the microservice architecture is that the services are loosely coupled (https://en.wikipedia.org/wiki/Loose_coupling). All interaction with a service happens via its API, which encapsulates its implementation details. This enables the implementation of the service to change without impacting its clients. Loosely coupled services are key to improving an application's development time attributes, including its maintainability and testability. They are much easier to understand, change, and test.

The requirement for services to be loosely coupled and to collaborate only via APIs prohibits services from communicating via a database. You must treat a service's persistent data like the fields of a class and keep them private. Keeping the data private enables a developer to change their service's database schema without having to spend time coordinating with developers working on other services. Not sharing database tables also improves runtime isolation. It ensures, for example, that one service can't hold database locks that block another service. Later on, though, you'll learn that one downside of not sharing databases is that maintaining data consistency and querying across services are more complex.

THE ROLE OF SHARED LIBRARIES

Developers often package functionality in a library (module) so that it can be reused by multiple applications without duplicating code. After all, where would we be today without Maven or npm repositories? You might be tempted to also use shared libraries in microservice architecture. On the surface, it looks like a good way to reduce code duplication in your services. But you need to ensure that you don't accidentally introduce coupling between your services.

Imagine, for example, that multiple services need to update the Order business object. One approach is to package that functionality as a library that's used by multiple services. On one hand, using a library eliminates code duplication. On the other hand, consider what happens when the requirements change in a way that affects the Order business object. You would need to simultaneously rebuild and redeploy those services. A much better approach would be to implement functionality that's likely to change, such as Order management, as a service.

You should strive to use libraries for functionality that's unlikely to change. For example, in a typical application it makes no sense for every service to implement a generic Money class. Instead, you should create a library that's used by the services.

THE SIZE OF A SERVICE IS MOSTLY UNIMPORTANT

One problem with the term *microservice* is that the first thing you hear is *micro*. This suggests that a service should be very small. This is also true of other size-based terms such as miniservice or nanoservice. In reality, size isn't a useful metric.

A much better goal is to define a well-designed service to be a service capable of being developed by a small team with minimal lead time and with minimal collaboration with other teams. In theory, a team might only be responsible for a single service, so that service is by no means *micro*. Conversely, if a service requires a large team or takes a long time to test, it probably makes sense to split the team and the service. Or if you constantly need to change a service because of changes to other services or if it's triggering changes in other services, that's a sign that it's not loosely coupled. You might even have built a distributed monolith.

The microservice architecture structures an application as a set of small, loosely coupled services. As a result, it improves the development time attributes—maintainability, testability, deployability, and so on—and enables an organization to develop better software faster. It also improves an application's scalability, although that's not the main goal. To develop a microservice architecture for your application, you need to identify the services and determine how they collaborate. Let's look at how to do that.

2.2   *Defining an application's microservice architecture*

How should we define a microservice architecture? As with any software development effort, the starting points are the written requirements, hopefully domain experts, and perhaps an existing application. Like much of software development, defining an architecture is more art than science. This section describes a simple, three-step process, shown in figure 2.5, for defining an application's architecture. It's important to remember, though, that it's not a process you can follow mechanically. It's likely to be iterative and involve a lot of creativity.

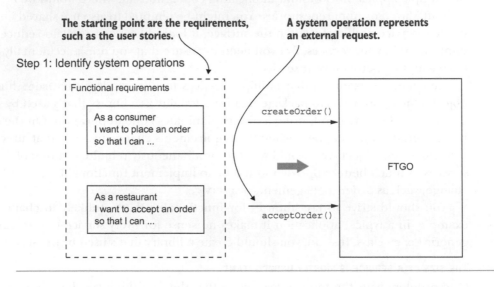

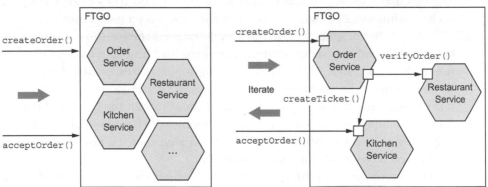

Figure 2.5   A three-step process for defining an application's microservice architecture

An application exists to handle requests, so the first step in defining its architecture is to distill the application's requirements into the key requests. But instead of describing the requests in terms of specific IPC technologies such as REST or messaging, I use the more abstract notion of system operation. A *system operation* is an abstraction of a request that the application must handle. It's either a command, which updates data, or a query, which retrieves data. The behavior of each command is defined in terms of an abstract domain model, which is also derived from the requirements. The system operations become the architectural scenarios that illustrate how the services collaborate.

The second step in the process is to determine the decomposition into services. There are several strategies to choose from. One strategy, which has its origins in the discipline of business architecture, is to define services corresponding to business capabilities. Another strategy is to organize services around domain-driven design subdomains. The end result is services that are organized around business concepts rather than technical concepts.

The third step in defining the application's architecture is to determine each service's API. To do that, you assign each system operation identified in the first step to a service. A service might implement an operation entirely by itself. Alternatively, it might need to collaborate with other services. In that case, you determine how the services collaborate, which typically requires services to support additional operations. You'll also need to decide which of the IPC mechanisms I describe in chapter 3 to implement each service's API.

There are several obstacles to decomposition. The first is network latency. You might discover that a particular decomposition would be impractical due to too many round-trips between services. Another obstacle to decomposition is that synchronous communication between services reduces availability. You might need to use the concept of self-contained services, described in chapter 3. The third obstacle is the requirement to maintain data consistency across services. You'll typically need to use sagas, discussed in chapter 4. The fourth and final obstacle to decomposition is so-called god classes, which are used throughout an application. Fortunately, you can use concepts from domain-driven design to eliminate god classes.

This section first describes how to identity an application's operations. After that, we'll look at strategies and guidelines for decomposing an application into services, and at obstacles to decomposition and how to address them. Finally, I'll describe how to define each service's API.

2.2.1 Identifying the system operations

The first step in defining an application's architecture is to define the system operations. The starting point is the application's requirements, including user stories and their associated user scenarios (note that these are different from the architectural scenarios). The system operations are identified and defined using the two-step process shown in figure 2.6. This process is inspired by the object-oriented design process covered in Craig Larman's book *Applying UML and Patterns* (Prentice Hall, 2004) (see www.craiglarman.com/wiki/index.php?title=Book_Applying_UML_and_Patterns for details). The first step creates the high-level domain model consisting of the key classes that provide a vocabulary with which to describe the system operations. The second step identifies the system operations and describes each one's behavior in terms of the domain model.

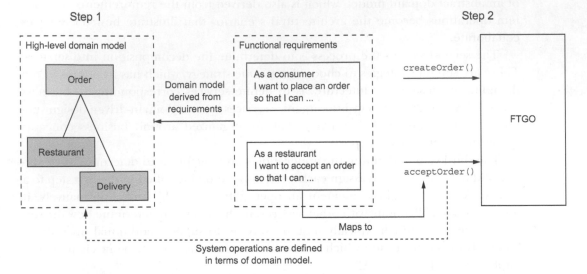

Figure 2.6   System operations are derived from the application's requirements using a two-step process. The first step is to create a high-level domain model. The second step is to define the system operations, which are defined in terms of the domain model.

The domain model is derived primarily from the nouns of the user stories, and the system operations are derived mostly from the verbs. You could also define the domain model using a technique called Event Storming, which I talk about in chapter 5. The behavior of each system operation is described in terms of its effect on one or more domain objects and the relationships between them. A system operation can create, update, or delete domain objects, as well as create or destroy relationships between them.

Let's look at how to define a high-level domain model. After that I'll define the system operations in terms of the domain model.

CREATING A HIGH-LEVEL DOMAIN MODEL

The first step in the process of defining the system operations is to sketch a high-level domain model for the application. Note that this domain model is much simpler than what will ultimately be implemented. The application won't even have a single domain model because, as you'll soon learn, each service has its own domain model. Despite being a drastic simplification, a high-level domain model is useful at this stage because it defines the vocabulary for describing the behavior of the system operations.

A domain model is created using standard techniques such as analyzing the nouns in the stories and scenarios and talking to the domain experts. Consider, for example, the `Place Order` story. We can expand that story into numerous user scenarios including this one:

```
Given a consumer
  And a restaurant
  And a delivery address/time that can be served by that restaurant
  And an order total that meets the restaurant's order minimum
When the consumer places an order for the restaurant
Then consumer's credit card is authorized
  And an order is created in the PENDING_ACCEPTANCE state
  And the order is associated with the consumer
  And the order is associated with the restaurant
```

The nouns in this user scenario hint at the existence of various classes, including `Consumer`, `Order`, `Restaurant`, and `CreditCard`.

Similarly, the `Accept Order` story can be expanded into a scenario such as this one:

```
Given an order that is in the PENDING_ACCEPTANCE state
  and a courier that is available to deliver the order
When a restaurant accepts an order with a promise to prepare by a particular
    time
Then the state of the order is changed to ACCEPTED
  And the order's promiseByTime is updated to the promised time
  And the courier is assigned to deliver the order
```

This scenario suggests the existence of `Courier` and `Delivery` classes. The end result after a few iterations of analysis will be a domain model that consists, unsurprisingly, of those classes and others, such as `MenuItem` and `Address`. Figure 2.7 is a class diagram that shows the key classes.

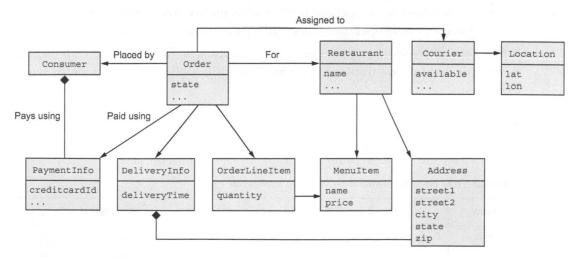

Figure 2.7   The key classes in the FTGO domain model

The responsibilities of each class are as follows:

- `Consumer`—A consumer who places orders.
- `Order`—An order placed by a consumer. It describes the order and tracks its status.
- `OrderLineItem`—A line item of an `Order`.
- `DeliveryInfo`—The time and place to deliver an order.
- `Restaurant`—A restaurant that prepares orders for delivery to consumers.
- `MenuItem`—An item on the restaurant's menu.
- `Courier`—A courier who deliver orders to consumers. It tracks the availability of the courier and their current location.
- `Address`—The address of a `Consumer` or a `Restaurant`.
- `Location`—The latitude and longitude of a `Courier`.

A class diagram such as the one in figure 2.7 illustrates one aspect of an application's architecture. But it isn't much more than a pretty picture without the scenarios to animate it. The next step is to define the system operations, which correspond to architectural scenarios.

DEFINING SYSTEM OPERATIONS

Once you've defined a high-level domain model, the next step is to identify the requests that the application must handle. The details of the UI are beyond the scope of this book, but you can imagine that in each user scenario, the UI will make requests to the backend business logic to retrieve and update data. FTGO is primarily a web application, which means that most requests are HTTP-based, but it's possible that some clients might use messaging. Instead of committing to a specific protocol, therefore, it makes sense to use the more abstract notion of a system operation to represent requests.

There are two types of system operations:

- *Commands*—System operations that create, update, and delete data
- *Queries*—System operations that read (query) data

Ultimately, these system operations will correspond to REST, RPC, or messaging endpoints, but for now thinking of them abstractly is useful. Let's first identify some commands.

A good starting point for identifying system commands is to analyze the verbs in the user stories and scenarios. Consider, for example, the `Place Order` story. It clearly suggests that the system must provide a `Create Order` operation. Many other stories individually map directly to system commands. Table 2.1 lists some of the key system commands.

Table 2.1   Key system commands for the FTGO application

Actor	Story	Command	Description
Consumer	Create Order	`createOrder()`	Creates an order
Restaurant	Accept Order	`acceptOrder()`	Indicates that the restaurant has accepted the order and is committed to preparing it by the indicated time

Table 2.1 Key system commands for the FTGO application *(continued)*

Actor	Story	Command	Description
Restaurant	Order Ready for Pickup	`noteOrderReadyForPickup()`	Indicates that the order is ready for pickup
Courier	Update Location	`noteUpdatedLocation()`	Updates the current location of the courier
Courier	Delivery picked up	`noteDeliveryPickedUp()`	Indicates that the courier has picked up the order
Courier	Delivery delivered	`noteDeliveryDelivered()`	Indicates that the courier has delivered the order

A command has a specification that defines its parameters, return value, and behavior in terms of the domain model classes. The behavior specification consists of preconditions that must be true when the operation is invoked, and post-conditions that are true after the operation is invoked. Here, for example, is the specification of the `createOrder()` system operation:

Operation	`createOrder` (consumer id, payment method, delivery address, delivery time, restaurant id, order line items)
Returns	`orderId`, ...
Preconditions	▪ The consumer exists and can place orders. ▪ The line items correspond to the restaurant's menu items. ▪ The delivery address and time can be serviced by the restaurant.
Post-conditions	▪ The consumer's credit card was authorized for the order total. ▪ An order was created in the `PENDING_ACCEPTANCE` state.

The preconditions mirror the *givens* in the `Place Order` user scenario described earlier. The post-conditions mirror the *thens* from the scenario. When a system operation is invoked it will verify the preconditions and perform the actions required to make the post-conditions true.

Here's the specification of the `acceptOrder()` system operation:

Operation	`acceptOrder(restaurantId, orderId, readyByTime)`
Returns	—
Preconditions	▪ The `order.status` is `PENDING_ACCEPTANCE`. ▪ A courier is available to deliver the order.
Post-conditions	▪ The `order.status` was changed to `ACCEPTED`. ▪ The `order.readyByTime` was changed to the `readyByTime`. ▪ The courier was assigned to deliver the order.

Its pre- and post-conditions mirror the user scenario from earlier.

Most of the architecturally relevant system operations are commands. Sometimes, though, queries, which retrieve data, are also important.

Besides implementing commands, an application must also implement queries. The queries provide the UI with the information a user needs to make decisions. At this stage, we don't have a particular UI design for FTGO application in mind, but consider, for example, the flow when a consumer places an order:

1 User enters delivery address and time.
2 System displays available restaurants.
3 User selects restaurant.
4 System displays menu.
5 User selects item and checks out.
6 System creates order.

This user scenario suggests the following queries:

- `findAvailableRestaurants(deliveryAddress, deliveryTime)`—Retrieves the restaurants that can deliver to the specified delivery address at the specified time
- `findRestaurantMenu(id)`—Retrieves information about a restaurant including the menu items

Of the two queries, `findAvailableRestaurants()` is probably the most architecturally significant. It's a complex query involving geosearch. The geosearch component of the query consists of finding all points—restaurants—that are near a location—the delivery address. It also filters out those restaurants that are closed when the order needs to be prepared and picked up. Moreover, performance is critical, because this query is executed whenever a consumer wants to place an order.

The high-level domain model and the system operations capture what the application does. They help drive the definition of the application's architecture. The behavior of each system operation is described in terms of the domain model. Each important system operation represents an architecturally significant scenario that's part of the description of the architecture.

Once the system operations have been defined, the next step is to identify the application's services. As mentioned earlier, there isn't a mechanical process to follow. There are, however, various decomposition strategies that you can use. Each one attacks the problem from a different perspective and uses its own terminology. But with all strategies, the end result is the same: an architecture consisting of services that are primarily organized around business rather than technical concepts.

Let's look at the first strategy, which defines services corresponding to business capabilities.

2.2.2 *Defining services by applying the Decompose by business capability pattern*

One strategy for creating a microservice architecture is to decompose by business capability. A concept from business architecture modeling, a *business capability* is something that a business does in order to generate value. The set of capabilities for a given business depends on the kind of business. For example, the capabilities of an insurance company typically include Underwriting, Claims management, Billing, Compliance, and so on. The capabilities of an online store include Order management, Inventory management, Shipping, and so on.

> **Pattern: Decompose by business capability**
> Define services corresponding to business capabilities. See http://microservices.io/patterns/decomposition/decompose-by-business-capability.html.

BUSINESS CAPABILITIES DEFINE WHAT AN ORGANIZATION DOES

An organization's business capabilities capture *what* an organization's business is. They're generally stable, as opposed to *how* an organization conducts its business, which changes over time, sometimes dramatically. That's especially true today, with the rapidly growing use of technology to automate many business processes. For example, it wasn't that long ago that you deposited checks at your bank by handing them to a teller. It then became possible to deposit checks using an ATM. Today you can conveniently deposit most checks using your smartphone. As you can see, the Deposit check business capability has remained stable, but the manner in which it's done has drastically changed.

IDENTIFYING BUSINESS CAPABILITIES

An organization's business capabilities are identified by analyzing the organization's purpose, structure, and business processes. Each business capability can be thought of as a service, except it's business-oriented rather than technical. Its specification consists of various components, including inputs, outputs, and service-level agreements. For example, the input to an Insurance underwriting capability is the consumer's application, and the outputs include approval and price.

A business capability is often focused on a particular business object. For example, the Claim business object is the focus of the Claim management capability. A capability can often be decomposed into sub-capabilities. For example, the Claim management capability has several sub-capabilities, including Claim information management, Claim review, and Claim payment management.

It is not difficult to imagine that the business capabilities for FTGO include the following:

- Supplier management
  - *Courier management*—Managing courier information
  - *Restaurant information management*—Managing restaurant menus and other information, including location and open hours

- Consumer management—Managing information about consumers
- Order taking and fulfillment
  - *Order management*—Enabling consumers to create and manage orders
  - *Restaurant order management*—Managing the preparation of orders at a restaurant
  - Logistics
  - *Courier availability management*—Managing the real-time availability of couriers to delivery orders
  - *Delivery management*—Delivering orders to consumers
- Accounting
  - *Consumer accounting*—Managing billing of consumers
  - *Restaurant accounting*—Managing payments to restaurants
  - *Courier accounting*—Managing payments to couriers
- …

The top-level capabilities include Supplier management, Consumer management, Order taking and fulfillment, and Accounting. There will likely be many other top-level capabilities, including marketing-related capabilities. Most top-level capabilities are decomposed into sub-capabilities. For example, Order taking and fulfillment is decomposed into five sub-capabilities.

One interesting aspect of this capability hierarchy is that there are three restaurant-related capabilities: Restaurant information management, Restaurant order management, and Restaurant accounting. That's because they represent three very different aspects of restaurant operations.

Next we'll look at how to use business capabilities to define services.

FROM BUSINESS CAPABILITIES TO SERVICES

Once you've identified the business capabilities, you then define a service for each capability or group of related capabilities. Figure 2.8 shows the mapping from capabilities to services for the FTGO application. Some top-level capabilities, such as the Accounting capability, are mapped to services. In other cases, sub-capabilities are mapped to services.

The decision of which level of the capability hierarchy to map to services is somewhat subjective. My justification for this particular mapping is as follows:

- I mapped the sub-capabilities of Supplier management to two services, because Restaurants and Couriers are very different types of suppliers.
- I mapped the Order taking and fulfillment capability to three services that are each responsible for different phases of the process. I combined the Courier availability management and Delivery management capabilities and mapped them to a single service because they're deeply intertwined.
- I mapped the Accounting capability to its own service, because the different types of accounting seem similar.

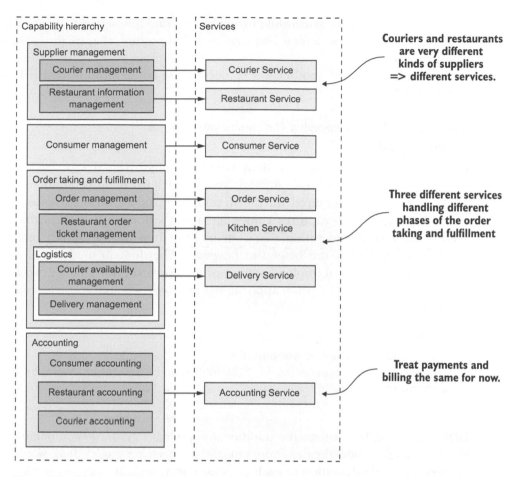

Figure 2.8 Mapping FTGO business capabilities to services. Capabilities at various levels of the capability hierarchy are mapped to services.

Later on, it may make sense to separate payments (of Restaurants and Couriers) and billing (of Consumers).

A key benefit of organizing services around capabilities is that because they're stable, the resulting architecture will also be relatively stable. The individual components of the architecture may evolve as the *how* aspect of the business changes, but the architecture remains unchanged.

Having said that, it's important to remember that the services shown in figure 2.8 are merely the first attempt at defining the architecture. They may evolve over time as we learn more about the application domain. In particular, an important step in the architecture definition process is investigating how the services collaborate in each of the key architectural services. You might, for example, discover that a particular decomposition is inefficient due to excessive interprocess communication and that you must combine services. Conversely, a service might grow in complexity to the point where it becomes worthwhile to split it into multiple services. What's more, in section 2.2.5, I describe several obstacles to decomposition that might cause you to revisit your decision.

Let's take a look at another way to decompose an application that is based on domain-driven design.

2.2.3   Defining services by applying the Decompose by sub-domain pattern

DDD, as described in the excellent book Domain-driven design by Eric Evans (Addison-Wesley Professional, 2003), is an approach for building complex software applications that is centered on the development of an object-oriented domain model. A *domain mode* captures knowledge about a domain in a form that can be used to solve problems within that domain. It defines the vocabulary used by the team, what DDD calls the *Ubiquitous Language*. The domain model is closely mirrored in the design and implementation of the application. DDD has two concepts that are incredibly useful when applying the microservice architecture: subdomains and bounded contexts.

> **Pattern: Decompose by subdomain**
> Define services corresponding to DDD subdomains. See http://microservices.io /patterns/decomposition/decompose-by-subdomain.html.

DDD is quite different than the traditional approach to enterprise modeling, which creates a single model for the entire enterprise. In such a model there would be, for example, a single definition of each business entity, such as customer, order, and so on. The problem with this kind of modeling is that getting different parts of an organization to agree on a single model is a monumental task. Also, it means that from the perspective of a given part of the organization, the model is overly complex for their needs. Moreover, the domain model can be confusing because different parts of the organization might use either the same term for different concepts or different terms for the same concept. DDD avoids these problems by defining multiple domain models, each with an explicit scope.

DDD defines a separate domain model for each subdomain. A subdomain is a part of the *domain*, DDD's term for the application's problem space. Subdomains are identified using the same approach as identifying business capabilities: analyze the business and identify the different areas of expertise. The end result is very likely to be subdomains that are similar to the business capabilities. The examples of subdomains in FTGO include Order taking, Order management, Kitchen management, Delivery, and Financials. As you can see, these subdomains are very similar to the business capabilities described earlier.

DDD calls the scope of a domain model a *bounded context*. A bounded context includes the code artifacts that implement the model. When using the microservice architecture, each bounded context is a service or possibly a set of services. We can create a microservice architecture by applying DDD and defining a service for each subdomain. Figure 2.9 shows how the subdomains map to services, each with its own domain model.

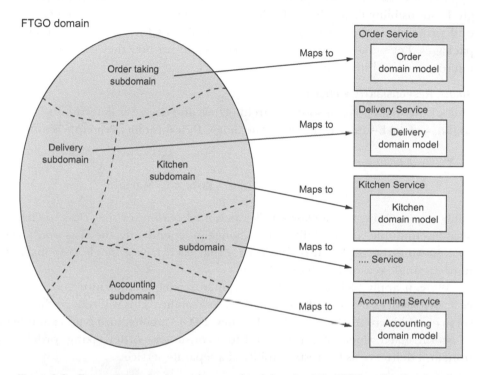

Figure 2.9 From subdomains to services: each subdomain of the FTGO application domain is mapped to a service, which has its own domain model.

DDD and the microservice architecture are in almost perfect alignment. The DDD concept of subdomains and bounded contexts maps nicely to services within a microservice architecture. Also, the microservice architecture's concept of autonomous teams owning services is completely aligned with the DDD's concept of each domain model being owned and developed by a single team. Even better, as I describe later in this section, the concept of a subdomain with its own domain model is a great way to eliminate god classes and thereby make decomposition easier.

Decompose by subdomain and Decompose by business capability are the two main patterns for defining an application's microservice architecture. There are, however, some useful guidelines for decomposition that have their roots in object-oriented design. Let's take a look at them.

2.2.4   *Decomposition guidelines*

So far in this chapter, we've looked at the main ways to define a microservice architecture. We can also adapt and use a couple of principles from object-oriented design when applying the microservice architecture pattern. These principles were created by Robert C. Martin and described in his classic book *Designing Object Oriented C++ Applications Using The Booch Method* (Prentice Hall, 1995). The first principle is the Single Responsibility Principle (SRP), for defining the responsibilities of a class. The second principle is the Common Closure Principle (CCP), for organizing classes into packages. Let's take a look at these principles and see how they can be applied to the microservice architecture.

SINGLE RESPONSIBILITY PRINCIPLE

One of the main goals of software architecture and design is determining the responsibilities of each software element. The Single Responsibility Principle is as follows:

> *A class should have only one reason to change.*
>
> Robert C. Martin

Each responsibility that a class has is a potential reason for that class to change. If a class has multiple responsibilities that change independently, the class won't be stable. By following the SRP, you define classes that each have a single responsibility and hence a single reason for change.

We can apply SRP when defining a microservice architecture and create small, cohesive services that each have a single responsibility. This will reduce the size of the services and increase their stability. The new FTGO architecture is an example of SRP in action. Each aspect of getting food to a consumer—order taking, order preparation, and delivery—is the responsibility of a separate service.

COMMON CLOSURE PRINCIPLE

The other useful principle is the Common Closure Principle:

> *The classes in a package should be closed together against the same kinds of changes. A change that affects a package affects all the classes in that package.*
>
> Robert C. Martin

The idea is that if two classes change in lockstep because of the same underlying reason, then they belong in the same package. Perhaps, for examplc, those classes implement a different aspect of a particular business rule. The goal is that when that business rule changes, developers only need to change code in a small number of packages (ideally only one). Adhering to the CCP significantly improves the maintainability of an application.

We can apply CCP when creating a microservice architecture and package components that change for the same reason into the same service. Doing this will minimize the number of services that need to be changed and deployed when some requirement changes. Ideally, a change will only affect a single team and a single service. CCP is the antidote to the distributed monolith anti-pattern.

SRP and CCP are 2 of the 11 principles developed by Bob Martin. They're particularly useful when developing a microservice architecture. The remaining nine principles are used when designing classes and packages. For more information about SRP, CCP, and the other OOD principles, see the article "The Principles of Object Oriented Design" on Bob Martin's website (http://butunclebob.com/ArticleS.UncleBob .PrinciplesOfOod).

Decomposition by business capability and by subdomain along with SRP and CCP are good techniques for decomposing an application into services. In order to apply them and successfully develop a microservice architecture, you must solve some transaction management and interprocess communication issues.

2.2.5   *Obstacles to decomposing an application into services*

On the surface, the strategy of creating a microservice architecture by defining services corresponding to business capabilities or subdomains looks straightforward. You may, however, encounter several obstacles:

- Network latency
- Reduced availability due to synchronous communication
- Maintaining data consistency across services
- Obtaining a consistent view of the data
- God classes preventing decomposition

Let's take a look at each obstacle, starting with network latency.

NETWORK LATENCY

Network latency is an ever-present concern in a distributed system. You might discover that a particular decomposition into services results in a large number of round-trips between two services. Sometimes, you can reduce the latency to an acceptable amount by implementing a batch API for fetching multiple objects in a single round trip. But in other situations, the solution is to combine services, replacing expensive IPC with language-level method or function calls.

SYNCHRONOUS INTERPROCESS COMMUNICATION REDUCES AVAILABILITY

Another problem is how to implement interservice communication in a way that doesn't reduce availability. For example, the most straightforward way to implement the createOrder() operation is for the Order Service to synchronously invoke the other services using REST. The drawback of using a protocol like REST is that it reduces the availability of the Order Service. It won't be able to create an order if any of those other services are unavailable. Sometimes this is a worthwhile trade-off, but in chapter 3 you'll learn that using asynchronous messaging, which eliminates tight coupling and improves availability, is often a better choice.

MAINTAINING DATA CONSISTENCY ACROSS SERVICES

Another challenge is maintaining data consistency across services. Some system operations need to update data in multiple services. For example, when a restaurant accepts an order, updates must occur in both the Kitchen Service and the Delivery Service. The Kitchen Service changes the status of the Ticket. The Delivery Service schedules delivery of the order. Both of these updates must be done atomically.

The traditional solution is to use a two-phase, commit-based, distributed transaction management mechanism. But as you'll see in chapter 4, this is not a good choice for modern applications, and you must use a very different approach to transaction management, a saga. A *saga* is a sequence of local transactions that are coordinated using messaging. Sagas are more complex than traditional ACID transactions but they work well in many situations. One limitation of sagas is that they are eventually consistent. If you need to update some data atomically, then it must reside within a single service, which can be an obstacle to decomposition.

OBTAINING A CONSISTENT VIEW OF THE DATA

Another obstacle to decomposition is the inability to obtain a truly consistent view of data across multiple databases. In a monolithic application, the properties of ACID transactions guarantee that a query will return a consistent view of the database. In contrast, in a microservice architecture, even though each service's database is consistent, you can't obtain a globally consistent view of the data. If you need a consistent view of some data, then it must reside in a single service, which can prevent decomposition. Fortunately, in practice this is rarely a problem.

GOD CLASSES PREVENT DECOMPOSITION

Another obstacle to decomposition is the existence of so-called god classes. *God classes* are the bloated classes that are used throughout an application (http://wiki.c2.com/ ?GodClass). A god class typically implements business logic for many different aspects of the application. It normally has a large number of fields mapped to a database table with many columns. Most applications have at least one of these classes, each representing a concept that's central to the domain: accounts in banking, orders in e-commerce, policies in insurance, and so on. Because a god class bundles together state and behavior for many different aspects of an application, it's an insurmountable obstacle to splitting any business logic that uses it into services.

The Order class is a great example of a god class in the FTGO application. That's not surprising—after all, the purpose of FTGO is to deliver food orders to customers. Most parts of the system involve orders. If the FTGO application had a single domain model, the Order class would be a very large class. It would have state and behavior corresponding to many different parts of the application. Figure 2.10 shows the structure of this class that would be created using traditional modeling techniques.

As you can see, the Order class has fields and methods corresponding to order processing, restaurant order management, delivery, and payments. This class also has a complex state model, due to the fact that one model has to describe state transitions

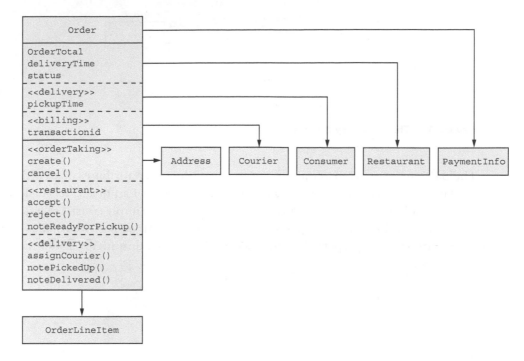

Figure 2.10   The Order god class is bloated with numerous responsibilities.

from disparate parts of the application. In its current form, this class makes it extremely difficult to split code into services.

One solution is to package the Order class into a library and create a central Order database. All services that process orders use this library and access the access database. The trouble with this approach is that it violates one of the key principles of the microservice architecture and results in undesirable, tight coupling. For example, any change to the Order schema requires the teams to update their code in lockstep.

Another solution is to encapsulate the Order database in an Order Service, which is invoked by the other services to retrieve and update orders. The problem with that design is that the Order Service would be a data service with an anemic domain model containing little or no business logic. Neither of these options is appealing, but fortunately, DDD provides a solution.

A much better approach is to apply DDD and treat each service as a separate subdomain with its own domain model. This means that each of the services in the FTGO application that has anything to do with orders has its own domain model with its version of the Order class. A great example of the benefit of multiple domain models is the Delivery Service. Its view of an Order, shown in figure 2.11, is extremely simple: pickup address, pickup time, delivery address, and delivery time. Moreover, rather than call it an Order, the Delivery Service uses the more appropriate name of Delivery.

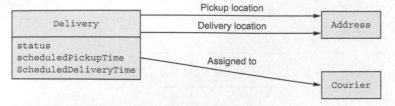

Figure 2.11   The `Delivery Service` domain model

The `Delivery Service` isn't interested in any of the other attributes of an order.

The `Kitchen Service` also has a much simpler view of an order. Its version of an `Order` is called a `Ticket`. As figure 2.12 shows, a `Ticket` simply consist of a status, the `requestedDeliveryTime`, a `prepareByTime`, and a list of line items that tell the restaurant what to prepare. It's unconcerned with the consumer, payment, delivery, and so on.

Figure 2.12   The `Kitchen Service` domain model

The `Order` service has the most complex view of an order, shown in figure 2.13. Even though it has quite a few fields and methods, it's still much simpler than the original version.

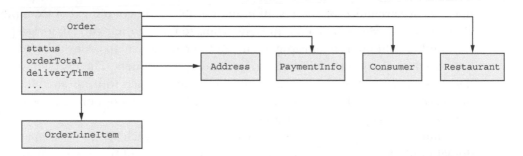

Figure 2.13   The `Order Service` domain model

The `Order` class in each domain model represents different aspects of the same `Order` business entity. The FTGO application must maintain consistency between these different objects in different services. For example, once the `Order Service` has authorized the consumer's credit card, it must trigger the creation of the Ticket in the Kitchen Service. Similarly, if the restaurant rejects the order via the Kitchen Service, it must be cancelled in the Order Service service, and the customer credited in the billing service. In chapter 4, you'll learn how to maintain consistency between services, using the previously mentioned event-driven mechanism sagas.

As well as creating technical challenges, having multiple domain models also impacts the implementation of the user experience. An application must translate between the user experience, which is its own domain model, and the domain models of each of the services. In the FTGO application, for example, the Order status displayed to a consumer is derived from Order information stored in multiple services. This translation is often handled by the API gateway, discussed in chapter 8. Despite these challenges, it's essential that you identify and eliminate god classes when defining a microservice architecture.

We'll now look at how to define the service APIs.

2.2.6 Defining service APIs

So far, we have a list of system operations and a list of a potential services. The next step is to define each service's API: its operations and events. A service API operation exists for one of two reasons: some operations correspond to system operations. They are invoked by external clients and perhaps by other services. The other operations exist to support collaboration between services. These operations are only invoked by other services.

A service publishes events primarily to enable it to collaborate with other services. Chapter 4 describes how events can be used to implement sagas, which maintain data consistency across services. And chapter 7 discusses how events can be used to update CQRS views, which support efficient querying. An application can also use events to notify external clients. For example, it could use WebSockets to deliver events to a browser.

The starting point for defining the service APIs is to map each system operation to a service. After that, we decide whether a service needs to collaborate with others to implement a system operation. If collaboration is required, we then determine what APIs those other services must provide in order to support the collaboration. Let's begin by looking at how to assign system operations to services.

ASSIGNING SYSTEM OPERATIONS TO SERVICES

The first step is to decide which service is the initial entry point for a request. Many system operations neatly map to a service, but sometimes the mapping is less obvious. Consider, for example, the noteUpdatedLocation() operation, which updates the courier location. On one hand, because it's related to couriers, this operation should be assigned to the Courier service. On the other hand, it's the Delivery Service that needs the courier location. In this case, assigning an operation to a service that needs the information provided by the operation is a better choice. In other situations, it might make sense to assign an operation to the service that has the information necessary to handle it.

Table 2.2 shows which services in the FTGO application are responsible for which operations.

Table 2.2 Mapping system operations to services in the FTGO application

Service	Operations
Consumer Service	createConsumer()
Order Service	createOrder()
Restaurant Service	findAvailableRestaurants()
Kitchen Service	▪ acceptOrder() ▪ noteOrderReadyForPickup()
Delivery Service	▪ noteUpdatedLocation() ▪ noteDeliveryPickedUp() ▪ noteDeliveryDelivered()

After having assigned operations to services, the next step is to decide how the services collaborate in order to handle each system operation.

DETERMINING THE APIS REQUIRED TO SUPPORT COLLABORATION BETWEEN SERVICES

Some system operations are handled entirely by a single service. For example, in the FTGO application, the Consumer Service handles the createConsumer() operation entirely by itself. But other system operations span multiple services. The data needed to handle one of these requests might, for instance, be scattered around multiple services. For example, in order to implement the createOrder() operation, the Order Service must invoke the following services in order to verify its preconditions and make the post-conditions become true:

- Consumer Service—Verify that the consumer can place an order and obtain their payment information.
- Restaurant Service—Validate the order line items, verify that the delivery address/time is within the restaurant's service area, verify order minimum is met, and obtain prices for the order line items.
- Kitchen Service—Create the Ticket.
- Accounting Service—Authorize the consumer's credit card.

Similarly, in order to implement the acceptOrder() system operation, the Kitchen Service must invoke the Delivery Service to schedule a courier to deliver the order. Table 2.3 shows the services, their revised APIs, and their collaborators. In order to fully define the service APIs, you need to analyze each system operation and determine what collaboration is required.

Table 2.3 The services, their revised APIs, and their collaborators

Service	Operations	Collaborators
Consumer Service	verifyConsumerDetails()	—
Order Service	createOrder()	▪ Consumer Service verifyConsumerDetails() ▪ Restaurant Service verifyOrderDetails() ▪ Kitchen Service createTicket() ▪ Accounting Service authorizeCard()
Restaurant Service	▪ findAvailableRestaurants() ▪ verifyOrderDetails()	—
Kitchen Service	▪ createTicket() ▪ acceptOrder() ▪ noteOrderReadyForPickup()	▪ Delivery Service scheduleDelivery()
Delivery Service	▪ scheduleDelivery() ▪ noteUpdatedLocation() ▪ noteDeliveryPickedUp() ▪ noteDeliveryDelivered()	—
Accounting Service	▪ authorizeCard()	—

So far, we've identified the services and the operations that each service implements. But it's important to remember that the architecture we've sketched out is very abstract. We've not selected any specific IPC technology. Moreover, even though the term *operation* suggests some kind of synchronous request/response-based IPC mechanism, you'll see that asynchronous messaging plays a significant role. Throughout this book I describe architecture and design concepts that influence how these services collaborate.

Chapter 3 describes specific IPC technologies, including synchronous communication mechanisms such as REST, and asynchronous messaging using a message broker. I discuss how synchronous communication can impact availability and introduce the concept of a self-contained service, which doesn't invoke other services synchronously. One way to implement a self-contained service is to use the CQRS pattern, covered in chapter 7. The Order Service could, for example, maintain a replica of the data owned by the Restaurant Service in order to eliminate the need for it to synchronously invoke the Restaurant Service to validate an order. It keeps the replica up-to-date by subscribing to events published by the Restaurant Service whenever it updates its data.

Chapter 4 introduces the saga concept and how it uses asynchronous messaging for coordinating the services that participate in the saga. As well as reliably updating data scattered across multiple services, a saga is also a way to implement a self-contained service. For example, I describe how the `createOrder()` operation is implemented using a saga, which invokes services such as the `Consumer Service`, `Kitchen Service`, and `Accounting Service` using asynchronous messaging.

Chapter 8 describes the concept of an API gateway, which exposes an API to external clients. An API gateway might implement a query operation using the API composition pattern, described in chapter 7, rather than simply route it to the service. Logic in the API gateway gathers the data needed by the query by calling multiple services and combining the results. In this situation, the system operation is assigned to the API gateway rather than a service. The services need to implement the query operations needed by the API gateway.

Summary

- Architecture determines your application's *-ilities*, including maintainability, testability, and deployability, which directly impact development velocity.
- The microservice architecture is an architecture style that gives an application high maintainability, testability, and deployability.
- Services in a microservice architecture are organized around business concerns—business capabilities or subdomains—rather than technical concerns.
- There are two patterns for decomposition:
  - Decompose by business capability, which has its origins in business architecture
  - Decompose by subdomain, based on concepts from domain-driven design
- You can eliminate god classes, which cause tangled dependencies that prevent decomposition, by applying DDD and defining a separate domain model for each service.

Interprocess communication in a microservice architecture

This chapter covers

- Applying the communication patterns: Remote procedure invocation, Circuit breaker, Client-side discovery, Self registration, Server-side discovery, Third party registration, Asynchronous messaging, Transactional outbox, Transaction log tailing, Polling publisher
- The importance of interprocess communication in a microservice architecture
- Defining and evolving APIs
- The various interprocess communication options and their trade-offs
- The benefits of services that communicate using asynchronous messaging
- Reliably sending messages as part of a database transaction

Mary and her team, like most other developers, had some experience with interprocess communication (IPC) mechanisms. The FTGO application has a REST API that's used by mobile applications and browser-side JavaScript. It also uses various cloud services, such as the Twilio messaging service and the Stripe payment service. But within a monolithic application like FTGO, modules invoke one another via language-level method or function calls. FTGO developers generally don't need to think about IPC unless they're working on the REST API or the modules that integrate with cloud services.

In contrast, as you saw in chapter 2, the microservice architecture structures an application as a set of services. Those services must often collaborate in order to handle a request. Because service instances are typically processes running on multiple machines, they must interact using IPC. It plays a much more important role in a microservice architecture than it does in a monolithic application. Consequently, as they migrate their application to microservices, Mary and the rest of the FTGO developers will need to spend a lot more time thinking about IPC.

There's no shortage of IPC mechanisms to chose from. Today, the fashionable choice is REST (with JSON). It's important, though, to remember that there are no silver bullets. You must carefully consider the options. This chapter explores various IPC options, including REST and messaging, and discusses the trade-offs.

The choice of IPC mechanism is an important architectural decision. It can impact application availability. What's more, as I explain in this chapter and the next, IPC even intersects with transaction management. I favor an architecture consisting of loosely coupled services that communicate with one another using asynchronous messaging. Synchronous protocols such as REST are used mostly to communicate with other applications.

I begin this chapter with an overview of interprocess communication in microservice architecture. Next, I describe remote procedure invocation-based IPC, of which REST is the most popular example. I cover important topics including service discovery and how to handle partial failure. After that, I describe asynchronous messaging-based IPC. I also talk about scaling consumers while preserving message ordering, correctly handling duplicate messages, and transactional messaging. Finally, I go through the concept of self-contained services that handle synchronous requests without communicating with other services in order to improve availability.

3.1 *Overview of interprocess communication in a microservice architecture*

There are lots of different IPC technologies to choose from. Services can use synchronous request/response-based communication mechanisms, such as HTTP-based REST or gRPC. Alternatively, they can use asynchronous, message-based communication mechanisms such as AMQP or STOMP. There are also a variety of different messages formats. Services can use human-readable, text-based formats such as JSON or XML. Alternatively, they could use a more efficient binary format such as Avro or Protocol Buffers.

Before getting into the details of specific technologies, I want to bring up several design issues you should consider. I start this section with a discussion of interaction styles, which are a technology-independent way of describing how clients and services interact. Next I discuss the importance of precisely defining APIs in a microservice architecture, including the concept of API-first design. After that, I discuss the important topic of API evolution. Finally, I discuss different options for message formats and how they can determine ease of API evolution. Let's begin by looking at interaction styles.

3.1.1 Interaction styles

It's useful to first think about the style of interaction between a service and its clients before selecting an IPC mechanism for a service's API. Thinking first about the interaction style will help you focus on the requirements and avoid getting mired in the details of a particular IPC technology. Also, as described in section 3.4, the choice of interaction style impacts the availability of your application. Furthermore, as you'll see in chapters 9 and 10, it helps you select the appropriate integration testing strategy.

There are a variety of client-service interaction styles. As table 3.1 shows, they can be categorized in two dimensions. The first dimension is whether the interaction is one-to-one or one-to-many:

- *One-to-one*—Each client request is processed by exactly one service.
- *One-to-many*—Each request is processed by multiple services.

The second dimension is whether the interaction is synchronous or asynchronous:

- *Synchronous*—The client expects a timely response from the service and might even block while it waits.
- *Asynchronous*—The client doesn't block, and the response, if any, isn't necessarily sent immediately.

Table 3.1   The various interaction styles can be characterized in two dimensions: one-to-one vs one-to-many and synchronous vs asynchronous.

	one-to-one	one-to-many
Synchronous	Request/response	—
Asynchronous	Asynchronous request/response One-way notifications	Publish/subscribe Publish/async responses

The following are the different types of one-to-one interactions:

- *Request/response*—A service client makes a request to a service and waits for a response. The client expects the response to arrive in a timely fashion. It might event block while waiting. This is an interaction style that generally results in services being tightly coupled.
- *Asynchronous request/response*—A service client sends a request to a service, which replies asynchronously. The client doesn't block while waiting, because the service might not send the response for a long time.

- *One-way notifications*—A service client sends a request to a service, but no reply is expected or sent.

It's important to remember that the synchronous request/response interaction style is mostly orthogonal to IPC technologies. A service can, for example, interact with another service using request/response style interaction with either REST or messaging. Even if two services are communicating using a message broker, the client service might be blocked waiting for a response. It doesn't necessarily mean they're loosely coupled. That's something I revisit later in this chapter when discussing the impact of inter-service communication on availability.

The following are the different types of one-to-many interactions:

- *Publish/subscribe*—A client publishes a notification message, which is consumed by zero or more interested services.
- *Publish/async responses*—A client publishes a request message and then waits for a certain amount of time for responses from interested services.

Each service will typically use a combination of these interaction styles. Many of the services in the FTGO application have both synchronous and asynchronous APIs for operations, and many also publish events.

Let's look at how to define a service's API.

3.1.2 *Defining APIs in a microservice architecture*

APIs or interfaces are central to software development. An application is comprised of modules. Each module has an interface that defines the set of operations that module's clients can invoke. A well-designed interface exposes useful functionality while hiding the implementation. It enables the implementation to change without impacting clients.

In a monolithic application, an interface is typically specified using a programming language construct such as a Java interface. A Java interface specifies a set of methods that a client can invoke. The implementation class is hidden from the client. Moreover, because Java is a statically typed language, if the interface changes to be incompatible with the client, the application won't compile.

APIs and interfaces are equally important in a microservice architecture. A service's API is a contract between the service and its clients. As described in chapter 2, a service's API consists of operations, which clients can invoke, and events, which are published by the service. An operation has a name, parameters, and a return type. An event has a type and a set of fields and is, as described in section 3.3, published to a message channel.

The challenge is that a service API isn't defined using a simple programming language construct. By definition, a service and its clients aren't compiled together. If a new version of a service is deployed with an incompatible API, there's no compilation error. Instead, there will be runtime failures.

Regardless of which IPC mechanism you choose, it's important to precisely define a service's API using some kind of *interface definition language* (IDL). Moreover, there are good arguments for using an API-first approach to defining services (see www .programmableweb.com/news/how-to-design-great-apis-api-first-design-and-raml/how-to/ 2015/07/10 for more). First you write the interface definition. Then you review the interface definition with the client developers. Only after iterating on the API definition do you then implement the service. Doing this up-front design increases your chances of building a service that meets the needs of its clients.

API-first design is essential

Even in small projects, I've seen problems occur because components don't agree on an API. For example, on one project the backend Java developer and the AngularJS frontend developer both said they had completed development. The application, however, didn't work. The REST and WebSocket API used by the frontend application to communicate with the backend was poorly defined. As a result, the two applications couldn't communicate!

The nature of the API definition depends on which IPC mechanism you're using. For example, if you're using messaging, the API consists of the message channels, the message types, and the message formats. If you're using HTTP, the API consists of the URLs, the HTTP verbs, and the request and response formats. Later in this chapter, I explain how to define APIs.

A service's API is rarely set in stone. It will likely evolve over time. Let's take a look at how to do that and consider the issues you'll face.

3.1.3 Evolving APIs

APIs invariably change over time as new features are added, existing features are changed, and (perhaps) old features are removed. In a monolithic application, it's relatively straightforward to change an API and update all the callers. If you're using a statically typed language, the compiler helps by giving a list of compilation errors. The only challenge may be the scope of the change. It might take a long time to change a widely used API.

In a microservices-based application, changing a service's API is a lot more difficult. A service's clients are other services, which are often developed by other teams. The clients may even be other applications outside of the organization. You usually can't force all clients to upgrade in lockstep with the service. Also, because modern applications are usually never down for maintenance, you'll typically perform a rolling upgrade of your service, so both old and new versions of a service will be running simultaneously.

It's important to have a strategy for dealing with these challenges. How you handle a change to an API depends on the nature of the change.

Use semantic versioning

The Semantic Versioning specification (http://semver.org) is a useful guide to versioning APIs. It's a set of rules that specify how version numbers are used and incremented. Semantic versioning was originally intended to be used for versioning of software packages, but you can use it for versioning APIs in a distributed system.

The Semantic Versioning specification (Semvers) requires a version number to consist of three parts: `MAJOR.MINOR.PATCH`. You must increment each part of a version number as follows:

- `MAJOR`—When you make an incompatible change to the API
- `MINOR`—When you make backward-compatible enhancements to the API
- `PATCH`—When you make a backward-compatible bug fix

There are a couple of places you can use the version number in an API. If you're implementing a REST API, you can, as mentioned below, use the major version as the first element of the URL path. Alternatively, if you're implementing a service that uses messaging, you can include the version number in the messages that it publishes. The goal is to properly version APIs and to evolve them in a controlled fashion. Let's look at how to handle minor and major changes.

Making minor, backward-compatible changes

Ideally, you should strive to only make backward-compatible changes. Backward-compatible changes are additive changes to an API:

- Adding optional attributes to request
- Adding attributes to a response
- Adding new operations

If you only ever make these kinds of changes, older clients will work with newer services, provided that they observe the Robustness principle (https://en.wikipedia.org/wiki/Robustness_principle), which states: "Be conservative in what you do, be liberal in what you accept from others." Services should provide default values for missing request attributes. Similarly, clients should ignore any extra response attributes. In order for this to be painless, clients and services must use a request and response format that supports the Robustness principle. Later in this section, I describe how text-based formats such as JSON and XML generally make it easier to evolve APIs.

Making major, breaking changes

Sometimes you must make major, incompatible changes to an API. Because you can't force clients to upgrade immediately, a service must simultaneously support old and new versions of an API for some period of time. If you're using an HTTP-based IPC mechanism, such as REST, one approach is to embed the major version number in the URL. For example, version 1 paths are prefixed with `'/v1/...'`, and version 2 paths with `'/v2/...'`.

Another option is to use HTTP's content negotiation mechanism and include the version number in the MIME type. For example, a client would request version 1.x of an Order using a request like this:

```
GET /orders/xyz HTTP/1.1
Accept: application/vnd.example.resource+json; version=1
...
```

This request tells the Order Service that the client expects a version 1.x response.

In order to support multiple versions of an API, the service's adapters that implement the APIs will contain logic that translates between the old and new versions. Also, as described in chapter 8, the API gateway will almost certainly use versioned APIs. It may even have to support numerous older versions of an API.

Now we'll look at the issue of message formats, the choice of which can impact how easy evolving an API will be.

3.1.4   Message formats

The essence of IPC is the exchange of messages. *Messages* usually contain data, and so an important design decision is the format of that data. The choice of message format can impact the efficiency of IPC, the usability of the API, and its evolvability. If you're using a messaging system or protocols such as HTTP, you get to pick your message format. Some IPC mechanisms—such as gRPC, which you'll learn about shortly—might dictate the message format. In either case, it's essential to use a cross-language message format. Even if you're writing your microservices in a single language today, it's likely that you'll use other languages in the future. You shouldn't, for example, use Java serialization.

There are two main categories of message formats: text and binary. Let's look at each one.

TEXT-BASED MESSAGE FORMATS

The first category is text-based formats such as JSON and XML. An advantage of these formats is that not only are they human readable, they're self describing. A JSON message is a collection of named properties. Similarly, an XML message is effectively a collection of named elements and values. This format enables a consumer of a message to pick out the values of interest and ignore the rest. Consequently, many changes to the message schema can easily be backward-compatible.

The structure of XML documents is specified by an XML schema (www.w3.org/XML/Schema). Over time, the developer community has come to realize that JSON also needs a similar mechanism. One popular option is to use the JSON Schema standard (http://json-schema.org). A JSON schema defines the names and types of a message's properties and whether they're optional or required. As well as being useful documentation, a JSON schema can be used by an application to validate incoming messages.

A downside of using a text-based messages format is that the messages tend to be verbose, especially XML. Every message has the overhead of containing the names of the attributes in addition to their values. Another drawback is the overhead of parsing text, especially when messages are large. Consequently, if efficiency and performance are important, you may want to consider using a binary format.

BINARY MESSAGE FORMATS

There are several different binary formats to choose from. Popular formats include Protocol Buffers (https://developers.google.com/protocol-buffers/docs/overview) and Avro (https://avro.apache.org). Both formats provide a typed IDL for defining the structure of your messages. A compiler then generates the code that serializes and deserializes the messages. You're forced to take an API-first approach to service design! Moreover, if you write your client in a statically typed language, the compiler checks that it uses the API correctly.

One difference between these two binary formats is that Protocol Buffers uses tagged fields, whereas an Avro consumer needs to know the schema in order to interpret messages. As a result, handling API evolution is easier with Protocol Buffers than with Avro. This blog post (http://martin.kleppmann.com/2012/12/05/schema-evolution-in-avro-protocol-buffers-thrift.html) is an excellent comparison of Thrift, Protocol Buffers, and Avro.

Now that we've looked at message formats, let's look at specific IPC mechanisms that transport the messages, starting with the Remote procedure invocation (RPI) pattern.

3.2 *Communicating using the synchronous Remote procedure invocation pattern*

When using a remote procedure invocation-based IPC mechanism, a client sends a request to a service, and the service processes the request and sends back a response. Some clients may block waiting for a response, and others might have a reactive, non-blocking architecture. But unlike when using messaging, the client assumes that the response will arrive in a timely fashion.

Figure 3.1 shows how RPI works. The business logic in the client invokes a *proxy interface*, implemented by an *RPI proxy* adapter class. The *RPI proxy* makes a request to the service. The request is handled by an *RPI server* adapter class, which invokes the service's business logic via an interface. It then sends back a reply to the *RPI proxy*, which returns the result to the client's business logic.

Pattern: Remote procedure invocation

A client invokes a service using a synchronous, remote procedure invocation-based protocol, such as REST (http://microservices.io/patterns/communication-style/messaging.html).

The *proxy interface* usually encapsulates the underlying communication protocol. There are numerous protocols to choose from. In this section, I describe REST and

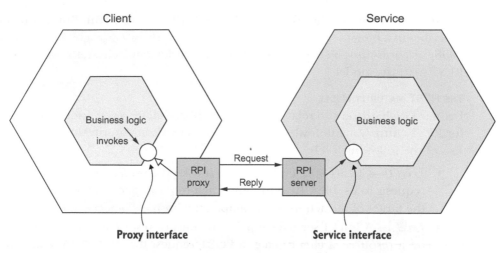

Figure 3.1   The client's business logic invokes an interface that is implemented by an *RPI proxy* adapter class. The *RPI proxy class* makes a request to the service. The *RPI server* adapter class handles the request by invoking the service's business logic.

gRPC. I cover how to improve the availability of your services by properly handling partial failure and explain why a microservices-based application that uses RPI must use a service discovery mechanism.

Let's first take a look at REST.

3.2.1   *Using REST*

Today, it's fashionable to develop APIs in the RESTful style (https://en.wikipedia .org/wiki/Representational_state_transfer). *REST* is an IPC mechanism that (almost always) uses HTTP. Roy Fielding, the creator of REST, defines REST as follows:

> *REST provides a set of architectural constraints that, when applied as a whole, emphasizes scalability of component interactions, generality of interfaces, independent deployment of components, and intermediary components to reduce interaction latency, enforce security, and encapsulate legacy systems.*
>
>   www.ics.uci.edu/~fielding/pubs/dissertation/top.htm

A key concept in REST is a *resource*, which typically represents a single business object, such as a Customer or Product, or a collection of business objects. REST uses the HTTP verbs for manipulating resources, which are referenced using a URL. For example, a GET request returns the representation of a resource, which is often in the form of an XML document or JSON object, although other formats such as binary can be used. A POST request creates a new resource, and a PUT request updates a resource. The Order Service, for example, has a POST /orders endpoint for creating an Order and a GET /orders/{orderId} endpoint for retrieving an Order.

Many developers claim their HTTP-based APIs are RESTful. But as Roy Fielding describes in a blog post, not all of them actually are (http://roy.gbiv.com/untangled/ 2008/rest-apis-must-be-hypertext-driven). To understand why, let's take a look at the REST maturity model.

THE REST MATURITY MODEL

Leonard Richardson (no relation to your author) defines a very useful maturity model for REST (http://martinfowler.com/articles/richardsonMaturityModel.html) that consists of the following levels:

- *Level 0*—Clients of a level 0 service invoke the service by making HTTP POST requests to its sole URL endpoint. Each request specifies the action to perform, the target of the action (for example, the business object), and any parameters.
- *Level 1*—A level 1 service supports the idea of resources. To perform an action on a resource, a client makes a POST request that specifies the action to perform and any parameters.
- *Level 2*—A level 2 service uses HTTP verbs to perform actions: GET to retrieve, POST to create, and PUT to update. The request query parameters and body, if any, specify the actions' parameters. This enables services to use web infrastructure such as caching for GET requests.
- *Level 3*—The design of a level 3 service is based on the terribly named HATEOAS (Hypertext As The Engine Of Application State) principle. The basic idea is that the representation of a resource returned by a GET request contains links for performing actions on that resource. For example, a client can cancel an order using a link in the representation returned by the GET request that retrieved the order. The benefits of HATEOAS include no longer having to hard-wire URLs into client code (www.infoq.com/news/2009/04/ hateoas-restful-api-advantages).

I encourage you to review the REST APIs at your organization to see which level they correspond to.

SPECIFYING REST APIS

As mentioned earlier in section 3.1, you must define your APIs using an interface definition language (IDL). Unlike older communication protocols like CORBA and SOAP, REST did not originally have an IDL. Fortunately, the developer community has rediscovered the value of an IDL for RESTful APIs. The most popular REST IDL is the Open API Specification (www.openapis.org), which evolved from the Swagger open source project. The Swagger project is a set of tools for developing and documenting REST APIs. It includes tools that generate client stubs and server skeletons from an interface definition.

THE CHALLENGE OF FETCHING MULTIPLE RESOURCES IN A SINGLE REQUEST

REST resources are usually oriented around business objects, such as `Consumer` and `Order`. Consequently, a common problem when designing a REST API is how to enable the client to retrieve multiple related objects in a single request. For example, imagine that a REST client wanted to retrieve an `Order` and the `Order`'s `Consumer`. A pure REST API would require the client to make at least two requests, one for the `Order` and another for its `Consumer`. A more complex scenario would require even more round-trips and suffer from excessive latency.

One solution to this problem is for an API to allow the client to retrieve related resources when it gets a resource. For example, a client could retrieve an `Order` and its `Consumer` using `GET /orders/order-id-1345?expand=consumer`. The query parameter specifies the related resources to return with the `Order`. This approach works well in many scenarios but it's often insufficient for more complex scenarios. It's also potentially time consuming to implement. This has led to the increasing popularity of alternative API technologies such as GraphQL (http://graphql.org) and Netflix Falcor (http://netflix.github.io/falcor/), which are designed to support efficient data fetching.

THE CHALLENGE OF MAPPING OPERATIONS TO HTTP VERBS

Another common REST API design problem is how to map the operations you want to perform on a business object to an HTTP verb. A REST API should use PUT for updates, but there may be multiple ways to update an order, including cancelling it, revising the order, and so on. Also, an update might not be idempotent, which is a requirement for using PUT. One solution is to define a sub-resource for updating a particular aspect of a resource. The `Order Service`, for example, has a `POST /orders/{orderId}/cancel` endpoint for cancelling orders, and a `POST /orders/{orderId}/revise` endpoint for revising orders. Another solution is to specify a verb as a URL query parameter. Sadly, neither solution is particularly RESTful.

This problem with mapping operations to HTTP verbs has led to the growing popularity of alternatives to REST, such as gPRC, discussed shortly in section 3.2.2. But first let's look at the benefits and drawbacks of REST.

BENEFITS AND DRAWBACKS OF REST

There are numerous benefits to using REST:

- It's simple and familiar.
- You can test an HTTP API from within a browser using, for example, the Postman plugin, or from the command line using curl (assuming JSON or some other text format is used).
- It directly supports request/response style communication.
- HTTP is, of course, firewall friendly.
- It doesn't require an intermediate broker, which simplifies the system's architecture.

There are some drawbacks to using REST:

- It only supports the request/response style of communication.
- Reduced availability. Because the client and service communicate directly without an intermediary to buffer messages, they must both be running for the duration of the exchange.

- Clients must know the locations (URLs) of the service instances(s). As described in section 3.2.4, this is a nontrivial problem in a modern application. Clients must use what is known as a *service discovery mechanism* to locate service instances.
- Fetching multiple resources in a single request is challenging.
- It's sometimes difficult to map multiple update operations to HTTP verbs.

Despite these drawbacks, REST seems to be the de facto standard for APIs, though there are a couple of interesting alternatives. GraphQL, for example, implements flexible, efficient data fetching. Chapter 8 discusses GraphQL and covers the API gateway pattern.

gRPC is another alternative to REST. Let's take a look at how it works.

3.2.2 Using gRPC

As mentioned in the preceding section, one challenge with using REST is that because HTTP only provides a limited number of verbs, it's not always straightforward to design a REST API that supports multiple update operations. An IPC technology that avoids this issue is gRPC (www.grpc.io), a framework for writing cross-language clients and servers (see https://en.wikipedia.org/wiki/Remote_procedure_call for more). gRPC is a binary message-based protocol, and this means—as mentioned earlier in the discussion of binary message formats—you're forced to take an API-first approach to service design. You define your gRPC APIs using a Protocol Buffers-based IDL, which is Google's language-neutral mechanism for serializing structured data. You use the Protocol Buffer compiler to generate client-side stubs and server-side skeletons. The compiler can generate code for a variety of languages, including Java, C#, NodeJS, and GoLang. Clients and servers exchange binary messages in the Protocol Buffers format using HTTP/2.

A gRPC API consists of one or more services and request/response message definitions. A *service definition* is analogous to a Java interface and is a collection of strongly typed methods. As well as supporting simple request/response RPC, gRPC support streaming RPC. A server can reply with a stream of messages to the client. Alternatively, a client can send a stream of messages to the server.

gRPC uses Protocol Buffers as the message format. Protocol Buffers is, as mentioned earlier, an efficient, compact, binary format. It's a tagged format. Each field of a Protocol Buffers message is numbered and has a type code. A message recipient can extract the fields that it needs and skip over the fields that it doesn't recognize. As a result, gRPC enables APIs to evolve while remaining backward-compatible.

Listing 3.1 shows an excerpt of the gRPC API for the Order Service. It defines several methods, including createOrder(). This method takes a CreateOrderRequest as a parameter and returns a CreateOrderReply.

Listing 3.1 An excerpt of the gRPC API for the Order Service

```
service OrderService {
  rpc createOrder(CreateOrderRequest) returns (CreateOrderReply) {}
```

```
  rpc cancelOrder(CancelOrderRequest) returns (CancelOrderReply) {}
  rpc reviseOrder(ReviseOrderRequest) returns (ReviseOrderReply) {}
  ...
}

message CreateOrderRequest {
  int64 restaurantId = 1;
  int64 consumerId = 2;
  repeated LineItem lineItems = 3;
  ...
}

message LineItem {
  string menuItemId = 1;
  int32 quantity = 2;
}


message CreateOrderReply {
  int64 orderId = 1;
}
...
```

CreateOrderRequest and CreateOrderReply are typed messages. For example, Create-OrderRequest message has a restaurantId field of type int64. The field's tag value is 1.
gRPC has several benefits:

- It's straightforward to design an API that has a rich set of update operations.
- It has an efficient, compact IPC mechanism, especially when exchanging large messages.
- Bidirectional streaming enables both RPI and messaging styles of communication.
- It enables interoperability between clients and services written in a wide range of languages.

gRPC also has several drawbacks:

- It takes more work for JavaScript clients to consume gRPC-based API than REST/JSON-based APIs.
- Older firewalls might not support HTTP/2.

gRPC is a compelling alternative to REST, but like REST, it's a synchronous communication mechanism, so it also suffers from the problem of partial failure. Let's take a look at what that is and how to handle it.

3.2.3 *Handling partial failure using the Circuit breaker pattern*

In a distributed system, whenever a service makes a synchronous request to another service, there is an ever-present risk of partial failure. Because the client and the service are separate processes, a service may not be able to respond in a timely way to a client's request. The service could be down because of a failure or for maintenance. Or the service might be overloaded and responding extremely slowly to requests.

Because the client is blocked waiting for a response, the danger is that the failure could cascade to the client's clients and so on and cause an outage.

> **Pattern: Circuit breaker**
> An RPI proxy that immediately rejects invocations for a timeout period after the number of consecutive failures exceeds a specified threshold. See http://microservices
> .io/patterns/reliability/circuit-breaker.html.

Consider, for example, the scenario shown in figure 3.2, where the Order Service is unresponsive. A mobile client makes a REST request to an API gateway, which, as discussed in chapter 8, is the entry point into the application for API clients. The API gateway proxies the request to the unresponsive Order Service.

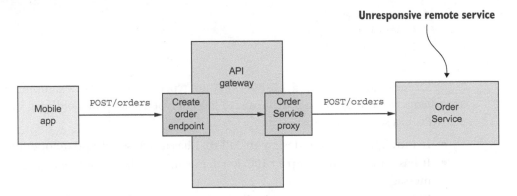

Figure 3.2 An API gateway must protect itself from unresponsive services, such as the Order Service.

A naive implementation of the OrderServiceProxy would block indefinitely, waiting for a response. Not only would that result in a poor user experience, but in many applications it would consume a precious resource, such as a thread. Eventually the API gateway would run out of resources and become unable to handle requests. The entire API would be unavailable.

It's essential that you design your services to prevent partial failures from cascading throughout the application. There are two parts to the solution:

- You must use design RPI proxies, such as OrderServiceProxy, to handle unresponsive remote services.
- You need to decide how to recover from a failed remote service.

First we'll look at how to write robust RPI proxies.

DEVELOPING ROBUST RPI PROXIES

Whenever one service synchronously invokes another service, it should protect itself using the approach described by Netflix (http://techblog.netflix.com/2012/02/fault-tolerance-in-high-volume.html). This approach consists of a combination of the following mechanisms:

- *Network timeouts*—Never block indefinitely and always use timeouts when waiting for a response. Using timeouts ensures that resources are never tied up indefinitely.
- *Limiting the number of outstanding requests from a client to a service*—Impose an upper bound on the number of outstanding requests that a client can make to a particular service. If the limit has been reached, it's probably pointless to make additional requests, and those attempts should fail immediately.
- *Circuit breaker pattern*—Track the number of successful and failed requests, and if the error rate exceeds some threshold, trip the circuit breaker so that further attempts fail immediately. A large number of requests failing suggests that the service is unavailable and that sending more requests is pointless. After a timeout period, the client should try again, and, if successful, close the circuit breaker.

Netflix Hystrix (https://github.com/Netflix/Hystrix) is an open source library that implements these and other patterns. If you're using the JVM, you should definitely consider using Hystrix when implementing RPI proxies. And if you're running in a non-JVM environment, you should use an equivalent library. For example, the Polly library is popular in the .NET community (https://github.com/App-vNext/Polly).

RECOVERING FROM AN UNAVAILABLE SERVICE

Using a library such as Hystrix is only part of the solution. You must also decide on a case-by-case basis how your services should recover from an unresponsive remote service. One option is for a service to simply return an error to its client. For example, this approach makes sense for the scenario shown in figure 3.2, where the request to create an `Order` fails. The only option is for the API gateway to return an error to the mobile client.

In other scenarios, returning a fallback value, such as either a default value or a cached response, may make sense. For example, chapter 7 describes how the API gateway could implement the `findOrder()` query operation by using the API composition pattern. As figure 3.3 shows, its implementation of the `GET /orders/{orderId}` endpoint invokes several services, including the `Order Service`, `Kitchen Service`, and `Delivery Service`, and combines the results.

It's likely that each service's data isn't equally important to the client. The data from the `Order Service` is essential. If this service is unavailable, the API gateway should return either a cached version of its data or an error. The data from the other services is less critical. A client can, for example, display useful information to the user even if the delivery status was unavailable. If the `Delivery Service` is unavailable,

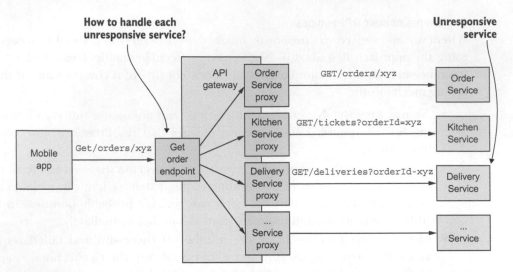

Figure 3.3   The API gateway implements the `GET /orders/{orderId}` endpoint using API composition. It calls several services, aggregates their responses, and sends a response to the mobile app. The code that implements the endpoint must have a strategy for handling the failure of each service that it calls.

the API gateway should return either a cached version of its data or omit it from the response.

It's essential that you design your services to handle partial failure, but that's not the only problem you need to solve when using RPI. Another problem is that in order for one service to invoke another service using RPI, it needs to know the network location of a service instance. On the surface this sounds simple, but in practice it's a challenging problem. You must use a service discovery mechanism. Let's look at how that works.

3.2.4   Using service discovery

Say you're writing some code that invokes a service that has a REST API. In order to make a request, your code needs to know the network location (IP address and port) of a service instance. In a traditional application running on physical hardware, the network locations of service instances are usually static. For example, your code could read the network locations from a configuration file that's occasionally updated. But in a modern, cloud-based microservices application, it's usually not that simple. As is shown in figure 3.4, a modern application is much more dynamic.

Service instances have dynamically assigned network locations. Moreover, the set of service instances changes dynamically because of autoscaling, failures, and upgrades. Consequently, your client code must use a service discovery.

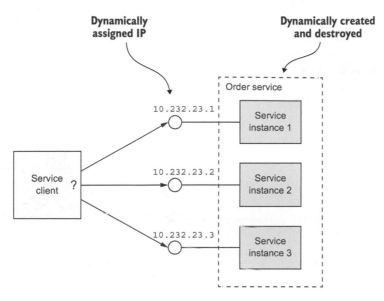

Figure 3.4   Service instances have dynamically assigned IP addresses.

OVERVIEW OF SERVICE DISCOVERY

As you've just seen, you can't statically configure a client with the IP addresses of the services. Instead, an application must use a dynamic service discovery mechanism. Service discovery is conceptually quite simple: its key component is a service registry, which is a database of the network locations of an application's service instances.

The service discovery mechanism updates the service registry when service instances start and stop. When a client invokes a service, the service discovery mechanism queries the service registry to obtain a list of available service instances and routes the request to one of them.

There are two main ways to implement service discovery:

- The services and their clients interact directly with the service registry.
- The deployment infrastructure handles service discovery. (I talk more about that in chapter 12.)

Let's look at each option.

APPLYING THE APPLICATION-LEVEL SERVICE DISCOVERY PATTERNS

One way to implement service discovery is for the application's services and their clients to interact with the service registry. Figure 3.5 shows how this works. A service instance registers its network location with the service registry. A service client invokes a service by first querying the service registry to obtain a list of service instances. It then sends a request to one of those instances.

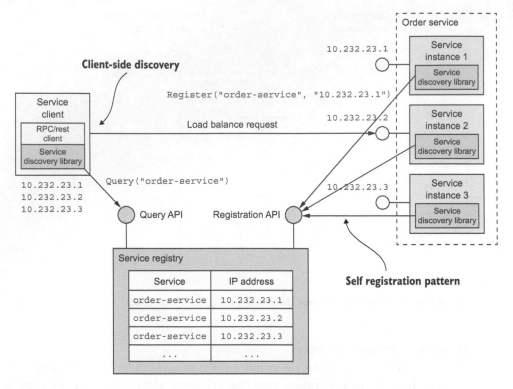

Figure 3.5   The service registry keeps track of the service instances. Clients query the service registry to find network locations of available service instances.

This approach to service discovery is a combination of two patterns. The first pattern is the Self registration pattern. A service instance invokes the service registry's registration API to register its network location. It may also supply a health check URL, described in more detail in chapter 11. The *health check* URL is an API endpoint that the service registry invokes periodically to verify that the service instance is healthy and available to handle requests. A service registry may require a service instance to periodically invoke a "heartbeat" API in order to prevent its registration from expiring.

Pattern: Self registration
A service instance registers itself with the service registry. See http://microservices.io/patterns/self-registration.html.

The second pattern is the Client-side discovery pattern. When a service client wants to invoke a service, it queries the service registry to obtain a list of the service's instances. To improve performance, a client might cache the service instances. The service client then uses a load-balancing algorithm, such as a round-robin or random, to select a service instance. It then makes a request to a select service instance.

> **Pattern: Client-side discovery**
>
> A service client retrieves the list of available service instances from the service registry and load balances across them. See http://microservices.io/patterns/client-side-discovery.html.

Application-level service discovery has been popularized by Netflix and Pivotal. Netflix developed and open sourced several components: Eureka, a highly available service registry, the Eureka Java client, and Ribbon, a sophisticated HTTP client that supports the Eureka client. Pivotal developed Spring Cloud, a Spring-based framework that makes it remarkably easy to use the Netflix components. Spring Cloud-based services automatically register with Eureka, and Spring Cloud-based clients automatically use Eureka for service discovery.

One benefit of application-level service discovery is that it handles the scenario when services are deployed on multiple deployment platforms. Imagine, for example, you've deployed only some of services on Kubernetes, discussed in chapter 12, and the rest is running in a legacy environment. Application-level service discovery using Eureka, for example, works across both environments, whereas Kubernetes-based service discovery only works within Kubernetes.

One drawback of application-level service discovery is that you need a service discovery library for every language—and possibly framework—that you use. Spring Cloud only helps Spring developers. If you're using some other Java framework or a non-JVM language such as NodeJS or GoLang, you must find some other service discovery framework. Another drawback of application-level service discovery is that you're responsible for setting up and managing the service registry, which is a distraction. As a result, it's usually better to use a service discovery mechanism that's provided by the deployment infrastructure.

APPLYING THE PLATFORM-PROVIDED SERVICE DISCOVERY PATTERNS

Later in chapter 12 you'll learn that many modern deployment platforms such as Docker and Kubernetes have a built-in service registry and service discovery mechanism. The deployment platform gives each service a DNS name, a virtual IP (VIP) address, and a DNS name that resolves to the VIP address. A service client makes a request to the DNS name/VIP, and the deployment platform automatically routes the request to one of the available service instances. As a result, service registration, service discovery, and request routing are entirely handled by the deployment platform. Figure 3.6 shows how this works.

The deployment platform includes a service registry that tracks the IP addresses of the deployed services. In this example, a client accesses the Order Service using the

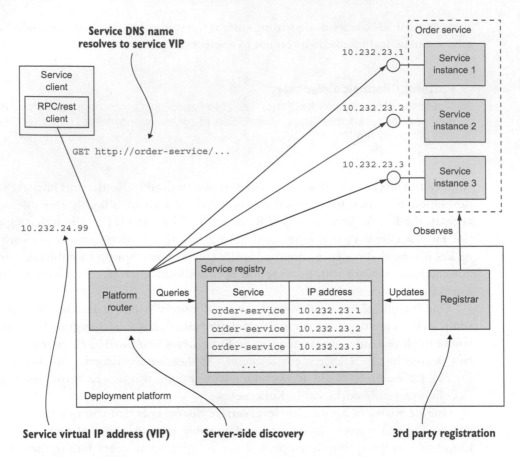

Figure 3.6   The platform is responsible for service registration, discovery, and request routing. Service instances are registered with the service registry by the *registrar*. Each service has a network location, a DNS name/virtual IP address. A client makes a request to the service's network location. The router queries the service registry and load balances requests across the available service instances.

DNS name `order-service`, which resolves to the virtual IP address `10.1.3.4`. The deployment platform automatically load balances requests across the three instances of the `Order Service`.

This approach is a combination of two patterns:

- *3rd party registration pattern*—Instead of a service registering itself with the service registry, a third party called the *registrar*, which is typically part of the deployment platform, handles the registration.
- *Server-side discovery pattern*—Instead of a client querying the service registry, it makes a request to a DNS name, which resolves to a request router that queries the service registry and load balances requests.

> **Pattern: 3rd party registration**
>
> Service instances are automatically registered with the service registry by a third party. See http://microservices.io/patterns/3rd-party-registration.html.

> **Pattern: Server-side discovery**
>
> A client makes a request to a router, which is responsible for service discovery. See http://microservices.io/patterns/server-side-discovery.html.

The key benefit of platform-provided service discovery is that all aspects of service discovery are entirely handled by the deployment platform. Neither the services nor the clients contain any service discovery code. Consequently, the service discovery mechanism is readily available to all services and clients regardless of which language or framework they're written in.

One drawback of platform-provided service discovery is that it only supports the discovery of services that have been deployed using the platform. For example, as mentioned earlier when describing application-level discovery, Kubernetes-based discovery only works for services running on Kubernetes. Despite this limitation, I recommend using platform-provided service discovery whenever possible.

Now that we've looked at synchronous IPC using REST or gRPC, let's take a look at the alternative: asynchronous, message-based communication.

3.3 Communicating using the Asynchronous messaging pattern

When using messaging, services communicate by asynchronously exchanging messages. A messaging-based application typically uses a *message broker*, which acts as an intermediary between the services, although another option is to use a brokerless architecture, where the services communicate directly with each other. A service client makes a request to a service by sending it a message. If the service instance is expected to reply, it will do so by sending a separate message back to the client. Because the communication is asynchronous, the client doesn't block waiting for a reply. Instead, the client is written assuming that the reply won't be received immediately.

> **Pattern: Messaging**
>
> A client invokes a service using asynchronous messaging. See http://microservices.io/patterns/communication-style/messaging.html.

I start this section with an overview of messaging. I show how to describe a messaging architecture independently of messaging technology. Next I compare and contrast brokerless and broker-based architectures and describe the criteria for selecting a message broker. I then discuss several important topics, including scaling consumers while preserving message ordering, detecting and discarding duplicate messages, and sending and receiving messages as part of a database transaction. Let's begin by looking at how messaging works.

3.3.1 Overview of messaging

A useful model of messaging is defined in the book *Enterprise Integration Patterns* (Addison-Wesley Professional, 2003) by Gregor Hohpe and Bobby Woolf. In this model, messages are exchanged over message channels. A sender (an application or service) writes a message to a channel, and a receiver (an application or service) reads messages from a channel. Let's look at messages and then look at channels.

ABOUT MESSAGES

A message consists of a header and a message body (www.enterpriseintegrationpatterns .com/Message.html). The *header* is a collection of name-value pairs, metadata that describes the data being sent. In addition to name-value pairs provided by the message's sender, the message header contains name-value pairs, such as a unique *message id* generated by either the sender or the messaging infrastructure, and an optional *return address*, which specifies the message channel that a reply should be written to. The message *body* is the data being sent, in either text or binary format.

There are several different kinds of messages:

- *Document*—A generic message that contains only data. The receiver decides how to interpret it. The reply to a command is an example of a document message.
- *Command*—A message that's the equivalent of an RPC request. It specifies the operation to invoke and its parameters.
- *Event*—A message indicating that something notable has occurred in the sender. An event is often a domain event, which represents a state change of a domain object such as an `Order`, or a `Customer`.

The approach to the microservice architecture described in this book uses commands and events extensively.

Let's now look at channels, the mechanism by which services communicate.

ABOUT MESSAGE CHANNELS

As figure 3.7 shows, messages are exchanged over channels (www.enterpriseintegra-tionpatterns.com/MessageChannel.html). The business logic in the sender invokes a *sending port* interface, which encapsulates the underlying communication mechanism. The *sending port* is implemented by a *message sender* adapter class, which sends a message to a receiver via a message channel. A *message channel* is an abstraction of the messaging infrastructure. A *message handler* adapter class in the receiver is invoked to handle the message. It invokes a *receiving port* interface implemented by the consumer's

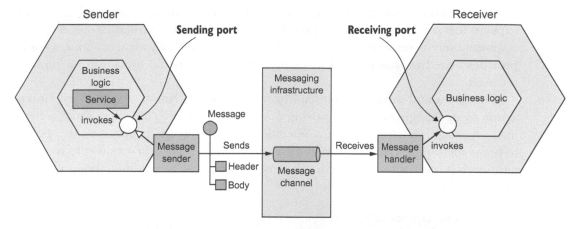

Figure 3.7   The business logic in the sender invokes a sending port interface, which is implemented by a message sender adapter. The message sender sends a message to a receiver via a message channel. The message channel is an abstraction of messaging infrastructure. A message handler adapter in the receiver is invoked to handle the message. It invokes the receiving port interface implemented by the receiver's business logic.

business logic. Any number of senders can send messages to a channel. Similarly, any number of receivers can receive messages from a channel.

There are two kinds of channels: point-to-point (www.enterpriseintegrationpatterns .com/PointToPointChannel.html) and publish-subscribe (www.enterpriseintegration- patterns.com/PublishSubscribeChannel.html):

- A *point-to-point* channel delivers a message to exactly one of the consumers that is reading from the channel. Services use point-to-point channels for the one- to-one interaction styles described earlier. For example, a command message is often sent over a point-to-point channel.
- A *publish-subscribe* channel delivers each message to all of the attached consum- ers. Services use publish-subscribe channels for the one-to-many interaction styles described earlier. For example, an event message is usually sent over a publish-subscribe channel.

3.3.2   *Implementing the interaction styles using messaging*

One of the valuable features of messaging is that it's flexible enough to support all the interaction styles described in section 3.1.1. Some interaction styles are directly imple- mented by messaging. Others must be implemented on top of messaging.

Let's look at how to implement each interaction style, starting with request/response and asynchronous request/response.

IMPLEMENTING REQUEST/RESPONSE AND ASYNCHRONOUS REQUEST/RESPONSE

When a client and service interact using either request/response or asynchronous request/response, the client sends a request and the service sends back a reply. The difference between the two interaction styles is that with request/response the client expects the service to respond immediately, whereas with asynchronous request/ response there is no such expectation. Messaging is inherently asynchronous, so only provides asynchronous request/response. But a client could block until a reply is received.

The client and service implement the asynchronous request/response style interaction by exchanging a pair of messages. As figure 3.8 shows, the client sends a command message, which specifies the operation to perform, and parameters, to a point-to-point messaging channel owned by a service. The service processes the requests and sends a reply message, which contains the outcome, to a point-to-point channel owned by the client.

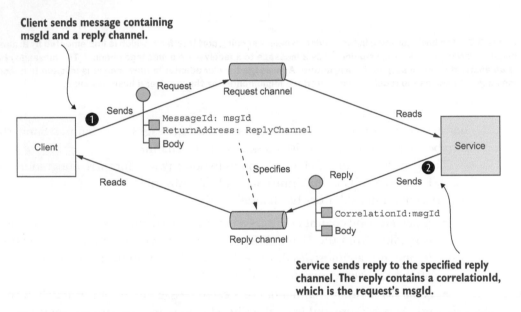

Figure 3.8   Implementing asynchronous request/response by including a reply channel and message identifier in the request message. The receiver processes the message and sends the reply to the specified reply channel.

The client must tell the service where to send a reply message and must match reply messages to requests. Fortunately, solving these two problems isn't that difficult. The client sends a command message that has a *reply channel* header. The server writes the reply message, which contains a *correlation id* that has the same value as *message identifier*, to the reply channel. The client uses the *correlation id* to match the reply message with the request.

Because the client and service communicate using messaging, the interaction is inherently asynchronous. In theory, a messaging client could block until it receives a reply, but in practice the client will process replies asynchronously. What's more, replies are typically processed by any one of the client's instances.

IMPLEMENTING ONE-WAY NOTIFICATIONS

Implementing one-way notifications is straightforward using asynchronous messaging. The client sends a message, typically a command message, to a point-to-point channel owned by the service. The service subscribes to the channel and processes the message. It doesn't send back a reply.

IMPLEMENTING PUBLISH/SUBSCRIBE

Messaging has built-in support for the publish/subscribe style of interaction. A client publishes a message to a publish-subscribe channel that is read by multiple consumers. As described in chapters 4 and 5, services use publish/subscribe to publish domain events, which represent changes to domain objects. The service that publishes the domain events owns a publish-subscribe channel, whose name is derived from the domain class. For example, the `Order Service` publishes `Order` events to an `Order` channel, and the `Delivery Service` publishes `Delivery` events to a `Delivery` channel. A service that's interested in a particular domain object's events only has to subscribe to the appropriate channel.

IMPLEMENTING PUBLISH/ASYNC RESPONSES

The publish/async responses interaction style is a higher-level style of interaction that's implemented by combining elements of publish/subscribe and request/response. A client publishes a message that specifies a *reply channel* header to a publish-subscribe channel. A consumer writes a reply message containing a *correlation id* to the reply channel. The client gathers the responses by using the *correlation id* to match the reply messages with the request.

Each service in your application that has an asynchronous API will use one or more of these implementation techniques. A service that has an asynchronous API for invoking operations will have a message channel for requests. Similarly, a service that publishes events will publish them to an event message channel.

As described in section 3.1.2, it's important to write an API specification for a service. Let's look at how to do that for an asynchronous API.

3.3.3 *Creating an API specification for a messaging-based service API*

The specification for a service's asynchronous API must, as figure 3.9 shows, specify the names of the message channels, the message types that are exchanged over each channel, and their formats. You must also describe the format of the messages using a standard such as JSON, XML, or Protobuf. But unlike with REST and Open API, there isn't a widely adopted standard for documenting the channels and the message types. Instead, you need to write an informal document.

A service's asynchronous API consists of operations, invoked by clients, and events, published by the services. They're documented in different ways. Let's take a look at each one, starting with operations.

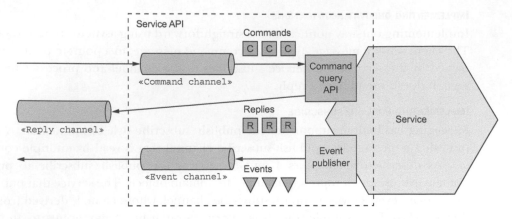

Figure 3.9   A service's asynchronous API consists of message channels and command, reply, and event message types.

DOCUMENTING ASYNCHRONOUS OPERATIONS

A service's operations can be invoked using one of two different interaction styles:

- *Request/async response-style API*—This consists of the service's command message channel, the types and formats of the command message types that the service accepts, and the types and formats of the reply messages sent by the service.
- *One-way notification-style API*—This consists of the service's command message channel and the types and format of the command message types that the service accepts.

A service may use the same request channel for both asynchronous request/response and one-way notification.

DOCUMENTING PUBLISHED EVENTS

A service can also publish events using a publish/subscribe interaction style. The specification of this style of API consists of the event channel and the types and formats of the event messages that are published by the service to the channel.

The messages and channels model of messaging is a great abstraction and a good way to design a service's asynchronous API. But in order to implement a service you need to choose a messaging technology and determine how to implement your design using its capabilities. Let's take a look at what's involved.

3.3.4   *Using a message broker*

A messaging-based application typically uses a *message broker*, an infrastructure service through which the service communicates. But a broker-based architecture isn't the only messaging architecture. You can also use a brokerless-based messaging architecture, in which the services communicate with one another directly. The two approaches, shown in figure 3.10, have different trade-offs, but usually a broker-based architecture is a better approach.

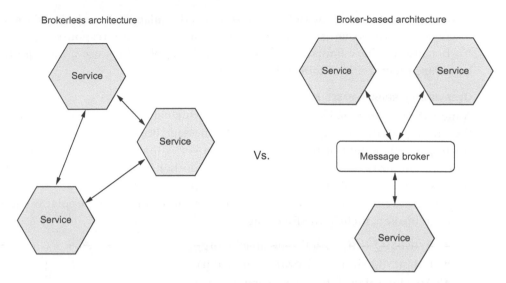

Figure 3.10   The services in brokerless architecture communicate directly, whereas the services in a broker-based architecture communicate via a message broker.

This book focuses on broker-based architecture, but it's worthwhile to take a quick look at the brokerless architecture, because there may be scenarios where you find it useful.

BROKERLESS MESSAGING

In a brokerless architecture, services can exchange messages directly. ZeroMQ (http://zeromq.org) is a popular brokerless messaging technology. It's both a specification and a set of libraries for different languages. It supports a variety of transports, including TCP, UNIX-style domain sockets, and multicast.

The brokerless architecture has some benefits:

- Allows lighter network traffic and better latency, because messages go directly from the sender to the receiver, instead of having to go from the sender to the message broker and from there to the receiver
- Eliminates the possibility of the message broker being a performance bottleneck or a single point of failure
- Features less operational complexity, because there is no message broker to set up and maintain

As appealing as these benefits may seem, brokerless messaging has significant drawbacks:

- Services need to know about each other's locations and must therefore use one of the discovery mechanisms describer earlier in section 3.2.4.
- It offers reduced availability, because both the sender and receiver of a message must be available while the message is being exchanged.
- Implementing mechanisms, such as guaranteed delivery, is more challenging.

In fact, some of these drawbacks, such as reduced availability and the need for service discovery, are the same as when using synchronous, response/response.

Because of these limitations, most enterprise applications use a message broker-based architecture. Let's look at how that works.

OVERVIEW OF BROKER-BASED MESSAGING

A message broker is an intermediary through which all messages flow. A sender writes the message to the message broker, and the message broker delivers it to the receiver. An important benefit of using a message broker is that the sender doesn't need to know the network location of the consumer. Another benefit is that a message broker buffers messages until the consumer is able to process them.

There are many message brokers to chose from. Examples of popular open source message brokers include the following:

- ActiveMQ (http://activemq.apache.org)
- RabbitMQ (https://www.rabbitmq.com)
- Apache Kafka (http://kafka.apache.org)

There are also cloud-based messaging services, such as AWS Kinesis (https://aws.amazon .com/kinesis/) and AWS SQS (https://aws.amazon.com/sqs/).

When selecting a message broker, you have various factors to consider, including the following:

- *Supported programming languages*—You probably should pick one that supports a variety of programming languages.
- *Supported messaging standards*—Does the message broker support any standards, such as AMQP and STOMP, or is it proprietary?
- *Messaging ordering*—Does the message broker preserve ordering of messages?
- *Delivery guarantees*—What kind of delivery guarantees does the broker make?
- *Persistence*—Are messages persisted to disk and able to survive broker crashes?
- *Durability*—If a consumer reconnects to the message broker, will it receive the messages that were sent while it was disconnected?
- *Scalability*—How scalable is the message broker?
- *Latency*—What is the end-to-end latency?
- *Competing consumers*—Does the message broker support competing consumers?

Each broker makes different trade-offs. For example, a very low-latency broker might not preserve ordering, make no guarantees to deliver messages, and only store messages in memory. A messaging broker that guarantees delivery and reliably stores messages on disk will probably have higher latency. Which kind of message broker is the best fit depends on your application's requirements. It's even possible that different parts of your application will have different messaging requirements.

It's likely, though, that messaging ordering and scalability are essential. Let's now look at how to implement message channels using a message broker.

IMPLEMENTING MESSAGE CHANNELS USING A MESSAGE BROKER

Each message broker implements the message channel concept in a different way. As table 3.2 shows, JMS message brokers such as ActiveMQ have queues and topics. AMQP-based message brokers such as RabbitMQ have exchanges and queues. Apache Kafka has topics, AWS Kinesis has streams, and AWS SQS has queues. What's more, some message brokers offer more flexible messaging than the message and channels abstraction described in this chapter.

Table 3.2   Each message broker implements the message channel concept in a different way.

Message broker	Point-to-point channel	Publish-subscribe channel
JMS	Queue	Topic
Apache Kafka	Topic	Topic
AMQP-based brokers, such as RabbitMQ	Exchange + Queue	Fanout exchange and a queue per consumer
AWS Kinesis	Stream	Stream
AWS SQS	Queue	—

Almost all the message brokers described here support both point-to-point and publish-subscribe channels. The one exception is AWS SQS, which only supports point-to-point channels.

Now let's look at the benefits and drawbacks of broker-based messaging.

BENEFITS AND DRAWBACKS OF BROKER-BASED MESSAGING

There are many advantages to using broker-based messaging:

- *Loose coupling*—A client makes a request by simply sending a message to the appropriate channel. The client is completely unaware of the service instances. It doesn't need to use a discovery mechanism to determine the location of a service instance.
- *Message buffering*—The message broker buffers messages until they can be processed. With a synchronous request/response protocol such as HTTP, both the client and service must be available for the duration of the exchange. With messaging, though, messages will queue up until they can be processed by the consumer. This means, for example, that an online store can accept orders from customers even when the order-fulfillment system is slow or unavailable. The messages will simply queue up until they can be processed.
- *Flexible communication*—Messaging supports all the interaction styles described earlier.
- *Explicit interprocess communication*—RPC-based mechanism attempts to make invoking a remote service look the same as calling a local service. But due to the laws of physics and the possibility of partial failure, they're in fact quite different.

Messaging makes these differences very explicit, so developers aren't lulled into a false sense of security.

There are some downsides to using messaging:

- *Potential performance bottleneck*—There is a risk that the message broker could be a performance bottleneck. Fortunately, many modern message brokers are designed to be highly scalable.
- *Potential single point of failure*—It's essential that the message broker is highly available—otherwise, system reliability will be impacted. Fortunately, most modern brokers have been designed to be highly available.
- *Additional operational complexity*—The messaging system is yet another system component that must be installed, configured, and operated.

Let's look at some design issues you might face.

3.3.5   *Competing receivers and message ordering*

One challenge is how to scale out message receivers while preserving message ordering. It's a common requirement to have multiple instances of a service in order to process messages concurrently. Moreover, even a single service instance will probably use threads to concurrently process multiple messages. Using multiple threads and service instances to concurrently process messages increases the throughput of the application. But the challenge with processing messages concurrently is ensuring that each message is processed once and in order.

For example, imagine that there are three instances of a service reading from the same point-to-point channel and that a sender publishes Order Created, Order Updated, and Order Cancelled event messages sequentially. A simplistic messaging implementation could concurrently deliver each message to a different receiver. Because of delays due to network issues or garbage collections, messages might be processed out of order, which would result in strange behavior. In theory, a service instance might process the Order Cancelled message before another service processes the Order Created message!

A common solution, used by modern message brokers like Apache Kafka and AWS Kinesis, is to use *sharded* (partitioned) channels. Figure 3.11 shows how this works. There are three parts to the solution:

1   A sharded channel consists of two or more shards, each of which behaves like a channel.
2   The sender specifies a shard key in the message's header, which is typically an arbitrary string or sequence of bytes. The message broker uses a shard key to assign the message to a particular shard/partition. It might, for example, select the shard by computing the hash of the shard key modulo the number of shards.
3   The messaging broker groups together multiple instances of a receiver and treats them as the same logical receiver. Apache Kafka, for example, uses the term *consumer group*. The message broker assigns each shard to a single receiver. It reassigns shards when receivers start up and shut down.

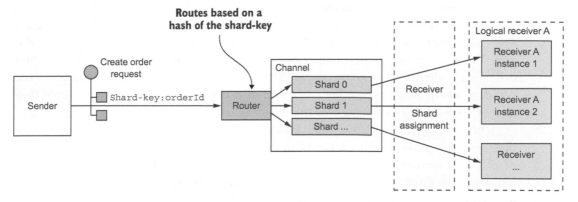

Figure 3.11 Scaling consumers while preserving message ordering by using a sharded (partitioned) message channel. The sender includes the shard key in the message. The message broker writes the message to a shard determined by the shard key. The message broker assigns each partition to an instance of the replicated receiver.

In this example, each `Order` event message has the `orderId` as its shard key. Each event for a particular order is published to the same shard, which is read by a single consumer instance. As a result, these messages are guaranteed to be processed in order.

3.3.6 *Handling duplicate messages*

Another challenge you must tackle when using messaging is dealing with duplicate messages. A message broker should ideally deliver each message only once, but guaranteeing exactly-once messaging is usually too costly. Instead, most message brokers promise to deliver a message *at least* once.

When the system is working normally, a message broker that guarantees at-least-once delivery will deliver each message only once. But a failure of a client, network, or message broker can result in a message being delivered multiple times. Say a client crashes after processing a message and updating its database—but before acknowledging the message. The message broker will deliver the unacknowledged message again, either to that client when it restarts or to another replica of the client.

Ideally, you should use a message broker that preserves ordering when redelivering messages. Imagine that the client processes an `Order Created` event followed by an `Order Cancelled` event for the same `Order`, and that somehow the `Order Created` event wasn't acknowledged. The message broker should redeliver both the `Order Created` and `Order Cancelled` events. If it only redelivers the `Order Created`, the client may undo the cancelling of the `Order`.

There are a couple of different ways to handle duplicate messages:

- Write idempotent message handlers.
- Track messages and discard duplicates.

Let's look at each option.

WRITING IDEMPOTENT MESSAGE HANDLERS

If the application logic that processes messages is idempotent, then duplicate messages are harmless. Application logic is *idempotent* if calling it multiple times with the same input values has no additional effect. For instance, cancelling an already-cancelled order is an idempotent operation. So is creating an order with a client-supplied ID. An idempotent message handler can be safely executed multiple times, provided that the message broker preserves ordering when redelivering messages.

Unfortunately, application logic is often not idempotent. Or you may be using a message broker that doesn't preserve ordering when redelivering messages. Duplicate or out-of-order messages can cause bugs. In this situation, you must write message handlers that track messages and discard duplicate messages.

TRACKING MESSAGES AND DISCARDING DUPLICATES

Consider, for example, a message handler that authorizes a consumer credit card. It must authorize the card exactly once for each order. This example of application logic has a different effect each time it's invoked. If duplicate messages caused the message handler to execute this logic multiple times, the application would behave incorrectly. The message handler that executes this kind of application logic must become idempotent by detecting and discarding duplicate messages.

A simple solution is for a message consumer to track the messages that it has processed using the message id and discard any duplicates. It could, for example, store the message id of each message that it consumed in a database table. Figure 3.12 shows how to do this using a dedicated table.

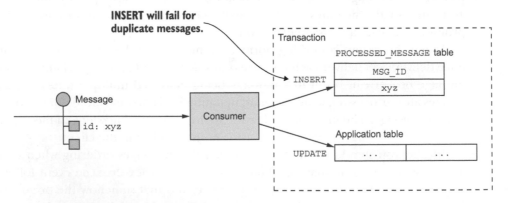

Figure 3.12   A consumer detects and discards duplicate messages by recording the IDs of processed messages in a database table. If a message has been processed before, the INSERT into the PROCESSED_MESSAGES table will fail.

When a consumer handles a message, it records the message id in the database table as part of the transaction that creates and updates business entities. In this example, the consumer inserts a row containing the message id into a PROCESSED_MESSAGES table. If a message is a duplicate, the INSERT will fail and the consumer can discard the message.

Another option is for a message handler to record `message ids` in an application table instead of a dedicated table. This approach is particularly useful when using a NoSQL database that has a limited transaction model, so it doesn't support updating two tables as part of a database transaction. Chapter 7 shows an example of this approach.

3.3.7   *Transactional messaging*

A service often needs to publish messages as part of a transaction that updates the database. For instance, throughout this book you see examples of services that publish domain events whenever they create or update business entities. Both the database update and the sending of the message must happen within a transaction. Otherwise, a service might update the database and then crash, for example, before sending the message. If the service doesn't perform these two operations atomically, a failure could leave the system in an inconsistent state.

The traditional solution is to use a distributed transaction that spans the database and the message broker. But as you'll learn in chapter 4, distributed transactions aren't a good choice for modern applications. Moreover, many modern brokers such as Apache Kafka don't support distributed transactions.

As a result, an application must use a different mechanism to reliably publish messages. Let's look at how that works.

USING A DATABASE TABLE AS A MESSAGE QUEUE

Let's imagine that your application is using a relational database. A straightforward way to reliably publish messages is to apply the Transactional outbox pattern. This pattern uses a database table as a temporary message queue. As figure 3.13 shows, a service that sends messages has an `OUTBOX` database table. As part of the database

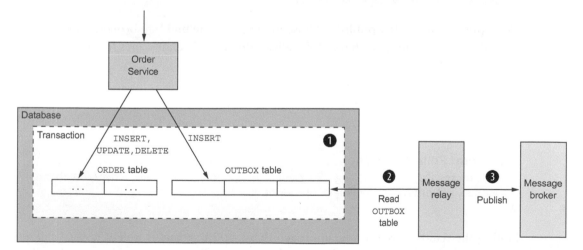

Figure 3.13   A service reliably publishes a message by inserting it into an `OUTBOX` **table as part of the transaction that updates the database. The** `Message Relay` **reads the** `OUTBOX` **table and publishes the messages to a message broker.**

transaction that creates, updates, and deletes business objects, the service sends messages by inserting them into the OUTBOX table. Atomicity is guaranteed because this is a local ACID transaction.

The OUTBOX table acts a temporary message queue. The MessageRelay is a component that reads the OUTBOX table and publishes the messages to a message broker.

> **Pattern: Transactional outbox**
> Publish an event or message as part of a database transaction by saving it in an OUT-BOX in the database. See http://microservices.io/patterns/data/transactional-outbox.html.

You can use a similar approach with some NoSQL databases. Each business entity stored as a record in the database has an attribute that is a list of messages that need to be published. When a service updates an entity in the database, it appends a message to that list. This is atomic because it's done with a single database operation. The challenge, though, is efficiently finding those business entities that have events and publishing them.

There are a couple of different ways to move messages from the database to the message broker. We'll look at each one.

PUBLISHING EVENTS BY USING THE POLLING PUBLISHER PATTERN
If the application uses a relational database, a very simple way to publish the messages inserted into the OUTBOX table is for the MessageRelay to poll the table for unpublished messages. It periodically queries the table:

```
SELECT * FROM OUTBOX ORDERED BY ... ASC
```

Next, the MessageRelay publishes those messages to the message broker, sending one to its destination message channel. Finally, it deletes those messages from the OUTBOX table:

```
BEGIN
 DELETE FROM OUTBOX WHERE ID in (....)
COMMIT
```

> **Pattern: Polling publisher**
> Publish messages by polling the outbox in the database. See http://microservices.io/patterns/data/polling-publisher.html.

Polling the database is a simple approach that works reasonably well at low scale. The downside is that frequently polling the database can be expensive. Also, whether you can use this approach with a NoSQL database depends on its querying capabilities. That's because rather than querying an OUTBOX table, the application must query the business entities, and that may or may not be possible to do efficiently. Because of these drawbacks and limitations, it's often better—and in some cases, necessary—to use the more sophisticated and performant approach of tailing the database transaction log.

PUBLISHING EVENTS BY APPLYING THE TRANSACTION LOG TAILING PATTERN

A sophisticated solution is for `MessageRelay` to *tail* the database transaction log (also called the commit log). Every committed update made by an application is represented as an entry in the database's transaction log. A transaction log miner can read the transaction log and publish each change as a message to the message broker. Figure 3.14 shows how this approach works.

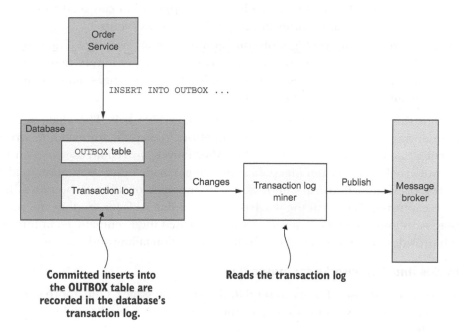

Figure 3.14   A service publishes messages inserted into the OUTBOX table by mining the database's transaction log.

The `Transaction Log Miner` reads the transaction log entries. It converts each relevant log entry corresponding to an inserted message into a message and publishes that message to the message broker. This approach can be used to publish messages written to an OUTBOX table in an RDBMS or messages appended to records in a NoSQL database.

Pattern: Transaction log tailing

Publish changes made to the database by tailing the transaction log. See http://micro-services.io/patterns/data/transaction-log-tailing.html.

There are a few examples of this approach in use:

- *Debezium* (http://debezium.io)—An open source project that publishes database changes to the Apache Kafka message broker.
- *LinkedIn Databus* (https://github.com/linkedin/databus)—An open source project that mines the Oracle transaction log and publishes the changes as events. LinkedIn uses Databus to synchronize various derived data stores with the system of record.
- *DynamoDB streams* (http://docs.aws.amazon.com/amazondynamodb/latest/developerguide/Streams.html)—DynamoDB streams contain the time-ordered sequence of changes (creates, updates, and deletes) made to the items in a DynamoDB table in the last 24 hours. An application can read those changes from the stream and, for example, publish them as events.
- *Eventuate Tram* (https://github.com/eventuate-tram/eventuate-tram-core)—Your author's very own open source transaction messaging library that uses MySQL binlog protocol, Postgres WAL, or polling to read changes made to an OUTBOX table and publish them to Apache Kafka.

Although this approach is obscure, it works remarkably well. The challenge is that implementing it requires some development effort. You could, for example, write low-level code that calls database-specific APIs. Alternatively, you could use an open source framework such as Debezium that publishes changes made by an application to MySQL, Postgres, or MongoDB to Apache Kafka. The drawback of using Debezium is that its focus is capturing changes at the database level and that APIs for sending and receiving messages are outside of its scope. That's why I created the Eventuate Tram framework, which provides the messaging APIs as well as transaction tailing and polling.

3.3.8   *Libraries and frameworks for messaging*

A service needs to use a library to send and receive messages. One approach is to use the message broker's client library, although there are several problems with using such a library directly:

- The client library couples business logic that publishes messages to the message broker APIs.
- A message broker's client library is typically low level and requires many lines of code to send or receive a message. As a developer, you don't want to repeatedly write boilerplate code. Also, as the author of this book I don't want the example code cluttered with low-level boilerplate.
- The client library usually provides only the basic mechanism to send and receive messages and doesn't support the higher-level interaction styles.

A better approach is to use a higher-level library or framework that hides the low-level details and directly supports the higher-level interaction styles. For simplicity, the examples in this book use my Eventuate Tram framework. It has a simple, easy-to-understand API that hides the complexity of using the message broker. Besides an API for sending and receiving messages, Eventuate Tram also supports higher-level interaction styles such as asynchronous request/response and domain event publishing.

What!? Why the Eventuate frameworks?

The code samples in this book use the open source Eventuate frameworks I've developed for transactional messaging, event sourcing, and sagas. I chose to use my frameworks because, unlike with, say, dependency injection and the Spring framework, there are no widely adopted frameworks for many of the features the microservice architecture requires. Without the Eventuate Tram framework, many examples would have to use the low-level messaging APIs directly, making them much more complicated and obscuring important concepts. Or they would use a framework that isn't widely adopted, which would also provoke criticism.

Instead, the examples use the Eventuate Tram frameworks, which have a simple, easy-to-understand API that hides the implementation details. You can use these frameworks in your applications. Alternatively, you can study the Eventuate Tram frameworks and reimplement the concepts yourself.

Eventuate Tram also implements two important mechanisms:

- *Transactional messaging*—It publishes messages as part of a database transaction.
- *Duplicate message detection*—The Eventuate Tram message consumer detects and discards duplicate messages, which is essential for ensuring that a consumer processes messages exactly once, as discussed in section 3.3.6.

Let's take a look at the Eventuate Tram APIs.

BASIC MESSAGING

The basic messaging API consists of two Java interfaces: `MessageProducer` and `Message-Consumer`. A producer service uses the `MessageProducer` interface to publish messages to message channels. Here's an example of using this interface:

```
MessageProducer messageProducer = ...;
String channel - ...;
String payload = ...;
messageProducer.send(destination, MessageBuilder.withPayload(payload).build())
```

A consumer service uses the `MessageConsumer` interface to subscribe to messages:

```
MessageConsumer messageConsumer;
messageConsumer.subscribe(subscriberId, Collections.singleton(destination),
    message -> { ... })
```

`MessageProducer` and `MessageConsumer` are the foundation of the higher-level APIs for asynchronous request/response and domain event publishing.

Let's talk about how to publish and subscribe to events.

DOMAIN EVENT PUBLISHING

Eventuate Tram has APIs for publishing and consuming domain events. Chapter 5 explains that domain events are events that are emitted by an *aggregate* (business object) when it's created, updated, or deleted. A service publishes a domain event using the DomainEventPublisher interface. Here is an example:

```
DomainEventPublisher domainEventPublisher;

String accountId = ...;

DomainEvent domainEvent = new AccountDebited(...);

domainEventPublisher.publish("Account", accountId, Collections.singletonList(
    domainEvent));
```

A service consumes domain events using the DomainEventDispatcher. An example follows:

```
DomainEventHandlers domainEventHandlers = DomainEventHandlersBuilder
        .forAggregateType("Order")
        .onEvent(AccountDebited.class, domainEvent -> { ... })
        .build();

new DomainEventDispatcher("eventDispatcherId",
        domainEventHandlers,
        messageConsumer);
```

Events aren't the only high-level messaging pattern supported by Eventuate Tram. It also supports command/reply-based messaging.

COMMAND/REPLY-BASED MESSAGING

A client can send a command message to a service using the CommandProducer interface. For example

```
CommandProducer commandProducer = ...;

Map<String, String> extraMessageHeaders = Collections.emptyMap();

String commandId = commandProducer.send("CustomerCommandChannel",
        new DoSomethingCommand(),
        "ReplyToChannel",
        extraMessageHeaders);
```

A service consumes command messages using the CommandDispatcher class. CommandDispatcher uses the MessageConsumer interface to subscribe to specified events. It dispatches each command message to the appropriate handler method. Here's an example:

```
CommandHandlers commandHandlers =CommandHandlersBuilder
        .fromChannel(commandChannel)
        .onMessage(DoSomethingCommand.class, (command) -
> { ... ; return withSuccess(); })
        .build();
```

```
CommandDispatcher dispatcher = new CommandDispatcher("subscribeId",
    commandHandlers, messageConsumer, messageProducer);
```

Throughout this book, you'll see code examples that use these APIs for sending and receiving messages.

As you've seen, the Eventuate Tram framework implements transactional messaging for Java applications. It provides a low-level API for sending and receiving messages transactionally. It also provides the higher-level APIs for publishing and consuming domain events and for sending and processing commands.

Let's now look at a service design approach that uses asynchronous messaging to improve availability.

3.4 Using asynchronous messaging to improve availability

As you've seen, a variety of IPC mechanisms have different trade-offs. One particular trade-off is how your choice of IPC mechanism impacts availability. In this section, you'll learn that synchronous communication with other services as part of request handling reduces application availability. As a result, you should design your services to use asynchronous messaging whenever possible.

Let's first look at the problem with synchronous communication and how it impacts availability.

3.4.1 Synchronous communication reduces availability

REST is an extremely popular IPC mechanism. You may be tempted to use it for inter-service communication. The problem with REST, though, is that it's a synchronous protocol: an HTTP client must wait for the service to send a response. Whenever services communicate using a synchronous protocol, the availability of the application is reduced.

To see why, consider the scenario shown in figure 3.15. The Order Service has a REST API for creating an Order. It invokes the Consumer Service and the Restaurant Service to validate the Order. Both of those services also have REST APIs.

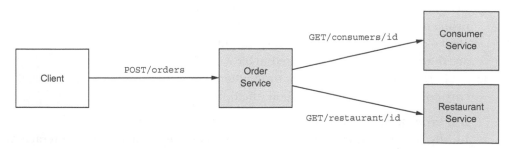

Figure 3.15 The Order Service invokes other services using REST. It's straightforward, but it requires all the services to be simultaneously available, which reduces the availability of the API.

The sequence of steps for creating an order is as follows:

1 Client makes an HTTP POST /orders request to the Order Service.
2 Order Service retrieves consumer information by making an HTTP GET /consumers/id request to the Consumer Service.
3 Order Service retrieves restaurant information by making an HTTP GET /restaurant/id request to the Restaurant Service.
4 Order Taking validates the request using the consumer and restaurant information.
5 Order Taking creates an Order.
6 Order Taking sends an HTTP response to the client.

Because these services use HTTP, they must all be simultaneously available in order for the FTGO application to process the CreateOrder request. The FTGO application couldn't create orders if any one of these three services is down. Mathematically speaking, the availability of a system operation is the product of the availability of the services that are invoked by that operation. If the Order Service and the two services that it invokes are 99.5% available, the overall availability is $99.5\%^3 = 98.5\%$, which is significantly less. Each additional service that participates in handling a request further reduces availability.

This problem isn't specific to REST-based communication. Availability is reduced whenever a service can only respond to its client after receiving a response from another service. This problem exists even if services communicate using request/response style interaction over asynchronous messaging. For example, the availability of the Order Service would be reduced if it sent a message to the Consumer Service via a message broker and then waited for a response.

If you want to maximize availability, you must minimize the amount of synchronous communication. Let's look at how to do that.

3.4.2   *Eliminating synchronous interaction*

There are a few different ways to reduce the amount of synchronous communication with other services while handling synchronous requests. One solution is to avoid the problem entirely by defining services that only have asynchronous APIs. That's not always possible, though. For example, public APIs are commonly RESTful. Services are therefore sometimes required to have synchronous APIs.

Fortunately, there are ways to handle synchronous requests without making synchronous requests. Let's talk about the options.

USE ASYNCHRONOUS INTERACTION STYLES
Ideally, all interactions should be done using the asynchronous interaction styles described earlier in this chapter. For example, say a client of the FTGO application used an asynchronous request/asynchronous response style of interaction to create orders. A client creates an order by sending a request message to the Order Service.

This service then asynchronously exchanges messages with other services and eventually sends a reply message to the client. Figure 3.16 shows the design.

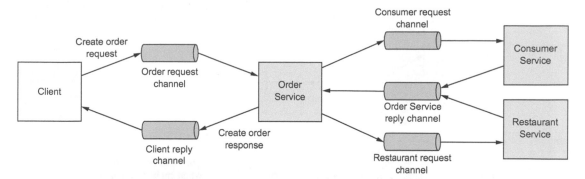

Figure 3.16   The FTGO application has higher availability if its services communicate using asynchronous messaging instead of synchronous calls.

The client and the services communicate asynchronously by sending messages via messaging channels. No participant in this interaction is ever blocked waiting for a response.

Such an architecture would be extremely resilient, because the message broker buffers messages until they can be consumed. The problem, however, is that services often have an external API that uses a synchronous protocol such as REST, so it must respond to requests immediately.

If a service has a synchronous API, one way to improve availability is to replicate data. Let's see how that works.

REPLICATE DATA

One way to minimize synchronous requests during request processing is to replicate data. A service maintains a replica of the data that it needs when processing requests. It keeps the replica up-to-date by subscribing to events published by the services that own the data. For example, `Order Service` could maintain a replica of data owned by `Consumer Service` and `Restaurant Service`. This would enable `Order Service` to handle a request to create an order without having to interact with those services. Figure 3.17 shows the design.

`Consumer Service` and `Restaurant Service` publish events whenever their data changes. `Order Service` subscribes to those events and updates its replica.

In some situations, replicating data is a useful approach. For example, chapter 5 describes how `Order Service` replicates data from `Restaurant Service` so that it can validate and price menu items. One drawback of replication is that it can sometimes require the replication of large amounts of data, which is inefficient. For example, it may not be practical for `Order Service` to maintain a replica of the data owned by `Consumer Service`, due to the large number of consumers. Another drawback of

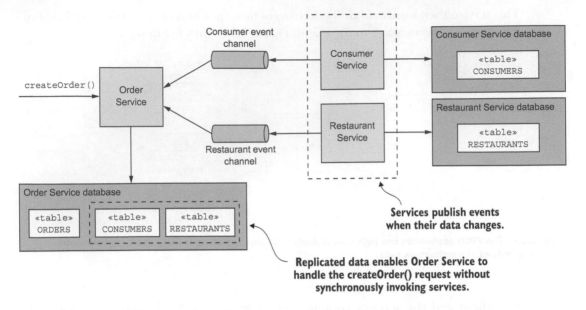

Services publish events when their data changes.

Replicated data enables Order Service to handle the createOrder() request without synchronously invoking services.

Figure 3.17 Order Service **is self-contained because it has replicas of the consumer and restaurant data.**

replication is that it doesn't solve the problem of how a service updates data owned by other services.

One way to solve that problem is for a service to delay interacting with other services until after it responds to its client. We'll next look at how that works.

FINISH PROCESSING AFTER RETURNING A RESPONSE

Another way to eliminate synchronous communication during request processing is for a service to handle a request as follows:

1 Validate the request using only the data available locally.
2 Update its database, including inserting messages into the OUTBOX table.
3 Return a response to its client.

While handling a request, the service doesn't synchronously interact with any other services. Instead, it asynchronously sends messages to other services. This approach ensures that the services are loosely coupled. As you'll learn in the next chapter, this is often implemented using a *saga*.

For example, if Order Service uses this approach, it creates an order in a PENDING state and then validates the order asynchronously by exchanging messages with other services. Figure 3.18 shows what happens when the createOrder() operation is invoked. The sequence of events is as follows:

1 Order Service creates an Order in a PENDING state.
2 Order Service returns a response to its client containing the order ID.
3 Order Service sends a ValidateConsumerInfo message to Consumer Service.

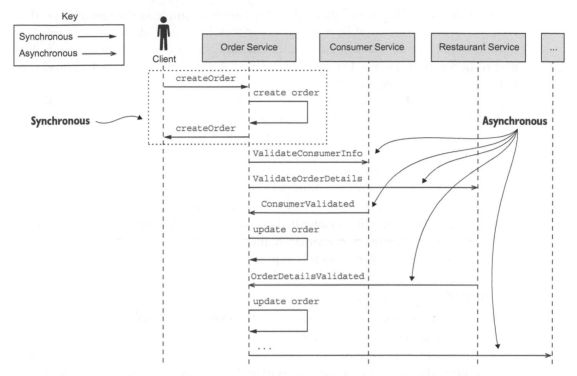

Figure 3.18 `Order Service` creates an order without invoking any other service. It then asynchronously validates the newly created `Order` by exchanging messages with other services, including `Consumer Service` and `Restaurant Service`.

4 `Order Service` sends a `ValidateOrderDetails` message to `Restaurant Service`.

5 `Consumer Service` receives a `ValidateConsumerInfo` message, verifies the consumer can place an order, and sends a `ConsumerValidated` message to `Order Service`.

6 `Restaurant Service` receives a `ValidateOrderDetails` message, verifies the menu item are valid and that the restaurant can deliver to the order's delivery address, and sends an `OrderDetailsValidated` message to `Order Service`.

7 `Order Service` receives `ConsumerValidated` and `OrderDetailsValidated` and changes the state of the order to `VALIDATED`.

8 ...

`Order Service` can receive the `ConsumerValidated` and `OrderDetailsValidated` messages in either order. It keeps track of which message it receives first by changing the state of the order. If it receives the `ConsumerValidated` first, it changes the state of the order to `CONSUMER_VALIDATED`, whereas if it receives the `OrderDetailsValidated` message first, it changes its state to `ORDER_DETAILS_VALIDATED`. `Order Service` changes the state of the `Order` to `VALIDATED` when it receives the other message.

After the Order has been validated, `Order Service` completes the rest of the order-creation process, discussed in the next chapter. What's nice about this approach is that even if `Consumer Service` is down, for example, `Order Service` still creates orders and responds to its clients. Eventually, `Consumer Service` will come back up and process any queued messages, and orders will be validated.

A drawback of a service responding before fully processing a request is that it makes the client more complex. For example, `Order Service` makes minimal guarantees about the state of a newly created order when it returns a response. It creates the order and returns immediately before validating the order and authorizing the consumer's credit card. Consequently, in order for the client to know whether the order was successfully created, either it must periodically poll or `Order Service` must send it a notification message. As complex as it sounds, in many situations this is the preferred approach—especially because it also addresses the distributed transaction management issues I discuss in the next chapter. In chapters 4 and 5, for example, I describe how `Order Service` uses this approach.

Summary

- The microservice architecture is a distributed architecture, so interprocess communication plays a key role.
- It's essential to carefully manage the evolution of a service's API. Backward-compatible changes are the easiest to make because they don't impact clients. If you make a breaking change to a service's API, it will typically need to support both the old and new versions until its clients have been upgraded.
- There are numerous IPC technologies, each with different trade-offs. One key design decision is to choose either a synchronous remote procedure invocation pattern or the asynchronous Messaging pattern. Synchronous remote procedure invocation-based protocols, such as REST, are the easiest to use. But services should ideally communicate using asynchronous messaging in order to increase availability.
- In order to prevent failures from cascading through a system, a service client that uses a synchronous protocol must be designed to handle partial failures, which are when the invoked service is either down or exhibiting high latency. In particular, it must use timeouts when making requests, limit the number of outstanding requests, and use the Circuit breaker pattern to avoid making calls to a failing service.
- An architecture that uses synchronous protocols must include a service discovery mechanism in order for clients to determine the network location of a service instance. The simplest approach is to use the service discovery mechanism implemented by the deployment platform: the Server-side discovery and 3rd party registration patterns. But an alternative approach is to implement service discovery at the application level: the Client-side discovery and Self registration

patterns. It's more work, but it does handle the scenario where services are running on multiple deployment platforms.

- A good way to design a messaging-based architecture is to use the messages and channels model, which abstracts the details of the underlying messaging system. You can then map that design to a specific messaging infrastructure, which is typically message broker–based.
- One key challenge when using messaging is atomically updating the database and publishing a message. A good solution is to use the Transactional outbox pattern and first write the message to the database as part of the database transaction. A separate process then retrieves the message from the database using either the Polling publisher pattern or the Transaction log tailing pattern and publishes it to the message broker.

Managing transactions with sagas

This chapter covers

- Why distributed transactions aren't a good fit for modern applications
- Using the Saga pattern to maintain data consistency in a microservice architecture
- Coordinating sagas using choreography and orchestration
- Using countermeasures to deal with the lack of isolation

When Mary started investigating the microservice architecture, one of her biggest concerns was how to implement transactions that span multiple services. Transactions are an essential ingredient of every enterprise application. Without transactions it would be impossible to maintain data consistency.

ACID (Atomicity, Consistency, Isolation, Durability) transactions greatly simplify the job of the developer by providing the illusion that each transaction has exclusive access to the data. In a microservice architecture, transactions that are within a single service can still use ACID transactions. The challenge, however, lies in implementing transactions for operations that update data owned by multiple services.

For example, as described in chapter 2, the `createOrder()` operation spans numerous services, including `Order Service`, `Kitchen Service`, and `Accounting Service`. Operations such as these need a transaction management mechanism that works across services.

Mary discovered that, as mentioned in chapter 2, the traditional approach to distributed transaction management isn't a good choice for modern applications. Instead of an ACID transactions, an operation that spans services must use what's known as a *saga*, a message-driven sequence of local transactions, to maintain data consistency. One challenge with sagas is that they are ACD (Atomicity, Consistency, Durability). They lack the isolation feature of traditional ACID transactions. As a result, an application must use what are known as *countermeasures*, design techniques that prevent or reduce the impact of concurrency anomalies caused by the lack of isolation.

In many ways, the biggest obstacle that Mary and the FTGO developers will face when adopting microservices is moving from a single database with ACID transactions to a multi-database architecture with ACD sagas. They're used to the simplicity of the ACID transaction model. But in reality, even monolithic applications such as the FTGO application typically don't use textbook ACID transactions. For example, many applications use a lower transaction isolation level in order to improve performance. Also, many important business processes, such as transferring money between accounts at different banks, are eventually consistent. Not even Starbucks uses two-phase commit (www.enterpriseintegrationpatterns.com/ramblings/18_starbucks.html).

I begin this chapter by looking at the challenges of transaction management in the microservice architecture and explain why the traditional approach to distributed transaction management isn't an option. Next I explain how to maintain data consistency using sagas. After that I look at the two different ways of coordinating sagas: *choreography*, where participants exchange events without a centralized point of control, and *orchestration*, where a centralized controller tells the saga participants what operation to perform. I discuss how to use countermeasures to prevent or reduce the impact of concurrency anomalies caused by the lack of isolation between sagas. Finally, I describe the implementation of an example saga.

Let's start by taking a look at the challenge of managing transactions in a microservice architecture.

4.1 Transaction management in a microservice architecture

Almost every request handled by an enterprise application is executed within a database transaction. Enterprise application developers use frameworks and libraries that simplify transaction management. Some frameworks and libraries provide a programmatic API for explicitly beginning, committing, and rolling back transactions. Other frameworks, such as the Spring framework, provide a declarative mechanism. Spring provides an `@Transactional` annotation that arranges for method invocations to be automatically executed within a transaction. As a result, it's straightforward to write transactional business logic.

Or, to be more precise, transaction management is straightforward in a monolithic application that accesses a single database. Transaction management is more challenging in a complex monolithic application that uses multiple databases and message brokers. And in a microservice architecture, transactions span multiple services, each of which has its own database. In this situation, the application must use a more elaborate mechanism to manage transactions. As you'll learn, the traditional approach of using distributed transactions isn't a viable option for modern applications. Instead, a microservices-based application must use sagas.

Before I explain sagas, let's first look at why transaction management is challenging in a microservice architecture.

4.1.1   *The need for distributed transactions in a microservice architecture*

Imagine that you're the FTGO developer responsible for implementing the `create-Order()` system operation. As described in chapter 2, this operation must verify that the consumer can place an order, verify the order details, authorize the consumer's credit card, and create an `Order` in the database. It's relatively straightforward to implement this operation in the monolithic FTGO application. All the data required to validate the order is readily accessible. What's more, you can use an ACID transaction to ensure data consistency. You might use Spring's `@Transactional` annotation on the `createOrder()` service method.

In contrast, implementing the same operation in a microservice architecture is much more complicated. As figure 4.1 shows, the needed data is scattered around multiple services. The `createOrder()` operation accesses data in numerous services. It reads data from `Consumer Service` and updates data in `Order Service`, `Kitchen Service`, and `Accounting Service`.

Because each service has its own database, you need to use a mechanism to maintain data consistency across those databases.

4.1.2   *The trouble with distributed transactions*

The traditional approach to maintaining data consistency across multiple services, databases, or message brokers is to use distributed transactions. The de facto standard for distributed transaction management is the X/Open Distributed Transaction Processing (DTP) Model (X/Open XA—see https://en.wikipedia.org/wiki/X/Open_XA). XA uses *two-phase commit* (2PC) to ensure that all participants in a transaction either commit or rollback. An XA-compliant technology stack consists of XA-compliant databases and message brokers, database drivers, and messaging APIs, and an interprocess communication mechanism that propagates the XA global transaction ID. Most SQL databases are XA compliant, as are some message brokers. Java EE applications can, for example, use JTA to perform distributed transactions.

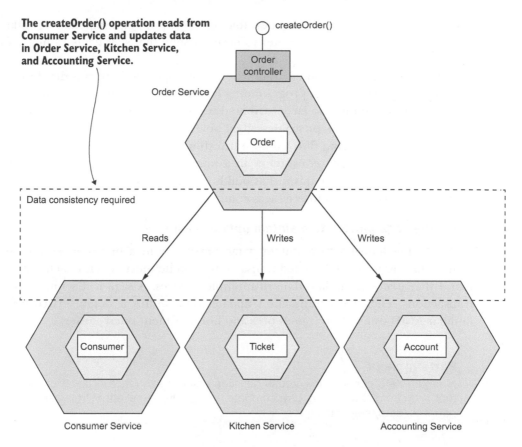

The createOrder() operation reads from Consumer Service and updates data in Order Service, Kitchen Service, and Accounting Service.

createOrder()

Order controller

Order Service

Order

Data consistency required

Reads   Writes   Writes

Consumer   Ticket   Account

Consumer Service   Kitchen Service   Accounting Service

Figure 4.1 The `createOrder()` operation updates data in several services. It must use a mechanism to maintain data consistency across those services.

As simple as this sounds, there are a variety of problems with distributed transactions. One problem is that many modern technologies, including NoSQL databases such as MongoDB and Cassandra, don't support them. Also, distributed transactions aren't supported by modern message brokers such as RabbitMQ and Apache Kafka. As a result, if you insist on using distributed transactions, you can't use many modern technologies.

Another problem with distributed transactions is that they are a form of synchronous IPC, which reduces availability. In order for a distributed transaction to commit, all the participating services must be available. As described in chapter 3, the availability is the product of the availability of all of the participants in the transaction. If a distributed transaction involves two services that are 99.5% available, then the overall availability is 99%, which is significantly less. Each additional service involved in a distributed transaction further reduces availability. There is even Eric Brewer's CAP theorem, which states that a system can only have two of the following three properties:

consistency, availability, and partition tolerance (https://en.wikipedia.org/wiki/CAP _theorem). Today, architects prefer to have a system that's available rather than one that's consistent.

On the surface, distributed transactions are appealing. From a developer's perspective, they have the same programming model as local transactions. But because of the problems mentioned so far, distributed transactions aren't a viable technology for modern applications. Chapter 3 described how to send messages as part of a database transaction without using distributed transactions. To solve the more complex problem of maintaining data consistency in a microservice architecture, an application must use a different mechanism that builds on the concept of loosely coupled, asynchronous services. This is where sagas come in.

4.1.3 *Using the Saga pattern to maintain data consistency*

Sagas are mechanisms to maintain data consistency in a microservice architecture without having to use distributed transactions. You define a saga for each system command that needs to update data in multiple services. A saga is a sequence of local transactions. Each local transaction updates data within a single service using the familiar ACID transaction frameworks and libraries mentioned earlier.

Pattern: Saga

Maintain data consistency across services using a sequence of local transactions that are coordinated using asynchronous messaging. See http://microservices.io/ patterns/data/saga.html.

The system operation initiates the first step of the saga. The completion of a local transaction triggers the execution of the next local transaction. Later, in section 4.2, you'll see how coordination of the steps is implemented using asynchronous messaging. An important benefit of asynchronous messaging is that it ensures that all the steps of a saga are executed, even if one or more of the saga's participants is temporarily unavailable.

Sagas differ from ACID transactions in a couple of important ways. As I describe in detail in section 4.3, they lack the isolation property of ACID transactions. Also, because each local transaction commits its changes, a saga must be rolled back using compensating transactions. I talk more about compensating transactions later in this section. Let's take a look at an example saga.

AN EXAMPLE SAGA: THE CREATE ORDER SAGA

The example saga used throughout this chapter is the Create Order Saga, which is shown in figure 4.2. The Order Service implements the createOrder() operation using this saga. The saga's first local transaction is initiated by the external request to create an order. The other five local transactions are each triggered by completion of the previous one.

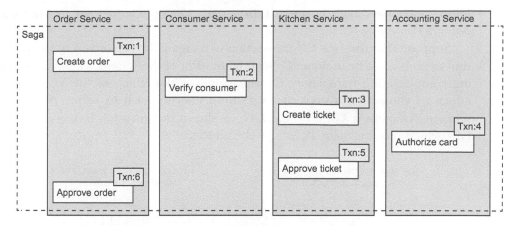

Figure 4.2   Creating an `Order` using a saga. The `createOrder()` operation is implemented by a saga that consists of local transactions in several services.

This saga consists of the following local transactions:

1   `Order Service`—Create an `Order` in an `APPROVAL_PENDING` state.
2   `Consumer Service`—Verify that the consumer can place an order.
3   `Kitchen Service`—Validate order details and create a `Ticket` in the `CREATE_PENDING`.
4   `Accounting Service`—Authorize consumer's credit card.
5   `Kitchen Service`—Change the state of the `Ticket` to `AWAITING_ACCEPTANCE`.
6   `Order Service`—Change the state of the `Order` to `APPROVED`.

Later, in section 4.2, I describe how the services that participate in a saga communicate using asynchronous messaging. A service publishes a message when a local transaction completes. This message then triggers the next step in the saga. Not only does using messaging ensure the saga participants are loosely coupled, it also guarantees that a saga completes. That's because if the recipient of a message is temporarily unavailable, the message broker buffers the message until it can be delivered.

On the surface, sagas seem straightforward, but there are a few challenges to using them. One challenge is the lack of isolation between sagas. Section 4.3 describes how to handle this problem. Another challenge is rolling back changes when an error occurs. Let's take a look at how to do that.

SAGAS USE COMPENSATING TRANSACTIONS TO ROLL BACK CHANGES
A great feature of traditional ACID transactions is that the business logic can easily roll back a transaction if it detects the violation of a business rule. It executes a ROLLBACK statement, and the database undoes all the changes made so far. Unfortunately, sagas can't be automatically rolled back, because each step commits its changes to the local database. This means, for example, that if the authorization of the credit card fails in the fourth step of the Create Order Saga, the FTGO application must explicitly

undo the changes made by the first three steps. You must write what are known as *compensating transactions.*

Suppose that the $(n + 1)^{th}$ transaction of a saga fails. The effects of the previous n transactions must be undone. Conceptually, each of those steps, T_i, has a corresponding compensating transaction, C_i, which undoes the effects of the T_i. To undo the effects of those first n steps, the saga must execute each C_i in reverse order. The sequence of steps is $T_1 \ldots T_n, C_n \ldots C_1$, as shown in figure 4.3. In this example, T_{n+1} fails, which requires steps $T_1 \ldots T_n$ to be undone.

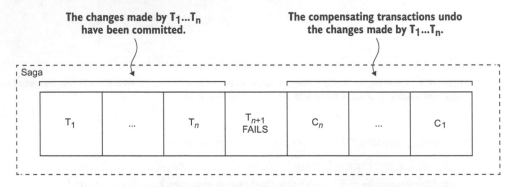

Figure 4.3   When a step of a saga fails because of a business rule violation, the saga must explicitly undo the updates made by previous steps by executing compensating transactions.

The saga executes the compensation transactions in reverse order of the forward transactions: $C_n \ldots C_1$. The mechanics of sequencing the C_is aren't any different than sequencing the T_is. The completion of C_i must trigger the execution of C_{i-1}.

Consider, for example, the `Create Order Saga`. This saga can fail for a variety of reasons:

- The consumer information is invalid or the consumer isn't allowed to create orders.
- The restaurant information is invalid or the restaurant is unable to accept orders.
- The authorization of the consumer's credit card fails.

If a local transaction fails, the saga's coordination mechanism must execute compensating transactions that reject the `Order` and possibly the `Ticket`. Table 4.1 shows the compensating transactions for each step of the `Create Order Saga`. It's important to note that not all steps need compensating transactions. Read-only steps, such as `verifyConsumerDetails()`, don't need compensating transactions. Nor do steps such as `authorizeCreditCard()` that are followed by steps that always succeed.

Section 4.3 discusses how the first three steps of the `Create Order Saga` are termed *compensatable transactions* because they're followed by steps that can fail, how the fourth step is termed the saga's *pivot transaction* because it's followed by steps that

Table 4.1 The compensating transactions for the `Create Order Saga`

Step	Service	Transaction	Compensating transaction
1	Order Service	createOrder()	rejectOrder()
2	Consumer Service	verifyConsumerDetails()	—
3	Kitchen Service	createTicket()	rejectTicket()
4	Accounting Service	authorizeCreditCard()	—
5	Kitchen Service	approveTicket()	—
6	Order Service	approveOrder()	—

never fail, and how the last two steps are termed *retriable transactions* because they always succeed.

To see how compensating transactions are used, imagine a scenario where the authorization of the consumer's credit card fails. In this scenario, the saga executes the following local transactions:

1 Order Service—Create an Order in an APPROVAL_PENDING state.
2 Consumer Service—Verify that the consumer can place an order.
3 Kitchen Service—Validate order details and create a Ticket in the CREATE _PENDING state.
4 Accounting Service—Authorize consumer's credit card, which fails.
5 Kitchen Service—Change the state of the Ticket to CREATE_REJECTED.
6 Order Service—Change the state of the Order to REJECTED.

The fifth and sixth steps are compensating transactions that undo the updates made by Kitchen Service and Order Service, respectively. A saga's coordination logic is responsible for sequencing the execution of forward and compensating transactions. Let's look at how that works.

4.2 Coordinating sagas

A saga's implementation consists of logic that coordinates the steps of the saga. When a saga is initiated by system command, the coordination logic must select and tell the first saga participant to execute a local transaction. Once that transaction completes, the saga's sequencing coordination selects and invokes the next saga participant. This process continues until the saga has executed all the steps. If any local transaction fails, the saga must execute the compensating transactions in reverse order. There are a couple of different ways to structure a saga's coordination logic:

- *Choreography*—Distribute the decision making and sequencing among the saga participants. They primarily communicate by exchanging events.

- *Orchestration*—Centralize a saga's coordination logic in a saga orchestrator class. A saga *orchestrator* sends command messages to saga participants telling them which operations to perform.

Let's look at each option, starting with choreography.

4.2.1 *Choreography-based sagas*

One way you can implement a saga is by using choreography. When using choreography, there's no central coordinator telling the saga participants what to do. Instead, the saga participants subscribe to each other's events and respond accordingly. To show how choreography-based sagas work, I'll first describe an example. After that, I'll discuss a couple of design issues that you must address. Then I'll discuss the benefits and drawbacks of using choreography.

IMPLEMENTING THE CREATE ORDER SAGA USING CHOREOGRAPHY

Figure 4.4 shows the design of the choreography-based version of the Create Order Saga. The participants communicate by exchanging events. Each participant, starting with the Order Service, updates its database and publishes an event that triggers the next participant.

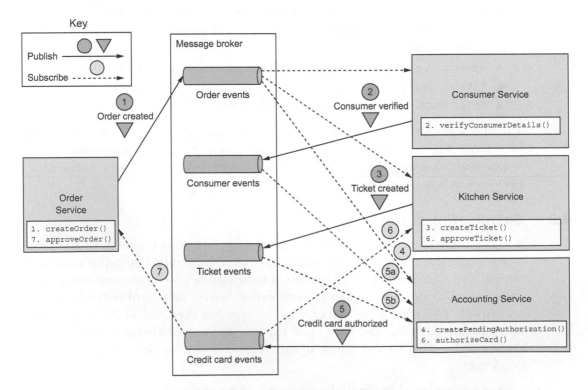

Figure 4.4 Implementing the Create Order Saga using choreography. The saga participants communicate by exchanging events.

The happy path through this saga is as follows:

1 `Order Service` creates an `Order` in the `APPROVAL_PENDING` state and publishes an `OrderCreated` event.

2 `Consumer Service` consumes the `OrderCreated` event, verifies that the consumer can place the order, and publishes a `ConsumerVerified` event.

3 `Kitchen Service` consumes the `OrderCreated` event, validates the `Order`, creates a `Ticket` in a `CREATE_PENDING` state, and publishes the `TicketCreated` event.

4 `Accounting Service` consumes the `OrderCreated` event and creates a `CreditCardAuthorization` in a `PENDING` state.

5 `Accounting Service` consumes the `TicketCreated` and `ConsumerVerified` events, charges the consumer's credit card, and publishes the `CreditCardAuthorized` event.

6 `Kitchen Service` consumes the `CreditCardAuthorized` event and changes the state of the `Ticket` to `AWAITING_ACCEPTANCE`.

7 `Order Service` receives the `CreditCardAuthorized` events, changes the state of the `Order` to `APPROVED`, and publishes an `OrderApproved` event.

The `Create Order Saga` must also handle the scenario where a saga participant rejects the `Order` and publishes some kind of failure event. For example, the authorization of the consumer's credit card might fail. The saga must execute the compensating transactions to undo what's already been done. Figure 4.5 shows the flow of events when the `AccountingService` can't authorize the consumer's credit card.

The sequence of events is as follows:

1 `Order Service` creates an `Order` in the `APPROVAL_PENDING` state and publishes an `OrderCreated` event.

2 `Consumer Service` consumes the `OrderCreated` event, verifies that the consumer can place the order, and publishes a `ConsumerVerified` event.

3 `Kitchen Service` consumes the `OrderCreated` event, validates the `Order`, creates a `Ticket` in a `CREATE_PENDING` state, and publishes the `TicketCreated` event.

4 `Accounting Service` consumes the `OrderCreated` event and creates a `CreditCardAuthorization` in a `PENDING` state.

5 `Accounting Service` consumes the `TicketCreated` and `ConsumerVerified` events, charges the consumer's credit card, and publishes a `Credit Card Authorization Failed` event.

6 `Kitchen Service` consumes the `Credit Card Authorization Failed` event and changes the state of the `Ticket` to `REJECTED`.

7 `Order Service` consumes the `Credit Card Authorization Failed` event and changes the state of the `Order` to `REJECTED`.

As you can see, the participants of choreography-based sagas interact using publish/ subscribe. Let's take a closer look at some issues you'll need to consider when implementing publish/subscribe-based communication for your sagas.

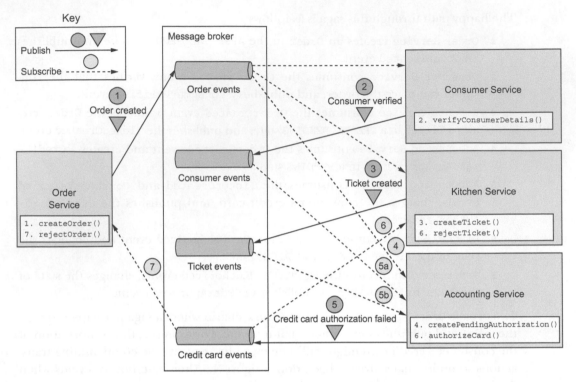

Figure 4.5 **The sequence of events in the `Create Order Saga` when the authorization of the consumer's credit card fails. `Accounting Service` publishes the `Credit Card Authorization Failed` event, which causes `Kitchen Service` to reject the `Ticket`, and `Order Service` to reject the `Order`.**

RELIABLE EVENT-BASED COMMUNICATION

There are a couple of interservice communication-related issues that you must consider when implementing choreography-based sagas. The first issue is ensuring that a saga participant updates its database and publishes an event as part of a database transaction. Each step of a choreography-based saga updates the database and publishes an event. For example, in the `Create Order Saga`, `Kitchen Service` receives a `Consumer Verified` event, creates a `Ticket`, and publishes a `Ticket Created` event. It's essential that the database update and the publishing of the event happen atomically. Consequently, to communicate reliably, the saga participants must use transactional messaging, described in chapter 3.

The second issue you need to consider is ensuring that a saga participant must be able to map each event that it receives to its own data. For example, when `Order Service` receives a `Credit Card Authorized` event, it must be able to look up the corresponding `Order`. The solution is for a saga participant to publish events containing a *correlation id*, which is data that enables other participants to perform the mapping.

For example, the participants of the `Create Order Saga` can use the `orderId` as a correlation ID that's passed from one participant to the next. `Accounting Service` publishes a `Credit Card Authorized` event containing the `orderId` from the `Ticket-Created` event. When `Order Service` receives a `Credit Card Authorized` event, it uses the `orderId` to retrieve the corresponding `Order`. Similarly, `Kitchen Service` uses the `orderId` from that event to retrieve the corresponding `Ticket`.

BENEFITS AND DRAWBACKS OF CHOREOGRAPHY-BASED SAGAS

Choreography-based sagas have several benefits:

- *Simplicity*—Services publish events when they create, update, or delete business objects.
- *Loose coupling*—The participants subscribe to events and don't have direct knowledge of each other.

And there are some drawbacks:

- *More difficult to understand*—Unlike with orchestration, there isn't a single place in the code that defines the saga. Instead, choreography distributes the implementation of the saga among the services. Consequently, it's sometimes difficult for a developer to understand how a given saga works.
- *Cyclic dependencies between the services*—The saga participants subscribe to each other's events, which often creates cyclic dependencies. For example, if you carefully examine figure 4.4, you'll see that there are cyclic dependencies, such as `Order Service` → `Accounting Service` → `Order Service`. Although this isn't necessarily a problem, cyclic dependencies are considered a design smell.
- *Risk of tight coupling*—Each saga participant needs to subscribe to all events that affect them. For example, `Accounting Service` must subscribe to all events that cause the consumer's credit card to be charged or refunded. As a result, there's a risk that it would need to be updated in lockstep with the order lifecycle implemented by `Order Service`.

Choreography can work well for simple sagas, but because of these drawbacks it's often better for more complex sagas to use orchestration. Let's look at how orchestration works.

4.2.2 *Orchestration-based sagas*

Orchestration is another way to implement sagas. When using orchestration, you define an orchestrator class whose sole responsibility is to tell the saga participants what to do. The saga orchestrator communicates with the participants using command/async reply-style interaction. To execute a saga step, it sends a command message to a participant telling it what operation to perform. After the saga participant has performed the operation, it sends a reply message to the orchestrator. The orchestrator then processes the message and determines which saga step to perform next.

To show how orchestration-based sagas work, I'll first describe an example. Then I'll describe how to model orchestration-based sagas as state machines. I'll discuss how to make use of transactional messaging to ensure reliable communication between the saga orchestrator and the saga participants. I'll then describe the benefits and drawbacks of using orchestration-based sagas.

IMPLEMENTING THE CREATE ORDER SAGA USING ORCHESTRATION

Figure 4.6 shows the design of the orchestration-based version of the Create Order Saga. The saga is orchestrated by the CreateOrderSaga class, which invokes the saga participants using asynchronous request/response. This class keeps track of the process and sends command messages to saga participants, such as Kitchen Service and Consumer Service. The CreateOrderSaga class reads reply messages from its reply channel and then determines the next step, if any, in the saga.

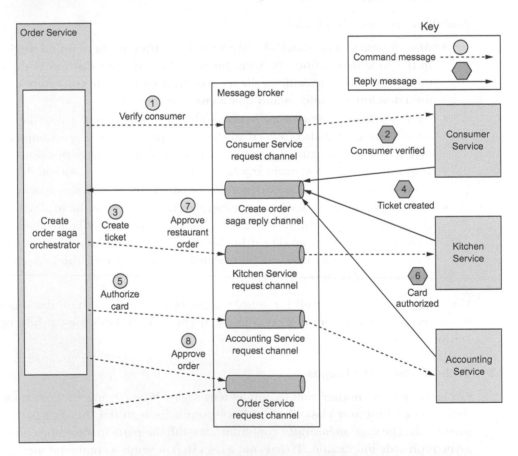

Figure 4.6 Implementing the Create Order Saga using orchestration. Order Service implements a saga orchestrator, which invokes the saga participants using asynchronous request/ response.

`Order Service` first creates an `Order` and a `Create Order Saga` orchestrator. After that, the flow for the happy path is as follows:

1 The saga orchestrator sends a `Verify Consumer` command to `Consumer Service`.
2 `Consumer Service` replies with a `Consumer Verified` message.
3 The saga orchestrator sends a `Create Ticket` command to `Kitchen Service`.
4 `Kitchen Service` replies with a `Ticket Created` message.
5 The saga orchestrator sends an `Authorize Card` message to `Accounting Service`.
6 `Accounting Service` replies with a `Card Authorized` message.
7 The saga orchestrator sends an `Approve Ticket` command to `Kitchen Service`.
8 The saga orchestrator sends an `Approve Order` command to `Order Service`.

Note that in final step, the saga orchestrator sends a command message to `Order Service`, even though it's a component of `Order Service`. In principle, the `Create Order Saga` could approve the `Order` by updating it directly. But in order to be consistent, the saga treats `Order Service` as just another participant.

Diagrams such as figure 4.6 each depict one scenario for a saga, but a saga is likely to have numerous scenarios. For example, the `Create Order Saga` has four scenarios. In addition to the happy path, the saga can fail due to a failure in either `Consumer Service`, `Kitchen Service`, or `Accounting Service`. It's useful, therefore, to model a saga as a state machine, because it describes all possible scenarios.

MODELING SAGA ORCHESTRATORS AS STATE MACHINES

A good way to model a saga orchestrator is as a state machine. A *state machine* consists of a set of states and a set of transitions between states that are triggered by events. Each transition can have an action, which for a saga is the invocation of a saga participant. The transitions between states are triggered by the completion of a local transaction performed by a saga participant. The current state and the specific outcome of the local transaction determine the state transition and what action, if any, to perform. There are also effective testing strategies for state machines. As a result, using a state machine model makes designing, implementing, and testing sagas easier.

Figure 4.7 shows the state machine model for the `Create Order Saga`. This state machine consists of numerous states, including the following:

- `Verifying Consumer`—The initial state. When in this state, the saga is waiting for the `Consumer Service` to verify that the consumer can place the order.
- `Creating Ticket`—The saga is waiting for a reply to the `Create Ticket` command.
- `Authorizing Card`—Waiting for `Accounting Service` to authorize the consumer's credit card.
- `Order Approved`—A final state indicating that the saga completed successfully.
- `Order Rejected`—A final state indicating that the `Order` was rejected by one of the participants.

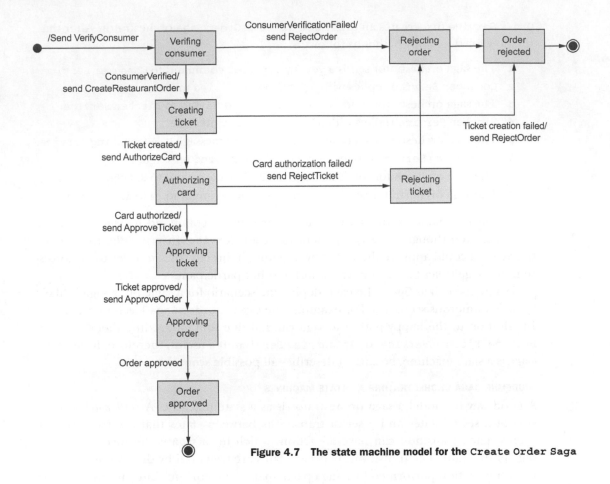

Figure 4.7   The state machine model for the `Create Order Saga`

The state machine also defines numerous state transitions. For example, the state machine transitions from the `Creating Ticket` state to either the `Authorizing Card` or the `Rejected Order` state. It transitions to the `Authorizing Card` state when it receives a successful reply to the `Create Ticket` command. Alternatively, if `Kitchen Service` couldn't create the `Ticket`, the state machine transitions to the `Rejected Order` state.

The state machine's initial action is to send the `VerifyConsumer` command to `Consumer Service`. The response from `Consumer Service` triggers the next state transition. If the consumer was successfully verified, the saga creates the `Ticket` and transitions to the `Creating Ticket` state. But if the consumer verification failed, the saga rejects the `Order` and transitions to the `Rejecting Order` state. The state machine undergoes numerous other state transitions, driven by the responses from saga participants, until it reaches a final state of either `Order Approved` or `Order Rejected`.

SAGA ORCHESTRATION AND TRANSACTIONAL MESSAGING

Each step of an orchestration-based saga consists of a service updating a database and publishing a message. For example, `Order Service` persists an `Order` and a `Create Order Saga` orchestrator and sends a message to the first saga participant. A saga participant, such as `Kitchen Service`, handles a command message by updating its database and sending a reply message. `Order Service` processes the participant's reply message by updating the state of the saga orchestrator and sending a command message to the next saga participant. As described in chapter 3, a service must use transactional messaging in order to atomically update the database and publish messages. Later on in section 4.4, I'll describe the implementation of the `Create Order Saga` orchestrator in more detail, including how it uses transaction messaging.

Let's take a look at the benefits and drawbacks of using saga orchestration.

BENEFITS AND DRAWBACKS OF ORCHESTRATION-BASED SAGAS

Orchestration-based sagas have several benefits:

- *Simpler dependencies*—One benefit of orchestration is that it doesn't introduce cyclic dependencies. The saga orchestrator invokes the saga participants, but the participants don't invoke the orchestrator. As a result, the orchestrator depends on the participants but not vice versa, and so there are no cyclic dependencies.

- *Less coupling*—Each service implements an API that is invoked by the orchestrator, so it does not need to know about the events published by the saga participants.

- *Improves separation of concerns and simplifies the business logic*—The saga coordination logic is localized in the saga orchestrator. The domain objects are simpler and have no knowledge of the sagas that they participate in. For example, when using orchestration, the `Order` class has no knowledge of any of the sagas, so it has a simpler state machine model. During the execution of the `Create Order Saga`, it transitions directly from the `APPROVAL_PENDING` state to the `APPROVED` state. The `Order` class doesn't have any intermediate states corresponding to the steps of the saga. As a result, the business is much simpler.

Orchestration also has a drawback: the risk of centralizing too much business logic in the orchestrator. This results in a design where the smart orchestrator tells the dumb services what operations to do. Fortunately, you can avoid this problem by designing orchestrators that are solely responsible for sequencing and don't contain any other business logic.

I recommend using orchestration for all but the simplest sagas. Implementing the coordination logic for your sagas is just one of the design problems you need to solve. Another, which is perhaps the biggest challenge that you'll face when using sagas, is handling the lack of isolation. Let's take a look at that problem and how to solve it.

4.3   *Handling the lack of isolation*

The *I* in ACID stands for *isolation.* The isolation property of ACID transactions ensures that the outcome of executing multiple transactions concurrently is the same as if they were executed in some serial order. The database provides the illusion that each ACID transaction has exclusive access to the data. Isolation makes it a lot easier to write business logic that executes concurrently.

The challenge with using sagas is that they lack the isolation property of ACID transactions. That's because the updates made by each of a saga's local transactions are immediately visible to other sagas once that transaction commits. This behavior can cause two problems. First, other sagas can change the data accessed by the saga while it's executing. And other sagas can read its data before the saga has completed its updates, and consequently can be exposed to inconsistent data. You can, in fact, consider a saga to be ACD:

- *Atomicity*—The saga implementation ensures that all transactions are executed or all changes are undone.
- *Consistency*—Referential integrity within a service is handled by local databases. Referential integrity across services is handled by the services.
- *Durability*—Handled by local databases.

This lack of isolation potentially causes what the database literature calls *anomalies.* An anomaly is when a transaction reads or writes data in a way that it wouldn't if transactions were executed one at time. When an anomaly occurs, the outcome of executing sagas concurrently is different than if they were executed serially.

On the surface, the lack of isolation sounds unworkable. But in practice, it's common for developers to accept reduced isolation in return for higher performance. An RDBMS lets you specify the isolation level for each transaction (https://dev.mysql .com/doc/refman/5.7/en/innodb-transaction-isolation-levels.html). The default isolation level is usually an isolation level that's weaker than full isolation, also known as serializable transactions. Real-world database transactions are often different from textbook definitions of ACID transactions.

The next section discusses a set of saga design strategies that deal with the lack of isolation. These strategies are known as *countermeasures.* Some countermeasures implement isolation at the application level. Other countermeasures reduce the business risk of the lack of isolation. By using countermeasures, you can write saga-based business logic that works correctly.

I'll begin the section by describing the anomalies that are caused by the lack of isolation. After that, I'll talk about countermeasures that either eliminate those anomalies or reduce their business risk.

4.3.1 Overview of anomalies

The lack of isolation can cause the following three anomalies:

- *Lost updates*—One saga overwrites without reading changes made by another saga.
- *Dirty reads*—A transaction or a saga reads the updates made by a saga that has not yet completed those updates.
- *Fuzzy/nonrepeatable reads*—Two different steps of a saga read the same data and get different results because another saga has made updates.

All three anomalies can occur, but the first two are the most common and the most challenging. Let's take a look at those two types of anomaly, starting with lost updates.

LOST UPDATES

A lost update anomaly occurs when one saga overwrites an update made by another saga. Consider, for example, the following scenario:

1 The first step of the `Create Order Saga` creates an `Order`.
2 While that saga is executing, the `Cancel Order Saga` cancels the `Order`.
3 The final step of the `Create Order Saga` approves the `Order`.

In this scenario, the `Create Order Saga` ignores the update made by the `Cancel Order Saga` and overwrites it. As a result, the FTGO application will ship an order that the customer had cancelled. Later in this section, I'll show how to prevent lost updates.

DIRTY READS

A dirty read occurs when one saga reads data that's in the middle of being updated by another saga. Consider, for example, a version of the FTGO application store where consumers have a credit limit. In this application, a saga that cancels an order consists of the following transactions:

- `Consumer Service`—Increase the available credit.
- `Order Service`—Change the state of the `Order` to cancelled.
- `Delivery Service`—Cancel the delivery.

Let's imagine a scenario that interleaves the execution of the `Cancel Order` and `Create Order` Sagas, and the `Cancel Order` Saga is rolled back because it's too late to cancel the delivery. It's possible that the sequence of transactions that invoke the `Consumer Service` is as follows:

1 `Cancel Order Saga`—Increase the available credit.
2 `Create Order Saga`—Reduce the available credit.
3 `Cancel Order Saga`—A compensating transaction that reduces the available credit.

In this scenario, the `Create Order Saga` does a dirty read of the available credit that enables the consumer to place an order that exceeds their credit limit. It's likely that this is an unacceptable risk to the business.

Let's look at how to prevent this and other kinds of anomalies from impacting an application.

4.3.2 *Countermeasures for handling the lack of isolation*

The saga transaction model is ACD, and its lack of isolation can result in anomalies that cause applications to misbehave. It's the responsibility of the developer to write sagas in a way that either prevents the anomalies or minimizes their impact on the business. This may sound like a daunting task, but you've already seen an example of a strategy that prevents anomalies. An Order's use of *_PENDING states, such as APPROVAL _PENDING, is an example of one such strategy. Sagas that update Orders, such as the Create Order Saga, begin by setting the state of an Order to *_PENDING. The *_PENDING state tells other transactions that the Order is being updated by a saga and to act accordingly.

An Order's use of *_PENDING states is an example of what the 1998 paper "Semantic ACID properties in multidatabases using remote procedure calls and update propagations" by Lars Frank and Torben U. Zahle calls a *semantic lock countermeasure* (https://dl.acm.org/citation.cfm?id=284472.284478). The paper describes how to deal with the lack of transaction isolation in multi-database architectures that don't use distributed transactions. Many of its ideas are useful when designing sagas. It describes a set of countermeasures for handling anomalies caused by lack of isolation that either prevent one or more anomalies or minimize their impact on the business. The countermeasures described by this paper are as follows:

- *Semantic lock*—An application-level lock.
- *Commutative updates*—Design update operations to be executable in any order.
- *Pessimistic view*—Reorder the steps of a saga to minimize business risk.
- *Reread value*—Prevent dirty writes by rereading data to verify that it's unchanged before overwriting it.
- *Version file*—Record the updates to a record so that they can be reordered.
- *By value*—Use each request's business risk to dynamically select the concurrency mechanism.

Later in this section, I describe each of these countermeasures, but first I want to introduce some terminology for describing the structure of a saga that's useful when discussing countermeasures.

THE STRUCTURE OF A SAGA

The countermeasures paper mentioned in the last section defines a useful model for the structure of a saga. In this model, shown in figure 4.8, a saga consists of three types of transactions:

- *Compensatable transactions*—Transactions that can potentially be rolled back using a compensating transaction.
- *Pivot transaction*—The go/no-go point in a saga. If the pivot transaction commits, the saga will run until completion. A pivot transaction can be a transaction that's neither compensatable nor retriable. Alternatively, it can be the last compensatable transaction or the first retriable transaction.

- *Retriable transactions*—Transactions that follow the pivot transaction and are guaranteed to succeed.

Compensatable transactions:
Must support roll back

Step	Service	Transaction	Compensation Transaction
1	Order Service	`createOrder()`	`rejectOrder()`
2	Consumer Service	`verifyConsumerDetails()`	–
3	Kitchen Service	`createTicket()`	`rejectTicket()`
4	Accounting Service	`authorizeCreditCard()`	–
5	Restaurant Order Service	`approveRestaurantOrder()`	–
6	Order Service	`approveOrder()`	–

Pivot transactions:
The saga's go/no-go transaction.
If it succeeds, then the saga runs
to completion.

Retriable transactions:
Guaranteed to complete

Figure 4.8 A saga consists of three different types of transactions: compensatable transactions, which can be rolled back, so have a compensating transaction, a pivot transaction, which is the saga's go/no-go point, and retriable transactions, which are transactions that don't need to be rolled back and are guaranteed to complete.

In the `Create Order Saga`, the `createOrder()`, `verifyConsumerDetails()`, and `createTicket()` steps are compensatable transactions. The `createOrder()` and `createTicket()` transactions have compensating transactions that undo their updates. The `verifyConsumerDetails()` transaction is read-only, so doesn't need a compensating transaction. The `authorizeCreditCard()` transaction is this saga's pivot transaction. If the consumer's credit card can be authorized, this saga is guaranteed to complete. The `approveTicket()` and `approveOrder()` steps are retriable transactions that follow the pivot transaction.

The distinction between compensatable transactions and retriable transactions is especially important. As you'll see, each type of transaction plays a different role in the countermeasures. Chapter 13 states that when migrating to microservices, the monolith must sometimes participate in sagas and that it's significantly simpler if the monolith only ever needs to execute retriable transactions.

Let's now look at each countermeasure, starting with the semantic lock countermeasure.

COUNTERMEASURE: SEMANTIC LOCK

When using the semantic lock countermeasure, a saga's compensatable transaction sets a flag in any record that it creates or updates. The flag indicates that the record isn't *committed* and could potentially change. The flag can either be a lock that prevents other transactions from accessing the record or a warning that indicates that other transactions should treat that record with suspicion. It's cleared by either a retriable transaction—saga is completing successfully—or by a compensating transaction: the saga is rolling back.

The `Order.state` field is a great example of a semantic lock. The `*_PENDING` states, such as `APPROVAL_PENDING` and `REVISION_PENDING`, implement a semantic lock. They tell other sagas that access an `Order` that a saga is in the process of updating the `Order`. For instance, the first step of the `Create Order Saga`, which is a compensatable transaction, creates an `Order` in an `APPROVAL_PENDING` state. The final step of the `Create Order Saga`, which is a retriable transaction, changes the field to `APPROVED`. A compensating transaction changes the field to `REJECTED`.

Managing the lock is only half the problem. You also need to decide on a case-by-case basis how a saga should deal with a record that has been locked. Consider, for example, the `cancelOrder()` system command. A client might invoke this operation to cancel an `Order` that's in the `APPROVAL_PENDING` state.

There are a few different ways to handle this scenario. One option is for the `cancelOrder()` system command to fail and tell the client to try again later. The main benefit of this approach is that it's simple to implement. The drawback, however, is that it makes the client more complex because it has to implement retry logic.

Another option is for `cancelOrder()` to block until the lock is released. A benefit of using semantic locks is that they essentially recreate the isolation provided by ACID transactions. Sagas that update the same record are serialized, which significantly reduces the programming effort. Another benefit is that they remove the burden of retries from the client. The drawback is that the application must manage locks. It must also implement a deadlock detection algorithm that performs a rollback of a saga to break a deadlock and re-execute it.

COUNTERMEASURE: COMMUTATIVE UPDATES

One straightforward countermeasure is to design the update operations to be commutative. Operations are *commutative* if they can be executed in any order. An `Account`'s `debit()` and `credit()` operations are commutative (if you ignore overdraft checks). This countermeasure is useful because it eliminates lost updates.

Consider, for example, a scenario where a saga needs to be rolled back after a compensatable transaction has debited (or credited) an account. The compensating transaction can simply credit (or debit) the account to undo the update. There's no possibility of overwriting updates made by other sagas.

COUNTERMEASURE: PESSIMISTIC VIEW

Another way to deal with the lack of isolation is the *pessimistic view* countermeasure. It reorders the steps of a saga to minimize business risk due to a dirty read. Consider, for example, the scenario earlier used to describe the dirty read anomaly. In that scenario, the `Create Order Saga` performed a dirty read of the available credit and created an order that exceeded the consumer credit limit. To reduce the risk of that happening, this countermeasure would reorder the Cancel Order Saga:

1 Order Service—Change the state of the Order to cancelled.
2 Delivery Service—Cancel the delivery.
3 Customer Service—Increase the available credit.

In this reordered version of the saga, the available credit is increased in a retriable transaction, which eliminates the possibility of a dirty read.

COUNTERMEASURE: REREAD VALUE

The *reread value* countermeasure prevents lost updates. A saga that uses this countermeasure rereads a record before updating it, verifies that it's unchanged, and then updates the record. If the record has changed, the saga aborts and possibly restarts. This countermeasure is a form of the Optimistic Offline Lock pattern (https://martinfowler.com/eaaCatalog/optimisticOfflineLock.html).

The Create Order Saga could use this countermeasure to handle the scenario where the Order is cancelled while it's in the process of being approved. The transaction that approves the Order verifies that the Order is unchanged since it was created earlier in the saga. If it's unchanged, the transaction approves the Order. But if the Order has been cancelled, the transaction aborts the saga, which causes its compensating transactions to be executed.

COUNTERMEASURE: VERSION FILE

The *version file* countermeasure is so named because it records the operations that are performed on a record so that it can reorder them. It's a way to turn noncommutative operations into commutative operations. To see how this countermeasure works, consider a scenario where the Create Order Saga executes concurrently with a Cancel Order Saga. Unless the sagas use the semantic lock countermeasure, it's possible that the Cancel Order Saga cancels the authorization of the consumer's credit card before the Create Order Saga authorizes the card.

One way for the Accounting Service to handle these out-of-order requests is for it to record the operations as they arrive and then execute them in the correct order. In this scenario, it would first record the Cancel Authorization request. Then, when the Accounting Service receives the subsequent Authorize Card request, it would notice that it had already received the Cancel Authorization request and skip authorizing the credit card.

COUNTERMEASURE: BY VALUE

The final countermeasure is the *by value* countermeasure. It's a strategy for selecting concurrency mechanisms based on business risk. An application that uses this countermeasure uses the properties of each request to decide between using sagas and distributed transactions. It executes low-risk requests using sagas, perhaps applying the countermeasures described in the preceding section. But it executes high-risk requests involving, for example, large amounts of money, using distributed transactions.

This strategy enables an application to dynamically make trade-offs about business risk, availability, and scalability.

It's likely that you'll need to use one or more of these countermeasures when implementing sagas in your application. Let's look at the detailed design and implementation of the Create Order Saga, which uses the semantic lock countermeasure.

4.4   The design of the Order Service and the Create Order Saga

Now that we've looked at various saga design and implementation issues, let's see an example. Figure 4.9 shows the design of Order Service. The service's business logic consists of traditional business logic classes, such as Order Service and the Order

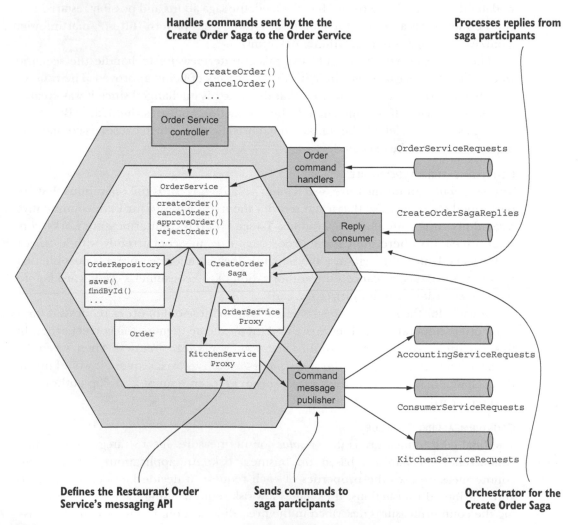

Figure 4.9   The design of the Order Service and its sagas

entity. There are also saga orchestrator classes, including the `CreateOrderSaga` class, which orchestrates `Create Order Saga`. Also, because `Order Service` participates in its own sagas, it has an `OrderCommandHandlers` adapter class that handles command messages by invoking `OrderService`.

Some parts of `Order Service` should look familiar. As in a traditional application, the core of the business logic is implemented by the `OrderService`, `Order`, and `Order-Repository` classes. In this chapter, I'll briefly describe these classes. I describe them in more detail in chapter 5.

What's less familiar about `Order Service` are the saga-related classes. This service is both a saga orchestrator and a saga participant. `Order Service` has several saga orchestrators, such as `CreateOrderSaga`. The saga orchestrators send command messages to a saga participant using a saga participant proxy class, such as `KitchenServiceProxy` and `OrderServiceProxy`. A saga participant proxy defines a saga participant's messaging API. `Order Service` also has an `OrderCommandHandlers` class, which handles the command messages sent by sagas to `Order Service`.

Let's look in more detail at the design, starting with the `OrderService` class.

4.4.1 *The OrderService class*

The `OrderService` class is a domain service called by the service's API layer. It's responsible for creating and managing orders. Figure 4.10 shows `OrderService` and some of its collaborators. `OrderService` creates and updates `Orders`, invokes the `OrderRepository` to persist `Orders`, and creates sagas, such as the `CreateOrderSaga`, using the `SagaManager`. The `SagaManager` class is one of the classes provided by the Eventuate Tram Saga framework, which is a framework for writing saga orchestrators and participants, and is discussed a little later in this section.

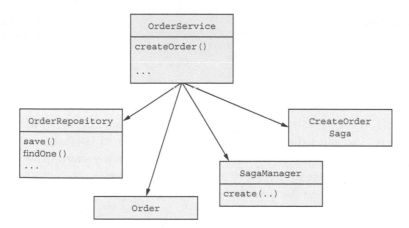

Figure 4.10 `OrderService` **creates and updates** `Orders`, **invokes the** `OrderRepository` **to persist** `Orders`, **and creates sagas, including the** `CreateOrderSaga`.

I'll discuss this class in more detail in chapter 5. For now, let's focus on the create-Order() method. The following listing shows OrderService's createOrder() method. This method first creates an Order and then creates an CreateOrderSaga to validate the order.

Listing 4.1   The OrderService class and its createOrder() method

```
@Transactional                              ◁──── Ensure that service
 public class OrderService {                        methods are transactional.

   @Autowired
   private SagaManager<CreateOrderSagaState> createOrderSagaManager;

   @Autowired
   private OrderRepository orderRepository;

   @Autowired
   private DomainEventPublisher eventPublisher;
                                                                    Create the
                                                                    Order.
   public Order createOrder(OrderDetails orderDetails) {
     ...
     ResultWithEvents<Order> orderAndEvents = Order.createOrder(...);   ◁─────
      Order order = orderAndEvents.result;
     orderRepository.save(order);              ◁──────| Persist the Order
                                                      | in the database.

     eventPublisher.publish(Order.class,                    ◁──── Publish domain
                       Long.toString(order.getId()),              events.
                       orderAndEvents.events);

     CreateOrderSagaState data =
         new CreateOrderSagaState(order.getId(), orderDetails);   ◁─────
      createOrderSagaManager.create(data, Order.class, order.getId());

     return order;                                           Create a
   }                                                         CreateOrderSaga.

   ...
 }
```

The createOrder() method creates an Order by calling the factory method Order.createOrder(). It then persists the Order using the OrderRepository, which is a JPA-based repository. It creates the CreateOrderSaga by calling SagaManager.create(), passing a CreateOrderSagaState containing the ID of the newly saved Order and the OrderDetails. The SagaManager instantiates the saga orchestrator, which causes it to send a command message to the first saga participant, and persists the saga orchestrator in the database.

Let's look at the CreateOrderSaga and its associated classes.

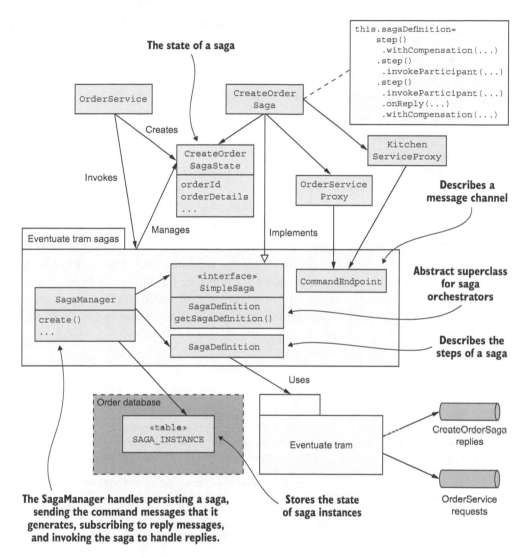

Figure 4.11 The `OrderService`'s sagas, such as `Create Order Saga`, are implemented using the Eventuate Tram Saga framework.

4.4.2　*The implementation of the Create Order Saga*

Figure 4.11 shows the classes that implement the `Create Order Saga`. The responsibilities of each class are as follows:

- `CreateOrderSaga`—A singleton class that defines the saga's state machine. It invokes the `CreateOrderSagaState` to create command messages and sends them to participants using message channels specified by the saga participant proxy classes, such as `KitchenServiceProxy`.

- `CreateOrderSagaState`—A saga's persistent state, which creates command messages.
- *Saga participant proxy classes, such as* `KitchenServiceProxy`—Each proxy class defines a saga participant's messaging API, which consists of the command channel, the command message types, and the reply types.

These classes are written using the Eventuate Tram Saga framework.

The Eventuate Tram Saga framework provides a domain-specific language (DSL) for defining a saga's state machine. It executes the saga's state machine and exchanges messages with saga participants using the Eventuate Tram framework. The framework also persists the saga's state in the database.

Let's take a closer look at the implementation of Create Order Saga, starting with the `CreateOrderSaga` class.

THE CREATEORDERSAGA ORCHESTRATOR

The `CreateOrderSaga` class implements the state machine shown earlier in figure 4.7. This class implements `SimpleSaga`, a base interface for sagas. The heart of the `CreateOrderSaga` class is the saga definition shown in the following listing. It uses the DSL provided by the Eventuate Tram Saga framework to define the steps of the Create Order Saga.

Listing 4.2   The definition of the `CreateOrderSaga`

```
public class CreateOrderSaga implements SimpleSaga<CreateOrderSagaState> {

  private SagaDefinition<CreateOrderSagaState> sagaDefinition;

  public CreateOrderSaga(OrderServiceProxy orderService,
                         ConsumerServiceProxy consumerService,
                         KitchenServiceProxy kitchenService,
                         AccountingServiceProxy accountingService) {
    this.sagaDefinition =
            step()
              .withCompensation(orderService.reject,
                            CreateOrderSagaState::makeRejectOrderCommand)
            .step()
              .invokeParticipant(consumerService.validateOrder,
                    CreateOrderSagaState::makeValidateOrderByConsumerCommand)
            .step()
              .invokeParticipant(kitchenService.create,
                    CreateOrderSagaState::makeCreateTicketCommand)
              .onReply(CreateTicketReply.class,
                    CreateOrderSagaState::handleCreateTicketReply)
              .withCompensation(kitchenService.cancel,
                  CreateOrderSagaState::makeCancelCreateTicketCommand)
            .step()
              .invokeParticipant(accountingService.authorize,
                    CreateOrderSagaState::makeAuthorizeCommand)
            .step()
              .invokeParticipant(kitchenService.confirmCreate,
                  CreateOrderSagaState::makeConfirmCreateTicketCommand)
```

```
                .step()
                 .invokeParticipant(orderService.approve,
                               CreateOrderSagaState::makeApproveOrderCommand)
                .build();
    }

  @Override
  public SagaDefinition<CreateOrderSagaState> getSagaDefinition() {
    return sagaDefinition;
  }
```

The `CreateOrderSaga`'s constructor creates the saga definition and stores it in the `sagaDefinition` field. The `getSagaDefinition()` method returns the saga definition.

To see how `CreateOrderSaga` works, let's look at the definition of the third step of the saga, shown in the following listing. This step of the saga invokes the Kitchen Service to create a `Ticket`. Its compensating transaction cancels that `Ticket`. The `step()`, `invokeParticipant()`, `onReply()`, and `withCompensation()` methods are part of the DSL provided by Eventuate Tram Saga.

Listing 4.3 The definition of the third step of the saga

```
public class CreateOrderSaga ...             Call handleCreateTicketReply() when
                                               a successful reply is received.
public CreateOrderSaga(..., KitchenServiceProxy kitchenService,
          ...) {
    ...                                   Define the forward
    .step()                               transaction.
      .invokeParticipant(kitchenService.create,
              CreateOrderSagaState::makeCreateTicketCommand)
      .onReply(CreateTicketReply.class,
              CreateOrderSagaState::handleCreateTicketReply)
      .withCompensation(kitchenService.cancel,
            CreateOrderSagaState::makeCancelCreateTicketCommand)

    ...                                   Define the compensating
  ;                                         transaction.
```

The call to `invokeParticipant()` defines the forward transaction. It creates the Create-Ticket command message by calling `CreateOrderSagaState.makeCreateTicket-Command()` and sends it to the channel specified by `kitchenService.create`. The call to `onReply()` specifies that `CreateOrderSagaState.handleCreateTicketReply()` should be called when a successful reply is received from Kitchen Service. This method stores the returned `ticketId` in the `CreateOrderSagaState`. The call to `withCompensation()` defines the compensating transaction. It creates a RejectTicket-Command command message by calling `CreateOrderSagaState.makeCancelCreate-Ticket()` and sends it to the channel specified by `kitchenService.create`.

The other steps of the saga are defined in a similar fashion. The CreateOrder-SagaState creates each message, which is sent by the saga to the messaging endpoint defined by a `KitchenServiceProxy`. Let's take a look at each of those classes, starting with `CreateOrderSagaState`.

THE CREATEORDERSAGASTATE CLASS

The `CreateOrderSagaState` class, shown in the following listing, represents the state of a saga instance. An instance of this class is created by `OrderService` and is persisted in the database by the Eventuate Tram Saga framework. Its primary responsibility is to create the messages that are sent to saga participants.

Listing 4.4 `CreateOrderSagaState` stores the state of a saga instance

```
public class CreateOrderSagaState {

  private Long orderId;

  private OrderDetails orderDetails;
  private long ticketId;

  public Long getOrderId() {
    return orderId;
  }                                                         Invoked by the
                                                            OrderService to
                                                            instantiate a
  private CreateOrderSagaState() {                          CreateOrderSagaState
  }

  public CreateOrderSagaState(Long orderId, OrderDetails orderDetails) {  ◁─┘
    this.orderId = orderId;
    this.orderDetails = orderDetails;
  }                                                  Creates a CreateTicket
                                                     command message
  CreateTicket makeCreateTicketCommand() {     ◁─┘
    return new CreateTicket(getOrderDetails().getRestaurantId(),
                 getOrderId(), makeTicketDetails(getOrderDetails())));
  }

  void handleCreateTicketReply(CreateTicketReply reply) {  ◁─┐  Saves the ID
    logger.debug("getTicketId {}", reply.getTicketId());        of the newly
    setTicketId(reply.getTicketId());                           created Ticket
  }

  CancelCreateTicket makeCancelCreateTicketCommand() {  ◁─┐  Creates
    return new CancelCreateTicket(getOrderId());              CancelCreateTicket
  }                                                           command message

  ...
```

The `CreateOrderSaga` invokes the `CreateOrderSagaState` to create the command messages. It sends those command messages to the endpoints defined by the `Saga-ParticipantProxy` classes. Let's take a look at one of those classes: `KitchenService-Proxy`.

THE KITCHENSERVICEPROXY CLASS

The `KitchenServiceProxy` class, shown in listing 4.5, defines the command message endpoints for `Kitchen Service`. There are three endpoints:

- `create`—Creates a `Ticket`
- `confirmCreate`—Confirms the creation
- `cancel`—Cancels a `Ticket`

Each `CommandEndpoint` specifies the command type, the command message's destination channel, and the expected reply types.

Listing 4.5 `KitchenServiceProxy` defines the command message endpoints for `Kitchen Service`

```java
public class KitchenServiceProxy {

    public final CommandEndpoint<CreateTicket> create =
            CommandEndpointBuilder
              .forCommand(CreateTicket.class)
              .withChannel(
                  KitchenServiceChannels.kitchenServiceChannel)
              .withReply(CreateTicketReply.class)
              .build();

    public final CommandEndpoint<ConfirmCreateTicket> confirmCreate =
            CommandEndpointBuilder
              .forCommand(ConfirmCreateTicket.class)
              .withChannel(
                    KitchenServiceChannels.kitchenServiceChannel)
              .withReply(Success.class)
              .build();

    public final CommandEndpoint<CancelCreateTicket> cancel =
            CommandEndpointBuilder
              .forCommand(CancelCreateTicket.class)
              .withChannel(
                    KitchenServiceChannels.kitchenServiceChannel)
              .withReply(Success.class)
              .build();

}
```

Proxy classes, such as `KitchenServiceProxy`, aren't strictly necessary. A saga could simply send command messages directly to participants. But proxy classes have two important benefits. First, a proxy class defines static typed endpoints, which reduces the chance of a saga sending the wrong message to a service. Second, a proxy class is a well-defined API for invoking a service that makes the code easier to understand and test. For example, chapter 10 describes how to write tests for `KitchenServiceProxy` that verify that `Order Service` correctly invokes `Kitchen Service`. Without `KitchenServiceProxy`, it would be impossible to write such a narrowly scoped test.

THE EVENTUATE TRAM SAGA FRAMEWORK

The Eventuate Tram Saga, shown in figure 4.12, is a framework for writing both saga orchestrators and saga participants. It uses transactional messaging capabilities of Eventuate Tram, discussed in chapter 3.

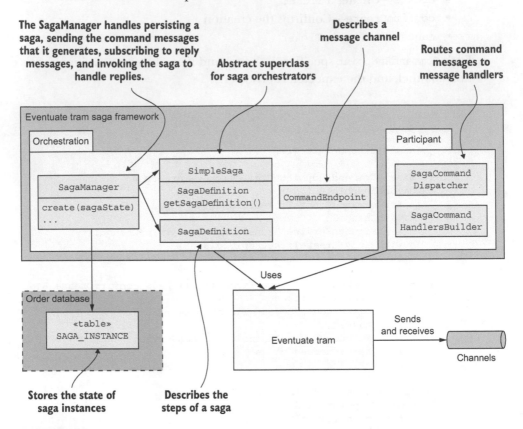

Figure 4.12   Eventuate Tram Saga is a framework for writing both saga orchestrators and saga participants.

The saga orchestration package is the most complex part of the framework. It provides SimpleSaga, a base interface for sagas, and a SagaManager class, which creates and manages saga instances. The SagaManager handles persisting a saga, sending the command messages that it generates, subscribing to reply messages, and invoking the saga to handle replies. Figure 4.13 shows the sequence of events when OrderService creates a saga. The sequence of events is as follows:

1 OrderService creates the CreateOrderSagaState.
2 It creates an instance of a saga by invoking the SagaManager.
3 The SagaManager executes the first step of the saga definition.
4 The CreateOrderSagaState is invoked to generate a command message.

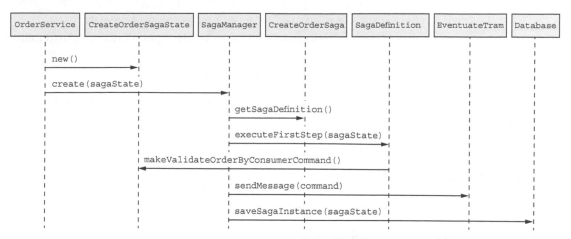

Figure 4.13 **The sequence of events when** `OrderService` **creates an instance of** `Create Order Saga`

5 The `SagaManager` sends the command message to the saga participant (the `Consumer Service`).

6 The `SagaManager` saves the saga instance in the database.

Figure 4.14 shows the sequence of events when `SagaManager` receives a reply from `Consumer Service`.

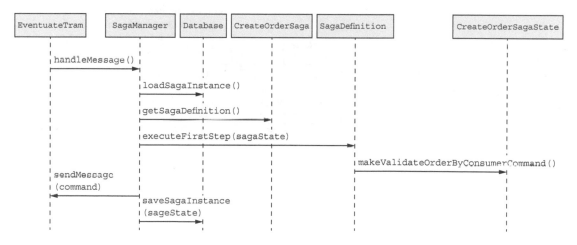

Figure 4.14 **The sequence of events when the** `SagaManager` **receives a reply message from a saga participant**

The sequence of events is as follows:

1 Eventuate Tram invokes `SagaManager` with the reply from `Consumer Service`.

2 `SagaManager` retrieves the saga instance from the database.

3 `SagaManager` executes the next step of the saga definition.

4   `CreateOrderSagaState` is invoked to generate a command message.

5   `SagaManager` sends the command message to the specified saga participant (`Kitchen Service`).

6   `SagaManager` saves the update saga instance in the database.

If a saga participant fails, `SagaManager` executes the compensating transactions in reverse order.

The other part of the Eventuate Tram Saga framework is the `saga participant` package. It provides the `SagaCommandHandlersBuilder` and `SagaCommandDispatcher` classes for writing saga participants. These classes route command messages to handler methods, which invoke the saga participants' business logic and generate reply messages. Let's take a look at how these classes are used by `Order Service`.

4.4.3   *The OrderCommandHandlers class*

`Order Service` participates in its own sagas. For example, `CreateOrderSaga` invokes `Order Service` to either approve or reject an `Order`. The `OrderCommandHandlers` class, shown in figure 4.15, defines the handler methods for the command messages sent by these sagas.

Each handler method invokes `OrderService` to update an `Order` and makes a reply message. The `SagaCommandDispatcher` class routes the command messages to the appropriate handler method and sends the reply.

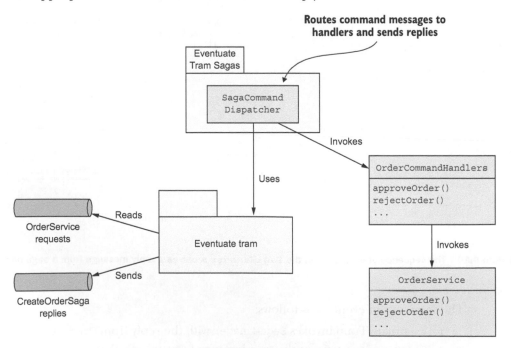

Figure 4.15   `OrderCommandHandlers` **implements command handlers for the commands that are sent by the various** `Order Service` **sagas.**

The following listing shows the `OrderCommandHandlers` class. Its `commandHandlers()` method maps command message types to handler methods. Each handler method takes a command message as a parameter, invokes `OrderService`, and returns a reply message.

Listing 4.6 The command handlers for `Order Service`

```
public class OrderCommandHandlers {

    @Autowired
    private OrderService orderService;

    public CommandHandlers commandHandlers() {        ◁── Route each command
        return SagaCommandHandlersBuilder                   message to the appropriate
            .fromChannel("orderService")                    handler method.
            .onMessage(ApproveOrderCommand.class, this::approveOrder)
            .onMessage(RejectOrderCommand.class, this::rejectOrder)
            ...
            .build();

    }

    public Message approveOrder(CommandMessage<ApproveOrderCommand> cm) {
        long orderId = cm.getCommand().getOrderId();
        orderService.approveOrder(orderId);          ◁── Change the state
        return withSuccess();         ◁─┐                of the Order to
    }                                   Return a generic   authorized.
                                        success message.

    public Message rejectOrder(CommandMessage<RejectOrderCommand> cm) {
        long orderId = cm.getCommand().getOrderId();
        orderService.rejectOrder(orderId);          ◁── Change the state of
        return withSuccess();                           the Order to rejected.
    }
}
```

The `approveOrder()` and `rejectOrder()` methods update the specified `Order` by invoking `OrderService`. The other services that participate in sagas have similar command handler classes that update their domain objects.

4.4.4 *The OrderServiceConfiguration class*

The `Order Service` uses the Spring framework. The following listing is an excerpt of the `OrderServiceConfiguration` class, which is an `@Configuration` class that instantiates and wires together the Spring `@Beans`.

Listing 4.7 The `OrderServiceConfiguration` is a Spring `@Configuration` class that defines the Spring `@Beans` for the `Order Service`.

```
@Configuration
public class OrderServiceConfiguration {

 @Bean
 public OrderService orderService(RestaurantRepository restaurantRepository,
```

```
                                    ...
                           SagaManager<CreateOrderSagaState>
                                   createOrderSagaManager,
                            ...) {
    return new OrderService(restaurantRepository,
                       ...
                       createOrderSagaManager
                       ...);
}


@Bean
public SagaManager<CreateOrderSagaState> createOrderSagaManager(CreateOrderS
    aga saga) {
 return new SagaManagerImpl<>(saga);
}


@Bean
public CreateOrderSaga createOrderSaga(OrderServiceProxy orderService,
                                  ConsumerServiceProxy consumerService,
                                  ...) {
    return new CreateOrderSaga(orderService, consumerService, ...);
}


@Bean
public OrderCommandHandlers orderCommandHandlers() {
 return new OrderCommandHandlers();
}


@Bean
public SagaCommandDispatcher  orderCommandHandlersDispatcher(OrderCommandHan
    dlers orderCommandHandlers) {
 return new SagaCommandDispatcher("orderService", orderCommandHandlers.comma
    ndHandlers());
}


@Bean
public KitchenServiceProxy kitchenServiceProxy() {
   return new KitchenServiceProxy();
}


@Bean
public OrderServiceProxy orderServiceProxy() {
   return new OrderServiceProxy();
}

 ...


}
```

This class defines several Spring @Beans including orderService, createOrder-
SagaManager, createOrderSaga, orderCommandHandlers, and orderCommandHandlers-
Dispatcher. It also defines Spring @Beans for the various proxy classes, including
kitchenServiceProxy and orderServiceProxy.

CreateOrderSaga is only one of Order Service's many sagas. Many of its other system operations also use sagas. For example, the cancelOrder() operation uses a Cancel Order Saga, and the reviseOrder() operation uses a Revise Order Saga. As a result, even though many services have an external API that uses a synchronous protocol, such as REST or gRPC, a large amount of interservice communication will use asynchronous messaging.

As you can see, transaction management and some aspects of business logic design are quite different in a microservice architecture. Fortunately, saga orchestrators are usually quite simple state machines, and you can use a saga framework to simplify your code. Nevertheless, transaction management is certainly more complicated than in a monolithic architecture. But that's usually a small price to pay for the tremendous benefits of microservices.

Summary

- Some system operations need to update data scattered across multiple services. Traditional, XA/2PC-based distributed transactions aren't a good fit for modern applications. A better approach is to use the Saga pattern. A saga is sequence of local transactions that are coordinated using messaging. Each local transaction updates data in a single service. Because each local transaction commits its changes, if a saga must roll back due to the violation of a business rule, it must execute compensating transactions to explicitly undo changes.

- You can use either choreography or orchestration to coordinate the steps of a saga. In a choreography-based saga, a local transaction publishes events that trigger other participants to execute local transactions. In an orchestration-based saga, a centralized saga orchestrator sends command messages to participants telling them to execute local transactions. You can simplify development and testing by modeling saga orchestrators as state machines. Simple sagas can use choreography, but orchestration is usually a better approach for complex sagas.

- Designing saga-based business logic can be challenging because, unlike ACID transactions, sagas aren't isolated from one another. You must often use countermeasures, which are design strategies that prevent concurrency anomalies caused by the ACD transaction model. An application may even need to use locking in order to simplify the business logic, even though that risks deadlocks.

Designing business logic in a microservice architecture

This chapter covers

- Applying the business logic organization patterns: Transaction script pattern and Domain model pattern
- Designing business logic with the Domain-driven design (DDD) aggregate pattern
- Applying the Domain event pattern in a microservice architecture

The heart of an enterprise application is the business logic, which implements the business rules. Developing complex business logic is always challenging. The FTGO application's business logic implements some quite complex business logic, especially for order management and delivery management. Mary had encouraged her team to apply object-oriented design principles, because in her experience this was the best way to implement complex business logic. Some of the business logic used the procedural Transcription script pattern. But the majority of the FTGO application's business logic is implemented in an object-oriented domain model that's mapped to the database using JPA.

Developing complex business logic is even more challenging in a microservice architecture where the business logic is spread over multiple services. You need to address two key challenges. First, a typical domain model is a tangled web of interconnected classes. Although this isn't a problem in a monolithic application, in a microservice architecture, where classes are scattered around different services, you need to eliminate object references that would otherwise span service boundaries. The second challenge is designing business logic that works within the transaction management constraints of a microservice architecture. Your business logic can use ACID transactions within services, but as described in chapter 4, it must use the Saga pattern to maintain data consistency across services.

Fortunately, we can address these issues by using the Aggregate pattern from DDD. The Aggregate pattern structures a service's business logic as a collection of aggregates. An *aggregate* is a cluster of objects that can be treated as a unit. There are two reasons why aggregates are useful when developing business logic in a microservice architecture:

- Aggregates avoid any possibility of object references spanning service boundaries, because an inter-aggregate reference is a primary key value rather than an object reference.
- Because a transaction can only create or update a single aggregate, aggregates fit the constraints of the microservices transaction model.

As a result, an ACID transaction is guaranteed to be within a single service.

I begin this chapter by describing the different ways of organizing business logic: the Transcription script pattern and the Domain model pattern. Next I introduce the concept of a DDD aggregate and explain why it's a good building block for a service's business logic. After that, I describe the Domain event pattern events and explain why it's useful for a service to publish events. I end this chapter with a couple of examples of business logic from `Kitchen Service` and `Order Service`.

Let's now look at business logic organization patterns.

5.1 *Business logic organization patterns*

Figure 5.1 shows the architecture of a typical service. As described in chapter 2, the business logic is the core of a hexagonal architecture. Surrounding the business logic are the inbound and outbound adapters. An *inbound adapter* handles requests from clients and invokes the business logic. An *outbound adapter*, which is invoked by the business logic, invokes other services and applications.

This service consists of the business logic and the following adapters:

- `REST API adapter`—An inbound adapter that implements a REST API which invokes the business logic
- `OrderCommandHandlers`—An inbound adapter that consumes command messages from a message channel and invokes the business logic
- `Database Adapter`—An outbound adapter that's invoked by the business logic to access the database
- `Domain Event Publishing Adapter`—An outbound adapter that publishes events to a message broker

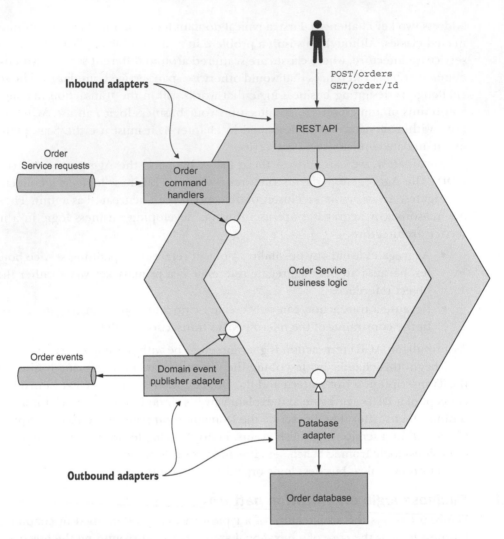

Figure 5.1 **The `Order Service` has a hexagonal architecture. It consists of the business logic and one or more adapters that interface with external applications and other services.**

The business logic is typically the most complex part of the service. When developing business logic, you should consciously organize your business logic in the way that's most appropriate for your application. After all, I'm sure you've experienced the frustration of having to maintain someone else's badly structured code. Most enterprise applications are written in an object-oriented language such as Java, so they consist of classes and methods. But using an object-oriented language doesn't guarantee that the business logic has an object-oriented design. The key decision you must make when developing business logic is whether to use an object-oriented approach or a procedural approach. There are two main patterns for organizing business logic: the procedural Transaction script pattern, and the object-oriented Domain model pattern.

5.1.1 Designing business logic using the Transaction script pattern

Although I'm a strong advocate of the object-oriented approach, there are some situations where it is overkill, such as when you are developing simple business logic. In such a situation, a better approach is to write procedural code and use what the book *Patterns of Enterprise Application Architecture* by Martin Fowler (Addison-Wesley Professional, 2002) calls the Transaction script pattern. Rather than doing any object-oriented design, you write a method called a *transaction script* to handle each request from the presentation tier. As figure 5.2 shows, an important characteristic of this approach is that the classes that implement behavior are separate from those that store state.

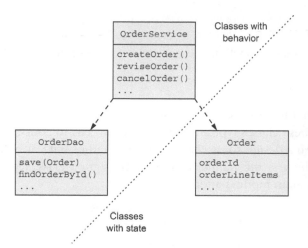

Figure 5.2 Organizing business logic as transaction scripts. In a typical transaction script–based design, one set of classes implements behavior and another set stores state. The transaction scripts are organized into classes that typically have no state. The scripts use data classes, which typically have no behavior.

When using the Transaction script pattern, the scripts are usually located in service classes, which in this example is the `OrderService` class. A service class has one method for each request/system operation. The method implements the business logic for that request. It accesses the database using data access objects (DAOs), such as the `OrderDao`. The data objects, which in this example is the `Order` class, are pure data with little or no behavior.

> **Pattern: Transaction script**
> Organize the business logic as a collection of procedural transaction scripts, one for each type of request.

This style of design is highly procedural and relies on few of the capabilities of object-oriented programming (OOP) languages. This what you would create if you were writing the application in C or another non-OOP language. Nevertheless, you shouldn't be ashamed to use a procedural design when it's appropriate. This approach works well for simple business logic. The drawback is that this tends not to be a good way to implement complex business logic.

5.1.2   *Designing business logic using the Domain model pattern*

The simplicity of the procedural approach can be quite seductive. You can write code without having to carefully consider how to organize the classes. The problem is that if your business logic becomes complex, you can end up with code that's a nightmare to maintain. In fact, in the same way that a monolithic application has a habit of continually growing, transaction scripts have the same problem. Consequently, unless you're writing an extremely simple application, you should resist the temptation to write procedural code and instead apply the Domain model pattern and develop an object-oriented design.

> **Pattern: Domain model**
> Organize the business logic as an object model consisting of classes that have state and behavior.

In an object-oriented design, the business logic consists of an object model, a network of relatively small classes. These classes typically correspond directly to concepts from the problem domain. In such a design some classes have only either state or behavior, but many contain both, which is the hallmark of a well-designed class. Figure 5.3 shows an example of the Domain model pattern.

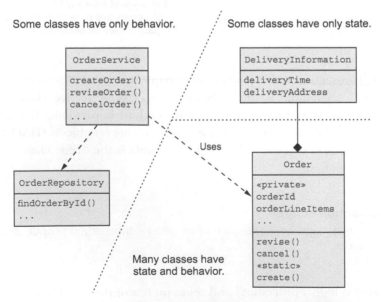

Figure 5.3   Organizing business logic as a domain model. The majority of the business logic consists of classes that have state and behavior.

As with the Transaction script pattern, an `OrderService` class has a method for each request/system operation. But when using the Domain model pattern, the service methods are usually simple. That's because a service method almost always delegates to persistent domain objects, which contain the bulk of the business logic. A service method might, for example, load a domain object from the database and invoke one of its methods. In this example, the `Order` class has both state and behavior. Moreover, its state is private and can only be accessed indirectly via its methods.

Using an object-oriented design has a number of benefits. First, the design is easy to understand and maintain. Instead of consisting of one big class that does everything, it consists of a number of small classes that each have a small number of responsibilities. In addition, classes such as `Account`, `BankingTransaction`, and `OverdraftPolicy` closely mirror the real world, which makes their role in the design easier to understand. Second, our object-oriented design is easier to test: each class can and should be tested independently. Finally, an object-oriented design is easier to extend because it can use well-known design patterns, such as the Strategy pattern and the Template method pattern, that define ways of extending a component without modifying the code.

The Domain model pattern works well, but there are a number of problems with this approach, especially in a microservice architecture. To address those problems, you need to use a refinement of OOD known as DDD.

5.1.3 *About Domain-driven design*

DDD, which is described in the book *Domain-Driven Design* by Eric Evans (Addison-Wesley Professional, 2003), is a refinement of OOD and is an approach for developing complex business logic. I introduced DDD in chapter 2 when discussing the usefulness of DDD subdomains when decomposing an application into services. When using DDD, each service has its own domain model, which avoids the problems of a single, application-wide domain model. Subdomains and the associated concept of Bounded Context are two of the strategic DDD patterns.

DDD also has some tactical patterns that are building blocks for domain models. Each pattern is a role that a class plays in a domain model and defines the characteristics of the class. The building blocks that have been widely adopted by developers include the following:

- *Entity*—An object that has a persistent identity. Two entities whose attributes have the same values are still different objects. In a Java EE application, classes that are persisted using JPA `@Entity` are usually DDD entities.
- *Value object*—An object that is a collection of values. Two value objects whose attributes have the same values can be used interchangeably. An example of a value object is a `Money` class, which consists of a currency and an amount.
- *Factory*—An object or method that implements object creation logic that's too complex to be done directly by a constructor. It can also hide the concrete

classes that are instantiated. A factory might be implemented as a static method of a class.

- *Repository*—An object that provides access to persistent entities and encapsulates the mechanism for accessing the database.
- *Service*—An object that implements business logic that doesn't belong in an entity or a value object.

These building blocks are used by many developers. Some are supported by frameworks such as JPA and the Spring framework. There is one more building block that has been generally ignored (myself included!) except by DDD purists: aggregates. As it turns out, aggregates are an extremely useful concept when developing microservices. Let's first look at some subtle problems with classic OOD that are solved by using aggregates.

5.2   Designing a domain model using the DDD aggregate pattern

In traditional object-oriented design, a domain model is a collection of classes and relationships between classes. The classes are usually organized into packages. For example, figure 5.4 shows part of a domain model for the FTGO application. It's a typical domain model consisting of a web of interconnected classes.

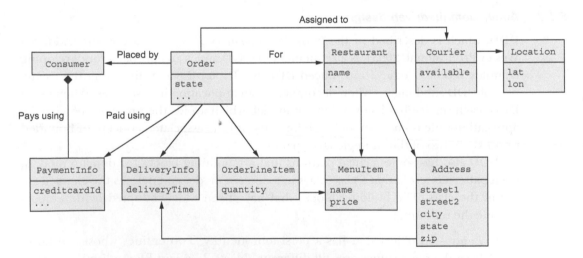

Figure 5.4   A traditional domain model is a web of interconnected classes. It doesn't explicitly specify the boundaries of business objects, such as `Consumer` **and** `Order`**.**

This example has several classes corresponding to business objects: `Consumer`, `Order`, `Restaurant`, and `Courier`. But interestingly, the explicit boundaries of each business object are missing from this kind of traditional domain model. It doesn't specify, for example, which classes are part of the `Order` business object. This lack of boundaries can sometimes cause problems, especially in microservice architecture.

I begin this section with an example problem caused by the lack of explicit boundaries. Next I describe the concept of an aggregate and how it has explicit boundaries. After that, I describe the rules that aggregates must obey and how they make aggregates a good fit for the microservice architecture. I then describe how to carefully choose the boundaries of your aggregates and why it matters. Finally, I discuss how to design business logic using aggregates. Let's first take a look at the problems caused by fuzzy boundaries.

5.2.1　*The problem with fuzzy boundaries*

Imagine, for example, that you want to perform an operation, such as a load or delete, on an `Order` business object. What exactly does that mean? What is the scope an operation? You would certainly load or delete the `Order` object. But in reality there's more to an `Order` than simply the `Order` object. There are also the order line items, the payment information, and so on. Figure 5.4 leaves the boundaries of a domain object to the developer's intuition.

Besides a conceptual fuzziness, the lack of explicit boundaries causes problems when updating a business object. A typical business object has *invariants*, business rules that must be enforced at all times. An `Order` has a minimum order amount, for example. The FTGO application must ensure that any attempt to update an order doesn't violate an invariant such as the minimum order amount. The challenge is that in order to enforce invariants, you must design your business logic carefully.

For example, let's look at how to ensure the order minimum is met when multiple consumers work together to create an order. Two consumers—Sam and Mary—are working together on an order and simultaneously decide that the order exceeds their budget. Sam reduces the quantity of samosas, and Mary reduces the quantity of naan bread. From the application's perspective, both consumers retrieve the order and its line items from the database. Both consumers then update a line item to reduce the cost of the order. From each consumer's perspective the order minimum is preserved. Here's the sequence of database transactions.

```
Consumer - Mary                          Consumer - Sam

BEGIN TXN                                BEGIN TXN

   SELECT ORDER_TOTAL FROM ORDER            SELECT ORDER_TOTAL FROM ORDER
     WHERE ORDER ID = X                        WHERE ORDER ID = X

   SELECT * FROM ORDER_LINE_ITEM            SELECT * FROM ORDER_LINE_ITEM
     WHERE ORDER_ID = X                        WHERE ORDER_ID = X
     ...                                       ...
END TXN                                  END TXN

Verify minimum is met
```

```
BEGIN TXN

   UPDATE ORDER_LINE_ITEM
     SET VERSION=..., QUANTITY=...
   WHERE VERSION = <loaded version>
     AND ID = ...

END TXN
```

```
Verify minimum is met

BEGIN TXN

   UPDATE ORDER_LINE_ITEM
     SET VERSION=..., QUANTITY=...
   WHERE VERSION = <loaded version>
     AND ID = ...

END TXN
```

Each consumer changes a line item using a sequence of two transactions. The first transaction loads the order and its line items. The UI verifies that the order minimum is satisfied before executing the second transaction. The second transaction updates the line item quantity using an optimistic offline locking check that verifies that the order line is unchanged since it was loaded by the first transaction.

In this scenario, Sam reduces the order total by $X and Mary reduces it by $Y. As a result, the Order is no longer valid, even though the application verified that the order still satisfied the order minimum after each consumer's update. As you can see, directly updating part of a business object can result in the violation of the business rules. DDD aggregates are intended to solve this problem.

5.2.2   *Aggregates have explicit boundaries*

An *aggregate* is a cluster of domain objects within a boundary that can be treated as a unit. It consists of a root entity and possibly one or more other entities and value objects. Many business objects are modeled as aggregates. For example, in chapter 2 we created a rough domain model by analyzing the nouns used in the requirements and by domain experts. Many of these nouns, such as Order, Consumer, and Restaurant, are aggregates.

Pattern: Aggregate
Organize a domain model as a collection of aggregates, each of which is a graph of objects that can be treated as a unit.

Figure 5.5 shows the Order aggregate and its boundary. An Order aggregate consists of an Order entity, one or more OrderLineItem value objects, and other value objects such as a delivery Address and PaymentInformation.

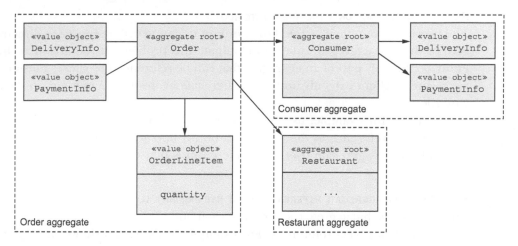

Figure 5.5 Structuring a domain model as a set of aggregates makes the boundaries explicit.

Aggregates decompose a domain model into chunks, which are individually easier to understand. They also clarify the scope of operations such as load, update, and delete. These operations act on the entire aggregate rather than on parts of it. An aggregate is often loaded in its entirety from the database, thereby avoiding any complications of lazy loading. Deleting an aggregate removes all of its objects from a database.

AGGREGATES ARE CONSISTENCY BOUNDARIES

Updating an entire aggregate rather than its parts solves the consistency issues, such as the example described earlier. Update operations are invoked on the aggregate root, which enforces invariants. Also, concurrency is handled by locking the aggregate root using, for example, a version number or a database-level lock. For example, instead of updating line items' quantities directly, a client must invoke a method on the root of the Order aggregate, which enforces invariants such as the minimum order amount. Note, though, that this approach doesn't require the entire aggregate to be updated in the database. An application might, for example, only update the rows corresponding to the Order object and the updated OrderLineItem.

IDENTIFYING AGGREGATES IS KEY

In DDD, a key part of designing a domain model is identifying aggregates, their boundaries, and their roots. The details of the aggregates' internal structure is secondary. The benefit of aggregates, however, goes far beyond modularizing a domain model. That's because aggregates must obey certain rules.

5.2.3 Aggregate rules

DDD requires aggregates to obey a set of rules. These rules ensure that an aggregate is a self-contained unit that can enforce its invariants. Let's look at each of the rules.

RULE #1: REFERENCE ONLY THE AGGREGATE ROOT

The previous example illustrated the perils of updating `OrderLineItems` directly. The goal of the first aggregate rule is to eliminate this problem. It requires that the root entity be the only part of an aggregate that can be referenced by classes outside of the aggregate. A client can only update an aggregate by invoking a method on the aggregate root.

A service, for example, uses a repository to load an aggregate from the database and obtain a reference to the aggregate root. It updates an aggregate by invoking a method on the aggregate root. This rule ensures that the aggregate can enforce its invariant.

RULE #2: INTER-AGGREGATE REFERENCES MUST USE PRIMARY KEYS

Another rule is that aggregates reference each other by identity (for example, primary key) instead of object references. For example, as figure 5.6 shows, an `Order` references its `Consumer` using a `consumerId` rather than a reference to the `Consumer` object. Similarly, an `Order` references a `Restaurant` using a `restaurantId`.

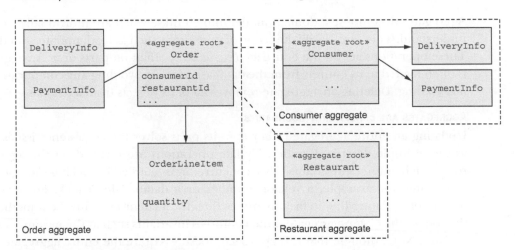

Figure 5.6   References between aggregates are by primary key rather than by object reference. The `Order` aggregate has the IDs of the `Consumer` and `Restaurant` aggregates. Within an aggregate, objects have references to one another.

This approach is quite different from traditional object modeling, which considers foreign keys in the domain model to be a design smell. It has a number of benefits. The use of identity rather than object references means that the aggregates are loosely coupled. It ensures that the aggregate boundaries between aggregates are well defined and avoids accidentally updating a different aggregate. Also, if an aggregate is part of another service, there isn't a problem of object references that span services.

This approach also simplifies persistence since the aggregate is the unit of storage. It makes it easier to store aggregates in a NoSQL database such as MongoDB. It also eliminates the need for transparent lazy loading and its associated problems. Scaling the database by sharding aggregates is relatively straightforward.

RULE #3: ONE TRANSACTION CREATES OR UPDATES ONE AGGREGATE

Another rule that aggregates must obey is that a transaction can only create or update a single aggregate. When I first read about it many years ago, this rule made no sense! At the time, I was developing traditional monolithic applications that used an RDBMS, so transactions could update multiple aggregates. Today, this constraint is perfect for the microservice architecture. It ensures that a transaction is contained within a service. This constraint also matches the limited transaction model of most NoSQL databases.

This rule makes it more complicated to implement operations that need to create or update multiple aggregates. But this is exactly the problem that sagas (described in chapter 4) are designed to solve. Each step of the saga creates or updates exactly one aggregate. Figure 5.7 shows how this works.

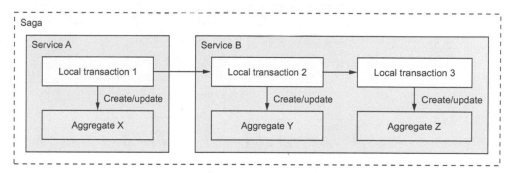

Figure 5.7   A transaction can only create or update a single aggregate, so an application uses a saga to update multiple aggregates. Each step of the saga creates or updates one aggregate.

In this example, the saga consists of three transactions. The first transaction updates aggregate X in service A. The other two transactions are both in service B. One transaction updates aggregate X, and the other updates aggregate Y.

An alternative approach to maintaining consistency across multiple aggregates within a single service is to cheat and update multiple aggregates within a transaction. For example, service B could update aggregates Y and Z in a single transaction. This is only possible when using a database, such as an RDBMS, that supports a rich transaction model. If you're using a NoSQL database that only has simple transactions, there's no other option except to use sagas.

Or is there? It turns out that aggregate boundaries are not set in stone. When developing a domain model, you get to choose where the boundaries lie. But like a 20th century colonial power drawing national boundaries, you need to be careful.

5.2.4　*Aggregate granularity*

When developing a domain model, a key decision you must make is how large to make each aggregate. On one hand, aggregates should ideally be small. Because updates to each aggregate are serialized, more fine-grained aggregates will increase the number of simultaneous requests that the application can handle, improving scalability. It will also improve the user experience because it reduces the chance of two users attempting conflicting updates of the same aggregate. On the other hand, because an aggregate is the scope of transaction, you may need to define a larger aggregate in order to make a particular update atomic.

For example, earlier I mentioned how in the FTGO application's domain model `Order` and `Consumer` are separate aggregates. An alternative design is to make `Order` part of the `Consumer` aggregate. Figure 5.8 shows this alternative design.

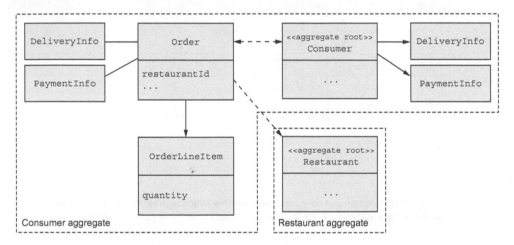

Figure 5.8　An alternative design defines a `Customer` aggregate that contains the `Customer` and `Order` classes. This design enables an application to atomically update a `Consumer` and one or more of its `Order`s.

A benefit of this larger `Consumer` aggregate is that the application can atomically update a `Consumer` and one or more of its `Order`s. A drawback of this approach is that it reduces scalability. Transactions that update different orders for the same customer would be serialized. Similarly, two users would conflict if they attempted to edit different orders for the same customer.

Another drawback of this approach in a microservice architecture is that it is an obstacle to decomposition. The business logic for `Order`s and `Consumer`s, for example, must be collocated in the same service, which makes the service larger. Because of these issues, making aggregates as fine-grained as possible is best.

5.2.5   *Designing business logic with aggregates*

In a typical (micro)service, the bulk of the business logic consists of aggregates. The rest of the business logic resides in the domain services and the sagas. The sagas orchestrate sequences of local transactions in order to enforce data consistency. The services are the entry points into the business logic and are invoked by inbound adapters. A service uses a repository to retrieve aggregates from the database or save aggregates to the database. Each repository is implemented by an outbound adapter that accesses the database. Figure 5.9 shows the aggregate-based design of the business logic for the `Order Service`.

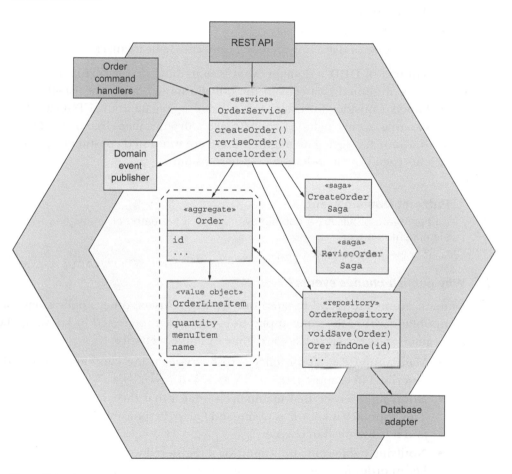

Figure 5.9   An aggregate-based design for the `Order Service` business logic

The business logic consists of the `Order` aggregate, the `OrderService` service class, the `OrderRepository`, and one or more sagas. The `OrderService` invokes the `Order-Repository` to save and load `Orders`. For simple requests that are local to the service, the service updates an `Order` aggregate. If an update request spans multiple services, the `OrderService` will also create a saga, as described in chapter 4.

We'll take a look at the code—but first, let's examine a concept that's closely related to aggregates: domain events.

5.3   *Publishing domain events*

Merriam-Webster (https://www.merriam-webster.com/dictionary/event) lists several definitions of the word *event*, including these:

1   Something that happens
2   A noteworthy happening
3   A social occasion or activity
4   An adverse or damaging medical occurrence, a heart attack or other cardiac event

In the context of DDD, a domain event is something that has happened to an aggregate. It's represented by a class in the domain model. An event usually represents a state change. Consider, for example, an `Order` aggregate in the FTGO application. Its state-changing events include `Order Created`, `Order Cancelled`, `Order Shipped`, and so forth. An `Order` aggregate might, if there are interested consumers, publish one of the events each time it undergoes a state transition.

> **Pattern: Domain event**
> An aggregate publishes a domain event when it's created or undergoes some other significant change.

5.3.1   *Why publish change events?*

Domain events are useful because other parties—users, other applications, or other components within the same application—are often interested in knowing about an aggregate's state changes. Here are some example scenarios:

- Maintaining data consistency across services using choreography-based sagas, described in chapter 4.
- Notifying a service that maintains a replica that the source data has changed. This approach is known as Command Query Responsibility Segregation (CQRS), and it's described in chapter 7.
- Notifying a different application via a registered webhook or via a message broker in order to trigger the next step in a business process.
- Notifying a different component of the same application in order, for example, to send a WebSocket message to a user's browser or update a text database such as ElasticSearch.
- Sending notifications—text messages or emails—to users informing them that their order has shipped, their Rx prescription is ready for pick up, or their flight is delayed.

- Monitoring domain events to verify that the application is behaving correctly.
- Analyzing events to model user behavior.

The trigger for the notification in all these scenarios is the state change of an aggregate in an application's database.

5.3.2 What is a domain event?

A *domain event* is a class with a name formed using a past-participle verb. It has properties that meaningfully convey the event. Each property is either a primitive value or a value object. For example, an OrderCreated event class has an orderId property.

A domain event typically also has metadata, such as the event ID, and a timestamp. It might also have the identity of the user who made the change, because that's useful for auditing. The metadata can be part of the event object, perhaps defined in a superclass. Alternatively, the event metadata can be in an envelope object that wraps the event object. The ID of the aggregate that emitted the event might also be part of the envelope rather than an explicit event property.

The OrderCreated event is an example of a domain event. It doesn't have any fields, because the Order's ID is part of the event envelope. The following listing shows the OrderCreated event class and the DomainEventEnvelope class.

Listing 5.1 The OrderCreated event and the DomainEventEnvelope class

```
interface DomainEvent {}

interface OrderDomainEvent extends DomainEvent {}

class OrderCreated implements OrderDomainEvent {}

class DomainEventEnvelope<T extends DomainEvent> {
  private String aggregateType;      ◁─┐
  private Object aggregateId;          │  The event's
  private T event;                     │  metadata
  ...
}
```

The DomainEvent interface is a marker interface that identifies a class as a domain event. OrderDomainEvent is a marker interface for events, such as OrderCreated, which are published by the Order aggregate. The DomainEventEnvelope is a class that contains event metadata and the event object. It's a generic class that's parameterized by the domain event type.

5.3.3 Event enrichment

Let's imagine, for example, that you're writing an event consumer that processes Order events. The OrderCreated event class shown previously captures the essence of what has happened. But your event consumer may need the order details when processing an

OrderCreated event. One option is for it to retrieve that information from the Order-Service. The drawback of an event consumer querying the service for the aggregate is that it incurs the overhead of a service request.

An alternative approach known as *event enrichment* is for events to contain information that consumers need. It simplifies event consumers because they no longer need to request that data from the service that published the event. In the OrderCreated event, the Order aggregate can enrich the event by including the order details. The following listing shows the enriched event.

Listing 5.2   The enriched OrderCreated event

```
class OrderCreated implements OrderEvent {
  private List<OrderLineItem> lineItems;
  private DeliveryInformation deliveryInformation;        ◁─┐ Data that its
  private PaymentInformation paymentInformation;             consumers
  private long restaurantId;                                 typically need
  private String restaurantName;
  ...
}
```

Because this version of the OrderCreated event contains the order details, an event consumer, such as the Order History Service (discussed in chapter 7) no longer needs to fetch that data when processing an OrderCreated event.

Although event enrichment simplifies consumers, the drawback is that it risks making the event classes less stable. An event class potentially needs to change whenever the requirements of its consumers change. This can reduce maintainability because this kind of change can impact multiple parts of the application. Satisfying every consumer can also be a futile effort. Fortunately, in many situations it's fairly obvious which properties to include in an event.

Now that we've covered the basics of domain events, let's look at how to discover them.

5.3.4   *Identifying domain events*

There are a few different strategies for identifying domain events. Often the requirements will describe scenarios where notifications are required. The requirements might include language such as "When X happens do Y." For example, one requirement in the FTGO application is "When an Order is placed send the consumer an email." A requirement for a notification suggests the existence of a domain event.

Another approach, which is increasing in popularity, is to use event storming. *Event storming* is an event-centric workshop format for understanding a complex domain. It involves gathering domain experts in a room, lots of sticky notes, and a very large surface—a whiteboard or paper roll—to stick the notes on. The result of event storming is an event-centric domain model consisting of aggregates and events.

Event storming consist of three main steps:

1 *Brainstorm events*—Ask the domain experts to brainstorm the domain events. Domain events are represented by orange sticky notes that are laid out in a rough timeline on the modeling surface.

2 *Identify event triggers*—Ask the domain experts to identify the trigger of each event, which is one of the following:
   - User actions, represented as a command using a blue sticky note
   - External system, represented by a purple sticky note
   - Another domain event
   - Passing of time

3 *Identify aggregates*—Ask the domain experts to identify the aggregate that consumes each command and emits the corresponding event. Aggregates are represented by yellow sticky notes.

Figure 5.10 shows the result of an event-storming workshop. In just a couple of hours, the participants identified numerous domain events, commands, and aggregates. It was a good first step in the process of creating a domain model.

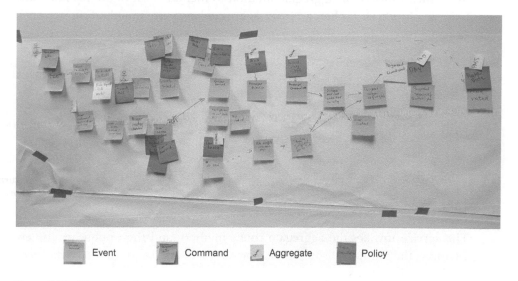

Figure 5.10 The result of an event-storming workshop that lasted a couple of hours. The sticky notes are events, which are laid out along a timeline; commands, which represent user actions; and aggregates, which emit events in response to a command.

Event storming is a useful technique for quickly creating a domain model.

Now that we've covered the basics of domain events, let's look at the mechanics of generating and publishing them.

5.3.5 Generating and publishing domain events

Communicating using domain events is a form of asynchronous messaging, discussed in chapter 3. But before the business logic can publish them to a message broker, it must first create them. Let's look at how to do that.

GENERATING DOMAIN EVENTS

Conceptually, domain events are published by aggregates. An aggregate knows when its state changes and hence what event to publish. An aggregate could invoke a messaging API directly. The drawback of this approach is that because aggregates can't use dependency injection, the messaging API would need to be passed around as a method argument. That would intertwine infrastructure concerns and business logic, which is extremely undesirable.

A better approach is to split responsibility between the aggregate and the service (or equivalent class) that invokes it. Services can use dependency injection to obtain a reference to the messaging API, easily publishing events. The aggregate generates the events whenever its state changes and returns them to the service. There are a couple of different ways an aggregate can return events back to the service. One option is for the return value of an aggregate method to include a list of events. For example, the following listing shows how a `Ticket` aggregate's `accept()` method can return a `Ticket-AcceptedEvent` to its caller.

Listing 5.3 The `Ticket` aggregate's `accept()` method

```
public class Ticket {

    public List<DomainEvent> accept(ZonedDateTime readyBy) {
        ...
        this.acceptTime = ZonedDateTime.now();             ⟵──┤ Updates
        this.readyBy = readyBy;                                │ the Ticket
        return singletonList(new TicketAcceptedEvent(readyBy)); ⟵┐ Returns
    }                                                            │ an event
}
```

The service invokes the aggregate root's method, and then publishes the events. For example, the following listing shows how `KitchenService` invokes `Ticket.accept()` and publishes the events.

Listing 5.4 `KitchenService` calls `Ticket.accept()`

```
public class KitchenService {

    @Autowired
    private TicketRepository ticketRepository;

    @Autowired
    private DomainEventPublisher domainEventPublisher;
```

```
public void accept(long ticketId, ZonedDateTime readyBy) {
  Ticket ticket =
      ticketRepository.findById(ticketId)
        .orElseThrow(() ->
              new TicketNotFoundException(ticketId));
  List<DomainEvent> events = ticket.accept(readyBy);
  domainEventPublisher.publish(Ticket.class, orderId, events);
}
```

Publishes domain events

The accept() method first invokes the TicketRepository to load the Ticket from the database. It then updates the Ticket by calling accept(). KitchenService then publishes events returned by Ticket by calling DomainEventPublisher.publish(), described shortly.

This approach is quite simple. Methods that would otherwise have a void return type now return List<Event>. The only potential drawback is that the return type of non-void methods is now more complex. They must return an object containing the original return value and List<Event>. You'll see an example of such a method soon.

Another option is for the aggregate root to accumulate events in a field. The service then retrieves the events and publishes them. For example, the following listing shows a variant of the Ticket class that works this way.

Listing 5.5 The Ticket extends a superclass, which records domain events

```
public class Ticket extends AbstractAggregateRoot {

  public void accept(ZonedDateTime readyBy) {
    ...
    this.acceptTime = ZonedDateTime.now();
    this.readyBy = readyBy;
    registerDomainEvent(new TicketAcceptedEvent(readyBy));
  }

}
```

Ticket extends AbstractAggregateRoot, which defines a registerDomainEvent() method that records the event. A service would call AbstractAggregateRoot.getDomainEvents() to retrieve those events.

My preference is for the first option: the method returning events to the service. But accumulating events in the aggregate root is also a viable option. In fact, the Spring Data Ingalls release train (https://spring.io/blog/2017/01/30/what-s-new-in-spring-data-release-ingalls) implements a mechanism that automatically publishes events to the Spring ApplicationContext. The main drawback is that to reduce code duplication, aggregate roots should extend a superclass such as AbstractAggregateRoot, which might conflict with a requirement to extend some other superclass. Another issue is that although it's easy for the aggregate root's methods to call registerDomainEvent(), methods in other classes in the aggregate would find it challenging. They would mostly likely need to somehow pass the events to the aggregate root.

HOW TO RELIABLY PUBLISH DOMAIN EVENTS?

Chapter 3 talks about how to reliably send messages as part of a local database transaction. Domain events are no different. A service must use transactional messaging to publish events to ensure that they're published as part of the transaction that updates the aggregate in the database. The Eventuate Tram framework, described in chapter 3, implements such a mechanism. It insert events into an OUTBOX table as part of the ACID transaction that updates the database. After the transaction commits, the events that were inserted into the OUTBOX table are then published to the message broker.

The Tram framework provides a DomainEventPublisher interface, shown in the following listing. It defines several overloaded publish() methods that take the aggregate type and ID as parameters, along with a list of domain events.

Listing 5.6   The Eventuate Tram framework's DomainEventPublisher interface

```
public interface DomainEventPublisher {
 void publish(String aggregateType, Object aggregateId,
    List<DomainEvent> domainEvents);
```

It uses the Eventuate Tram framework's MessageProducer interface to publish those events transactionally.

A service could call the DomainEventPublisher publisher directly. But one drawback of doing so is that it doesn't ensure that a service only publishes valid events. KitchenService, for example, should only publish events that implement Ticket-DomainEvent, which is the marker interface for the Ticket aggregate's events. A better option is for services to implement a subclass of AbstractAggregateDomainEvent-Publisher, which is shown in listing 5.7. AbstractAggregateDomainEventPublisher is an abstract class that provides a type-safe interface for publishing domain events. It's a generic class that has two type parameters, A, the aggregate type, and E, the marker interface type for the domain events. A service publishes events by calling the publish() method, which has two parameters: an aggregate of type A and a list of events of type E.

Listing 5.7   The abstract superclass of type-safe domain event publishers

```
public abstract class AbstractAggregateDomainEventPublisher<A, E extends Doma
    inEvent> {
  private Function<A, Object> idSupplier;
  private DomainEventPublisher eventPublisher;
  private Class<A> aggregateType;

  protected AbstractAggregateDomainEventPublisher(
    DomainEventPublisher eventPublisher,
    Class<A> aggregateType,
    Function<A, Object> idSupplier) {
    this.eventPublisher = eventPublisher;
    this.aggregateType = aggregateType;
```

```
    this.idSupplier = idSupplier;
  }

  public void publish(A aggregate, List<E> events) {
    eventPublisher.publish(aggregateType, idSupplier.apply(aggregate),
      (List<DomainEvent>) events);
  }

}
```

The `publish()` method retrieves the aggregate's ID and invokes `DomainEventPublisher` `.publish()`. The following listing shows the `TicketDomainEventPublisher`, which publishes domain events for the `Ticket` aggregate.

Listing 5.8 A type-safe interface for publishing `Ticket` aggregates' domain events

```
public class TicketDomainEventPublisher extends
    AbstractAggregateDomainEventPublisher<Ticket, TicketDomainEvent> {

  public TicketDomainEventPublisher(DomainEventPublisher eventPublisher) {
    super(eventPublisher, Ticket.class, Ticket::getId);
  }

}
```

This class only publishes events that are a subclass of `TicketDomainEvent`.

Now that we've looked at how to publish domain events, let's see how to consume them.

5.3.6 *Consuming domain events*

Domain events are ultimately published as messages to a message broker, such as Apache Kafka. A consumer could use the broker's client API directly. But it's more convenient to use a higher-level API such as the Eventuate Tram framework's `Domain-EventDispatcher`, described in chapter 3. A `DomainEventDispatcher` dispatches domain events to the appropriate handle method. Listing 5.9 shows an example event handler class. `KitchenServiceEventConsumer` subscribes to events published by `Restaurant Service` whenever a restaurant's menu is updated. It's responsible for keeping `Kitchen Service`'s replica of the data up-to-date.

Listing 5.9 Dispatching events to event handler methods

```
public class KitchenServiceEventConsumer {
  @Autowired
  private RestaurantService restaurantService;
                                                              Maps events to
  public DomainEventHandlers domainEventHandlers() {    ◁──┘  event handlers
    return DomainEventHandlersBuilder
      .forAggregateType("net.chrisrichardson.ftgo.restaurantservice.Restaurant")
      .onEvent(RestaurantMenuRevised.class, this::reviseMenu)
```

```
      .build();
  }

  public void reviseMenu(DomainEventEnvelope<RestaurantMenuRevised> de) {     ⟵
    long id = Long.parseLong(de.getAggregateId());
    RestaurantMenu revisedMenu = de.getEvent().getRevisedMenu();
    restaurantService.reviseMenu(id, revisedMenu);
  }
}
```

**An event handler for the
RestaurantMenuRevised
event**

The `reviseMenu()` method handles `RestaurantMenuRevised` events. It calls `restaurant-Service.reviseMenu()`, which updates the restaurant's menu. That method returns a list of domain events, which are published by the event handler.

Now that we've looked at aggregates and domain events, it's time to consider some example business logic that's implemented using aggregates.

5.4 *Kitchen Service business logic*

The first example is `Kitchen Service`, which enables a restaurant to manage their orders. The two main aggregates in this service are the `Restaurant` and `Ticket` aggregates. The `Restaurant` aggregate knows the restaurant's menu and opening hours and can validate orders. A `Ticket` represents an order that a restaurant must prepare for pickup by a courier. Figure 5.11 shows these aggregates and other key parts of the service's business logic, as well as the service's adapters.

In addition to the aggregates, the other main parts of `Kitchen Service`'s business logic are `KitchenService`, `TicketRepository`, and `RestaurantRepository`. `Kitchen-Service` is the business logic's entry. It defines methods for creating and updating the `Restaurant` and `Ticket` aggregates. `TicketRepository` and `RestaurantRepository` define methods for persisting `Tickets` and `Restaurants` respectively.

The `Kitchen Service` service has three inbound adapters:

- `REST API`—The REST API invoked by the user interface used by workers at the restaurant. It invokes `KitchenService` to create and update `Tickets`.
- `KitchenServiceCommandHandler`—The asynchronous request/response-based API that's invoked by sagas. It invokes `KitchenService` to create and update `Tickets`.
- `KitchenServiceEventConsumer`—Subscribes to events published by `Restaurant Service`. It invokes `KitchenService` to create and update `Restaurants`.

The service also has two outbound adapters:

- `DB adapter`—Implements the `TicketRepository` and the `RestaurantRepository` interfaces and accesses the database.
- `DomainEventPublishingAdapter`—Implements the `DomainEventPublisher` interface and publishes `Ticket` domain events.

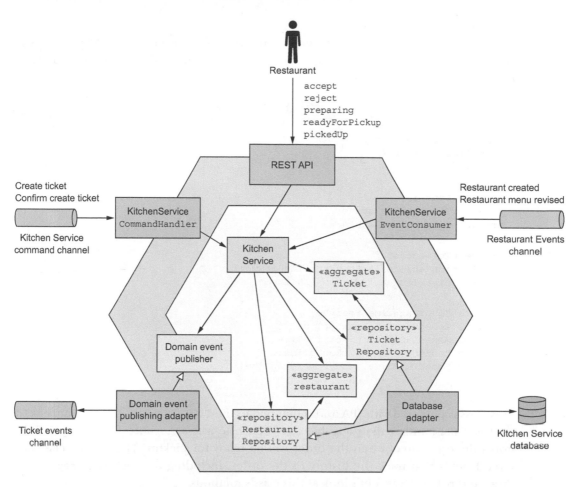

Figure 5.11 **The design of** `Kitchen Service`

Let's take a closer look at the design of `KitchenService`, starting with the `Ticket` aggregate.

5.4.1 *The Ticket aggregate*

`Ticket` is one of the aggregates of `Kitchen Service`. As described in chapter 2, when talking about the concept of a Bounded Context, this aggregate represents the restaurant kitchen's view of an order. It doesn't contain information about the consumer, such as their identity, the delivery information, or payment details. It's focused on enabling a restaurant's kitchen to prepare the `Order` for pickup. Moreover, `Kitchen-Service` doesn't generate a unique ID for this aggregate. Instead, it uses the ID supplied by `OrderService`.

Let's first look at the structure of this class and then we'll examine its methods.

STRUCTURE OF THE TICKET CLASS

The following listing shows an excerpt of the code for this class. The `Ticket` class is similar to a traditional domain class. The main difference is that references to other aggregates are by primary key.

Listing 5.10 Part of the `Ticket` class, which is a JPA entity

```java
@Entity(table="tickets")
public class Ticket {

  @Id
  private Long id;
  private TicketState state;
  private Long restaurantId;

  @ElementCollection
  @CollectionTable(name="ticket_line_items")
  private List<TicketLineItem> lineItems;

  private ZonedDateTime readyBy;
  private ZonedDateTime acceptTime;
  private ZonedDateTime preparingTime;
  private ZonedDateTime pickedUpTime;
  private ZonedDateTime readyForPickupTime;
  ...
```

This class is persisted with JPA and is mapped to the TICKETS table. The `restaurantId` field is a `Long` rather than an object reference to a `Restaurant`. The `readyBy` field stores the estimate of when the order will be ready for pickup. The `Ticket` class has several fields that track the history of the order, including `acceptTime`, `preparing-Time`, and `pickupTime`. Let's look at this class's methods.

BEHAVIOR OF THE TICKET AGGREGATE

The `Ticket` aggregate defines several methods. As you saw earlier, it has a static `create()` method, which is a factory method that creates a `Ticket`. There are also some methods that are invoked when the restaurant updates the state of the order:

- `accept()`—The restaurant has accepted the order.
- `preparing()`—The restaurant has started preparing the order, which means the order can no longer be changed or cancelled.
- `readyForPickup()`—The order can now be picked up.

The following listing shows some of its methods.

> ### Listing 5.11 Some of the `Ticket`'s methods

```
public class Ticket {

public static ResultWithAggregateEvents<Ticket, TicketDomainEvent>
    create(Long id, TicketDetails details) {
  return new ResultWithAggregateEvents<>(new Ticket(id, details), new
    TicketCreatedEvent(id, details));
}

public List<TicketPreparationStartedEvent> preparing() {
  switch (state) {
    case ACCEPTED:
      this.state = TicketState.PREPARING;
      this.preparingTime = ZonedDateTime.now();
      return singletonList(new TicketPreparationStartedEvent());
    default:
      throw new UnsupportedStateTransitionException(state);
  }
}

public List<TicketDomainEvent> cancel() {
    switch (state) {
      case CREATED:
      case ACCEPTED:
        this.state = TicketState.CANCELLED;
        return singletonList(new TicketCancelled());
      case READY_FOR_PICKUP:
        throw new TicketCannotBeCancelledException();

      default:
        throw new UnsupportedStateTransitionException(state);

    }
  }
}
```

The create() method creates a Ticket. The preparing() method is called when the restaurant starts preparing the order. It changes the state of the order to PREPARING, records the time, and publishes an event. The cancel() method is called when a user attempts to cancel an order. If the cancellation is allowed, this method changes the state of the order and returns an event. Otherwise, it throws an exception. These methods are invoked in response to REST API requests as well as events and command messages. Let's look at the classes that invoke the aggregate's method.

THE KITCHENSERVICE DOMAIN SERVICE

KitchenService is invoked by the service's inbound adapters. It defines various methods for changing the state of an order, including accept(), reject(), preparing(), and others. Each method loads the specifies aggregate, calls the corresponding method on the aggregate root, and publishes any domain events. The following listing shows its accept() method.

Listing 5.12   The service's `accept()` method updates `Ticket`

```
public class KitchenService {

  @Autowired
  private TicketRepository ticketRepository;

  @Autowired
  private TicketDomainEventPublisher domainEventPublisher;

  public void accept(long ticketId, ZonedDateTime readyBy) {
    Ticket ticket =
        ticketRepository.findById(ticketId)
          .orElseThrow(() ->
                    new TicketNotFoundException(ticketId));
    List<TicketDomainEvent> events = ticket.accept(readyBy);
    domainEventPublisher.publish(ticket, events);        ◁──┐  Publish
  }                                                          │  domain
                                                             │  events
}
```

The `accept()` method is invoked when the restaurant accepts a new order. It has two parameters:

- `orderId`—ID of the order to accept
- `readyBy`—Estimated time when the order will be ready for pickup

This method retrieves the `Ticket` aggregate and calls its `accept()` method. It publishes any generated events.

Now let's look at the class that handles asynchronous commands.

THE KITCHENSERVICECOMMANDHANDLER CLASS

The `KitchenServiceCommandHandler` class is an adapter that's responsible for handling command messages sent by the various sagas implemented by `Order Service`. This class defines a handler method for each command, which invokes `KitchenService` to create or update a `Ticket`. The following listing shows an excerpt of this class.

Listing 5.13   Handling command messages sent by sagas

```
public class KitchenServiceCommandHandler {

  @Autowired
  private KitchenService kitchenService;
                                                           Maps command messages
                                                           to message handlers
  public CommandHandlers commandHandlers() {    ◁──┘
    return CommandHandlersBuilder
          .fromChannel("orderService")
          .onMessage(CreateTicket.class, this::createTicket)
          .onMessage(ConfirmCreateTicket.class,
                  this::confirmCreateTicket)
```

```
                      .onMessage(CancelCreateTicket.class,
                            this::cancelCreateTicket)
                      .build();
            }

            private Message createTicket(CommandMessage<CreateTicket>
                                                        cm) {
              CreateTicket command = cm.getCommand();
              long restaurantId = command.getRestaurantId();
              Long ticketId = command.getOrderId();
              TicketDetails ticketDetails =
                  command.getTicketDetails();

              try {                                            Invokes KitchenService
                Ticket ticket =                                to create the Ticket
                  kitchenService.createTicket(restaurantId,
                                    ticketId, ticketDetails);
                CreateTicketReply reply =
                          new CreateTicketReply(ticket.getId());   Sends back a
                return withSuccess(reply);                         successful reply
              } catch (RestaurantDetailsVerificationException e) {
                return withFailure();
              }                                    Sends back a
            }                                      failure reply

            private Message confirmCreateTicket
                  (CommandMessage<ConfirmCreateTicket> cm) {      Confirms
                Long ticketId = cm.getCommand().getTicketId();    the order
                kitchenService.confirmCreateTicket(ticketId);
                return withSuccess();
            }

            ...
```

All the command handler methods invoke `KitchenService` and reply with either a success or a failure reply.

Now that you've seen the business logic for a relatively simple service, we'll look at a more complex example: `Order Service`.

5.5 *Order Service business logic*

As mentioned in earlier chapters, `Order Service` provides an API for creating, updating, and canceling orders. This API is primarily invoked by the consumer. Figure 5.12 shows the high-level design of the service. The `Order` aggregate is the central aggregate of `Order Service`. But there's also a `Restaurant` aggregate, which is a partial replica of data owned by `Restaurant Service`. It enables `Order Service` to validate and price an `Order`'s line items.

In addition to the `Order` and `Restaurant` aggregates, the business logic consists of `OrderService`, `OrderRepository`, `RestaurantRepository`, and various sagas such as the `CreateOrderSaga` described in chapter 4. `OrderService` is the primary entry point into the business logic and defines methods for creating and updated `Orders`

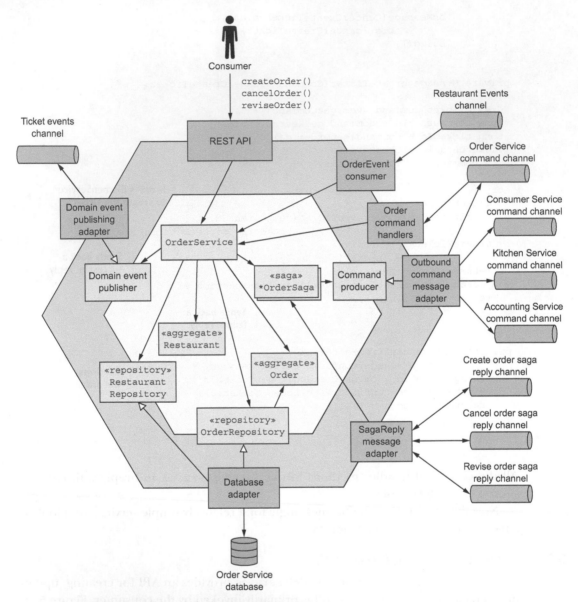

Figure 5.12   The design of the `Order Service`. It has a REST API for managing orders. It exchanges messages and events with other services via several message channels.

and `Restaurants`. `OrderRepository` defines methods for persisting `Orders`, and `RestaurantRepository` has methods for persisting `Restaurants`. `Order Service` has several inbound adapters:

- `REST API`—The REST API invoked by the user interface used by consumers. It invokes `OrderService` to create and update `Orders`.

- `OrderEventConsumer`—Subscribes to events published by `Restaurant Service`. It invokes `OrderService` to create and update its replica of `Restaurants`.
- `OrderCommandHandlers`—The asynchronous request/response-based API that's invoked by sagas. It invokes `OrderService` to update `Orders`.
- `SagaReplyAdapter`—Subscribes to the saga reply channels and invokes the sagas.

The service also has some outbound adapters:

- `DB adapter`—Implements the `OrderRepository` interface and accesses the `Order Service` database
- `DomainEventPublishingAdapter`—Implements the `DomainEventPublisher` interface and publishes `Order` domain events
- `OutboundCommandMessageAdapter`—Implements the `CommandPublisher` interface and sends command messages to saga participants

Let's first take a closer look at the `Order` aggregate and then examine `OrderService`.

5.5.1 *The Order Aggregate*

The `Order` aggregate represents an order placed by a consumer. We'll first look at the structure of the `Order` aggregate and then check out its methods.

THE STRUCTURE OF THE ORDER AGGREGATE

Figure 5.13 shows the structure of the `Order` aggregate. The `Order` class is the root of the `Order` aggregate. The `Order` aggregate also consists of value objects such as `Order-LineItem`, `DeliveryInfo`, and `PaymentInfo`.

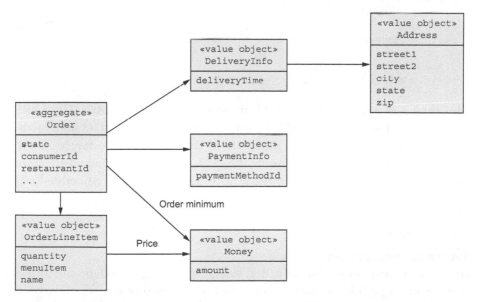

Figure 5.13   The design of the `Order` aggregate, which consists of the `Order` aggregate root and various value objects.

The `Order` class has a collection of `OrderLineItems`. Because the `Order`'s `Consumer` and `Restaurant` are other aggregates, it references them by primary key value. The `Order` class has a `DeliveryInfo` class, which stores the delivery address and the desired delivery time, and a `PaymentInfo`, which stores the payment info. The following listing shows the code.

Listing 5.14   The `Order` class and its fields

```
@Entity
@Table(name="orders")
@Access(AccessType.FIELD)
public class Order {

  @Id
  @GeneratedValue
  private Long id;

  @Version
  private Long version;

  private OrderState state;
  private Long consumerId;
  private Long restaurantId;

  @Embedded
  private OrderLineItems orderLineItems;

  @Embedded
  private DeliveryInformation deliveryInformation;

  @Embedded
  private PaymentInformation paymentInformation;

  @Embedded
  private Money orderMinimum;
```

This class is persisted with JPA and is mapped to the `ORDERS` table. The `id` field is the primary key. The `version` field is used for optimistic locking. The state of an `Order` is represented by the `OrderState` enumeration. The `DeliveryInformation` and `Payment-Information` fields are mapped using the `@Embedded` annotation and are stored as columns of the `ORDERS` table. The `orderLineItems` field is an embedded object that contains the order line items. The `Order` aggregate consists of more than just fields. It also implements business logic, which can be described by a state machine. Let's take a look at the state machine.

THE ORDER AGGREGATE STATE MACHINE

In order to create or update an order, `Order Service` must collaborate with other services using sagas. Either `OrderService` or the first step of the saga invokes an `Order` method that verifies that the operation can be performed and changes the state of the `Order` to a pending state. A *pending* state, as explained in chapter 4, is an example of a semantic lock countermeasure, which helps ensure that sagas are isolated from one another. Eventually, once the saga has invoked the participating services, it then updates the Order to reflect the outcome. For example, as described in chapter 4, the Create Order Saga has multiple participant services, including Consumer Service, Accounting Service, and Kitchen Service. OrderService first creates an Order in an APPROVAL_PENDING state, and then later changes its state to either APPROVED or REJECTED. The behavior of an Order can be modeled as the state machine shown in figure 5.14.

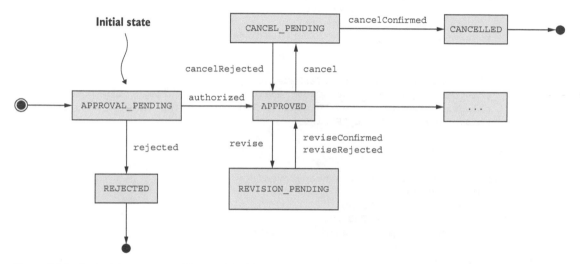

Figure 5.14   Part of the state machine model of the Order **aggregate**

Similarly, other Order Service operations such as revise() and cancel() first change the Order to a pending state and use a saga to verify that the operation can be performed. Then, once the saga has verified that the operation can be performed, it changes the Order transitions to some other state that reflects the successful outcome of the operation. If the verification of the operation fails, the Order reverts to the previous state. For example, the cancel() operation first transitions the Order to the CANCEL_PENDING state. If the order can be cancelled, the Cancel Order Saga changes the state of the Order to the CANCELLED state. Otherwise, if a cancel() operation is rejected because, for example, it's too late to cancel the order, then the Order transitions back to the APPROVED state.

Let's now look at the how the Order aggregate implements this state machine.

THE ORDER AGGREGATE'S METHODS

The Order class has several groups of methods, each of which corresponds to a saga. In each group, one method is invoked at the start of the saga, and the other methods are invoked at the end. I'll first discuss the business logic that creates an Order. After that we'll look at how an Order is updated. The following listing shows the Order's methods that are invoked during the process of creating an Order.

Listing 5.15   The methods that are invoked during order creation

```
public class Order { ...

  public static ResultWithDomainEvents<Order, OrderDomainEvent>
   createOrder(long consumerId, Restaurant restaurant,
                                   List<OrderLineItem> orderLineItems) {
    Order order = new Order(consumerId, restaurant.getId(), orderLineItems);
    List<OrderDomainEvent> events = singletonList(new OrderCreatedEvent(
           new OrderDetails(consumerId, restaurant.getId(), orderLineItems,
                   order.getOrderTotal()),
           restaurant.getName()));
    return new ResultWithDomainEvents<>(order, events);
  }

  public Order(OrderDetails orderDetails) {
    this.orderLineItems = new OrderLineItems(orderDetails.getLineItems());
    this.orderMinimum = orderDetails.getOrderMinimum();
    this.state = APPROVAL_PENDING;
  }
  ...

  public List<DomainEvent> noteApproved() {
    switch (state) {
      case APPROVAL_PENDING:
        this.state = APPROVED;
        return singletonList(new OrderAuthorized());
      ...
      default:
        throw new UnsupportedStateTransitionException(state);
    }
  }

  public List<DomainEvent> noteRejected() {
    switch (state) {
      case APPROVAL_PENDING:
        this.state = REJECTED;
        return singletonList(new OrderRejected());
        ...
      default:
        throw new UnsupportedStateTransitionException(state);
    }
  }

}
```

The `createOrder()` method is a static factory method that creates an Order and publishes an `OrderCreatedEvent`. The `OrderCreatedEvent` is enriched with the details of the `Order`, including the line items, the total amount, the restaurant ID, and the restaurant name. Chapter 7 discusses how `Order History Service` uses `Order` events, including `OrderCreatedEvent`, to maintain an easily queried replica of `Orders`.

The initial state of the Order is APPROVAL_PENDING. When the CreateOrderSaga completes, it will invoke either noteApproved() or noteRejected(). The note-Approved() method is invoked when the consumer's credit card has been successfully authorized. The noteRejected() method is called when one of the services rejects the order or authorization fails. As you can see, the state of the Order aggregate determines the behavior of most of its methods. Like the Ticket aggregate, it also emits events.

In addition to createOrder(), the Order class defines several update methods. For example, the Revise Order Saga revises an order by first invoking the revise() method and then, once it's verified that the revision can be made, it invokes the confirm-Revised() method. The following listing shows these methods.

Listing 5.16 The Order method for revising an Order

```
class Order ...

  public List<OrderDomainEvent> revise(OrderRevision orderRevision) {
    switch (state) {

      case APPROVED:
        LineItemQuantityChange change =
                orderLineItems.lineItemQuantityChange(orderRevision);
        if (change.newOrderTotal.isGreaterThanOrEqual(orderMinimum)) {
          throw new OrderMinimumNotMetException();
        }
        this.state = REVISION_PENDING;
        return singletonList(new OrderRevisionProposed(orderRevision,
                        change.currentOrderTotal, change.newOrderTotal));

      default:
        throw new UnsupportedStateTransitionException(state);
    }
  }

  public List<OrderDomainEvent> confirmRevision(OrderRevision orderRevision) {
    switch (state) {
      case REVISION_PENDING:
        LineItemQuantityChange licd =
          orderLineItems.lineItemQuantityChange(orderRevision);

        orderRevision
            .getDeliveryInformation()
            .ifPresent(newDi -> this.deliveryInformation = newDi);

        if (!orderRevision.getRevisedLineItemQuantities().isEmpty()) {
          orderLineItems.updateLineItems(orderRevision);
        }

        this.state = APPROVED;
        return singletonList(new OrderRevised(orderRevision,
                        licd.currentOrderTotal, licd.newOrderTotal));
```

```
        default:
          throw new UnsupportedStateTransitionException(state);
      }
    }

}
```

The `revise()` method is called to initiate the revision of an order. Among other things, it verifies that the revised order won't violate the order minimum and changes the state of the order to `REVISION_PENDING`. Once Revise Order Saga has successfully updated `Kitchen Service` and `Accounting Service`, it then calls `confirmRevision()` to complete the revision.

These methods are invoked by `OrderService`. Let's take a look at that class.

5.5.2   *The OrderService class*

The `OrderService` class defines methods for creating and updating `Orders`. It's the main entry point into the business logic and is invoked by various inbound adapters, such as the REST API. Most of its methods create a saga to orchestrate the creation and updating of `Order` aggregates. As a result, this service is more complicated than the `KitchenService` class discussed earlier. The following listing shows an excerpt of this class. `OrderService` is injected with various dependencies, including `OrderRepository`, `OrderDomainEventPublisher`, and several saga managers. It defines several methods, including `createOrder()` and `reviseOrder()`.

> **Listing 5.17   The `OrderService` class has methods for creating and managing orders**

```
@Transactional
public class OrderService {

  @Autowired
  private OrderRepository orderRepository;

  @Autowired
  private SagaManager<CreateOrderSagaState, CreateOrderSagaState>
    createOrderSagaManager;

  @Autowired
  private SagaManager<ReviseOrderSagaState, ReviseOrderSagaData>
    reviseOrderSagaManagement;

  @Autowired
  private OrderDomainEventPublisher orderAggregateEventPublisher;

  public Order createOrder(OrderDetails orderDetails) {

    Restaurant restaurant = restaurantRepository.findById(restaurantId)
            .orElseThrow(() -
      > new RestaurantNotFoundException(restaurantId));
```

```
    List<OrderLineItem> orderLineItems =              ◄─┐  Creates the Order
        makeOrderLineItems(lineItems, restaurant);        │  aggregate

    ResultWithDomainEvents<Order, OrderDomainEvent> orderAndEvents =
            Order.createOrder(consumerId, restaurant, orderLineItems);

    Order order = orderAndEvents.result;                              Publishes
                                          ┌─ Persists the Order       domain
    orderRepository.save(order);        ◄─┘  in the database          events

    orderAggregateEventPublisher.publish(order, orderAndEvents.events);  ◄─┘

    OrderDetails orderDetails =
      new OrderDetails(consumerId, restaurantId, orderLineItems,
                          order.getOrderTotal());
    CreateOrderSagaState data = new CreateOrderSagaState(order.getId(),
            orderDetails);

    createOrderSagaManager.create(data, Order.class, order.getId());    ◄──┐

    return order;                                         Creates the Create
  }                                                            Order Saga │

  public Order reviseOrder(Long orderId, Long expectedVersion,
                              OrderRevision orderRevision)  {
    public Order reviseOrder(long orderId, OrderRevision orderRevision) {
      Order order = orderRepository.findById(orderId)                   ◄─┐
              .orElseThrow(() -> new OrderNotFoundException(orderId));    │
      ReviseOrderSagaData sagaData =
        new ReviseOrderSagaData(order.getConsumerId(), orderId,        Retrieves
              null, orderRevision);                                    the Order │
      reviseOrderSagaManager.create(sagaData);        ◄─┐  Creates the
      return order;                                       │  Revise Order
    }                                                     │  Saga
  }
```

The createOrder() method first creates and persists an Order aggregate. It then publishes the domain events emitted by the aggregate. Finally, it creates a CreateOrderSaga. The reviseOrder() retrieves the Order and then creates a ReviseOrderSaga.

In many ways, the business logic for a microservices-based application is not that different from that of a monolithic application. It's comprised of classes such as services, JPA-backed entities, and repositories. There are some differences, though. A domain model is organized as a set of DDD aggregates that impose various design constraints. Unlike in a traditional object model, references between classes in different aggregates are in terms of primary key value rather than object references. Also, a transaction can only create or update a single aggregate. It's also useful for aggregates to publish domain events when their state changes.

Another major difference is that services often use sagas to maintain data consistency across multiple services. For example, Kitchen Service merely participates in sagas, it doesn't initiate them. In contrast, Order Service relies heavily on sagas when creating and updating orders. That's because `Orders` must be transactionally consistent with data owned by other services. As a result, most `OrderService` methods create a saga rather than update an `Order` directly.

This chapter has covered how to implement business logic using a traditional approach to persistence. That has involved integrating messaging and event publishing with database transaction management. The event publishing code is intertwined with the business logic. The next chapter looks at event sourcing, an event-centric approach to writing business logic where event generation is integral to the business logic rather than being bolted on.

Summary

- The procedural Transaction script pattern is often a good way to implement simple business logic. But when implementing complex business logic you should consider using the object-oriented Domain model pattern.
- A good way to organize a service's business logic is as a collection of DDD aggregates. DDD aggregates are useful because they modularize the domain model, eliminate the possibility of object reference between services, and ensure that each ACID transaction is within a service.
- An aggregate should publish domain events when it's created or updated. Domain events have a wide variety of uses. Chapter 4 discusses how they can implement choreography-based sagas. And, in chapter 7, I talk about how to use domain events to update replicated data. Domain event subscribers can also notify users and other applications, and publish WebSocket messages to a user's browser.

6
Developing business logic with event sourcing

Mary liked the idea, described in chapter 5, of structuring business logic as a collection of DDD aggregates that publish domain events. She could imagine the use of those events being extremely useful in a microservice architecture. Mary planned to use events to implement choreography-based sagas, which maintain data consistency across services and are described in chapter 4. She also expected to use CQRS views, replicas that support efficient querying that are described in chapter 7.

She was, however, worried that the event publishing logic might be error prone. On one hand, the event publishing logic is reasonably straightforward. Each of an aggregate's methods that initializes or changes the state of the aggregate returns a list of events. The domain service then publishes those events. But on the other

183

hand, the event publishing logic is bolted on to the business logic. The business logic continues to work even when the developer forgets to publish an event. Mary was concerned that this way of publishing events might be a source of bugs.

Many years ago, Mary had learned about *event sourcing*, an event-centric way of writing business logic and persisting domain objects. At the time she was intrigued by its numerous benefits, including how it preserves the complete history of the changes to an aggregate, but it remained a curiosity. Given the importance of domain events in microservice architecture, she now wonders whether it would be worthwhile to explore using event sourcing in the FTGO application. After all, event sourcing eliminates a source of programming errors by guaranteeing that an event will be published whenever an aggregate is created or updated.

I begin this chapter by describing how event sourcing works and how you can use it to write business logic. I describe how event sourcing persists each aggregate as a sequence of events in what is known as an *event store*. I discuss the benefits and drawbacks of event sourcing and cover how to implement an event store. I describe a simple framework for writing event sourcing-based business logic. After that, I discuss how event sourcing is a good foundation for implementing sagas. Let's start by looking at how to develop business logic with event sourcing.

6.1   Developing business logic using event sourcing

Event sourcing is a different way of structuring the business logic and persisting aggregates. It persists an aggregate as a sequence of events. Each event represents a state change of the aggregate. An application recreates the current state of an aggregate by replaying the events.

> **Pattern: Event sourcing**
> Persist an aggregate as a sequence of domain events that represent state changes.
> See http://microservices.io/patterns/data/event-sourcing.html.

Event sourcing has several important benefits. For example, it preserves the history of aggregates, which is valuable for auditing and regulatory purposes. And it reliably publishes domain events, which is particularly useful in a microservice architecture. Event sourcing also has drawbacks. It involves a learning curve, because it's a different way to write your business logic. Also, querying the event store is often difficult, which requires you to use the CQRS pattern, described in chapter 7.

I begin this section by describing the limitations of traditional persistence. I then describe event sourcing in detail and talk about how it overcomes those limitations. After that, I show how to implement the Order aggregate using event sourcing. Finally, I describe the benefits and drawbacks of event sourcing.

Let's first look at the limitations of the traditional approach to persistence.

6.1.1 *The trouble with traditional persistence*

The traditional approach to persistence maps classes to database tables, fields of those classes to table columns, and instances of those classes to rows in those tables. For example, figure 6.1 shows how the Order aggregate, described in chapter 5, is mapped to the ORDER table. Its OrderLineItems are mapped to the ORDER_LINE_ITEM table.

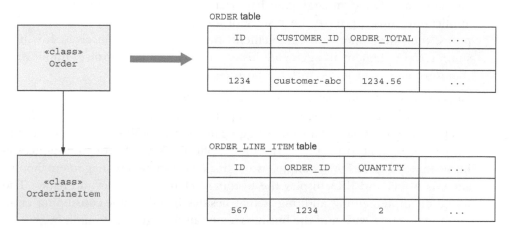

ORDER table

ID	CUSTOMER_ID	ORDER_TOTAL	...
1234	customer-abc	1234.56	...

ORDER_LINE_ITEM table

ID	ORDER_ID	QUANTITY	...
567	1234	2	...

Figure 6.1   The traditional approach to persistence maps classes to tables and objects to rows in those tables.

The application persists an order instance as rows in the ORDER and ORDER_LINE_ITEM tables. It might do that using an ORM framework such as JPA or a lower-level framework such as MyBATIS.

This approach clearly works well because most enterprise applications store data this way. But it has several drawbacks and limitations:

- Object-Relational impedance mismatch.
- Lack of aggregate history.
- Implementing audit logging is tedious and error prone.
- Event publishing is bolted on to the business logic.

Let's look at each of these problems, starting with the Object-Relational impedance mismatch problem.

OBJECT-RELATIONAL IMPEDANCE MISMATCH

One age-old problem is the so-called *Object-Relational impedance mismatch* problem. There's a fundamental conceptual mismatch between the tabular relational schema and the graph structure of a rich domain model with its complex relationships. Some aspects of this problem are reflected in polarized debates over the suitability of Object/Relational mapping (ORM) frameworks. For example, Ted Neward has said that "Object-Relational mapping is the Vietnam of Computer Science" (http://blogs.tedneward.com/post/the-vietnam-of-computer-science/). To be fair, I've used

Hibernate successfully to develop applications where the database schema has been derived from the object model. But the problems are deeper than the limitations of any particular ORM framework.

LACK OF AGGREGATE HISTORY

Another limitation of traditional persistence is that it only stores the current state of an aggregate. Once an aggregate has been updated, its previous state is lost. If an application must preserve the history of an aggregate, perhaps for regulatory purposes, then developers must implement this mechanism themselves. It is time consuming to implement an aggregate history mechanism and involves duplicating code that must be synchronized with the business logic.

IMPLEMENTING AUDIT LOGGING IS TEDIOUS AND ERROR PRONE

Another issue is audit logging. Many applications must maintain an audit log that tracks which users have changed an aggregate. Some applications require auditing for security or regulatory purposes. In other applications, the history of user actions is an important feature. For example, issue trackers and task-management applications such as Asana and JIRA display the history of changes to tasks and issues. The challenge of implementing auditing is that besides being a time-consuming chore, the auditing logging code and the business logic can diverge, resulting in bugs.

EVENT PUBLISHING IS BOLTED ON TO THE BUSINESS LOGIC

Another limitation of traditional persistence is that it usually doesn't support publishing domain events. Domain events, discussed in chapter 5, are events that are published by an aggregate when its state changes. They're a useful mechanism for synchronizing data and sending notifications in microservice architecture. Some ORM frameworks, such as Hibernate, can invoke application-provided callbacks when data objects change. But there's no support for automatically publishing messages as part of the transaction that updates the data. Consequently, as with history and auditing, developers must bolt on event-generation logic, which risks not being synchronized with the business logic. Fortunately, there's a solution to these issues: event sourcing.

6.1.2 *Overview of event sourcing*

Event sourcing is an event-centric technique for implementing business logic and persisting aggregates. An aggregate is stored in the database as a series of events. Each event represents a state change of the aggregate. An aggregate's business logic is structured around the requirement to produce and consume these events. Let's see how that works.

EVENT SOURCING PERSISTS AGGREGATES USING EVENTS

Earlier, in section 6.1.1, I discussed how traditional persistence maps aggregates to tables, their fields to columns, and their instances to rows. Event sourcing is a very different approach to persisting aggregates that builds on the concept of domain events. It persists each aggregate as a sequence of events in the database, known as an event store.

Consider, for example, the Order aggregate. As figure 6.2 shows, rather than store each Order as a row in an ORDER table, event sourcing persists each Order aggregate as one or more rows in an EVENTS table. Each row is a domain event, such as Order Created, Order Approved, Order Shipped, and so on.

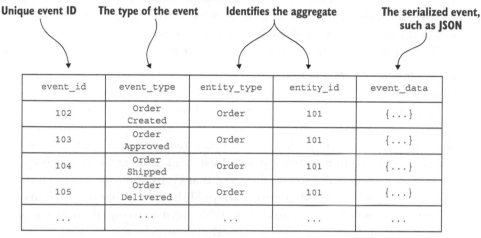

event_id	event_type	entity_type	entity_id	event_data
102	Order Created	Order	101	{...}
103	Order Approved	Order	101	{...}
104	Order Shipped	Order	101	{...}
105	Order Delivered	Order	101	{...}
...	...	...	...	...

EVENTS table

Figure 6.2 Event sourcing persists each aggregate as a sequence of events. A RDBMS-based application can, for example, store the events in an EVENTS table.

When an application creates or updates an aggregate, it inserts the events emitted by the aggregate into the EVENTS table. An application loads an aggregate from the event store by retrieving its events and replaying them. Specifically, loading an aggregate consists of the following three steps:

1. Load the events for the aggregate.
2. Create an aggregate instance by using its default constructor.
3. Iterate through the events, calling apply().

For example, the Eventuate Client framework, covered later in section 6.2.2, uses code similar to the following to reconstruct an aggregate:

```
Class aggregateClass = ...;
Aggregate aggregate = aggregateClass.newInstance();
for (Event event : events) {
  aggregate = aggregate.applyEvent(event);
}
// use aggregate...
```

It creates an instance of the class and iterates through the events, calling the aggregate's applyEvent() method. If you're familiar with functional programming, you may recognize this as a *fold or reduce* operation.

It may be strange and unfamiliar to reconstruct the in-memory state of an aggregate by loading the events and replaying events. But in some ways, it's not all that different from how an ORM framework such as JPA or Hibernate loads an entity. An ORM framework loads an object by executing one or more SELECT statements to retrieve the current persisted state, instantiating objects using their default constructors. It uses reflection to initialize those objects. What's different about event sourcing is that the reconstruction of the in-memory state is accomplished using events.

Let's now look at the requirements event sourcing places on domain events.

EVENTS REPRESENT STATE CHANGES

Chapter 5 defines domain events as a mechanism for notifying subscribers of changes to aggregates. Events can either contain minimal data, such as just the aggregate ID, or can be enriched to contain data that's useful to a typical consumer. For example, the Order Service can publish an OrderCreated event when an order is created. An OrderCreated event may only contain the orderId. Alternatively, the event could contain the complete order so consumers of that event don't have to fetch the data from the Order Service. Whether events are published and what those events contain are driven by the needs of the consumers. With event sourcing, though, it's primarily the aggregate that determines the events and their structure.

Events aren't optional when using event sourcing. Every state change of an aggregate, including its creation, is represented by a domain event. Whenever the aggregate's state changes, it must emit an event. For example, an Order aggregate must emit an OrderCreated event when it's created, and an Order* event whenever it is updated. This is a much more stringent requirement than before, when an aggregate only emitted events that were of interest to consumers.

What's more, an event must contain the data that the aggregate needs to perform the state transition. The state of an aggregate consists of the values of the fields of the objects that comprise the aggregate. A state change might be as simple as changing the value of the field of an object, such as Order.state. Alternatively, a state change can involve adding or removing objects, such as revising an Order's line items.

Suppose, as figure 6.3 shows, that the current state of the aggregate is S and the new state is S'. An event E that represents the state change must contain the data such that when an Order is in state S, calling order.apply(E) will update the Order to state S'. In the next section you'll see that apply() is a method that performs the state change represented by an event.

Some events, such as the Order Shipped event, contain little or no data and just represent the state transition. The apply() method handles an Order Shipped event by changing the Order's status field to SHIPPED. Other events, however, contain a lot of data. An OrderCreated event, for example, must contain all the data needed by the apply() method to initialize an Order, including its line items, payment information, delivery information, and so on. Because events are used to persist an aggregate, you no longer have the option of using a minimal OrderCreated event that contains the orderId.

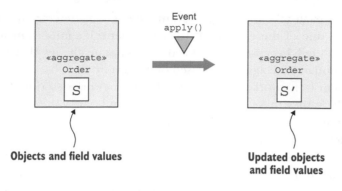

Figure 6.3 Applying event `E` when the `Order` is in state `S` must change the `Order` state to `S'`. The event must contain the data necessary to perform the state change.

AGGREGATE METHODS ARE ALL ABOUT EVENTS

The business logic handles a request to update an aggregate by calling a command method on the aggregate root. In a traditional application, a command method typically validates its arguments and then updates one or more of the aggregate's fields. Command methods in an event sourcing-based application work because they must generate events. As figure 6.4 shows, the outcome of invoking an aggregate's command method is a sequence of events that represent the state changes that must be made. These events are persisted in the database and applied to the aggregate to update its state.

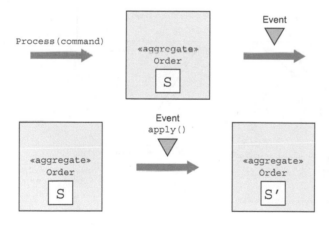

Figure 6.4 Processing a command generates events without changing the state of the aggregate. An aggregate is updated by applying an event.

The requirement to generate events and apply them requires a restructuring—albeit mechanical—of the business logic. Event sourcing refactors a command method into two or more methods. The first method takes a command object parameter, which represents the request, and determines what state changes need to be performed. It validates its arguments, and without changing the state of the aggregate, returns a list of events representing the state changes. This method typically throws an exception if the command cannot be performed.

The other methods each take a particular event type as a parameter and update the aggregate. There's one of these methods for each event. It's important to note that these methods can't fail, because an event represents a state change that *has* happened. Each method updates the aggregate based on the event.

The Eventuate Client framework, an event-sourcing framework described in more detail in section 6.2.2, names these methods `process()` and `apply()`. A `process()` method takes a command object, which contains the arguments of the update request, as a parameter and returns a list of events. An `apply()` method takes an event as a parameter and returns void. An aggregate will define multiple overloaded versions of these methods: one `process()` method for each command class and one `apply()` method for each event type emitted by the aggregate. Figure 6.5 shows an example.

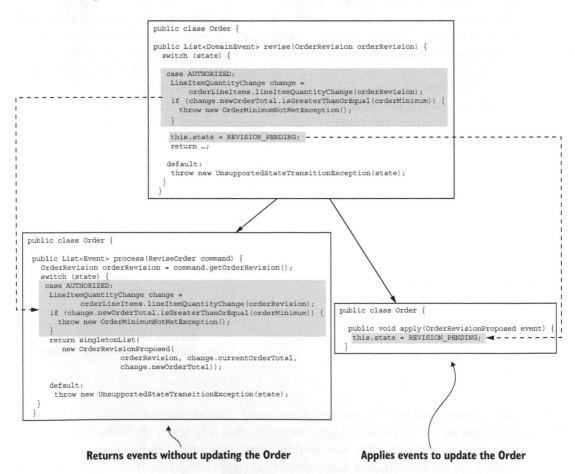

Returns events without updating the Order   **Applies events to update the Order**

Figure 6.5   Event sourcing splits a method that updates an aggregate into a `process()` method, which takes a command and returns events, and one or more `apply()` methods, which take an event and update the aggregate.

In this example, the reviseOrder() method is replaced by a process() method and an apply() method. The process() method takes a ReviseOrder command as a parameter. This command class is defined by applying *Introduce Parameter Object* refactoring (https://refactoring.com/catalog/introduceParameterObject.html) to the reviseOrder() method. The process() method either returns an OrderRevisionProposed event, or throws an exception if it's too late to revise the Order or if the proposed revision doesn't meet the order minimum. The apply() method for the OrderRevisionProposed event changes the state of the Order to REVISION_PENDING.

An aggregate is created using the following steps:

1 Instantiate aggregate root using its default constructor.
2 Invoke process() to generate the new events.
3 Update the aggregate by iterating through the new events, calling its apply().
4 Save the new events in the event store.

An aggregate is updated using the following steps:

1 Load aggregate's events from the event store.
2 Instantiate the aggregate root using its default constructor.
3 Iterate through the loaded events, calling apply() on the aggregate root.
4 Invoke its process() method to generate new events.
5 Update the aggregate by iterating through the new events, calling apply().
6 Save the new events in the event store.

To see this in action, let's now look at the event sourcing version of the Order aggregate.

EVENT SOURCING-BASED ORDER AGGREGATE

Listing 6.1 shows the Order aggregate's fields and the methods responsible for creating it. The event sourcing version of the Order aggregate has some similarities to the JPA-based version shown in chapter 5. Its fields are almost identical, and it emits similar events. What's different is that its business logic is implemented in terms of processing commands that emit events and applying those events, which updates its state. Each method that creates or updates the JPA-based aggregate, such as createOrder() and reviseOrder(), is replaced in the event sourcing version by process() and apply() methods.

> **Listing 6.1   The Order aggregate's fields and its methods that initialize an instance**

```
public class Order {

  private OrderState state;
  private Long consumerId;
  private Long restaurantId;
  private OrderLineItems orderLineItems;
  private DeliveryInformation deliveryInformation;
  private PaymentInformation paymentInformation;
  private Money orderMinimum;
```

```
public Order() {                              Validates the command and
}                                             returns an OrderCreatedEvent

public List<Event> process(CreateOrderCommand command) {    ◄─────┐
    ... validate command ...
    return events(new OrderCreatedEvent(command.getOrderDetails()));
}

public void apply(OrderCreatedEvent event) {                ◄─────────────┐
    OrderDetails orderDetails = event.getOrderDetails();
    this.orderLineItems = new OrderLineItems(orderDetails.getLineItems());
    this.orderMinimum = orderDetails.getOrderMinimum();
    this.state = APPROVAL_PENDING;
}                                        Apply the OrderCreatedEvent by
                                         initializing the fields of the Order.
```

This class's fields are similar to those of the JPA-based `Order`. The only difference is that the aggregate's id isn't stored in the aggregate. The `Order`'s methods are quite different. The `createOrder()` factory method has been replaced by `process()` and `apply()` methods. The `process()` method takes a `CreateOrder` command and emits an `OrderCreated` event. The `apply()` method takes the `OrderCreated` and initializes the fields of the `Order`.

We'll now look at the slightly more complex business logic for revising an order. Previously this business logic consisted of three methods: `reviseOrder()`, `confirm-Revision()`, and `rejectRevision()`. The event sourcing version replaces these three methods with three `process()` methods and some `apply()` methods. The following listing shows the event sourcing version of `reviseOrder()` and `confirmRevision()`.

Listing 6.2   The `process()` and `apply()` methods that revise an `Order` aggregate

```
public class Order {                                        Verify that the Order
                                                            can be revised and
public List<Event> process(ReviseOrder command) {   ◄────── that the revised
    OrderRevision orderRevision = command.getOrderRevision();   order meets the
    switch (state) {                                        order minimum.
        case APPROVED:
            LineItemQuantityChange change =
                    orderLineItems.lineItemQuantityChange(orderRevision);
            if (change.newOrderTotal.isGreaterThanOrEqual(orderMinimum)) {
                throw new OrderMinimumNotMetException();
            }
            return singletonList(new OrderRevisionProposed(orderRevision,
                                change.currentOrderTotal, change.newOrderTotal));

        default:
            throw new UnsupportedStateTransitionException(state);
    }
}
                                                    Change the state of the Order
                                                    to REVISION_PENDING.
public void apply(OrderRevisionProposed event) {   ◄──────┘
    this.state = REVISION_PENDING;
}
```

```java
public List<Event> process(ConfirmReviseOrder command) {         ◁──┐ Verify that the
  OrderRevision orderRevision = command.getOrderRevision();            revision can be
  switch (state) {                                                     confirmed and
    case REVISION_PENDING:                                             return an Order-
      LineItemQuantityChange licd =                                    Revised event.
            orderLineItems.lineItemQuantityChange(orderRevision);
      return singletonList(new OrderRevised(orderRevision,
            licd.currentOrderTotal, licd.newOrderTotal));
    default:
      throw new UnsupportedStateTransitionException(state);
  }
}


                                                            ┌─ Revise the
public void apply(OrderRevised event) {             ◁───────┘  Order.
  OrderRevision orderRevision = event.getOrderRevision();
  if (!orderRevision.getRevisedLineItemQuantities().isEmpty()) {
    orderLineItems.updateLineItems(orderRevision);
  }
  this.state = APPROVED;
}
```

As you can see, each method has been replaced by a process() method and one or more apply() methods. The reviseOrder() method has been replaced by process (ReviseOrder) and apply(OrderRevisionProposed). Similarly, confirmRevision() has been replaced by process(ConfirmReviseOrder) and apply(OrderRevised).

6.1.3   *Handling concurrent updates using optimistic locking*

It's not uncommon for two or more requests to simultaneously update the same aggregate. An application that uses traditional persistence often uses optimistic locking to prevent one transaction from overwriting another's changes. *Optimistic locking* typically uses a version column to detect whether an aggregate has changed since it was read. The application maps the aggregate root to a table that has a VERSION column, which is incremented whenever the aggregate is updated. The application updates the aggregate using an UPDATE statement like this:

```
UPDATE AGGREGATE_ROOT_TABLE
SET VERSION = VERSION + 1 ...
WHERE VERSION = <original version>
```

This UPDATE statement will only succeed if the version is unchanged from when the application read the aggregate. If two transactions read the same aggregate, the first one that updates the aggregate will succeed. The second one will fail because the version number has changed, so it won't accidentally overwrite the first transaction's changes.

   An event store can also use optimistic locking to handle concurrent updates. Each aggregate instance has a version that's read along with the events. When the application inserts events, the event store verifies that the version is unchanged. A simple approach is to use the number of events as the version number. Alternatively, as you'll see below in section 6.2, an event store could maintain an explicit version number.

6.1.4 *Event sourcing and publishing events*

Strictly speaking, event sourcing persists aggregates as events and reconstructs the current state of an aggregate from those events. You can also use event sourcing as a reliable event publishing mechanism. Saving an event in the event store is an inherently atomic operation. We need to implement a mechanism to deliver all persisted events to interested consumers.

Chapter 3 describes a couple of different mechanisms—polling and transaction log tailing—for publishing messages that are inserted into the database as part of a transaction. An event sourcing-based application can publish events using one of these mechanisms. The main difference is that it permanently stores events in an EVENTS table rather than temporarily saving events in an OUTBOX table and then deleting them. Let's take a look at each approach, starting with polling.

USING POLLING TO PUBLISH EVENTS

If events are stored in the EVENTS table shown in figure 6.6, an event publisher can poll the table for new events by executing a SELECT statement and publish the events to a message broker. The challenge is determining which events are new. For example, imagine that eventIds are monotonically increasing. The superficially appealing approach is for the event publisher to record the last eventId that it has processed. It would then retrieve new events using a query like this: SELECT * FROM EVENTS where event_id > ? ORDER BY event_id ASC.

The problem with this approach is that transactions can commit in an order that's different from the order in which they generate events. As a result, the event publisher can accidentally skip over an event. Figure 6.6 shows such as a scenario.

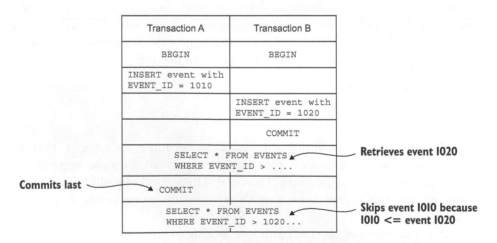

Figure 6.6   A scenario where an event is skipped because its transaction *A* commits after transaction *B*. Polling sees eventId=1020 and then later skips eventId=1010.

In this scenario, Transaction *A* inserts an event with an EVENT_ID of 1010. Next, transaction *B* inserts an event with an EVENT_ID of 1020 and then commits. If the event publisher were now to query the EVENTS table, it would find event 1020. Later on, after transaction *A* committed and event 1010 became visible, the event publisher would ignore it.

One solution to this problem is to add an extra column to the EVENTS table that tracks whether an event has been published. The event publisher would then use the following process:

1 Find unpublished events by executing this SELECT statement: SELECT * FROM EVENTS where PUBLISHED = 0 ORDER BY event_id ASC.

2 Publish events to the message broker.

3 Mark the events as having been published: UPDATE EVENTS SET PUBLISHED = 1 WHERE EVENT_ID in.

This approach prevents the event publisher from skipping events.

USING TRANSACTION LOG TAILING TO RELIABLY PUBLISH EVENTS

More sophisticated event stores use *transaction log tailing*, which, as chapter 3 describes, guarantees that events will be published and is also more performant and scalable. For example, Eventuate Local, an open source event store, uses this approach. It reads events inserted into an EVENTS table from the database transaction log and publishes them to the message broker. Section 6.2 discusses how Eventuate Local works in more detail.

6.1.5 *Using snapshots to improve performance*

An Order aggregate has relatively few state transitions, so it only has a small number of events. It's efficient to query the event store for those events and reconstruct an Order aggregate. Long-lived aggregates, though, can have a large number of events. For example, an Account aggregate potentially has a large number of events. Over time, it would become increasingly inefficient to load and fold those events.

A common solution is to periodically persist a snapshot of the aggregate's state. Figure 6.7 shows an example of using a snapshot. The application restores the state of

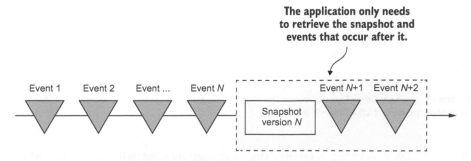

Figure 6.7 Using a snapshot improves performance by eliminating the need to load all events. An application only needs to load the snapshot and the events that occur after it.

an aggregate by loading the most recent snapshot and only those events that have occurred since the snapshot was created.

In this example, the snapshot version is *N*. The application only needs to load the snapshot and the two events that follow it in order to restore the state of the aggregate. The previous *N* events are not loaded from the event store.

When restoring the state of an aggregate from a snapshot, an application first creates an aggregate instance from the snapshot and then iterates through the events, applying them. For example, the Eventuate Client framework, described in section 6.2.2, uses code similar to the following to reconstruct an aggregate:

```
Class aggregateClass = ...;
Snapshot snapshot = ...;
Aggregate aggregate = recreateFromSnapshot(aggregateClass, snapshot);
for (Event event : events) {
  aggregate = aggregate.applyEvent(event);
}
// use aggregate...
```

When using snapshots, the aggregate instance is recreated from the snapshot instead of being created using its default constructor. If an aggregate has a simple, easily serializable structure, the snapshot can be, for example, its JSON serialization. More complex aggregates can be snapshotted using the Memento pattern (https://en.wikipedia.org/wiki/Memento_pattern).

The `Customer` aggregate in the online store example has a very simple structure: the customer's information, their credit limit, and their credit reservations. A snapshot of a `Customer` is the JSON serialization of its state. Figure 6.8 shows how to recreate a `Customer` from a snapshot corresponding to the state of a `Customer` as of event #103. The `Customer Service` needs to load the snapshot and the events that have occurred after event #103.

EVENTS

event_id	event_type	entity_type	entity_id	event_data
...	...	...	...	...
103	...	Customer	101	{...}
104	Credit Reserved	Customer	101	{...}
105	Address Changed	Customer	101	{...}
106	Credit Reserved	Customer	101	{...}

SNAPSHOTS

event_id	entity_type	event_id	snapshot_data
...	...	...	...
103	Customer	101	{name: "..." , ...}
...	...	...	...
...	...	...	...

Figure 6.8 The `Customer Service` recreates the `Customer` by deserializing the snapshot's JSON and then loading and applying events #104 through #106.

The `Customer Service` recreates the `Customer` by deserializing the snapshot's JSON and then loading and applying events #104 through #106.

6.1.6 *Idempotent message processing*

Services often consume messages from other applications or other services. A service might, for example, consume domain events published by aggregates or command messages sent by a saga orchestrator. As described in chapter 3, an important issue when developing a message consumer is ensuring that it's idempotent, because a message broker might deliver the same message multiple times.

A message consumer is idempotent if it can safely be invoked with the same message multiple times. The Eventuate Tram framework, for example, implements idempotent message handling by detecting and discarding duplicate messages. It records the *ids* of processed messages in a PROCESSED_MESSAGES table as part of the local ACID transaction used by the business logic to create or update aggregates. If the ID of a message is in the PROCESSED_MESSAGES table, it's a duplicate and can be discarded. Event sourcing-based business logic must implement an equivalent mechanism. How this is done depends on whether the event store uses an RDBMS or a NoSQL database.

IDEMPOTENT MESSAGE PROCESSING WITH AN RDBMS-BASED EVENT STORE

If an application uses an RDBMS-based event store, it can use an identical approach to detect and discard duplicates messages. It inserts the message ID into the PROCESSED _MESSAGES table as part of the transaction that inserts events into the EVENTS table.

IDEMPOTENT MESSAGE PROCESSING WHEN USING A NoSQL-BASED EVENT STORE

A NoSQL-based event store, which has a limited transaction model, must use a different mechanism to implement idempotent message handling. A message consumer must somehow atomically persist events and record the message ID. Fortunately, there's a simple solution. A message consumer stores the message's ID in the events that are generated while processing it. It detects duplicates by verifying that none of an aggregate's events contains the message ID.

One challenge with using this approach is that processing a message might not generate any events. The lack of events means there's no record of a message having been processed. A subsequent redelivery and reprocessing of the same message might result in incorrect behavior. For example, consider the following scenario:

1 Message A is processed but doesn't update an aggregate.
2 Message B is processed, and the message consumer updates the aggregate.
3 Message A is redelivered, and because there's no record of it having been processed, the message consumer updates the aggregate.
4 Message B is processed again....

In this scenario, the redelivery of events results in a different and possibly erroneous outcome.

One way to avoid this problem is to always publish an event. If an aggregate doesn't emit an event, an application saves a pseudo event solely to record the message ID. Event consumers must ignore these pseudo events.

6.1.7   *Evolving domain events*

Event sourcing, at least conceptually, stores events forever—which is a double-edged sword. On one hand, it provides the application with an audit log of changes that's guaranteed to be accurate. It also enables an application to reconstruct the historical state of an aggregate. On the other hand, it creates a challenge, because the structure of events often changes over time.

An application must potentially deal with multiple versions of events. For example, a service that loads an `Order` aggregate could potentially need to fold multiple versions of events. Similarly, an event subscriber might potentially see multiple versions.

Let's first look at the different ways that events can change, and then I'll describe a commonly used approach for handling changes.

EVENT SCHEMA EVOLUTION

Conceptually, an event sourcing application has a schema that's organized into three levels:

- Consists of one or more aggregates
- Defines the events that each aggregate emits
- Defines the structure of the events

Table 6.1 shows the different types of changes that can occur at each level.

Table 6.1   The different ways that an application's events can evolve

Level	Change	Backward compatible
Schema	Define a new aggregate type	Yes
Remove aggregate	Remove an existing aggregate	No
Rename aggregate	Change the name of an aggregate type	No
Aggregate	Add a new event type	Yes
Remove event	Remove an event type	No
Rename event	Change the name of an event type	No
Event	Add a new field	Yes
Delete field	Delete a field	No
Rename field	Rename a field	No
Change type of field	Change the type of a field	No

These changes occur naturally as a service's domain model evolves over time—for example, when a service's requirements change or as its developers gain deeper insight into a domain and improve the domain model. At the schema level, developers add, remove, and rename aggregate classes. At the aggregate level, the types of events emitted by a particular aggregate can change. Developers can change the structure of an event type by adding, removing, and changing the name or type of a field.

Fortunately, many of these types of changes are backward-compatible changes. For example, adding a field to an event is unlikely to impact consumers. A consumer ignores unknown fields. Other changes, though, aren't backward compatible. For example, changing the name of an event or the name of a field requires consumers of that event type to be changed.

MANAGING SCHEMA CHANGES THROUGH UPCASTING

In the SQL database world, changes to a database schema are commonly handled using schema migrations. Each schema change is represented by a *migration*, a SQL script that changes the schema and migrates the data to a new schema. The schema migrations are stored in a version control system and applied to a database using a tool such as Flyway.

An event sourcing application can use a similar approach to handle non-backward-compatible changes. But instead of migrating events to the new schema version in situ, event sourcing frameworks transform events when they're loaded from the event store. A component commonly called an *upcaster* updates individual events from an old version to a newer version. As a result, the application code only ever deals with the current event schema.

Now that we've looked at how event sourcing works, let's consider its benefits and drawbacks.

6.1.8 Benefits of event sourcing

Event sourcing has both benefits and drawbacks. The benefits include the following:

- Reliably publishes domain events
- Preserves the history of aggregates
- Mostly avoids the O/R impedance mismatch problem
- Provides developers with a time machine

Let's examine each benefit in more detail.

RELIABLY PUBLISHES DOMAIN EVENTS

A major benefit of event sourcing is that it reliably publishes events whenever the state of an aggregate changes. That's a good foundation for an event-driven microservice architecture. Also, because each event can store the identity of the user who made the change, event sourcing provides an audit log that's guaranteed to be accurate. The stream of events can be used for a variety of other purposes, including notifying users, application integration, analytics, and monitoring.

PRESERVES THE HISTORY OF AGGREGATES

Another benefit of event sourcing is that it stores the entire history of each aggregate. You can easily implement temporal queries that retrieve the past state of an aggregate. To determine the state of an aggregate at a given point in time, you fold the events that occurred up until that point. It's straightforward, for example, to calculate the available credit of a customer at some point in the past.

MOSTLY AVOIDS THE O/R IMPEDANCE MISMATCH PROBLEM

Event sourcing persists events rather than aggregating them. Events typically have a simple, easily serializable structure. As mentioned earlier, a service can snapshot a complex aggregate by serializing a memento of its state, which adds a level of indirection between an aggregate and its serialized representation.

PROVIDES DEVELOPERS WITH A TIME MACHINE

Event sourcing stores a history of everything that's happened in the lifetime of an application. Imagine that the FTGO developers need to implement a new requirement to customers who added an item to their shopping cart and then removed it. A traditional application wouldn't preserve this information, so could only market to customers who add and remove items after the feature is implemented. In contrast, an event sourcing-based application can immediately market to customers who have done this in the past. It's as if event sourcing provides developers with a time machine for traveling to the past and implementing unanticipated requirements.

6.1.9   *Drawbacks of event sourcing*

Event sourcing isn't a silver bullet. It has the following drawbacks:

- It has a different programming model that has a learning curve.
- It has the complexity of a messaging-based application.
- Evolving events can be tricky.
- Deleting data is tricky.
- Querying the event store is challenging.

Let's look at each drawback.

DIFFERENT PROGRAMMING MODEL THAT HAS A LEARNING CURVE

It's a different and unfamiliar programming model, and that means a learning curve. In order for an existing application to use event sourcing, you must rewrite its business logic. Fortunately, that's a fairly mechanical transformation that you can do when you migrate your application to microservices.

COMPLEXITY OF A MESSAGING-BASED APPLICATION

Another drawback of event sourcing is that message brokers usually guarantee at-least-once delivery. Event handlers that aren't idempotent must detect and discard duplicate events. The event sourcing framework can help by assigning each event a monotonically increasing ID. An event handler can then detect duplicate events by tracking the highest-seen event ID. This even happens automatically when event handlers update aggregates.

EVOLVING EVENTS CAN BE TRICKY

With event sourcing, the schema of events (and snapshots!) will evolve over time. Because events are stored forever, aggregates potentially need to fold events corresponding to multiple schema versions. There's a real risk that aggregates may become bloated with code to deal with all the different versions. As mentioned in section 6.1.7, a good solution to this problem is to upgrade events to the latest version when they're loaded from the event store. This approach separates the code that upgrades events from the aggregate, which simplifies the aggregates because they only need to apply the latest version of the events.

DELETING DATA IS TRICKY

Because one of the goals of event sourcing is to preserve the history of aggregates, it intentionally stores data forever. The traditional way to delete data when using event sourcing is to do a soft delete. An application deletes an aggregate by setting a *deleted* flag. The aggregate will typically emit a `Deleted` event, which notifies any interested consumers. Any code that accesses that aggregate can check the flag and act accordingly.

Using a soft delete works well for many kinds of data. One challenge, however, is complying with the General Data Protection Regulation (GDPR), a European data protection and privacy regulation that grants individuals the right to erasure (https://gdpr-info.eu/art-17-gdpr/). An application must have the ability to forget a user's personal information, such as their email address. The issue with an event sourcing-based application is that the email address might either be stored in an `AccountCreated` event or used as the primary key of an aggregate. The application somehow must forget about the user without deleting the events.

Encryption is one mechanism you can use to solve this problem. Each user has an encryption key, which is stored in a separate database table. The application uses that encryption key to encrypt any events containing the user's personal information before storing them in an event store. When a user requests to be erased, the application deletes the encryption key record from the database table. The user's personal information is effectively deleted, because the events can no longer be decrypted.

Encrypting events solves most problems with erasing a user's personal information. But if some aspect of a user's personal information, such as email address, is used as an aggregate ID, throwing away the encryption key may not be sufficient. For example, section 6.2 describes an event store that has an `entities` table whose primary key is the aggregate ID. One solution to this problem is to use the technique of *pseudonymization*, replacing the email address with a UUID token and using that as the aggregate ID. The application stores the association between the UUID token and the email address in a database table. When a user requests to be erased, the application deletes the row for their email address from that table. This prevents the application from mapping the UUID back to the email address.

Imagine you need to find customers who have exhausted their credit limit. Because there isn't a column containing the credit, you can't write SELECT * FROM CUSTOMER WHERE CREDIT_LIMIT = 0. Instead, you must use a more complex and potentially inefficient query that has a nested SELECT to compute the credit limit by folding events that set the initial credit and adjusting it. To make matters worse, a NoSQL-based event store will typically only support primary key-based lookup. Consequently, you must implement queries using the CQRS approach described in chapter 7.

6.2   *Implementing an event store*

An application that uses event sourcing stores its events in an event store. An *event store* is a hybrid of a database and a message broker. It behaves as a database because it has an API for inserting and retrieving an aggregate's events by primary key. And it behaves as a message broker because it has an API for subscribing to events.

There are a few different ways to implement an event store. One option is to implement your own event store and event sourcing framework. You can, for example, persist events in an RDBMS. A simple, albeit low-performance, way to publish events is for subscribers to poll the EVENTS table for events. But, as noted in section 6.1.4, one challenge is ensuring that a subscriber processes all events in order.

Another option is to use a special-purpose event store, which typically provides a rich set of features and better performance and scalability. There are several of these to chose from:

- *Event Store*—A .NET-based open source event store developed by Greg Young, an event sourcing pioneer (https://eventstore.org).
- *Lagom*—A microservices framework developed by Lightbend, the company formerly known as Typesafe (www.lightbend.com/lagom-framework).
- *Axon*—An open source Java framework for developing event-driven applications that use event sourcing and CQRS (www.axonframework.org).
- *Eventuate*—Developed by my startup, Eventuate (http://eventuate.io). There are two versions of Eventuate: Eventuate SaaS, a cloud service, and Eventuate Local, an Apache Kafka/RDBMS-based open source project.

Although these frameworks differ in the details, the core concepts remain the same. Because Eventuate is the framework I'm most familiar with, that's the one I cover here. It has a straightforward, easy-to-understand architecture that illustrates event sourcing concepts. You can use it in your applications, reimplement the concepts yourself, or apply what you learn here to build applications with one of the other event sourcing frameworks.

I begin the following sections by describing how the Eventuate Local event store works. Then I describe the Eventuate Client framework for Java, an easy-to-use framework for writing event sourcing-based business logic that uses the Eventuate Local event store.

6.2.1   *How the Eventuate Local event store works*

Eventuate Local is an open source event store. Figure 6.9 shows the architecture. Events are stored in a database, such as MySQL. Applications insert and retrieve aggregate events by primary key. Applications consume events from a message broker, such as Apache Kafka. A transaction log tailing mechanism propagates events from the database to the message broker.

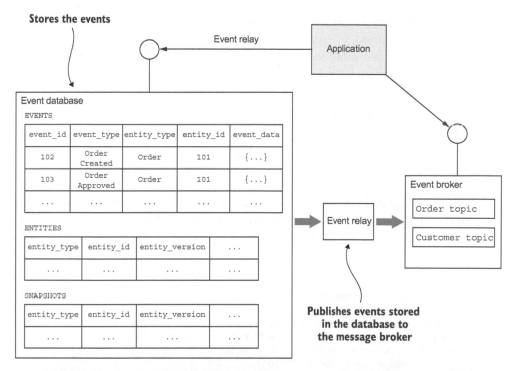

Figure 6.9   The architecture of Eventuate Local. It consists of an event database (such as MySQL) that stores the events, an event broker (like Apache Kafka) that delivers events to subscribers, and an event relay that publishes events stored in the event database to the event broker.

Let's look at the different Eventuate Local components, starting with the database schema.

THE SCHEMA OF EVENTUATE LOCAL'S EVENT DATABASE

The event database consists of three tables:

- events—Stores the events
- entities—One row per entity
- snapshots—Stores snapshots

The central table is the events table. The structure of this table is very similar to the table shown in figure 6.2. Here's its definition:

```
create table events (
  event_id varchar(1000) PRIMARY KEY,
  event_type varchar(1000),
  event_data varchar(1000) NOT NULL,
  entity_type VARCHAR(1000) NOT NULL,
  entity_id VARCHAR(1000) NOT NULL,
  triggering_event VARCHAR(1000)
);
```

The triggering_event column is used to detect duplicate events/messages. It stores the ID of the message/event whose processing generated this event.

The entities table stores the current version of each entity. It's used to implement optimistic locking. Here's the definition of this table:

```
create table entities (
  entity_type VARCHAR(1000),
  entity_id VARCHAR(1000),
  entity_version VARCHAR(1000) NOT NULL,
  PRIMARY KEY(entity_type, entity_id)
);
```

When an entity is created, a row is inserted into this table. Each time an entity is updated, the entity_version column is updated.

The snapshots table stores the snapshots of each entity. Here's the definition of this table:

```
create table snapshots (
  entity_type VARCHAR(1000),
  entity_id VARCHAR(1000),
  entity_version VARCHAR(1000),
  snapshot_type VARCHAR(1000) NOT NULL,
  snapshot_json VARCHAR(1000) NOT NULL,
  triggering_events VARCHAR(1000),
  PRIMARY KEY(entity_type, entity_id, entity_version)
)
```

The entity_type and entity_id columns specify the snapshot's entity. The snapshot _json column is the serialized representation of the snapshot, and the snapshot_type is its type. The entity_version specifies the version of the entity that this is a snapshot of.

The three operations supported by this schema are find(), create(), and update(). The find() operation queries the snapshots table to retrieve the latest snapshot, if any. If a snapshot exists, the find() operation queries the events table to find all events whose event_id is greater than the snapshot's entity_version. Otherwise, find() retrieves all events for the specified entity. The find() operation also queries the entity table to retrieve the entity's current version.

The create() operation inserts a row into the entity table and inserts the events into the events table. The update() operation inserts events into the events table. It also performs an optimistic locking check by updating the entity version in the entities table using this UPDATE statement:

```
UPDATE entities SET entity_version = ?
WHERE entity_type = ? and entity_id = ? and entity_version = ?
```

This statement verifies that the version is unchanged since it was retrieved by the find() operation. It also updates the entity_version to the new version. The update() operation performs these updates within a transaction in order to ensure atomicity.

Now that we've looked at how Eventuate Local stores an aggregate's events and snapshots, let's see how a client subscribes to events using Eventuate Local's event broker.

CONSUMING EVENTS BY SUBSCRIBING TO EVENTUATE LOCAL'S EVENT BROKER

Services consume events by subscribing to the event broker, which is implemented using Apache Kafka. The event broker has a topic for each aggregate type. As described in chapter 3, a *topic* is a partitioned message channel. This enables consumers to scale horizontally while preserving message ordering. The aggregate ID is used as the partition key, which preserves the ordering of events published by a given aggregate. To consume an aggregate's events, a service subscribes to the aggregate's topic.

Let's now look at the event relay—the glue between the event database and the event broker.

THE EVENTUATE LOCAL EVENT RELAY PROPAGATES EVENTS FROM THE DATABASE TO THE MESSAGE BROKER

The event relay propagates events inserted into the event database to the event broker. It uses transaction log tailing whenever possible and polling for other databases. For example, the MySQL version of the event relay uses the MySQL master/slave replication protocol. The event relay connects to the MySQL server as if it were a slave and reads the MySQL binlog, a record of updates made to the database. Inserts into the EVENTS table, which correspond to events, are published to the appropriate Apache Kafka topic. The event relay ignores any other kinds of changes.

The event relay is deployed as a standalone process. In order to restart correctly, it periodically saves the current position in the binlog—filename and offset—in a special Apache Kafka topic. On startup, it first retrieves the last recorded position from the topic. The event relay then starts reading the MySQL binlog from that position.

The event database, message broker, and event relay comprise the event store. Let's now look at the framework a Java application uses to access the event store.

6.2.2 *The Eventuate client framework for Java*

The Eventuate client framework enables developers to write event sourcing-based applications that use the Eventuate Local event store. The framework, shown in figure 6.10, provides the foundation for developing event sourcing-based aggregates, services, and event handlers.

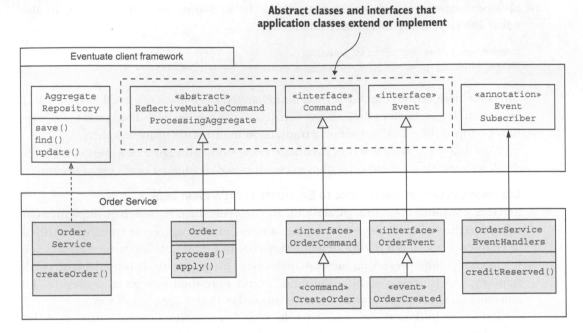

Figure 6.10   The main classes and interfaces provided by the Eventuate client framework for Java

The framework provides base classes for aggregates, commands, and events. There's also an AggregateRepository class that provides CRUD functionality. And the framework has an API for subscribing to events.

Let's briefly look at each of the types shown in figure 6.10.

DEFINING AGGREGATES WITH THE REFLECTIVEMUTABLECOMMANDPROCESSINGAGGREGATE CLASS

ReflectiveMutableCommandProcessingAggregate is the base class for aggregates. It's a generic class that has two type parameters: the first is the concrete aggregate class, and the second is the superclass of the aggregate's command classes. As its rather long name suggests, it uses reflection to dispatch command and events to the appropriate method. Commands are dispatched to a process() method, and events to an apply() method.

The Order class you saw earlier extends ReflectiveMutableCommandProcessing-Aggregate. The following listing shows the Order class.

Listing 6.3   The Eventuate version of the Order class

```
public class Order extends ReflectiveMutableCommandProcessingAggregate<Order,
    OrderCommand> {

  public List<Event> process(CreateOrderCommand command) { ... }

  public void apply(OrderCreatedEvent event) { ... }
```

```
    ...
}
```

The two type parameters passed to `ReflectiveMutableCommandProcessingAggregate` are `Order` and `OrderCommand`, which is the base interface for `Order`'s commands.

DEFINING AGGREGATE COMMANDS

An aggregate's command classes must extend an aggregate-specific base interface, which itself must extend the `Command` interface. For example, the `Order` aggregate's commands extend `OrderCommand`:

```
public interface OrderCommand extends Command {
}

public class CreateOrderCommand implements OrderCommand { ... }
```

The `OrderCommand` interface extends `Command`, and the `CreateOrderCommand` command class extends `OrderCommand`.

DEFINING DOMAIN EVENTS

An aggregate's event classes must extend the `Event` interface, which is a marker interface with no methods. It's also useful to define a common base interface, which extends `Event` for all of an aggregate's event classes. For example, here's the definition of the `OrderCreated` event:

```
interface OrderEvent extends Event {

}

public class OrderCreated extends OrderEvent { ... }
```

The `OrderCreated` event class extends `OrderEvent`, which is the base interface for the `Order` aggregate's event classes. The `OrderEvent` interface extends `Event`.

CREATING, FINDING, AND UPDATING AGGREGATES WITH THE AGGREGATEREPOSITORY CLASS

The framework provides several ways to create, find, and update aggregates. The simplest approach, which I describe here, is to use an `AggregateRepository`. `AggregateRepository` is a generic class that's parameterized by the aggregate class and the aggregate's base command class. It provides three overloaded methods:

- `save()`—Creates an aggregate
- `find()`—Finds an aggregate
- `update()`—Updates an aggregate

The `save()` and `update()` methods are particularly convenient because they encapsulate the boilerplate code required for creating and updating aggregates. For instance, `save()` takes a command object as a parameter and performs the following steps:

1 Instantiates the aggregate using its default constructor
2 Invokes `process()` to process the command

  3   Applies the generated events by calling `apply()`

  4   Saves the generated events in the event store

The `update()` method is similar. It has two parameters, an aggregate ID and a command, and performs the following steps:

  1   Retrieves the aggregate from the event store

  2   Invokes `process()` to process the command

  3   Applies the generated events by calling `apply()`

  4   Saves the generated events in the event store

The `AggregateRepository` class is primarily used by services, which create and update aggregates in response to external requests. For example, the following listing shows how `OrderService` uses an `AggregateRepository` to create an `Order`.

Listing 6.4   `OrderService` uses an `AggregateRepository`

```
public class OrderService {
  private AggregateRepository<Order, OrderCommand> orderRepository;

  public OrderService(AggregateRepository<Order, OrderCommand> orderRepository)
  {
    this.orderRepository = orderRepository;
  }

  public EntityWithIdAndVersion<Order> createOrder(OrderDetails orderDetails) {
    return orderRepository.save(new CreateOrder(orderDetails));
  }
}
```

`OrderService` is injected with an `AggregateRepository` for `Orders`. Its `create()` method invokes `AggregateRepository.save()` with a `CreateOrder` command.

SUBSCRIBING TO DOMAIN EVENTS

The Eventuate Client framework also provides an API for writing event handlers. Listing 6.5 shows an event handler for `CreditReserved` events. The `@EventSubscriber` annotation specifies the ID of the durable subscription. Events that are published when the subscriber isn't running will be delivered when it starts up. The `@EventHandler-Method` annotation identifies the `creditReserved()` method as an event handler.

Listing 6.5   An event handler for `OrderCreatedEvent`

```
@EventSubscriber(id="orderServiceEventHandlers")
public class OrderServiceEventHandlers {

  @EventHandlerMethod
  public void creditReserved(EventHandlerContext<CreditReserved> ctx) {
    CreditReserved event = ctx.getEvent();
    ...
  }
```

An event handler has a parameter of type `EventHandlerContext`, which contains the event and its metadata.

Now that we've looked at how to write event sourcing-based business logic using the Eventuate client framework, let's look at how to use event sourcing-based business logic with sagas.

6.3 *Using sagas and event sourcing together*

Imagine you've implemented one or more services using event sourcing. You've probably written services similar to the one shown in listing 6.4. But if you've read chapter 4, you know that services often need to initiate and participate in *sagas*, sequences of local transactions used to maintain data consistency across services. For example, `Order Service` uses a saga to validate an `Order`. `Kitchen Service`, `Consumer Service`, and `Accounting Service` participate in that saga. Consequently, you must integrate sagas and event sourcing-based business logic.

Event sourcing makes it easy to use choreography-based sagas. The participants exchange the domain events emitted by their aggregates. Each participant's aggregates handle events by processing commands and emitting new events. You need to write the aggregates and the event handler classes, which update the aggregates.

But integrating event sourcing-based business logic with orchestration-based sagas can be more challenging. That's because the event store's concept of a transaction might be quite limited. When using some event stores, an application can only create or update a single aggregate and publish the resulting event(s). But each step of a saga consists of several actions that must be performed atomically:

- *Saga creation*—A service that initiates a saga must atomically create or update an aggregate and create the saga orchestrator. For example, `Order Service`'s `createOrder()` method must create an `Order` aggregate and a `CreateOrderSaga`.
- *Saga orchestration*—A saga orchestrator must atomically consume replies, update its state, and send command messages.
- *Saga participants*—Saga participants, such as `Kitchen Service` and `Order Service`, must atomically consume messages, detect and discard duplicates, create or update aggregates, and send reply messages.

Because of this mismatch between these requirements and the transactional capabilities of an event store, integrating orchestration-based sagas and event sourcing potentially creates some interesting challenges.

A key factor in determining the ease of integrating event sourcing and orchestration-based sagas is whether the event store uses an RDBMS or a NoSQL database. The Eventuate Tram saga framework described in chapter 4 and the underlying Tram messaging framework described in chapter 3 rely on flexible ACID transactions provided by the RDBMS. The saga orchestrator and the saga participants use ACID transactions to atomically update their databases and exchange messages. If the application uses an RDBMS-based event store, such as Eventuate Local, then it can *cheat* and invoke the

Eventuate Tram saga framework and update the event store within an ACID transaction. But if the event store uses a NoSQL database, which can't participate in the same transaction as the Eventuate Tram saga framework, it will have to take a different approach.

Let's take a closer look at some of the different scenarios and issues you'll need to address:

- Implementing choreography-based sagas
- Creating an orchestration-based saga
- Implementing an event sourcing-based saga participant
- Implementing saga orchestrators using event sourcing

We'll begin by looking at how to implement choreography-based sagas using event sourcing.

6.3.1 *Implementing choreography-based sagas using event sourcing*

The event-driven nature of event sourcing makes it quite straightforward to implement choreography-based sagas. When an aggregate is updated, it emits an event. An event handler for a different aggregate can consume that event and update its aggregate. The event sourcing framework automatically makes each event handler idempotent.

For example, chapter 4 discusses how to implement Create Order Saga using choreography. ConsumerService, KitchenService, and AccountingService subscribe to the OrderService's events and vice versa. Each service has an event handler similar to the one shown in listing 6.5. The event handler updates the corresponding aggregate, which emits another event.

Event sourcing and choreography-based sagas work very well together. Event sourcing provides the mechanisms that sagas need, including messaging-based IPC, message de-duplication, and atomic updating of state and message sending. Despite its simplicity, choreography-based sagas have several drawbacks. I talk about some drawbacks in chapter 4, but there's a drawback that's specific to event sourcing.

The problem with using events for saga choreography is that events now have a dual purpose. Event sourcing uses events to represent state changes, but using events for saga choreography requires an aggregate to emit an event even if there is no state change. For example, if updating an aggregate would violate a business rule, then the aggregate must emit an event to report the error. An even worse problem is when a saga participant can't create an aggregate. There's no aggregate that can emit an error event.

Because of these kinds of issues, it's best to implement more complex sagas using orchestration. The following sections explain how to integrate orchestration-based sagas and event sourcing. As you'll see, it involves solving some interesting problems.

Let's first look at how a service method such as OrderService.createOrder() creates a saga orchestrator.

6.3.2 *Creating an orchestration-based saga*

Saga orchestrators are created by some service methods. Other service methods, such as `OrderService.createOrder()`, do two things: create or update an aggregate *and* create a saga orchestrator. The service must perform both actions in a way that guarantees that if it does the first action, then the second action will be done eventually. How the service ensures that both of these actions are performed depends on the kind of event store it uses.

CREATING A SAGA ORCHESTRATOR WHEN USING AN **RDBMS**-BASED EVENT STORE

If a service uses an RDBMS-based event store, it can update the event store and create a saga orchestrator within the same ACID transaction. For example, imagine that the `OrderService` uses Eventuate Local and the Eventuate Tram saga framework. Its `createOrder()` method would look like this:

```
class OrderService

                                            Ensure the createOrder() executes
                                               within a database transaction.
    @Autowired
    private SagaManager<CreateOrderSagaState> createOrderSagaManager;

    @Transactional
     public EntityWithIdAndVersion<Order> createOrder(OrderDetails orderDetails) {
       EntityWithIdAndVersion<Order> order =
           orderRepository.save(new CreateOrder(orderDetails));          Create the Order
                                                                         aggregate.
       CreateOrderSagaState data =
           new CreateOrderSagaState(order.getId(), orderDetails);      Create the
                                                                       CreateOrderSaga.

       createOrderSagaManager.create(data, Order.class, order.getId());

       return order;
    }
...
```

It's a combination of the `OrderService` in listing 6.4 and the `OrderService` described in chapter 4. Because Eventuate Local uses an RDBMS, it can participate in the same ACID transaction as the Eventuate Tram saga framework. But if a service uses a NoSQL-based event store, creating a saga orchestrator isn't as straightforward.

CREATING A SAGA ORCHESTRATOR WHEN USING A **NoSQL**-BASED EVENT STORE

A service that uses a NoSQL-based event store will most likely be unable to atomically update the event store and create a saga orchestrator. The saga orchestration framework might use an entirely different database. Even if it uses the same NoSQL database, the application won't be able to create or update two different objects atomically because of the NoSQL database's limited transaction model. Instead, a service must have an event handler that creates the saga orchestrator in response to a domain event emitted by the aggregate.

For example, figure 6.11 shows how `Order Service` creates a `CreateOrderSaga` using an event handler for the `OrderCreated` event. `Order Service` first creates an

`Order` aggregate and persists it in the event store. The event store publishes the `Order-Created` event, which is consumed by the event handler. The event handler invokes the Eventuate Tram saga framework to create a `CreateOrderSaga`.

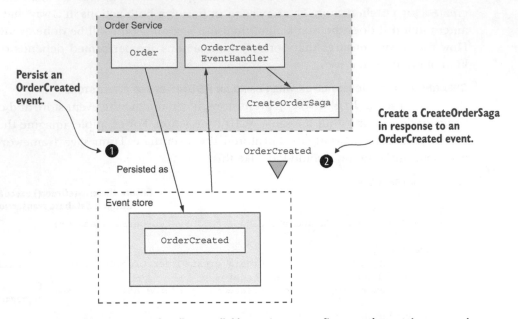

Figure 6.11   Using an event handler to reliably create a saga after a service creates an event sourcing-based aggregate

One issue to keep in mind when writing an event handler that creates a saga orchestrator is that it must handle duplicate events. At-least-once message delivery means that the event handler that creates the saga might be invoked multiple times. It's important to ensure that only one saga instance is created.

A straightforward approach is to derive the ID of the saga from a unique attribute of the event. There are a couple of different options. One is to use the ID of the aggregate that emits the event as the ID of the saga. This works well for sagas that are created in response to aggregate creation events.

Another option is to use the event ID as the saga ID. Because event IDs are unique, this will guarantee that the saga ID is unique. If an event is a duplicate, the event handler's attempt to create the saga will fail because the ID already exists. This option is useful when multiple instances of the same saga can exist for a given aggregate instance.

A service that uses an RDBMS-based event store can also use the same event-driven approach to create sagas. A benefit of this approach is that it promotes loose coupling because services such as `OrderService` no longer explicitly instantiate sagas.

Now that we've looked at how to reliably create a saga orchestrator, let's see how event sourcing-based services can participate in orchestration-based sagas.

6.3.3 *Implementing an event sourcing-based saga participant*

Imagine that you used event sourcing to implement a service that needs to participate in an orchestration-based saga. Not surprisingly, if your service uses an RDBMS-based event store such as Eventuate Local, you can easily ensure that it atomically processes saga command messages and sends replies. It can update the event store as part of the ACID transaction initiated by the Eventuate Tram framework. But you must use an entirely different approach if your service uses an event store that can't participate in the same transaction as the Eventuate Tram framework.

You must address a couple of different issues:

- Idempotent command message handling
- Atomically sending a reply message

Let's first look at how to implement idempotent command message handlers.

IDEMPOTENT COMMAND MESSAGE HANDLING

The first problem to solve is how an event sourcing-based saga participant can detect and discard duplicate messages in order to implement idempotent command message handling. Fortunately, this is an easy problem to address using the idempotent message handling mechanism described earlier. A saga participant records the message ID in the events that are generated when processing the message. Before updating an aggregate, the saga participant verifies that it hasn't processed the message before by looking for the message ID in the events.

ATOMICALLY SENDING REPLY MESSAGES

The second problem to solve is how an event sourcing-based saga participant can atomically send replies. In principle, a saga orchestrator could subscribe to the events emitted by an aggregate, but there are two problems with this approach. The first is that a saga command might not actually change the state of an aggregate. In this scenario, the aggregate won't emit an event, so no reply will be sent to the saga orchestrator. The second problem is that this approach requires the saga orchestrator to treat saga participants that use event sourcing differently from those that don't. That's because in order to receive domain events, the saga orchestrator must subscribe to the aggregate's event channel in addition to its own reply channel.

A better approach is for the saga participant to continue to send a reply message to the saga orchestrator's reply channel. But rather than send the reply message directly, a saga participant uses a two-step process:

1. When a saga command handler creates or updates an aggregate, it arranges for a SagaReplyRequested pseudo event to be saved in the event store along with the real events emitted by the aggregate.
2. An event handler for the SagaReplyRequested pseudo event uses the data contained in the event to construct the reply message, which it then writes to the saga orchestrator's reply channel.

Let's look at an example to see how this works.

EXAMPLE EVENT SOURCING-BASED SAGA PARTICIPANT

This example looks at Accounting Service, one of the participants of Create Order Saga. Figure 6.12 shows how Accounting Service handles the Authorize Command sent by the saga. Accounting Service is implemented using the Eventuate Saga framework. The Eventuate Saga framework is an open source framework for writing sagas that use event sourcing. It's built on the Eventuate Client framework.

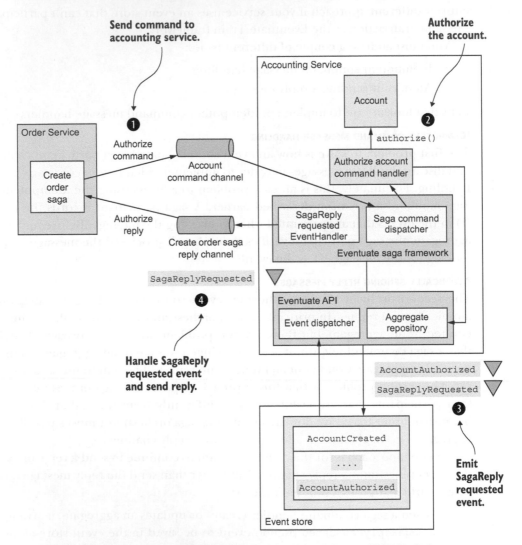

Figure 6.12   How the event sourcing-based Accounting Service participates in Create Order Saga

This figure shows how Create Order Saga and AccountingService interact. The sequence of events is as follows:

1 Create Order Saga sends an `AuthorizeAccount` command to Accounting-Service via a messaging channel. The Eventuate Saga framework's `SagaCommand-Dispatcher` invokes `AccountingServiceCommandHandler` to handle the command message.

2 `AccountingServiceCommandHandler` sends the command to the specified Account aggregate.

3 The aggregate emits two events, `AccountAuthorized` and `SagaReplyRequested-Event`.

4 `SagaReplyRequestedEventHandler` handles `SagaReplyRequestedEvent` by sending a reply message to `CreateOrderSaga`.

The `AccountingServiceCommandHandler` shown in the following listing handles the `AuthorizeAccount` command message by calling `AggregateRepository.update()` to update the Account aggregate.

Listing 6.6 Handles command messages sent by sagas

```
public class AccountingServiceCommandHandler {

  @Autowired
  private AggregateRepository<Account, AccountCommand> accountRepository;

  public void authorize(CommandMessage<AuthorizeCommand> cm) {
    AuthorizeCommand command = cm.getCommand();
    accountRepository.update(command.getOrderId(),
          command,
          replyingTo(cm)
            .catching(AccountDisabledException.class,
                  () -> withFailure(new AccountDisabledReply()))
            .build());
  }

  ...
```

The `authorize()` method invokes an `AggregateRepository` to update the Account aggregate. The third argument to `update()`, which is the `UpdateOptions`, is computed by this expression:

```
replyingTo(cm)
    .catching(AccountDisabledException.class,
          () -> withFailure(new AccountDisabledReply()))
    .build()
```

These `UpdateOptions` configure the `update()` method to do the following:

1 Use the *message id* as an idempotency key to ensure that the message is processed exactly once. As mentioned earlier, the Eventuate framework stores the idempotency key in all generated events, enabling it to detect and ignore duplicate attempts to update an aggregate.

2   Add a `SagaReplyRequestedEvent` pseudo event to the list of events saved in the event store. When `SagaReplyRequestedEventHandler` receives the `SagaReply-RequestedEvent` pseudo event, it sends a reply to the `CreateOrderSaga`'s reply channel.

3   Send an `AccountDisabledReply` instead of the default error reply when the aggregate throws an `AccountDisabledException`.

Now that we've looked at how to implement saga participants using event sourcing, let's find out how to implement saga orchestrators.

6.3.4   *Implementing saga orchestrators using event sourcing*

So far in this section, I've described how event sourcing-based services can initiate and participate in sagas. You can also use event sourcing to implement saga orchestrators. This will enable you to develop applications that are entirely based on an event store.

There are three key design problems you must solve when implementing a saga orchestrator:

1   How can you persist a saga orchestrator?
2   How can you atomically change the state of the orchestrator and send command messages?
3   How can you ensure that a saga orchestrator processes reply messages exactly once?

Chapter 4 discusses how to implement an RDBMS-based saga orchestrator. Let's look at how to solve these problems when using event sourcing.

PERSISTING A SAGA ORCHESTRATOR USING EVENT SOURCING

A saga orchestrator has a very simple lifecycle. First, it's created. Then it's updated in response to replies from saga participants. We can, therefore, persist a saga using the following events:

- `SagaOrchestratorCreated`—The saga orchestrator has been created.
- `SagaOrchestratorUpdated`—The saga orchestrator has been updated.

A saga orchestrator emits a `SagaOrchestratorCreated` event when it's created and a `SagaOrchestratorUpdated` event when it has been updated. These events contain the data necessary to re-create the state of the saga orchestrator. For example, the events for `CreateOrderSaga`, described in chapter 4, would contain a serialized (for example, JSON) `CreateOrderSagaState`.

SENDING COMMAND MESSAGES RELIABLY

Another key design issue is how to atomically update the state of the saga and send a command. As described in chapter 4, the Eventuate Tram-based saga implementation does this by updating the orchestrator and inserting the command message into a `message` table as part of the same transaction. An application that uses an

RDBMS-based event store, such as Eventuate Local, can use the same approach. An application that uses a NoSQL-based event store, such as Eventuate SaaS, can use an analogous approach, despite having a very limited transaction model.

The trick is to persist a `SagaCommandEvent`, which represents a command to send. An event handler then subscribes to `SagaCommandEvents` and sends each command message to the appropriate channel. Figure 6.13 shows how this works.

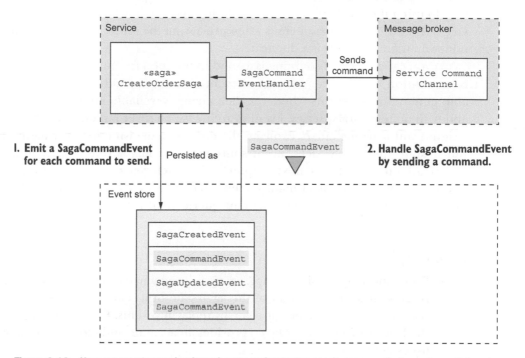

Figure 6.13 How an event sourcing-based saga orchestrator sends commands to saga participants

The saga orchestrator uses a two-step process to send commands:

1 A saga orchestrator emits a `SagaCommandEvent` for each command that it wants to send. `SagaCommandEvent` contains all the data needed to send the command, such as the destination channel and the command object. These events are persisted in the event store.
2 An event handler processes these `SagaCommandEvents` and sends command messages to the destination message channel.

This two-step approach guarantees that the command will be sent at least once.

Because the event store provides at-least-once delivery, an event handler might be invoked multiple times with the same event. That will cause the event handler for `SagaCommandEvents` to send duplicate command messages. Fortunately, though, a saga participant can easily detect and discard duplicate commands using the following mechanism. The ID of `SagaCommandEvent`, which is guaranteed to be unique, is used as the ID of the command message. As a result, the duplicate messages will have the same ID. A saga participant that receives a duplicate command message will discard it using the mechanism described earlier.

PROCESSING REPLIES EXACTLY ONCE

A saga orchestrator also needs to detect and discard duplicate reply messages, which it can do using the mechanism described earlier. The orchestrator stores the reply message's ID in the events that it emits when processing the reply. It can then easily determine whether a message is a duplicate.

As you can see, event sourcing is a good foundation for implementing sagas. This is in addition to the other benefits of event sourcing, including the inherently reliable generation of events whenever data changes, reliable audit logging, and the ability to do temporal queries. Event sourcing isn't a silver bullet, though. It involves a significant learning curve. Evolving the event schema isn't always straightforward. But despite these drawbacks, event sourcing has a major role to play in a microservice architecture. In the next chapter, we'll switch gears and look at how to tackle a different distributed data management challenge in a microservice architecture: queries. I'll describe how to implement queries that retrieve data scattered across multiple services.

Summary

- Event sourcing persists an aggregate as a sequence of events. Each event represents either the creation of the aggregate or a state change. An application recreates the state of an aggregate by replaying events. Event sourcing preserves the history of a domain object, provides an accurate audit log, and reliably publishes domain events.
- Snapshots improve performance by reducing the number of events that must be replayed.
- Events are stored in an event store, a hybrid of a database and a message broker. When a service saves an event in an event store, it delivers the event to subscribers.
- Eventuate Local is an open source event store based on MySQL and Apache Kafka. Developers use the Eventuate client framework to write aggregates and event handlers.
- One challenge with using event sourcing is handling the evolution of events. An application potentially must handle multiple event versions when replaying events. A good solution is to use upcasting, which upgrades events to the latest version when they're loaded from the event store.
- Deleting data in an event sourcing application is tricky. An application must use techniques such as encryption and pseudonymization in order to comply with regulations like the European Union's GDPR that requires an application to erase an individual's data.

- Event sourcing is a simple way to implement choreography-based sagas. Services have event handlers that listen to the events published by event sourcing-based aggregates.
- Event sourcing is a good way to implement saga orchestrators. As a result, you can write applications that exclusively use an event store.

Implementing queries in a microservice architecture

This chapter covers

- The challenges of querying data in a microservice architecture
- When and how to implement queries using the API composition pattern
- When and how to implement queries using the Command query responsibility segregation (CQRS) pattern

Mary and her team were just starting to get comfortable with the idea of using sagas to maintain data consistency. Then they discovered that transaction management wasn't the only distributed data-related challenge they had to worry about when migrating the FTGO application to microservices. They also had to figure out how to implement queries.

In order to support the UI, the FTGO application implements a variety of query operations. Implementing these queries in the existing monolithic application is relatively straightforward, because it has a single database. For the most part, all the FTGO developers needed to do was write SQL SELECT statements and define the necessary indexes. As Mary discovered, writing queries in a microservice architecture is challenging. Queries often need to retrieve data that's scattered among the databases owned by multiple services. You can't, however, use a traditional distributed query mechanism, because even if it were technically possible, it violates encapsulation.

Consider, for example, the query operations for the FTGO application described in chapter 2. Some queries retrieve data that's owned by just one service. The find-ConsumerProfile() query, for example, returns data from Consumer Service. But other FTGO query operations, such as findOrder() and findOrderHistory(), return data owned by multiple services. Implementing these query operations is not as straightforward.

There are two different patterns for implementing query operations in a microservice architecture:

- *The API composition pattern*—This is the simplest approach and should be used whenever possible. It works by making clients of the services that own the data responsible for invoking the services and combining the results.
- *The Command query responsibility segregation (CQRS) pattern*—This is more powerful than the API composition pattern, but it's also more complex. It maintains one or more view databases whose sole purpose is to support queries.

After discussing these two patterns, I will talk about how to design CQRS views, followed by the implementation of an example view. Let's start by taking a look at the API composition pattern.

7.1 Querying using the API composition pattern

The FTGO application implements numerous query operations. Some queries, as mentioned earlier, retrieve data from a single service. Implementing these queries is usually straightforward—although later in this chapter, when I cover the CQRS pattern, you'll see examples of single service queries that are challenging to implement.

There are also queries that retrieve data from multiple services. In this section, I describe the findOrder() query operation, which is an example of a query that retrieves data from multiple services. I explain the challenges that often crop up when implementing this type of query in a microservice architecture. I then describe the API composition pattern and show how you can use it to implement queries such as findOrder().

7.1.1 The findOrder() query operation

The findOrder() operation retrieves an order by its primary key. It takes an orderId as a parameter and returns an OrderDetails object, which contains information about the order. As shown in figure 7.1, this operation is called by a frontend module, such as a mobile device or a web application, that implements the *Order Status* view.

The information displayed by the *Order Status* view includes basic information about the order, including its status, payment status, status of the order from the

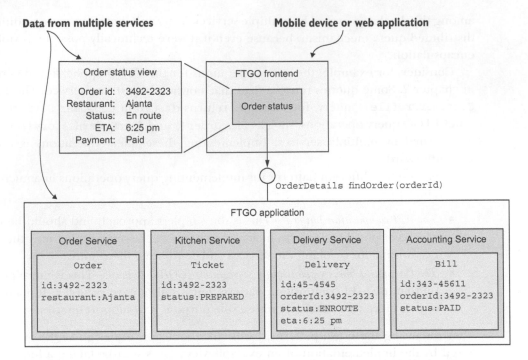

Figure 7.1 The findOrder() operation is invoked by a FTGO frontend module and returns the details of an Order.

restaurant's perspective, and delivery status, including its location and estimated delivery time if in transit.

Because its data resides in a single database, the monolithic FTGO application can easily retrieve the order details by executing a single SELECT statement that joins the various tables. In contrast, in the microservices-based version of the FTGO application, the data is scattered around the following services:

- Order Service—Basic order information, including the details and status
- Kitchen Service—Status of the order from the restaurant's perspective and the estimated time it will be ready for pickup
- Delivery Service—The order's delivery status, estimated delivery information, and its current location
- Accounting Service—The order's payment status

Any client that needs the order details must ask all of these services.

7.1.2 *Overview of the API composition pattern*

One way to implement query operations, such as findOrder(), that retrieve data owned by multiple services is to use the API composition pattern. This pattern implements a query operation by invoking the services that own the data and combining the results. Figure 7.2 shows the structure of this pattern. It has two types of participants:

- *An API composer*—This implements the query operation by querying the provider services.
- *A provider service*—This is a service that owns some of the data that the query returns.

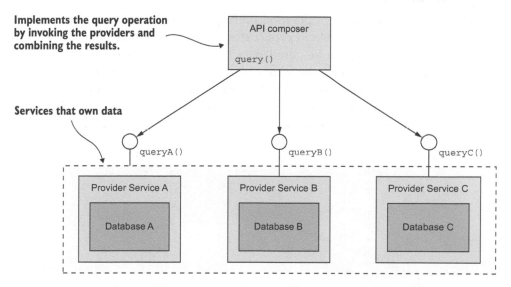

Figure 7.2   The API composition pattern consists of an API composer and two or more provider services. The API composer implements a query by querying the providers and combining the results.

Figure 7.2 shows three provider services. The API composer implements the query by retrieving data from the provider services and combining the results. An API composer might be a client, such as a web application, that needs the data to render a web page. Alternatively, it might be a service, such as an API gateway and its Backends for frontends variant described in chapter 8, which exposes the query operation as an API endpoint.

> **Pattern: API composition**
> Implement a query that retrieves data from several services by querying each service via its API and combining the results. See http://microservices.io/patterns/data/api-composition.html.

Whether you can use this pattern to implement a particular query operation depends on several factors, including how the data is partitioned, the capabilities of the APIs exposed by the services that own the data, and the capabilities of the databases used by the services. For instance, even if the *Provider services* have APIs for retrieving the required data, the aggregator might need to perform an inefficient, in-memory join of large datasets. Later on, you'll see examples of query operations that can't be implemented using this pattern. Fortunately, though, there are many scenarios where this pattern is applicable. To see it in action, we'll look at an example.

7.1.3 Implementing the findOrder() query operation using the API composition pattern

The findOrder() query operation corresponds to a simple primary key-based equi-join query. It's reasonable to expect that each of the *Provider services* has an API endpoint for retrieving the required data by orderId. Consequently, the findOrder() query operation is an excellent candidate to be implemented by the API composition pattern. The *API composer* invokes the four services and combines the results together. Figure 7.3 shows the design of the Find Order Composer.

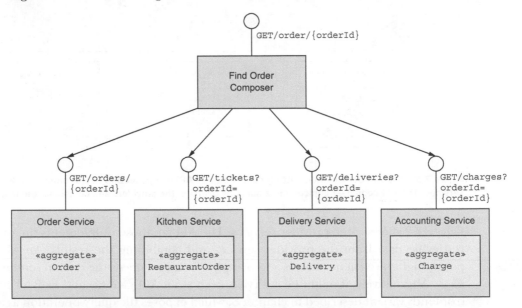

Figure 7.3   Implementing findOrder() using the API composition pattern

In this example, the *API composer* is a service that exposes the query as a REST endpoint. The *Provider services* also implement REST APIs. But the concept is the same if the services used some other interprocess communication protocol, such as gRPC, instead of HTTP. The Find Order Composer implements a REST endpoint GET /order/{orderId}. It invokes the four services and joins the responses using the orderId. Each *Provider service* implements a REST endpoint that returns a response corresponding to a single aggregate. The OrderService retrieves its version of an Order by primary key and the other services use the orderId as a foreign key to retrieve their aggregates.

As you can see, the API composition pattern is quite simple. Let's look at a couple of design issues you must address when applying this pattern.

7.1.4 API composition design issues

When using this pattern, you have to address a couple of design issues:

- Deciding which component in your architecture is the query operation's *API composer*
- How to write efficient aggregation logic

Let's look at each issue.

WHO PLAYS THE ROLE OF THE API COMPOSER?

One decision that you must make is who plays the role of the query operation's *API composer.* You have three options. The first option, shown in figure 7.4, is for a client of the services to be the *API composer.*

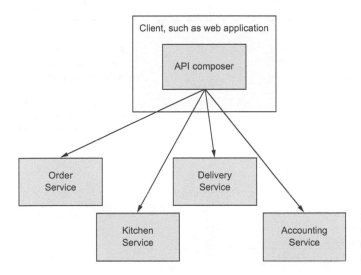

Figure 7.4   Implementing API composition in a client. The client queries the provider services to retrieve the data.

A frontend client such as a web application, that implements the Order Status view and is running on the same LAN, could efficiently retrieve the order details using this pattern. But as you'll learn in chapter 8, this option is probably not practical for clients that are outside of the firewall and access services via a slower network.

The second option, shown in figure 7.5, is for an API gateway, which implements the application's external API, to play the role of an *API composer* for a query operation.

This option makes sense if the query operation is part of the application's external API. Instead of routing a request to another service, the API gateway implements the API composition logic. This approach enables a client, such as a mobile device, that's running outside of the firewall to efficiently retrieve data from numerous services with a single API call. I discuss the API gateway in chapter 8.

The third option, shown in figure 7.6, is to implement an *API composer* as a standalone service.

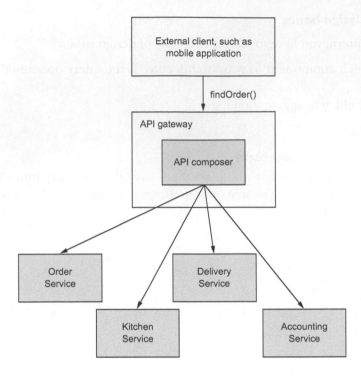

Figure 7.5   Implementing API composition in the API gateway. The API queries the provider services to retrieve the data, combines the results, and returns a response to the client.

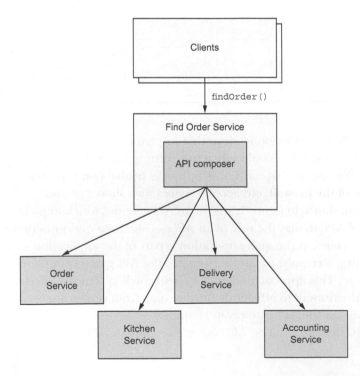

Figure 7.6   Implement a query operation used by multiple clients and services as a standalone service.

You should use this option for a query operation that's used internally by multiple services. This operation can also be used for externally accessible query operations whose aggregation logic is too complex to be part of an API gateway.

API COMPOSERS SHOULD USE A REACTIVE PROGRAMMING MODEL

When developing a distributed system, minimizing latency is an ever-present concern. Whenever possible, an *API composer* should call provider services in parallel in order to minimize the response time for a query operation. The `Find Order Aggregator` should, for example, invoke the four services concurrently because there are no dependencies between the calls. Sometimes, though, an *API composer* needs the result of one *Provider service* in order to invoke another service. In this case, it will need to invoke some—but hopefully not all—of the *provider services* sequentially.

The logic to efficiently execute a mixture of sequential and parallel service invocations can be complex. In order for an *API composer* to be maintainable as well as performant and scalable, it should use a reactive design based on Java `Completable-Future`'s, RxJava observables, or some other equivalent abstraction. I discuss this topic further in chapter 8 when I cover the API gateway pattern.

7.1.5 The benefits and drawbacks of the API composition pattern

This pattern is a simple and intuitive way to implement query operations in a microservice architecture. But it has some drawbacks:

- Increased overhead
- Risk of reduced availability
- Lack of transactional data consistency

Let's take a look at them.

INCREASED OVERHEAD

One drawback of this pattern is the overhead of invoking multiple services and querying multiple databases. In a monolithic application, a client can retrieve data with a single request, which will often execute a single database query. In comparison, using the API composition pattern involves multiple requests and database queries. As a result, more computing and network resources are required, increasing the cost of running the application.

RISK OF REDUCED AVAILABILITY

Another drawback of this pattern is reduced availability. As described in chapter 3, the availability of an operation declines with the number of services that are involved. Because the implementation of a query operation involves at least three services—the *API composer* and at least two provider services—its availability will be significantly less than that of a single service. For example, if the availability of an individual service is 99.5%, then the availability of the `findOrder()` endpoint, which invokes four provider services, is $99.5\%^{(4+1)} = 97.5\%$!

There are couple of strategies you can use to improve availability. The first strategy is for the *API composer* to return previously cached data when a *Provider service* is unavailable. An *API composer* sometimes caches the data returned by a *Provider service* in order to improve performance. It can also use this cache to improve availability. If a provider is unavailable, the *API composer* can return data from the cache, though it may be potentially stale.

Another strategy for improving availability is for the *API composer* to return incomplete data. For example, imagine that Kitchen Service is temporarily unavailable. The *API Composer* for the findOrder() query operation could omit that service's data from the response, because the UI can still display useful information. You'll see more details on API design, caching, and reliability in chapter 8.

LACK OF TRANSACTIONAL DATA CONSISTENCY

Another drawback of the API composition pattern is the lack of data consistency. A monolithic application typically executes a query operation using a single database transaction. ACID transactions—subject to the fine print about isolation levels—ensure that an application has a consistent view of the data, even if it executes multiple database queries. In contrast, the API composition pattern executes multiple database queries against multiple databases. There's a risk, therefore, that a query operation will return inconsistent data.

For example, an Order retrieved from Order Service might be in the CANCELLED state, whereas the corresponding Ticket retrieved from Kitchen Service might not yet have been cancelled. The *API composer* must resolve this discrepancy, which increases the code complexity. To make matters worse, an *API composer* might not always be able to detect inconsistent data, and will return it to the client.

Despite these drawbacks, the API composition pattern is extremely useful. You can use it to implement many query operations. But there are some query operations that can't be efficiently implemented using this pattern. A query operation might, for example, require the *API composer* to perform an in-memory join of large datasets.

It's usually better to implement these types of query operations using the CQRS pattern. Let's take a look at how this pattern works.

7.2   *Using the CQRS pattern*

Many enterprise applications use an RDBMS as the transactional system of record and a text search database, such as Elasticsearch or Solr, for text search queries. Some applications keep the databases synchronized by writing to both simultaneously. Others periodically copy data from the RDBMS to the text search engine. Applications with this architecture leverage the strengths of multiple databases: the transactional properties of the RDBMS and the querying capabilities of the text database.

Pattern: Command query responsibility segregation

Implement a query that needs data from several services by using events to maintain a read-only view that replicates data from the services. See http://microservices .io/patterns/data/cqrs.html.

CQRS is a generalization of this kind of architecture. It maintains one or more view databases—not just text search databases—that implement one or more of the application's queries. To understand why this is useful, we'll look at some queries that can't be efficiently implemented using the API composition pattern. I'll explain how CQRS works and then talk about the benefits and drawbacks of CQRS. Let's take a look at when you need to use CQRS.

7.2.1 Motivations for using CQRS

The API composition pattern is a good way to implement many queries that must retrieve data from multiple services. Unfortunately, it's only a partial solution to the problem of querying in a microservice architecture. That's because there are multiple service queries the API composition pattern can't implement efficiently.

What's more, there are also single service queries that are challenging to implement. Perhaps the service's database doesn't efficiently support the query. Alternatively, it sometimes makes sense for a service to implement a query that retrieves data owned by a different service. Let's take a look at these problems, starting with a multi-service query that can't be efficiently implemented using API composition.

IMPLEMENTING THE findOrderHistory() QUERY OPERATION

The `findOrderHistory()` operation retrieves a consumer's order history. It has several parameters:

- `consumerId`—Identifies the consumer
- `pagination`—Page of results to return
- `filter`—Filter criteria, including the max age of the orders to return, an optional order status, and optional keywords that match the restaurant name and menu items

This query operation returns an `OrderHistory` object that contains a summary of the matching orders sorted by increasing age. It's called by the module that implements the `Order History` view. This view displays a summary of each order, which includes the order number, order status, order total, and estimated delivery time.

On the surface, this operation is similar to the `findOrder()` query operation. The only difference is that it returns multiple orders instead of just one. It may appear that the *API composer* only has to execute the same query against each *Provider service* and combine the results. Unfortunately, it's not that simple.

That's because not all services store the attributes that are used for filtering or sorting. For example, one of the `findOrderHistory()` operation's filter criteria is a keyword that matches against a menu item. Only two of the services, `Order Service` and `Kitchen Service`, store an `Order`'s menu items. Neither `Delivery Service` nor `Accounting Service` stores the menu items, so can't filter their data using this keyword. Similarly, neither `Kitchen Service` nor `Delivery Service` can sort by the `orderCreationDate` attribute.

There are two ways an *API composer* could solve this problem. One solution is for the *API composer* to do an in-memory join, as shown in figure 7.7. It retrieves all orders for the consumer from `Delivery Service` and `Accounting Service` and performs a join with the orders retrieved from `Order Service` and `Kitchen Service`.

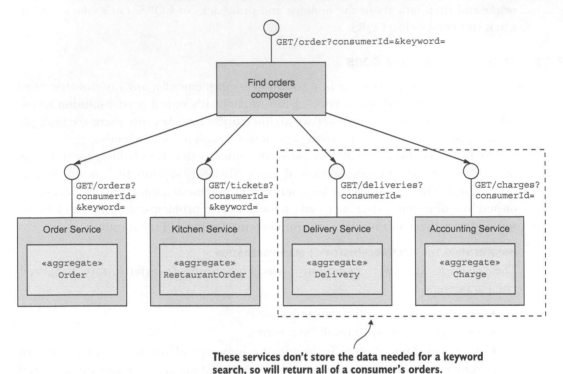

Figure 7.7 **API composition can't efficiently retrieve a consumer's orders, because some providers, such as `Delivery Service`, don't store the attributes used for filtering.**

The drawback of this approach is that it potentially requires the *API composer* to retrieve and join large datasets, which is inefficient.

The other solution is for the *API composer* to retrieve matching orders from `Order Service` and `Kitchen Service` and then request orders from the other services by ID. But this is only practical if those services have a bulk fetch API. Requesting orders individually will likely be inefficient because of excessive network traffic.

Queries such as `findOrderHistory()` require the *API composer* to duplicate the functionality of an RDBMS's query execution engine. On one hand, this potentially moves work from the less scalable database to the more scalable application. On the other hand, it's less efficient. Also, developers should be writing business functionality, not a query execution engine.

Next I show you how to apply the CQRS pattern and use a separate datastore, which is designed to efficiently implement the `findOrderHistory()` query operation.

But first, let's look at an example of a query operation that's challenging to implement, despite being local to a single service.

A CHALLENGING SINGLE SERVICE QUERY: FINDAVAILABLERESTAURANTS()

As you've just seen, implementing queries that retrieve data from multiple services can be challenging. But even queries that are local to a single service can be difficult to implement. There are a couple of reasons why this might be the case. One is because, as discussed shortly, sometimes it's not appropriate for the service that owns the data to implement the query. The other reason is that sometimes a service's database (or data model) doesn't efficiently support the query.

Consider, for example, the findAvailableRestaurants() query operation. This query finds the restaurants that are available to deliver to a given address at a given time. The heart of this query is a geospatial (location-based) search for restaurants that are within a certain distance of the delivery address. It's a critical part of the order process and is invoked by the UI module that displays the available restaurants.

The key challenge when implementing this query operation is performing an efficient geospatial query. How you implement the findAvailableRestaurants() query depends on the capabilities of the database that stores the restaurants. For example, it's straightforward to implement the findAvailableRestaurants() query using either MongoDB or the Postgres and MySQL geospatial extensions. These databases support geospatial datatypes, indexes, and queries. When using one of these databases, Restaurant Service persists a Restaurant as a database record that has a location attribute. It finds the available restaurants using a geospatial query that's optimized by a geospatial index on the location attribute.

If the FTGO application stores restaurants in some other kind of database, implementing the findAvailableRestaurant() query is more challenging. It must maintain a replica of the restaurant data in a form that's designed to support the geospatial query. The application could, for example, use the Geospatial Indexing Library for DynamoDB (https://github.com/awslabs/dynamodb-geo) that uses a table as a geospatial index. Alternatively, the application could store a replica of the restaurant data in an entirely different type of database, a situation very similar to using a text search database for text queries.

The challenge with using replicas is keeping them up-to-date whenever the original data changes. As you'll learn below, CQRS solves the problem of synchronizing replicas.

THE NEED TO SEPARATE CONCERNS

Another reason why single service queries are challenging to implement is that sometimes the service that owns the data shouldn't be the one that implements the query. The findAvailableRestaurants() query operation retrieves data that is owned by Restaurant Service. This service enables restaurant owners to manage their restaurant's profile and menu items. It stores various attributes of a restaurant, including its name, address, cuisines, menu, and opening hours. Given that this service owns the data, it makes sense, at least on the surface, for it to implement this query operation. But data ownership isn't the only factor to consider.

You must also take into account the need to separate concerns and avoid overloading services with too many responsibilities. For example, the primary responsibility of the team that develops `Restaurant Service` is enabling restaurant managers to maintain their restaurants. That's quite different from implementing a high-volume, critical query. What's more, if they were responsible for the `findAvailable-Restaurants()` query operation, the team would constantly live in fear of deploying a change that prevented consumers from placing orders.

It makes sense for `Restaurant Service` to merely provide the restaurant data to another service that implements the `findAvailableRestaurants()` query operation and is most likely owned by the `Order Service` team. As with the `findOrderHistory()` query operation, and when needing to maintain geospatial index, there's a requirement to maintain an eventually consistent replica of some data in order to implement a query. Let's look at how to accomplish that using CQRS.

7.2.2   *Overview of CQRS*

The examples described in section 7.2.1 highlighted three problems that are commonly encountered when implementing queries in a microservice architecture:

- Using the API composition pattern to retrieve data scattered across multiple services results in expensive, inefficient in-memory joins.
- The service that owns the data stores the data in a form or in a database that doesn't efficiently support the required query.
- The need to separate concerns means that the service that owns the data isn't the service that should implement the query operation.

The solution to all three of these problems is to use the CQRS pattern.

CQRS SEPARATES COMMANDS FROM QUERIES

Command Query Responsibility Segregation, as the name suggests, is all about *segregation*, or the separation of concerns. As figure 7.8 shows, it splits a persistent data model and the modules that use it into two parts: the command side and the query side. The command side modules and data model implement create, update, and delete operations (abbreviated CUD—for example, HTTP POSTs, PUTs, and DELETEs). The query-side modules and data model implement queries (such as HTTP GETs). The query side keeps its data model synchronized with the command-side data model by subscribing to the events published by the command side.

Both the non-CQRS and CQRS versions of the service have an API consisting of various CRUD operations. In a non-CQRS-based service, those operations are typically implemented by a domain model that's mapped to a database. For performance, a few queries might bypass the domain model and access the database directly. A single persistent data model supports both commands and queries.

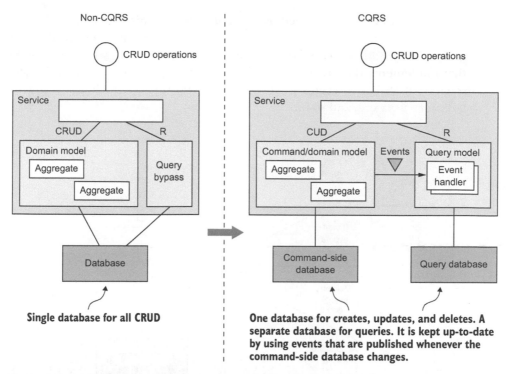

Figure 7.8 On the left is the non-CQRS version of the service, and on the right is the CQRS version. CQRS restructures a service into command-side and query-side modules, which have separate databases.

In a CQRS-based service, the command-side domain model handles CRUD operations and is mapped to its own database. It may also handle simple queries, such as non-join, primary key-based queries. The command side publishes domain events whenever its data changes. These events might be published using a framework such as Eventuate Tram or using event sourcing.

A separate query model handles the nontrivial queries. It's much simpler than the command side because it's not responsible for implementing the business rules. The query side uses whatever kind of database makes sense for the queries that it must support. The query side has event handlers that subscribe to domain events and update the database or databases. There may even be multiple query models, one for each type of query.

CQRS AND QUERY-ONLY SERVICES

Not only can CQRS be applied within a service, but you can also use this pattern to define query services. A query service has an API consisting of only query operations—no command operations. It implements the query operations by querying a database that it keeps up-to-date by subscribing to events published by one or more other services. A query-side service is a good way to implement a view that's built by subscribing to events published by multiple services. This kind of view doesn't belong to any particular service, so it makes sense to implement it as a standalone service. A good example of such a service is `Order History Service`, which is a query service that implements the `findOrderHistory()` query operation. As figure 7.9 shows, this service subscribes to events published by several services, including `Order Service`, `Delivery Service`, and so on.

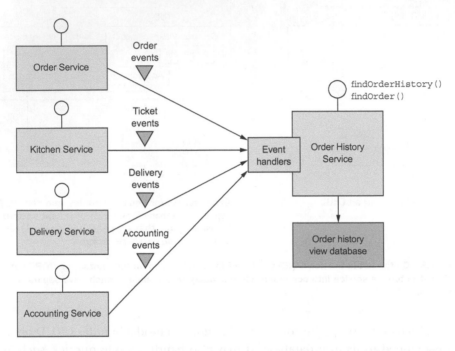

Figure 7.9   The design of `Order History Service`, which is a query-side service. It implements the `findOrderHistory()` query operation by querying a database, which it maintains by subscribing to events published by multiple other services.

`Order History Service` has event handlers that subscribe to events published by several services and update the `Order History View Database`. I describe the implementation of this service in more detail in section 7.4.

A query service is also a good way to implement a view that replicates data owned by a single service yet because of the need to separate concerns isn't part of that service. For example, the FTGO developers can define an `Available Restaurants Service`, which implements the `findAvailableRestaurants()` query operation described earlier. It subscribes to events published by `Restaurant Service` and updates a database designed for efficient geospatial queries.

In many ways, CQRS is an event-based generalization of the popular approach of using RDBMS as the system of record and a text search engine, such as Elasticsearch, to handle text queries. What's different is that CQRS uses a broader range of database types—not just a text search engine. Also, CQRS query-side views are updated in near real time by subscribing to events.

Let's now look at the benefits and drawbacks of CQRS.

7.2.3 The benefits of CQRS

CQRS has both benefits and drawbacks. The benefits are as follows:

- Enables the efficient implementation of queries in a microservice architecture
- Enables the efficient implementation of diverse queries
- Makes querying possible in an event sourcing-based application
- Improves separation of concerns

ENABLES THE EFFICIENT IMPLEMENTATION OF QUERIES IN A MICROSERVICE ARCHITECTURE

One benefit of the CQRS pattern is that it efficiently implements queries that retrieve data owned by multiple services. As described earlier, using the API composition pattern to implement queries sometimes results in expensive, inefficient in-memory joins of large datasets. For those queries, it's more efficient to use an easily queried CQRS view that pre-joins the data from two or more services.

ENABLES THE EFFICIENT IMPLEMENTATION OF DIVERSE QUERIES

Another benefit of CQRS is that it enables an application or service to efficiently implement a diverse set of queries. Attempting to support all queries using a single persistent data model is often challenging and in some cases impossible. Some NoSQL databases have very limited querying capabilities. Even when a database has extensions to support a particular kind of query, using a specialized database is often more efficient. The CQRS pattern avoids the limitations of a single datastore by defining one or more views, each of which efficiently implements specific queries.

ENABLES QUERYING IN AN EVENT SOURCING-BASED APPLICATION

CQRS also overcomes a major limitation of event sourcing. An event store only supports primary key-based queries. The CQRS pattern addresses this limitation by defining one or more views of the aggregates, which are kept up-to-date, by subscribing to the streams of events that are published by the event sourcing-based aggregates. As a result, an event sourcing-based application invariably uses CQRS.

IMPROVES SEPARATION OF CONCERNS

Another benefit of CQRS is that it separates concerns. A domain model and its corresponding persistent data model don't handle both commands and queries. The CQRS pattern defines separate code modules and database schemas for the command and query sides of a service. By separating concerns, the command side and query side are likely to be simpler and easier to maintain.

Moreover, CQRS enables the service that implements a query to be different than the service that owns the data. For example, earlier I described how even though `Restaurant Service` owns the data that's queried by the `findAvailableRestaurants` query operation, it makes sense for another service to implement such a critical, high-volume query. A CQRS query service maintains a view by subscribing to the events published by the service or services that own the data.

7.2.4 *The drawbacks of CQRS*

Even though CQRS has several benefits, it also has significant drawbacks:

- More complex architecture
- Dealing with the replication lag

Let's look at these drawbacks, starting with the increased complexity.

MORE COMPLEX ARCHITECTURE

One drawback of CQRS is that it adds complexity. Developers must write the query-side services that update and query the views. There is also the extra operational complexity of managing and operating the extra datastores. What's more, an application might use different types of databases, which adds further complexity for both developers and operations.

DEALING WITH THE REPLICATION LAG

Another drawback of CQRS is dealing with the "lag" between the command-side and the query-side views. As you might expect, there's delay between when the command side publishes an event and when that event is processed by the query side and the view updated. A client application that updates an aggregate and then immediately queries a view may see the previous version of the aggregate. It must often be written in a way that avoids exposing these potential inconsistencies to the user.

One solution is for the command-side and query-side APIs to supply the client with version information that enables it to tell that the query side is out-of-date. A client can poll the query-side view until it's up-to-date. Shortly I'll discuss how the service APIs can enable a client to do this.

A UI application such as a native mobile application or single page JavaScript application can handle replication lag by updating its local model once the command is successful without issuing a query. It can, for example, update its model using data returned by the command. Hopefully, when a user action triggers a query, the view will be up-to-date. One drawback of this approach is that the UI code may need to duplicate server-side code in order to update its model.

As you can see, CQRS has both benefits and drawbacks. As mentioned earlier, you should use the API composition whenever possible and use CQRS only when you must.

Now that you've seen the benefits and drawbacks of CQRS, let's now look at how to design CQRS views.

7.3 *Designing CQRS views*

A CQRS view module has an API consisting of one more query operations. It implements these query operations by querying a database that it maintains by subscribing to events published by one or more services. As figure 7.10 shows, a view module consists of a view database and three submodules.

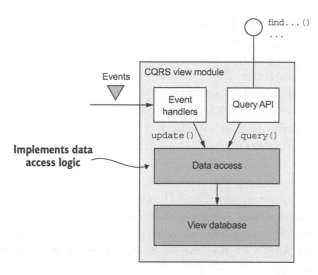

Figure 7.10   The design of a CQRS view module. Event handlers update the view database, which is queried by the Query API module.

The data access module implements the database access logic. The event handlers and query API modules use the data access module to update and query the database. The event handlers module subscribes to events and updates the database. The query API module implements the query API.

You must make some important design decisions when developing a view module:

- You must choose a database and design the schema.
- When designing the data access module, you must address various issues, including ensuring that updates are idempotent and handling concurrent updates.
- When implementing a new view in an existing application or changing the schema of an existing application, you must implement a mechanism to efficiently build or rebuild the view.
- You must decide how to enable a client of the view to cope with the replication lag, described earlier.

Let's look at each of these issues.

7.3.1   *Choosing a view datastore*

A key design decision is the choice of database and the design of the schema. The primary purpose of the database and the data model is to efficiently implement the view module's query operations. It's the characteristics of those queries that are the primary consideration when selecting a database. But the database must also efficiently implement the update operations performed by the event handlers.

SQL vs. NoSQL databases

Not that long ago, there was one type of database to rule them all: the SQL-based RDBMS. As the Web grew in popularity, though, various companies discovered that an RDBMS couldn't satisfy their web scale requirements. That led to the creation of the so-called NoSQL databases. A *NoSQL database* typically has a limited form of transactions and less general querying capabilities. For certain use cases, these databases have certain advantages over SQL databases, including a more flexible data model and better performance and scalability.

A NoSQL database is often a good choice for a CQRS view, which can leverage its strengths and ignore its weaknesses. A CQRS view benefits from the richer data model, and performance of a NoSQL database. It's unaffected by the limitations of a NoSQL database, because it only uses simple transactions and executes a fixed set of queries.

Having said that, sometimes it makes sense to implement a CQRS view using a SQL database. A modern RDBMS running on modern hardware has excellent performance. Developers, database administrators, and IT operations are, in general, much more familiar with SQL databases than they are with NoSQL databases. As mentioned earlier, SQL databases often have extensions for non-relational features, such as geospatial datatypes and queries. Also, a CQRS view might need to use a SQL database in order to support a reporting engine.

As you can see in table 7.1, there are lots of different options to choose from. And to make the choice even more complicated, the differences between the different types of database are starting to blur. For example, MySQL, which is an RDBMS, has excellent support for JSON, which is one of the strengths of MongoDB, a JSON-style document-oriented database.

Table 7.1 Query-side view stores

If you need	Use	Example
PK-based lookup of JSON objects	A document store such as MongoDB or DynamoDB, or a key value store such as Redis	Implement order history by maintaining a MongoDB document containing the per-customer.
Query-based lookup of JSON objects	A document store such as MongoDB or DynamoDB	Implement customer view using MongoDB or DynamoDB.
Text queries	A text search engine such as Elasticsearch	Implement text search for orders by maintaining a per-order Elasticsearch document.
Graph queries	A graph database such as Neo4j	Implement fraud detection by maintaining a graph of customers, orders, and other data.
Traditional SQL reporting/BI	An RDBMS	Standard business reports and analytics.

Now that I've discussed the different kinds of databases you can use to implement a CQRS view, let's look at the problem of how to efficiently update a view.

SUPPORTING UPDATE OPERATIONS

Besides efficiently implementing queries, the view data model must also efficiently implement the update operations executed by the event handlers. Usually, an event handler will update or delete a record in the view database using its primary key. For example, soon I'll describe the design of a CQRS view for the `findOrderHistory()` query. It stores each `Order` as a database record using the `orderId` as the primary key. When this view receives an event from `Order Service`, it can straightforwardly update the corresponding record.

Sometimes, though, it will need to update or delete a record using the equivalent of a foreign key. Consider, for instance, the event handlers for `Delivery*` events. If there is a one-to-one correspondence between a `Delivery` and an `Order`, then `Delivery.id` might be the same as `Order.id`. If it is, then `Delivery*` event handlers can easily update the order's database record.

But suppose a `Delivery` has its own primary key or there is a one-to-many relationship between an `Order` and a `Delivery`. Some `Delivery*` events, such as the `DeliveryCreated` event, will contain the `orderId`. But other events, such as a `DeliveryPickedUp` event, might not. In this scenario, an event handler for `DeliveryPickedUp` will need to update the order's record using the `deliveryId` as the equivalent of a foreign key.

Some types of database efficiently support foreign-key-based update operations. For example, if you're using an RDBMS or MongoDB, you create an index on the necessary columns. However, non-primary key-based updates are not straightforward when using other NOSQL databases. The application will need to maintain some kind of database-specific mapping from a foreign key to a primary key in order to determine which record to update. For example, an application that uses DynamoDB, which only supports primary key-based updates and deletes, must first query a DynamoDB secondary index (discussed shortly) to determine the primary keys of the items to update or delete.

7.3.2 *Data access module design*

The event handlers and the query API module don't access the datastore directly. Instead they use the data access module, which consists of a data access object (DAO) and its helper classes. The DAO has several responsibilities. It implements the update operations invoked by the event handlers and the query operations invoked by the query module. The DAO maps between the data types used by the higher-level code and the database API. It also must handle concurrent updates and ensure that updates are idempotent.

Let's look at these issues, starting with how to handle concurrent updates.

HANDLING CONCURRENCY

Sometimes a DAO must handle the possibility of multiple concurrent updates to the same database record. If a view subscribes to events published by a single aggregate type, there won't be any concurrency issues. That's because events published by a particular aggregate instance are processed sequentially. As a result, a record corresponding to an aggregate instance won't be updated concurrently. But if a view subscribes to events published by multiple aggregate types, then it's possible that multiple events handlers update the same record simultaneously.

For example, an event handler for an `Order*` event might be invoked at the same time as an event handler for a `Delivery*` event for the same order. Both event handlers then simultaneously invoke the DAO to update the database record for that `Order`. A DAO must be written in a way that ensures that this situation is handled correctly. It must not allow one update to overwrite another. If a DAO implements updates by reading a record and then writing the updated record, it must use either pessimistic or optimistic locking. In the next section you'll see an example of a DAO that handles concurrent updates by updating database records without reading them first.

IDEMPOTENT EVENT HANDLERS

As mentioned in chapter 3, an event handler may be invoked with the same event more than once. This is generally not a problem if a query-side event handler is idempotent. An event handler is idempotent if handling duplicate events results in the correct outcome. In the worst case, the view datastore will temporarily be out-of-date. For example, an event handler that maintains the `Order History` view might be invoked with the (admittedly improbable) sequence of events shown in figure 7.11: `Delivery-PickedUp`, `DeliveryDelivered`, `DeliveryPickedUp`, and `DeliveryDelivered`. After delivering the `DeliveryPickedUp` and `DeliveryDelivered` events the first time, the message broker, perhaps because of a network error, starts delivering the events from an earlier point in time, and so redelivers `DeliveryPickedUp` and `DeliveryDelivered`.

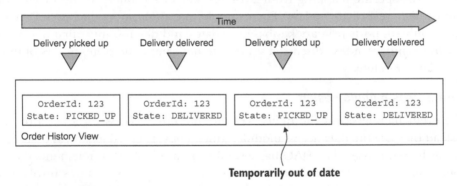

Figure 7.11 The `DeliveryPickedUp` and `DeliveryDelivered` events are delivered twice, which causes the order state in view to be temporarily out-of-date.

After the event handler processes the second `DeliveryPickedUp` event, the `Order History` view temporarily contains the out-of-date state of the `Order` until the `Delivery-Delivered` is processed. If this behavior is undesirable, then the event handler should detect and discard duplicate events, like a non-idempotent event handler.

An event handler isn't idempotent if duplicate events result in an incorrect outcome. For example, an event handler that increments the balance of a bank account isn't idempotent. A non-idempotent event handler must, as explained in chapter 3, detect and discard duplicate events by recording the IDs of events that it has processed in the view datastore.

In order to be reliable, the event handler must record the event ID and update the datastore atomically. How to do this depends on the type of database. If the view database store is a SQL database, the event handler could insert processed events into a `PROCESSED_EVENTS` table as part of the transaction that updates the view. But if the view datastore is a NoSQL database that has a limited transaction model, the event handler must save the event in the datastore "record" (for example, a MongoDB document or DynamoDB table item) that it updates.

It's important to note that the event handler doesn't need to record the ID of every event. If, as is the case with Eventuate, events have a monotonically increasing ID, then each record only needs to store the `max(eventId)` that's received from a given aggregate instance. Furthermore, if the record corresponds to a single aggregate instance, then the event handler only needs to record `max(eventId)`. Only records that represent joins of events from multiple aggregates must contain a map from [`aggregate type, aggregate id`] to `max(eventId)`.

For example, you'll soon see that the DynamoDB implementation of the `Order History` view contains items that have attributes for tracking events that look like this:

```
{...
    "Order3949384394-039434903" : "0000015e0c6fc18f-0242ac1100e50002",
    "Delivery3949384394-039434903" : "0000015e0c6fc264-0242ac1100e50002",
}
```

This view is a join of events published by various services. The name of each of these event-tracking attributes is «aggregateType»«aggregateId», and the value is the `eventId`. Later on, I describe how this works in more detail.

ENABLING A CLIENT APPLICATION TO USE AN EVENTUALLY CONSISTENT VIEW

As I said earlier, one issue with using CQRS is that a client that updates the command side and then immediately executes a query might not see its own update. The view is eventually consistent because of the unavoidable latency of the messaging infrastructure.

The command and query module APIs can enable the client to detect an inconsistency using the following approach. A command-side operation returns a token containing the ID of the published event to the client. The client then passes the token to a query operation, which returns an error if the view hasn't been updated by that event. A view module can implement this mechanism using the duplicate event-detection mechanism.

7.3.3 *Adding and updating CQRS views*

CQRS views will be added and updated throughout the lifetime of an application. Sometimes you need to add a new view to support a new query. At other times you might need to re-create a view because the schema has changed or you need to fix a bug in code that updates the view.

Adding and updating views is conceptually quite simple. To create a new view, you develop the query-side module, set up the datastore, and deploy the service. The query side module's event handlers process all the events, and eventually the view will be up-to-date. Similarly, updating an existing view is also conceptually simple: you change the event handlers and rebuild the view from scratch. The problem, however, is that this approach is unlikely to work in practice. Let's look at the issues.

BUILD CQRS VIEWS USING ARCHIVED EVENTS

One problem is that message brokers can't store messages indefinitely. Traditional message brokers such as RabbitMQ delete a message once it's been processed by a consumer. Even more modern brokers such as Apache Kafka, that retain messages for a configurable retention period, aren't intended to store events indefinitely. As a result, a view can't be built by only reading all the needed events from the message broker. Instead, an application must also read older events that have been archived in, for example, AWS S3. You can do this by using a scalable big data technology such as Apache Spark.

BUILD CQRS VIEWS INCREMENTALLY

Another problem with view creation is that the time and resources required to process all events keep growing over time. Eventually, view creation will become too slow and expensive. The solution is to use a two-step incremental algorithm. The first step periodically computes a snapshot of each aggregate instance based on its previous snapshot and events that have occurred since that snapshot was created. The second step creates a view using the snapshots and any subsequent events.

7.4   *Implementing a CQRS view with AWS DynamoDB*

Now that we've looked at the various design issues you must address when using CQRS, let's consider an example. This section describes how to implement a CQRS view for the findOrderHistory() operation using DynamoDB. AWS DynamoDB is a scalable, NoSQL database that's available as a service on the Amazon cloud. The DynamoDB data model consists of tables that contain items that, like JSON objects, are collections of hierarchical name-value pairs. AWS DynamoDB is a fully managed database, and you can scale the throughput capacity of a table up and down dynamically.

The CQRS view for the findOrderHistory() consumes events from multiple services, so it's implemented as a standalone Order View Service. The service has an API that implements two operations: findOrderHistory() and findOrder(). Even though findOrder() can be implemented using API composition, this view provides this operation for free. Figure 7.12 shows the design of the service. Order History Service is structured as a set of modules, each of which implements a particular responsibility in order to simplify development and testing. The responsibility of each module is as follows:

- OrderHistoryEventHandlers—Subscribes to events published by the various services and invokes the OrderHistoryDAO
- OrderHistoryQuery API *module*—Implements the REST endpoints described earlier

- `OrderHistoryDataAccess`—Contains the `OrderHistoryDAO`, which defines the methods that update and query the `ftgo-order-history` DynamoDB table and its helper classes
- `ftgo-order-history` *DynamoDB table*—The table that stores the orders

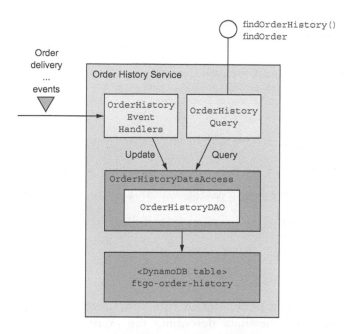

Figure 7.12 The design of `OrderHistoryService`. `OrderHistory-EventHandlers` updates the database in response to events. The `OrderHistoryQuery` module implements the query operations by querying the database. These two modules use the `OrderHistory-DataAccess` module to access the database.

Let's look at the design of the event handlers, the DAO, and the DynamoDB table in more detail.

7.4.1   The OrderHistoryEventHandlers module

This module consists of the event handlers that consume events and update the DynamoDB table. As the following listing shows, the event handlers are simple methods. Each method is a one-liner that invokes an `OrderHistoryDao` method with arguments that are derived from the event.

Listing 7.1   Event handlers that call the `OrderHistoryDao`

```
public class OrderHistoryEventHandlers {

  private OrderHistoryDao orderHistoryDao;

  public OrderHistoryEventHandlers(OrderHistoryDao orderHistoryDao) {
    this.orderHistoryDao = orderHistoryDao;
  }

  public void handleOrderCreated(DomainEventEnvelope<OrderCreated> dee) {
    orderHistoryDao.addOrder(makeOrder(dee.getAggregateId(), dee.getEvent()),
                             makeSourceEvent(dee));
  }

  private Order makeOrder(String orderId, OrderCreatedEvent event) {
    ...
  }

  public void handleDeliveryPickedUp(DomainEventEnvelope<DeliveryPickedUp>
                                           dee) {
   orderHistoryDao.notePickedUp(dee.getEvent().getOrderId(),
         makeSourceEvent(dee));
  }

  ...
```

Each event handler has a single parameter of type `DomainEventEnvelope`, which contains the event and some metadata describing the event. For example, the `handleOrderCreated()` method is invoked to handle an `OrderCreated` event. It calls `orderHistoryDao.addOrder()` to create an `Order` in the database. Similarly, the `handleDeliveryPickedUp()` method is invoked to handle a `DeliveryPickedUp` event. It calls `orderHistoryDao.notePickedUp()` to update the status of the `Order` in the database.

Both methods call the helper method `makeSourceEvent()`, which constructs a `SourceEvent` containing the type and ID of the aggregate that emitted the event and the event ID. In the next section you'll see that `OrderHistoryDao` uses `SourceEvent` to ensure that update operations are idempotent.

Let's now look at the design of the DynamoDB table and after that examine `OrderHistoryDao`.

7.4.2   *Data modeling and query design with DynamoDB*

Like many NoSQL databases, DynamoDB has data access operations that are much less powerful than those that are provided by an RDBMS. Consequently, you must carefully design how the data is stored. In particular, the queries often dictate the design of the schema. We need to address several design issues:

- Designing the `ftgo-order-history` table
- Defining an index for the `findOrderHistory` query

- Implementing the `findOrderHistory` query
- Paginating the query results
- Updating orders
- Detecting duplicate events

We'll look at each one in turn.

DESIGNING THE FTGO-ORDER-HISTORY TABLE

The DynamoDB storage model consists of tables, which contain items, and indexes, which provide alternative ways to access a table's items (discussed shortly). An *item* is a collection of named attributes. An *attribute value* is either a scalar value such as a string, a multivalued collection of strings, or a collection of named attributes. Although an item is the equivalent to a row in an RDBMS, it's a lot more flexible and can store an entire aggregate.

This flexibility enables the `OrderHistoryDataAccess` module to store each `Order` as a single item in a DynamoDB table called `ftgo-order-history`. Each field of the `Order` class is mapped to an item attribute, as shown in figure 7.13. Simple fields such as `orderCreationTime` and `status` are mapped to single-value item attributes. The `lineItems` field is mapped to an attribute that is a list of maps, one map per time line. It can be considered to be a JSON array of objects.

```
ftgo-order-history table
```

Primary key					
orderId	consumerId	orderCreationTime	status	lineItems	. . .
. . .	xyz-abc	22939283232	CREATED	[{...}, {...}, ...]	. . .
. . .	. . .	. . .	. . .	....	. . .

Figure 7.13   Preliminary structure of the DynamoDB `OrderHistory` table

An important part of the definition of a table is its primary key. A DynamoDB application inserts, updates, and retrieves a table's items by primary key. It would seem to make sense for the primary key to be `orderId`. This enables `Order History Service` to insert, update, and retrieve an order by `orderId`. But before finalizing this decision, let's first explore how a table's primary key impacts the kinds of data access operations it supports.

DEFINING AN INDEX FOR THE FINDORDERHISTORY QUERY

This table definition supports primary key-based reads and writes of `Orders`. But it doesn't support a query such as `findOrderHistory()` that returns multiple matching orders sorted by increasing age. That's because, as you will see later in this section, this query uses the DynamoDB `query()` operation, which requires a table to have a composite primary key consisting of two scalar attributes. The first attribute is a partition key. The *partition key* is so called because DynamoDB's Z-axis scaling (described in chapter 1) uses it to select an item's storage partition. The second attribute is the *sort* key. A query() operation returns those items that have the specified partition key, have a sort key in the specified range, and match the optional filter expression. It returns items in the order specified by the sort key.

The findOrderHistory() query operation returns a consumer's orders sorted by increasing age. It therefore requires a primary key that has the consumerId as the partition key and the orderCreationDate as the sort key. But it doesn't make sense for (consumerId, orderCreationDate) to be the primary key of the ftgo-order-history table, because it's not unique.

The solution is for findOrderHistory() to query what DynamoDB calls a *secondary index* on the ftgo-order-history table. This index has (consumerId, orderCreation-Date) as its non-unique key. Like an RDBMS index, a DynamoDB index is automatically updated whenever its table is updated. But unlike a typical RDBMS index, a DynamoDB index can have non-key attributes. *Non-key attributes* improve performance because they're returned by the query, so the application doesn't have to fetch them from the table. Also, as you'll soon see, they can be used for filtering. Figure 7.14 shows the structure of the table and this index.

The index is part of the definition of the ftgo-order-history table and is called ftgo-order-history-by-consumer-id-and-creation-time. The index's attributes

ftgo-order-history-by-consumer-id-and-creation-time   global secondary index

consumerId	orderCreationTime	orderId	status	...
xyz-abc	22939283232	cde-fgh	CREATED	...
...	...	...	...	...

ftgo-order-history table

orderId	consumerId	orderCreationTime	status	lineItems	...
cde-fgh	xyz-abc	22939283232	CREATED	[{...}. {...}, ...]	...
...	...	...	...	....	...

Figure 7.14   The design of the OrderHistory table and index

include the primary key attributes, `consumerId` and `orderCreationTime`, and non-key attributes, including `orderId` and `status`.

The `ftgo-order-history-by-consumer-id-and-creation-time` index enables the `OrderHistoryDaoDynamoDb` to efficiently retrieve a consumer's orders sorted by increasing age.

Let's now look at how to retrieve only those orders that match the filter criteria.

IMPLEMENTING THE findOrderHistory QUERY

The `findOrderHistory()` query operation has a `filter` parameter that specifies the search criteria. One filter criterion is the maximum age of the orders to return. This is easy to implement because the DynamoDB `Query` operation's *key condition expression* supports a range restriction on the sort key. The other filter criteria correspond to non-key attributes and can be implemented using a *filter expression*, which is a Boolean expression. A DynamoDB `Query` operation returns only those items that satisfy the filter expression. For example, to find `Orders` that are `CANCELLED`, the `OrderHistoryDao-DynamoDb` uses a query expression `orderStatus = :orderStatus`, where `:orderStatus` is a placeholder parameter.

The keyword filter criteria is more challenging to implement. It selects orders whose restaurant name or menu items match one of the specified keywords. The `OrderHistoryDaoDynamoDb` enables the keyword search by tokenizing the restaurant name and menu items and storing the set of keywords in a set-valued attribute called `keywords`. It finds the orders that match the keywords by using a filter expression that uses the `contains()` function, for example `contains(keywords, :keyword1)` `OR contains(keywords, :keyword2)`, where `:keyword1` and `:keyword2` are placeholders for the specified keywords.

PAGINATING THE QUERY RESULTS

Some consumers will have a large number of orders. It makes sense, therefore, for the `findOrderHistory()` query operation to use pagination. The DynamoDB `Query` operation has an operation `pageSize` parameter, which specifies the maximum number of items to return. If there are more items, the result of the query has a non-null `Last-EvaluatedKey` attribute. A DAO can retrieve the next page of items by invoking the query with the `exclusiveStartKey` parameter set to `LastEvaluatedKey`.

As you can see, DynamoDB doesn't support position-based pagination. Consequently, `Order History Service` returns an opaque pagination token to its client. The client uses this pagination token to request the next page of results.

Now that I've described how to query DynamoDB for orders, let's look at how to insert and update them.

UPDATING ORDERS

DynamoDB supports two operations for adding and updating items: `PutItem()` and `UpdateItem()`. The `PutItem()` operation creates or replaces an entire item by its primary key. In theory, `OrderHistoryDaoDynamoDb` could use this operation to insert and update orders. One challenge, however, with using `PutItem()` is ensuring that simultaneous updates to the same item are handled correctly.

Consider, for example, the scenario where two event handlers simultaneously attempt to update the same item. Each event handler calls `OrderHistoryDaoDynamoDb` to load the item from DynamoDB, change it in memory, and update it in DynamoDB using `PutItem()`. One event handler could potentially overwrite the change made by the other event handler. `OrderHistoryDaoDynamoDb` can prevent lost updates by using DynamoDB's optimistic locking mechanism. But an even simpler and more efficient approach is to use the `UpdateItem()` operation.

The `UpdateItem()` operation updates individual attributes of the item, creating the item if necessary. Since different event handlers update different attributes of the `Order` item, using `UpdateItem` makes sense. This operation is also more efficient because there's no need to first retrieve the order from the table.

One challenge with updating the database in response to events is, as mentioned earlier, detecting and discarding duplicate events. Let's look at how to do that when using DynamoDB.

DETECTING DUPLICATE EVENTS

All of `Order History Service`'s event handlers are idempotent. Each one sets one or more attributes of the `Order` item. `Order History Service` could, therefore, simply ignore the issue of duplicate events. The downside of ignoring the issue, though, is that `Order` item will sometimes be temporarily out-of-date. That's because an event handler that receives a duplicate event will set an `Order` item's attributes to previous values. The `Order` item won't have the correct values until later events are redelivered.

As described earlier, one way to prevent data from becoming out-of-date is to detect and discard duplicate events. `OrderHistoryDaoDynamoDb` can detect duplicate events by recording in each item the events that have caused it to be updated. It can then use the `UpdateItem()` operation's conditional update mechanism to only update an item if an event isn't a duplicate.

A conditional update is only performed if a *condition expression* is true. A *condition expression* tests whether an attribute exists or has a particular value. The `OrderHistoryDaoDynamoDb` DAO can track events received from each aggregate instance using an attribute called «aggregateType»«aggregateId» whose value is the highest received event ID. An event is a duplicate if the attribute exists and its value is less than or equal to the event ID. The `OrderHistoryDaoDynamoDb` DAO uses this condition expression:

```
attribute_not_exists(«aggregateType»«aggregateId»)
    OR «aggregateType»«aggregateId» < :eventId
```

The *condition expression* only allows the update if the attribute doesn't exist or the `eventId` is greater than the last processed event ID.

For example, suppose an event handler receives a `DeliveryPickup` event whose ID is `123323-343434` from a `Delivery` aggregate whose ID is `3949384394-039434903`. The name of the tracking attribute is `Delivery3949384394-039434903`. The event handler should consider the event to be a duplicate if the value of this attribute is greater than or equal to `123323-343434`. The `query()` operation invoked by the event handler updates the `Order` item using this condition expression:

```
attribute_not_exists(Delivery3949384394-039434903)
    OR Delivery3949384394-039434903 < :eventId
```

Now that I've described the DynamoDB data model and query design, let's take a look at `OrderHistoryDaoDynamoDb`, which defines the methods that update and query the `ftgo-order-history` table.

7.4.3 *The OrderHistoryDaoDynamoDb class*

The `OrderHistoryDaoDynamoDb` class implements methods that read and write items in the `ftgo-order-history` table. Its update methods are invoked by `OrderHistory-EventHandlers`, and its query methods are invoked by `OrderHistoryQuery` API. Let's take a look at some example methods, starting with the `addOrder()` method.

THE ADDORDER() METHOD

The `addOrder()` method, which is shown in listing 7.2, adds an order to the `ftgo-order-history` table. It has two parameters: `order` and `sourceEvent`. The `order` parameter is the `Order` to add, which is obtained from the `OrderCreated` event. The `sourceEvent` parameter contains the `eventId` and the type and ID of the aggregate that emitted the event. It's used to implement the conditional update.

Listing 7.2 The `addOrder()` method adds or updates an `Order`

```java
public class OrderHistoryDaoDynamoDb ...                    The primary key of the
                                                           Order item to update
    @Override
    public boolean addOrder(Order order, Optional<SourceEvent> eventSource) {
        UpdateItemSpec spec = new UpdateItemSpec()
                .withPrimaryKey("orderId", order.getOrderId())
                .withUpdateExpression("SET orderStatus = :orderStatus, " +      ← The update
                        "creationDate = :cd, consumerId = :consumerId, lineItems =" +   expression that
                        " :lineItems, keywords = :keywords, restaurantName = " +        updates the
                        ":restaurantName")                                              attributes
                .withValueMap(new Maps()                  ← The values of the
                        .add(":orderStatus", order.getStatus().toString())     placeholders in
                        .add(":cd", order.getCreationDate().getMillis())       the update
                        .add(":consumerId", order.getConsumerId())             expression
                        .add(":lineItems", mapLineItems(order.getLineItems()))
                        .add(":keywords", mapKeywords(order))
                        .add(":restaurantName", order.getRestaurantName())
                        .map())
                .withReturnValues(ReturnValue.NONE);
        return idempotentUpdate(spec, eventSource);
    }
```

The addOrder() method creates an UpdateSpec, which is part of the AWS SDK and describes the update operation. After creating the UpdateSpec, it calls idempotent-Update(), a helper method that performs the update after adding a condition expression that guards against duplicate updates.

THE NOTEPICKEDUP() METHOD

The notePickedUp() method, shown in listing 7.3, is called by the event handler for the DeliveryPickedUp event. It changes the deliveryStatus of the Order item to PICKED_UP.

Listing 7.3 The notePickedUp() method changes the order status to PICKED_UP

```
public class OrderHistoryDaoDynamoDb ...

@Override
public void notePickedUp(String orderId, Optional<SourceEvent> eventSource) {
 UpdateItemSpec spec = new UpdateItemSpec()
         .withPrimaryKey("orderId", orderId)
         .withUpdateExpression("SET #deliveryStatus = :deliveryStatus")
         .withNameMap(Collections.singletonMap("#deliveryStatus",
             DELIVERY_STATUS_FIELD))
         .withValueMap(Collections.singletonMap(":deliveryStatus",
             DeliveryStatus.PICKED_UP.toString()))
         .withReturnValues(ReturnValue.NONE);
 idempotentUpdate(spec, eventSource);
}
```

This method is similar to addOrder(). It creates an UpdateItemSpec and invokes idempotentUpdate(). Let's look at the idempotentUpdate() method.

THE IDEMPOTENTUPDATE() METHOD

The following listing shows the idempotentUpdate() method, which updates the item after possibly adding a condition expression to the UpdateItemSpec that guards against duplicate updates.

Listing 7.4 The idempotentUpdate() method ignores duplicate events

```
public class OrderHistoryDaoDynamoDb ...

private boolean idempotentUpdate(UpdateItemSpec spec, Optional<SourceEvent>
        eventSource) {
 try {
  table.updateItem(eventSource.map(es -> es.addDuplicateDetection(spec))
          .orElse(spec));
  return true;
 } catch (ConditionalCheckFailedException e) {
  // Do nothing
  return false;
 }
}
```

If the `sourceEvent` is supplied, `idempotentUpdate()` invokes `SourceEvent.add-DuplicateDetection()` to add to `UpdateItemSpec` the condition expression that was described earlier. The `idempotentUpdate()` method catches and ignores the `ConditionalCheckFailedException`, which is thrown by `updateItem()` if the event was a duplicate.

Now that we've seen the code that updates the table, let's look at the query method.

THE FINDORDERHISTORY() METHOD

The `findOrderHistory()` method, shown in listing 7.5, retrieves the consumer's orders by querying the `ftgo-order-history` table using the `ftgo-order-history-by-consumer-id-and-creation-time` secondary index. It has two parameters: `consumerId` specifies the consumer, and `filter` specifies the search criteria. This method creates `QuerySpec`—which, like `UpdateSpec`, is part of the AWS SDK—from its parameters, queries the index, and transforms the returned items into an `OrderHistory` object.

Listing 7.5 The `findOrderHistory()` method retrieves a consumer's matching orders

```
public class OrderHistoryDaoDynamoDb ...

@Override
public OrderHistory findOrderHistory(String consumerId, OrderHistoryFilter
        filter) {

QuerySpec spec = new QuerySpec()
        .withScanIndexForward(false)              // Specifies that query must return the orders in order of increasing age
        .withHashKey("consumerId", consumerId)
        .withRangeKeyCondition(new RangeKeyCondition("creationDate")
                        .gt(filter.getSince().getMillis()));       // The maximum age of the orders to return

filter.getStartKeyToken().ifPresent(token ->
        spec.withExclusiveStartKey(toStartingPrimaryKey(token)));

Map<String, Object> valuesMap = new HashMap<>();

String filterExpression = Expressions.and(
        keywordFilterExpression(valuesMap, filter.getKeywords()),
        statusFilterExpression(valuesMap, filter.getStatus()));   // Construct a filter expression and placeholder value map from the OrderHistoryFilter.

if (!valuesMap.isEmpty())
 spec.withValueMap(valuesMap);

if (StringUtils.isNotBlank(filterExpression)) {
 spec.withFilterExpression(filterExpression);
}

filter.getPageSize().ifPresent(spec::withMaxResultSize);   // Limit the number of results if the caller has specified a page size.

ItemCollection<QueryOutcome> result = index.query(spec);

return new OrderHistory(
        StreamSupport.stream(result.spliterator(), false)
```

```
      .map(this::toOrder)
        .collect(toList()),
  Optional.ofNullable(result
        .getLastLowLevelResult()
        .getQueryResult().getLastEvaluatedKey())
    .map(this::toStartKeyToken));
}
```

Create an Order from
an item returned by
the query.

After building a `QuerySpec`, this method then executes a query and builds an `Order-History`, which contains the list of `Orders`, from the returned items.

The `findOrderHistory()` method implements pagination by serializing the value returned by `getLastEvaluatedKey()` into a JSON token. If a client specifies a start token in `OrderHistoryFilter`, then `findOrderHistory()` serializes it and invokes `withExclusiveStartKey()` to set the start key.

As you can see, you must address numerous issues when implementing a CQRS view, including picking a database, designing the data model that efficiently implements updates and queries, handling concurrent updates, and dealing with duplicate events. The only complex part of the code is the DAO, because it must properly handle concurrency and ensure that updates are idempotent.

Summary

- Implementing queries that retrieve data from multiple services is challenging because each service's data is private.

- There are two ways to implement these kinds of query: the API composition pattern and the Command query responsibility segregation (CQRS) pattern.

- The API composition pattern, which gathers data from multiple services, is the simplest way to implement queries and should be used whenever possible.

- A limitation of the API composition pattern is that some complex queries require inefficient in-memory joins of large datasets.

- The CQRS pattern, which implements queries using view databases, is more powerful but more complex to implement.

- A CQRS view module must handle concurrent updates as well as detect and discard duplicate events.

- CQRS improves separation of concerns by enabling a service to implement a query that returns data owned by a different service.

- Clients must handle the eventual consistency of CQRS views.

External API patterns

The FTGO application, like many other applications, has a REST API. Its clients include the FTGO mobile applications, JavaScript running in the browser, and applications developed by partners. In such a monolithic architecture, the API that's exposed to clients is the monolith's API. But when once the FTGO team starts deploying microservices, there's no longer one API, because each service has its own API. Mary and her team must decide what kind of API the FTGO application should now expose to its clients. For example, should clients be aware of the existence of services and make requests to them directly?

The task of designing an application's external API is made even more challenging by the diversity of its clients. Different clients typically require different data. A desktop browser-based UI usually displays far more information than a mobile application. Also, different clients access the services over different kinds of networks. The clients within the firewall use a high-performance LAN, and the clients outside of the firewall use the internet or mobile network, which will have lower performance. Consequently, as you'll learn, it often doesn't make sense to have a single, one-size-fits-all API.

This chapter begins by describing various external API design issues. I then describe the external API patterns. I cover the API gateway pattern and then the Backends for frontends pattern. After that, I discuss how to design and implement an API gateway. I review the various options that are available, which include off-the-shelf API gateway products and frameworks for developing your own. I describe the design and implementation of an API gateway that's built using the Spring Cloud Gateway framework. I also describe how to build an API gateway using GraphQL, a framework that provides graph-based query language.

8.1   *External API design issues*

In order to explore the various API-related issues, let's consider the FTGO application. As figure 8.1 shows, this application's services are consumed by a variety of clients. Four kinds of clients consume the services' APIs:

- Web applications, such as `Consumer web application`, which implements the browser-based UI for consumers, `Restaurant web application`, which implements the browser-based UI for restaurants, and `Admin web application`, which implements the internal administrator UI
- JavaScript applications running in the browser
- Mobile applications, one for consumers and the other for couriers
- Applications written by third-party developers

The web applications run inside the firewall, so they access the services over a high-bandwidth, low-latency LAN. The other clients run outside the firewall, so they access the services over the lower-bandwidth, higher-latency internet or mobile network.

One approach to API design is for clients to invoke the services directly. On the surface, this sounds quite straightforward—after all, that's how clients invoke the API of a monolithic application. But this approach is rarely used in a microservice architecture because of the following drawbacks:

- The fine-grained service APIs require clients to make multiple requests to retrieve the data they need, which is inefficient and can result in a poor user experience.
- The lack of encapsulation caused by clients knowing about each service and its API makes it difficult to change the architecture and the APIs.
- Services might use IPC mechanisms that aren't convenient or practical for clients to use, especially those clients outside the firewall.

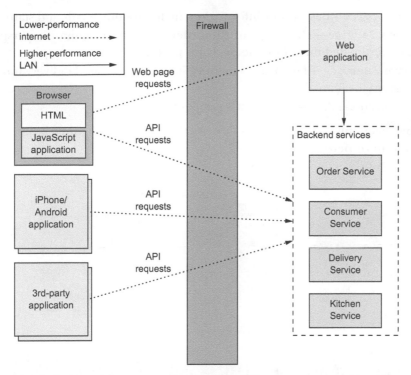

Figure 8.1 The FTGO application's services and their clients. There are several different types of clients. Some are inside the firewall, and others are outside. Those outside the firewall access the services over the lower-performance Internet/mobile network. Those clients inside the firewall use a higher-performance LAN.

To learn more about these drawbacks, let's take a look at how the FTGO mobile application for consumers retrieves data from the services.

8.1.1 API design issues for the FTGO mobile client

Consumers use the FTGO mobile client to place and manage their orders. Imagine you're developing the mobile client's View Order view, which displays an order. As described in chapter 7, the information displayed by this view includes basic order information, including its status, payment status, status of the order from the restaurant's perspective, and delivery status, including its location and estimated delivery time if in transit.

The monolithic version of the FTGO application has an API endpoint that returns the order details. The mobile client retrieves the information it needs by making a single request. In contrast, in the microservices version of the FTGO application, the order details are, as described previously, scattered across several services, including the following:

- `Order Service`—Basic order information, including the details and status
- `Kitchen Service`—The status of the order from the restaurant's perspective and the estimated time it will be ready for pickup
- `Delivery Service`—The order's delivery status, its estimated delivery time, and its current location
- `Accounting Service`—The order's payment status

If the mobile client invokes the services directly, then it must, as figure 8.2 shows, make multiple calls to retrieve this data.

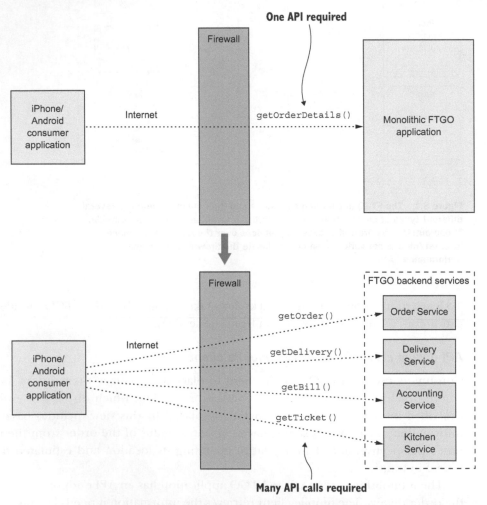

Figure 8.2   A client can retrieve the order details from the monolithic FTGO application with a single request. But the client must make multiple requests to retrieve the same information in a microservice architecture.

In this design, the mobile application is playing the role of API composer. It invokes multiple services and combines the results. Although this approach seems reasonable, it has several serious problems.

POOR USER EXPERIENCE DUE TO THE CLIENT MAKING MULTIPLE REQUESTS

The first problem is that the mobile application must sometimes make multiple requests to retrieve the data it wants to display to the user. The chatty interaction between the application and the services can make the application seem unresponsive, especially when it uses the internet or a mobile network. The internet has much lower bandwidth and higher latency than a LAN, and mobile networks are even worse. The latency of a mobile network (and internet) is typically 100x greater than a LAN.

The higher latency might not be a problem when retrieving the order details, because the mobile application minimizes the delay by executing the requests concurrently. The overall response time is no greater than that of a single request. But in other scenarios, a client may need to execute requests sequentially, which will result in a poor user experience.

What's more, poor user experience due to network latency is not the only issue with a chatty API. It requires the mobile developer to write potentially complex API composition code. This work is a distraction from their primary task of creating a great user experience. Also, because each network request consumes power, a chatty API drains the mobile device's battery faster.

LACK OF ENCAPSULATION REQUIRES FRONTEND DEVELOPERS TO CHANGE THEIR CODE IN LOCKSTEP WITH THE BACKEND

Another drawback of a mobile application directly accessing the services is the lack of encapsulation. As an application evolves, the developers of a service sometimes change an API in a way that breaks existing clients. They might even change how the system is decomposed into services. Developers may add new services and split or merge existing services. But if knowledge about the services is baked into a mobile application, it can be difficult to change the services' APIs.

Unlike when updating a server-side application, it takes hours or perhaps even days to roll out a new version of a mobile application. Apple or Google must approve the upgrade and make it available for download. Users might not download the upgrade immediately—if ever. And you may not want to force reluctant users to upgrade. The strategy of exposing service APIs to mobile creates a significant obstacle to evolving those APIs.

SERVICES MIGHT USE CLIENT-UNFRIENDLY IPC MECHANISMS

Another challenge with a mobile application directly calling services is that some services could use protocols that aren't easily consumed by a client. Client applications that run outside the firewall typically use protocols such as HTTP and WebSockets. But as described in chapter 3, service developers have many protocols to choose from—not just HTTP. Some of an application's services might use gRPC, whereas others could use the AMQP messaging protocol. These kinds of protocols work well internally, but might not be easily consumed by a mobile client. Some aren't even firewall friendly.

8.1.2 *API design issues for other kinds of clients*

I picked the mobile client because it's a great way to demonstrate the drawbacks of clients accessing services directly. But the problems created by exposing services to clients aren't specific to just mobile clients. Other kinds of clients, especially those outside the firewall, also encounter these problems. As described earlier, the FTGO application's services are consumed by web applications, browser-based JavaScript applications, and third-party applications. Let's take a look at the API design issues with these clients.

API DESIGN ISSUES FOR WEB APPLICATIONS

Traditional server-side web applications, which handle HTTP requests from browsers and return HTML pages, run within the firewall and access the services over a LAN. Network bandwidth and latency aren't obstacles to implementing API composition in a web application. Also, web applications can use non-web-friendly protocols to access the services. The teams that develop web applications are part of the same organization and often work in close collaboration with the teams writing the backend services, so a web application can easily be updated whenever the backend services are changed. Consequently, it's feasible for a web application to access the backend services directly.

API DESIGN ISSUES FOR BROWSER-BASED JAVASCRIPT APPLICATIONS

Modern browser applications use some amount of JavaScript. Even if the HTML is primarily generated by a server-side web application, it's common for JavaScript running in the browser to invoke services. For example, all of the FTGO application web applications—`Consumer`, `Restaurant`, and `Admin`—contain JavaScript that invokes the backend services. The `Consumer` web application, for instance, dynamically refreshes the `Order Details` page using JavaScript that invokes the service APIs.

On one hand, browser-based JavaScript applications are easy to update when service APIs change. On the other hand, JavaScript applications that access the services over the internet have the same problems with network latency as mobile applications. To make matters worse, browser-based UIs, especially those for the desktop, are usually more sophisticated and need to compose more services than mobile applications. It's likely that the `Consumer` and `Restaurant` applications, which access services over the internet, won't be able to compose service APIs efficiently.

DESIGNING APIS FOR THIRD-PARTY APPLICATIONS

FTGO, like many other organizations, exposes an API to third-party developers. The developers can use the FTGO API to write applications that place and manage orders. These third-party applications access the APIs over the internet, so API composition is likely to be inefficient. But the inefficiency of API composition is a relatively minor problem compared to the much larger challenge of designing an API that's used by third-party applications. That's because third-party developers need an API that's stable.

Very few organizations can force third-party developers to upgrade to a new API. Organizations that have an unstable API risk losing developers to a competitor. Consequently, you must carefully manage the evolution of an API that's used by third-party developers. You typically have to maintain older versions for a long time—possibly forever.

This requirement is a huge burden for an organization. It's impractical to make the developers of the backend services responsible for maintaining long-term backward compatibility. Rather than expose services directly to third-party developers, organizations should have a separate public API that's developed by a separate team. As you'll learn later, the public API is implemented by an architectural component known as an *API gateway*. Let's look at how an API gateway works.

8.2 The API gateway pattern

As you've just seen, there are numerous drawbacks with services accessing services directly. It's often not practical for a client to perform API composition over the internet. The lack of encapsulation makes it difficult for developers to change service decomposition and APIs. Services sometimes use communication protocols that aren't suitable outside the firewall. Consequently, a much better approach is to use an API gateway.

> **Pattern: API gateway**
> Implement a service that's the entry point into the microservices-based application from external API clients. See http://microservices.io/patterns/apigateway.html.

An *API gateway* is a service that's the entry point into the application from the outside world. It's responsible for request routing, API composition, and other functions, such as authentication. This section covers the API gateway pattern. I discuss its benefits and drawbacks and describe various design issues you must address when developing an API gateway.

8.2.1 Overview of the API gateway pattern

Section 8.1.1 described the drawbacks of clients, such as the FTGO mobile application, making multiple requests in order to display information to the user. A much better approach is for a client to make a single request to an API gateway, a service that serves as the single entry point for API requests into an application from outside the firewall. It's similar to the Facade pattern from object-oriented design. Like a facade, an API gateway encapsulates the application's internal architecture and provides an API to its clients. It may also have other responsibilities, such as authentication, monitoring, and rate limiting. Figure 8.3 shows the relationship between the clients, the API gateway, and the services.

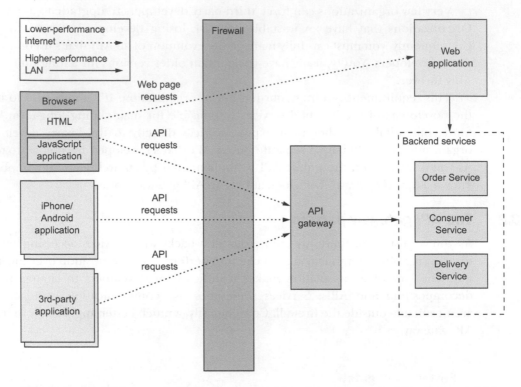

Figure 8.3   The API gateway is the single entry point into the application for API calls from outside the firewall.

The API gateway is responsible for request routing, API composition, and protocol translation. All API requests from *external* clients first go to the API gateway, which routes some requests to the appropriate service. The API gateway handles other requests using the API composition pattern and by invoking multiple services and aggregating the results. It may also translate between client-friendly protocols such as HTTP and WebSockets and client-unfriendly protocols used by the services.

REQUEST ROUTING

One of the key functions of an API gateway is *request routing*. An API gateway implements some API operations by routing requests to the corresponding service. When it receives a request, the API gateway consults a routing map that specifies which service to route the request to. A routing map might, for example, map an HTTP method and path to the HTTP URL of a service. This function is identical to the reverse proxying features provided by web servers such as NGINX.

API COMPOSITION

An API gateway typically does more than simply reverse proxying. It might also implement some API operations using API composition. The FTGO API gateway, for example, implements the `Get Order Details` API operation using API composition. As figure 8.4 shows, the mobile application makes one request to the API gateway, which fetches the order details from multiple services.

The FTGO API gateway provides a coarse-grained API that enables mobile clients to retrieve the data they need with a single request. For example, the mobile client makes a single `getOrderDetails()` request to the API gateway.

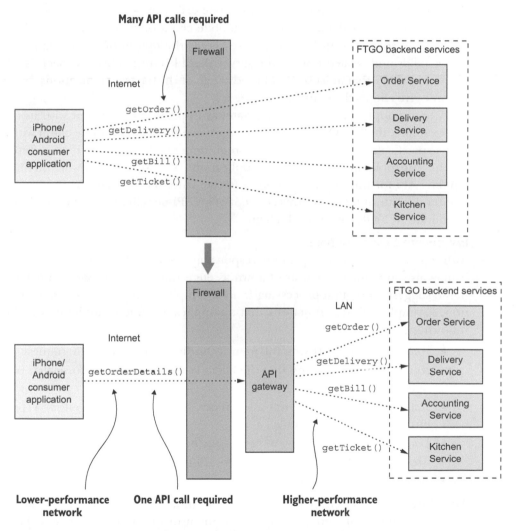

Figure 8.4   An API gateway often does API composition, which enables a client such as a mobile device to efficiently retrieve data using a single API request.

PROTOCOL TRANSLATION

An API gateway might also perform protocol translation. It might provide a RESTful API to external clients, even though the application services use a mixture of protocols internally, including REST and gRPC. When needed, the implementation of some API operations translates between the RESTful external API and the internal gRPC-based APIs.

THE API GATEWAY PROVIDES EACH CLIENT WITH CLIENT-SPECIFIC API

An API gateway could provide a single one-size-fits-all (OSFA) API. The problem with a single API is that different clients often have different requirements. For instance, a third-party application might require the Get Order Details API operation to return the complete Order details, whereas a mobile client only needs a subset of the data. One way to solve this problem is to give clients the option of specifying in a request which fields and related objects the server should return. This approach is adequate for a public API that must serve a broad range of third-party applications, but it often doesn't give clients the control they need.

A better approach is for the API gateway to provide each client with its own API. For example, the FTGO API gateway can provide the FTGO mobile client with an API that's specifically designed to meet its requirements. It may even have different APIs for the Android and iPhone mobile applications. The API gateway will also implement a public API for third-party developers to use. Later on, I'll describe the Backends for frontends pattern that takes this concept of an API-per-client even further by defining a separate API gateway for each client.

IMPLEMENTING EDGE FUNCTIONS

Although an API gateway's primary responsibilities are API routing and composition, it may also implement what are known as edge functions. An *edge function* is, as the name suggests, a request-processing function implemented at the edge of an application. Examples of edge functions that an application might implement include the following:

- *Authentication*—Verifying the identity of the client making the request.
- *Authorization*—Verifying that the client is authorized to perform that particular operation.
- *Rate limiting*—Limiting how many requests per second from either a specific client and/or from all clients.
- *Caching*—Cache responses to reduce the number of requests made to the services.
- *Metrics collection*—Collect metrics on API usage for billing analytics purposes.
- *Request logging*—Log requests.

There are three different places in your application where you could implement these edge functions. First, you can implement them in the backend services. This might make sense for some functions, such as caching, metrics collection, and possibly authorization. But it's generally more secure if the application authenticates requests on the edge before they reach the services.

The second option is to implement these edge functions in an edge service that's upstream from the API gateway. The edge service is the first point of contact for an external client. It authenticates the request and performs other edge processing before passing it to the API gateway.

An important benefit of using a dedicated edge service is that it separates concerns. The API gateway focuses on API routing and composition. Another benefit is that it centralizes responsibility for critical edge functions such as authentication. That's particularly valuable when an application has multiple API gateways that are possibly written using a variety of languages and frameworks. I'll talk more about that later. The drawback of this approach is that it increases network latency because of the extra hop. It also adds to the complexity of the application.

As a result, it's often convenient to use the third option and implement these edge functions, especially authorization, in the API gateway itself. There's one less network hop, which improves latency. There are also fewer moving parts, which reduces complexity. Chapter 11 describes how the API gateway and the services collaborate to implement security.

API GATEWAY ARCHITECTURE

An API gateway has a layered, modular architecture. Its architecture, shown in figure 8.5, consists of two layers: the API layer and a common layer. The API layer consists of one or more independent API modules. Each API module implements an API for a

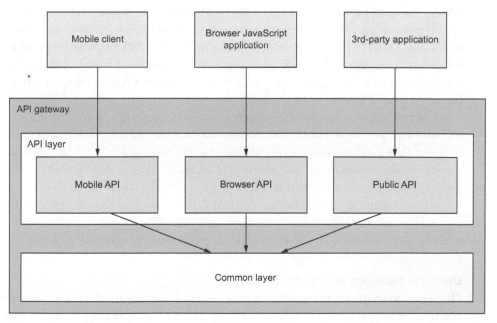

Figure 8.5 An API gateway has a layered modular architecture. The API for each client is implemented by a separate module. The common layer implements functionality common to all APIs, such as authentication.

particular client. The common layer implements shared functionality, including edge functions such as authentication.

In this example, the API gateway has three API modules:

- *Mobile API*—Implements the API for the FTGO mobile client
- *Browser API*—Implements the API for the JavaScript application running in the browser
- *Public API*—Implements the API for third-party developers

An API module implements each API operation in one of two ways. Some API operations map directly to single service API operation. An API module implements these operations by routing requests to the corresponding service API operation. It might route requests using a generic routing module that reads a configuration file describing the routing rules.

An API module implements other, more complex API operations using API composition. The implementation of this API operation consists of custom code. Each API operation implementation handles requests by invoking multiple services and combining the results.

API GATEWAY OWNERSHIP MODEL

An important question that you must answer is who is responsible for the development of the API gateway and its operation? There are a few different options. One is for a separate team to be responsible for the API gateway. The drawback to that is that it's similar to SOA, where an Enterprise Service Bus (ESB) team was responsible for all ESB development. If a developer working on the mobile application needs access to a particular service, they must submit a request to the API gateway team and wait for them to expose the API. This kind of centralized bottleneck in the organization is very much counter to the philosophy of the microservice architecture, which promotes loosely coupled autonomous teams.

A better approach, which has been promoted by Netflix, is for the client teams—the mobile, web, and public API teams—to own the API module that exposes their API. An API gateway team is responsible for developing the Common module and for the operational aspects of the gateway. This ownership model, shown in figure 8.6, gives the teams control over their APIs.

When a team needs to change their API, they check in the changes to the source repository for the API gateway. To work well, the API gateway's deployment pipeline must be fully automated. Otherwise, the client teams will often be blocked waiting for the API gateway team to deploy the new version.

USING THE BACKENDS FOR FRONTENDS PATTERN

One concern with an API gateway is that responsibility for it is blurred. Multiple teams contribute to the same code base. An API gateway team is responsible for its operation. Though not as bad as a SOA ESB, this blurring of responsibilities is counter to the microservice architecture philosophy of "if you build it, you own it."

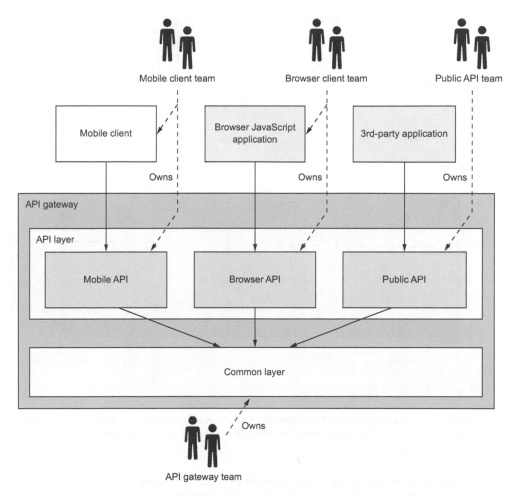

Figure 8.6 A client team owns their API module. As they change the client, they can change the API module and not ask the API gateway team to make the changes.

The solution is to have an API gateway for each client, the so-called Backends for frontends (BFF) pattern, which was pioneered by Phil Calçado (http://philcalcado.com/) and his colleagues at SoundCloud. As figure 8.7 shows, each API module becomes its own standalone API gateway that's developed and operated by a single client team.

Pattern: Backends for frontends
Implement a separate API gateway for each type of client. See http://microservices.io/patterns/apigateway.html.

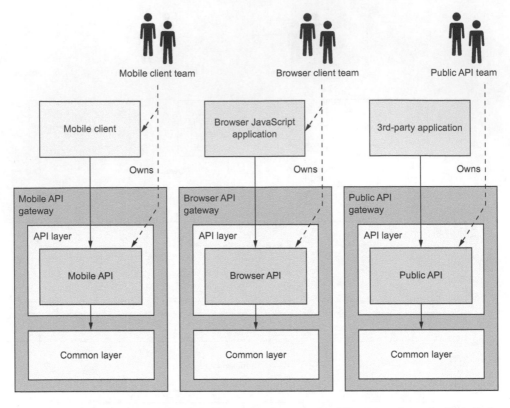

Figure 8.7   The Backends for frontends pattern defines a separate API gateway for each client. Each client team owns their API gateway. An API gateway team owns the common layer.

The public API team owns and operates their API gateway, the mobile team owns and operates theirs, and so on. In theory, different API gateways could be developed using different technology stacks. But that risks duplicating code for common functionality, such as the code that implements edge functions. Ideally, all API gateways use the same technology stack. The common functionality is a shared library implemented by the API gateway team.

Besides clearly defining responsibilities, the BFF pattern has other benefits. The API modules are isolated from one another, which improves reliability. One misbehaving API can't easily impact other APIs. It also improves observability, because different API modules are different processes. Another benefit of the BFF pattern is that each API is independently scalable. The BFF pattern also reduces startup time because each API gateway is a smaller, simpler application.

8.2.2 Benefits and drawbacks of an API gateway

As you might expect, the API gateway pattern has both benefits and drawbacks.

BENEFITS OF AN API GATEWAY

A major benefit of using an API gateway is that it encapsulates internal structure of the application. Rather than having to invoke specific services, clients talk to the gateway. The API gateway provides each client with a client-specific API, which reduces the number of round-trips between the client and application. It also simplifies the client code.

DRAWBACKS OF AN API GATEWAY

The API gateway pattern also has some drawbacks. It is yet another highly available component that must be developed, deployed, and managed. There's also a risk that the API gateway becomes a development bottleneck. Developers must update the API gateway in order to expose their services's API. It's important that the process for updating the API gateway be as lightweight as possible. Otherwise, developers will be forced to wait in line in order to update the gateway. Despite these drawbacks, though, for most real-world applications, it makes sense to use an API gateway. If necessary, you can use the Backends for frontends pattern to enable the teams to develop and deploy their APIs independently.

8.2.3 Netflix as an example of an API gateway

A great example of an API gateway is the Netflix API. The Netflix streaming service is available on hundreds of different kinds of devices including televisions, Blu-ray players, smartphones, and many more gadgets. Initially, Netflix attempted to have a one-size-fits-all style API for its streaming service (www.programmableweb.com/news/why-rest-keeps-me-night/2012/05/15). But the company soon discovered that didn't work well because of the diverse range of devices and their different needs. Today, Netflix uses an API gateway that implements a separate API for each device. The client device team develops and owns the API implementation.

In the first version of the API gateway, each client team implemented their API using Groovy scripts that perform routing and API composition. Each script invoked one or more service APIs using Java client libraries provided by the service teams. On one hand, this works well, and client developers have written thousands of scripts. The Netflix API gateway handles billions of requests per day, and on average each API call fans out to six or seven backend services. On the other hand, Netflix has found this monolithic architecture to be somewhat cumbersome.

As a result, Netflix is now moving to an API gateway architecture similar to the Backends for frontends pattern. In this new architecture, client teams write API modules using NodeJS. Each API module runs its own Docker container, but the scripts don't invoke the services directly. Rather, they invoke a second "API gateway," which exposes the service APIs using Netflix Falcor. *Netflix Falcor* is an API technology that does declarative, dynamic API composition and enables a client to invoke multiple services using a single request. This new architecture has a number of benefits. The API modules are isolated from one another, which improves reliability and observability, and the client API module is independently scalable.

8.2.4 API gateway design issues

Now that we've looked at the API gateway pattern and its benefits and drawbacks, let's examine various API gateway design issues. There are several issues to consider when designing an API gateway:

- Performance and scalability
- Writing maintainable code by using reactive programming abstractions
- Handling partial failure
- Being a good citizen in the application's architecture

We'll look at each one.

PERFORMANCE AND SCALABILITY

An API gateway is the application's front door. All external requests must first pass through the gateway. Although most companies don't operate at the scale of Netflix, which handles billions of requests per day, the performance and scalability of the API gateway is usually very important. A key design decision that affects performance and scalability is whether the API gateway should use synchronous or asynchronous I/O.

In the *synchronous* I/O model , each network connection is handled by a dedicated thread. This is a simple programming model and works reasonably well. For example, it's the basis of the widely used Java EE servlet framework, although this framework provides the option of completing a request asynchronously. One limitation of synchronous I/O, however, is that operating system threads are heavyweight, so there is a limit on the number of threads, and hence concurrent connections, that an API gateway can have.

The other approach is to use the *asynchronous* (nonblocking) I/O model . In this model, a single event loop thread dispatches I/O requests to event handlers. You have a variety of asynchronous I/O technologies to choose from. On the JVM you can use one of the NIO-based frameworks such as Netty, Vertx, Spring Reactor, or JBoss Undertow. One popular non-JVM option is NodeJS, a platform built on Chrome's JavaScript engine.

Nonblocking I/O is much more scalable because it doesn't have the overhead of using multiple threads. The drawback, though, is that the asynchronous, callback-based programming model is much more complex. The code is more difficult to write, understand, and debug. Event handlers must return quickly to avoid blocking the event loop thread.

Also, whether using nonblocking I/O has a meaningful overall benefit depends on the characteristics of the API gateway's request-processing logic. Netflix had mixed results when it rewrote Zuul, its edge server, to use NIO (see https://medium.com/netflix-techblog/zuul-2-the-netflix-journey-to-asynchronous-non-blocking-systems-45947377fb5c).

On one hand, as you would expect, using NIO reduced the cost of each network connection, due to the fact that there's no longer a dedicated thread for each one. Also, a Zuul cluster that ran I/O-intensive logic—such as request routing—had a 25% increase in throughput and a 25% reduction in CPU utilization. On the other hand, a Zuul cluster that ran CPU-intensive logic—such as decryption and compression—showed no improvement.

USE REACTIVE PROGRAMMING ABSTRACTIONS

As mentioned earlier, API composition consists of invoking multiple backend services. Some backend service requests depend entirely on the client request's parameters. Others might depend on the results of other service requests. One approach is for an API endpoint handler method to call the services in the order determined by the dependencies. For example, the following listing shows the handler for the `findOrder()` request that's written this way. It calls each of the four services, one after the other.

> **Listing 8.1 Fetching the order details by calling the backend services sequentially**

```
@RestController
public class OrderDetailsController {
@RequestMapping("/order/{orderId}")
public OrderDetails getOrderDetails(@PathVariable String orderId) {

  OrderInfo orderInfo = orderService.findOrderById(orderId);

  TicketInfo ticketInfo = kitchenService
        .findTicketByOrderId(orderId);

  DeliveryInfo deliveryInfo = deliveryService
        .findDeliveryByOrderId(orderId);

  BillInfo billInfo = accountingService
        .findBillByOrderId(orderId);

  OrderDetails orderDetails =
      OrderDetails.makeOrderDetails(orderInfo, ticketInfo,
                                    deliveryInfo, billInfo);

  return orderDetails;
}
...
```

The drawback of calling the services sequentially is that the response time is the sum of the service response times. In order to minimize response time, the composition logic should, whenever possible, invoke services concurrently. In this example, there are no dependencies between the service calls. All services should be invoked concurrently, which significantly reduces response time. The challenge is to write concurrent code that's maintainable.

This is because the traditional way to write scalable, concurrent code is to use callbacks. Asynchronous, event-driven I/O is inherently callback-based. Even a Servlet

API-based API composer that invokes services concurrently typically uses callbacks. It could execute requests concurrently by calling `ExecutorService.submitCallable()`. The problem there is that this method returns a `Future`, which has a blocking API. A more scalable approach is for an API composer to call `ExecutorService.submit` `(Runnable)` and for each `Runnable` to invoke a callback with the outcome of the request. The callback accumulates results, and once all of them have been received it sends back the response to the client.

Writing API composition code using the traditional asynchronous callback approach quickly leads you to callback hell. The code will be tangled, difficult to understand, and error prone, especially when composition requires a mixture of parallel and sequential requests. A much better approach is to write API composition code in a declarative style using a reactive approach. Examples of reactive abstractions for the JVM include the following:

- Java 8 `CompletableFutures`
- Project Reactor `Monos`
- RxJava (Reactive Extensions for Java) `Observables`, created by Netflix specifically to solve this problem in its API gateway
- Scala `Futures`

A NodeJS-based API gateway would use JavaScript promises or RxJS, which is reactive extensions for JavaScript. Using one of these reactive abstractions will enable you to write concurrent code that's simple and easy to understand. Later in this chapter, I show an example of this style of coding using Project Reactor `Monos` and version 5 of the Spring Framework.

HANDLING PARTIAL FAILURES

As well as being scalable, an API gateway must also be reliable. One way to achieve reliability is to run multiple instances of the gateway behind a load balancer. If one instance fails, the load balancer will route requests to the other instances.

Another way to ensure that an API gateway is reliable is to properly handle failed requests and requests that have unacceptably high latency. When an API gateway invokes a service, there's always a chance that the service is slow or unavailable. An API gateway may wait a very long time, perhaps indefinitely, for a response, which consumes resources and prevents it from sending a response to its client. An outstanding request to a failed service might even consume a limited, precious resource such as a thread and ultimately result in the API gateway being unable to handle any other requests. The solution, as described in chapter 3, is for an API gateway to use the Circuit breaker pattern when invoking services.

BEING A GOOD CITIZEN IN THE ARCHITECTURE

In chapter 3 I described patterns for service discovery, and in chapter 11, I cover patterns for observability. The service discovery patterns enable a service client, such as an API gateway, to determine the network location of a service instance so that it can invoke it. The observability patterns enable developers to monitor the behavior of an application and troubleshoot problems. An API gateway, like other services in the architecture, must implement the patterns that have been selected for the architecture.

8.3 Implementing an API gateway

Let's now look at how to implement an API gateway. As mentioned earlier, the responsibilities of an API gateway are as follows:

- *Request routing*—Routes requests to services using criteria such as HTTP request method and path. The API gateway must route using the HTTP request method when the application has one or more CQRS query services. As discussed in chapter 7, in such an architecture commands and queries are handled by separate services.
- *API composition*—Implements a GET REST endpoint using the API composition pattern, described in chapter 7. The request handler combines the results of invoking multiple services.
- *Edge functions*—Most notable among these is authentication.
- *Protocol translation*—Translates between client-friendly protocols and the client-unfriendly protocols used by services.
- Being a good citizen in the application's architecture.

There are a couple of different ways to implement an API gateway:

- *Using an off-the-shelf API gateway product/service*—This option requires little or no development but is the least flexible. For example, an off-the-shelf API gateway typically does not support API composition
- *Developing your own API gateway using either an API gateway framework or a web framework as the starting point*—This is the most flexible approach, though it requires some development effort.

Let's look at these options, starting with using an off-the-shelf API gateway product or service.

8.3.1 Using an off-the-shelf API gateway product/service

Several off-the-self services and products implement API gateway features. Let's first look at a couple of services that are provided by AWS. After that, I'll discuss some products that you can download, configure, and run yourself.

AWS API GATEWAY

The AWS API gateway, one of the many services provided by Amazon Web Services, is a service for deploying and managing APIs. An AWS API gateway API is a set of REST resources, each of which supports one or more HTTP methods. You configure the API gateway to route each (Method, Resource) to a backend service. A backend service is either an AWS Lambda Function, described later in chapter 12, an application-defined HTTP service, or an AWS service. If necessary, you can configure the API gateway to transform request and response using a template-based mechanism. The AWS API gateway can also authenticate requests.

The AWS API gateway fulfills some of the requirements for an API gateway that I listed earlier. The API gateway is provided by AWS, so you're not responsible for installation and operations. You configure the API gateway, and AWS handles everything else, including scaling.

Unfortunately, the AWS API gateway has several drawbacks and limitations that cause it to not fulfill other requirements. It doesn't support API composition, so you'd need to implement API composition in the backend services. The AWS API gateway only supports HTTP(S) with a heavy emphasis on JSON. It only supports the Server-side discovery pattern, described in chapter 3. An application will typically use an AWS Elastic Load Balancer to load balance requests across a set of EC2 instances or ECS containers. Despite these limitations, unless you need API composition, the AWS API gateway is a good implementation of the API gateway pattern.

AWS APPLICATION LOAD BALANCER

Another AWS service that provides API gateway-like functionality is the AWS Application Load Balancer, which is a load balancer for HTTP, HTTPS, WebSocket, and HTTP/2 (https://aws.amazon.com/blogs/aws/new-aws-application-load-balancer/). When configuring an Application Load Balancer, you define routing rules that route requests to backend services, which must be running on AWS EC2 instances.

Like the AWS API gateway, the AWS Application Load Balancer meets some of the requirements for an API gateway. It implements basic routing functionality. It's hosted, so you're not responsible for installation or operations. Unfortunately, it's quite limited. It doesn't implement HTTP method-based routing. Nor does it implement API composition or authentication. As a result, the AWS Application Load Balancer doesn't meet the requirements for an API gateway.

USING AN API GATEWAY PRODUCT

Another option is to use an API gateway product such as Kong or Traefik . These are open source packages that you install and operate yourself. Kong is based on the NGINX HTTP server, and Traefik is written in GoLang. Both products let you configure flexible routing rules that use the HTTP method, headers, and path to select the backend service. Kong lets you configure plugins that implement edge functions such as authentication. Traefik can even integrate with some service registries, described in chapter 3.

Although these products implement edge functions and powerful routing capabilities, they have some drawbacks. You must install, configure, and operate them yourself. They don't support API composition. And if you want the API gateway to perform API composition, you must develop your own API gateway.

8.3.2 *Developing your own API gateway*

Developing an API gateway isn't particularly difficult. It's basically a web application that proxies requests to other services. You can build one using your favorite web framework. There are, however, two key design problems that you'll need to solve:

- Implementing a mechanism for defining routing rules in order to minimize the complex coding
- Correctly implementing the HTTP proxying behavior, including how HTTP headers are handled

Consequently, a better starting point for developing an API gateway is to use a framework designed for that purpose. Its built-in functionality significantly reduces the amount of code you need to write.

We'll take a look at Netflix Zuul, an open source project by Netflix, and then consider the Spring Cloud Gateway, an open source project from Pivotal.

USING NETFLIX ZUUL

Netflix developed the Zuul framework to implement edge functions such as routing, rate limiting, and authentication (https://github.com/Netflix/zuul). The Zuul framework uses the concept of *filters*, reusable request interceptors that are similar to servlet filters or NodeJS Express middleware. Zuul handles an HTTP request by assembling a chain of applicable filters that then transform the request, invoke backend services, and transform the response before it's sent back to the client. Although you can use Zuul directly, using Spring Cloud Zuul, an open source project from Pivotal, is far easier. Spring Cloud Zuul builds on Zuul and through convention-over-configuration makes developing a Zuul-based server remarkably easy.

Zuul handles the routing and edge functionality. You can extend Zuul by defining Spring MVC controllers that implement API composition. But a major limitation of Zuul is that it can only implement path-based routing. For example, it's incapable of routing `GET /orders` to one service and `POST /orders` to a different service. Consequently, Zuul doesn't support the query architecture described in chapter 7.

ABOUT SPRING CLOUD GATEWAY

None of the options I've described so far meet all the requirements. In fact, I had given up in my search for an API gateway framework and had started developing an API gateway based on Spring MVC. But then I discovered the Spring Cloud Gateway project (https://cloud.spring.io/spring-cloud-gateway/). It's an API gateway framework built on top of several frameworks, including Spring Framework 5, Spring Boot 2, and Spring Webflux, which is a reactive web framework that's part of Spring Framework 5 and built on Project Reactor. Project Reactor is an NIO-based reactive framework for the JVM that provides the Mono abstraction used a little later in this chapter.

Spring Cloud Gateway provides a simple yet comprehensive way to do the following:

- Route requests to backend services.
- Implement request handlers that perform API composition.
- Handle edge functions such as authentication.

Figure 8.8 shows the key parts of an API gateway built using this framework.

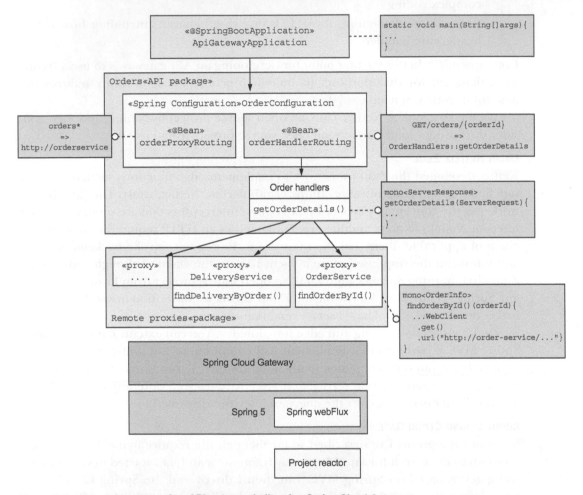

Figure 8.8   The architecture of an API gateway built using Spring Cloud Gateway

The API gateway consists of the following packages:

- `ApiGatewayMain` *package*—Defines the Main program for the API gateway.
- *One or more API packages*—An API package implements a set of API endpoints. For example, the `Orders` package implements the `Order`-related API endpoints.
- *Proxy package*—Consists of proxy classes that are used by the API packages to invoke the services.

The `OrderConfiguration` class defines the Spring beans responsible for routing `Order`-related requests. A routing rule can match against some combination of the HTTP method, the headers, and the path. The `orderProxyRoutes` `@Bean` defines rules that map API operations to backend service URLs. For example, it routes paths beginning with `/orders` to the `Order Service`.

The `orderHandlers` `@Bean` defines rules that override those defined by `orderProxyRoutes`. These rules map API operations to handler methods, which are the Spring WebFlux equivalent of Spring MVC controller methods. For example, `orderHandlers` maps the operation `GET /orders/{orderId}` to the `OrderHandlers::getOrderDetails()` method.

The `OrderHandlers` class implements various request handler methods, such as `OrderHandlers::getOrderDetails()`. This method uses API composition to fetch the order details (described earlier). The handle methods invoke backend services using remote proxy classes, such as `OrderService`. This class defines methods for invoking the `OrderService`.

Let's take a look at the code, starting with the `OrderConfiguration` class.

THE ORDERCONFIGURATION CLASS

The `OrderConfiguration` class, shown in listing 8.2, is a Spring `@Configuration` class. It defines the Spring `@Beans` that implement the `/orders` endpoints. The `orderProxyRouting` and `orderHandlerRouting` `@Beans` use the Spring WebFlux routing DSL to define the request routing. The `orderHandlers` `@Bean` implements the request handlers that perform API composition.

Listing 8.2 The Spring `@Beans` that implement the `/orders` endpoints

```
@Configuration
@EnableConfigurationProperties(OrderDestinations.class)
public class OrderConfiguration {

  @Bean
  public RouteLocator orderProxyRouting(OrderDestinations orderDestinations) {
    return Routes.locator()
            .route("orders")
            .uri(orderDestinations.orderServiceUrl)
            .predicate(path("/orders").or(path("/orders/*")))
            .and()
            ...
            .build();
  }

  @Bean
  public RouterFunction<ServerResponse>
            orderHandlerRouting(OrderHandlers orderHandlers) {
    return RouterFunctions.route(GET("/orders/{orderId}"),
                    orderHandlers::getOrderDetails);
  }
```

By default, route all requests whose path begins with /orders to the URL orderDestinations.orderServiceUrl.

Route a GET /orders/{orderId} to orderHandlers::getOrderDetails.

```
@Bean
public OrderHandlers orderHandlers(OrderService orderService,
                        KitchenService kitchenService,
                        DeliveryService deliveryService,
                        AccountingService accountingService) {
    return new OrderHandlers(orderService, kitchenService,          ◁
                        deliveryService, accountingService);
}
```

The @Bean, which implements the custom request-handling logic

```
}
```

OrderDestinations, shown in the following listing, is a Spring @Configuration-Properties class that enables the externalized configuration of backend service URLs.

Listing 8.3   The externalized configuration of backend service URLs

```
@ConfigurationProperties(prefix = "order.destinations")
public class OrderDestinations {

  @NotNull
  public String orderServiceUrl;

  public String getOrderServiceUrl() {
    return orderServiceUrl;
  }

  public void setOrderServiceUrl(String orderServiceUrl) {
    this.orderServiceUrl = orderServiceUrl;
  }
  ...
}
```

You can, for example, specify the URL of the Order Service either as the order .destinations.orderServiceUrl property in a properties file or as an operating system environment variable, ORDER_DESTINATIONS_ORDER_SERVICE_URL.

THE ORDERHANDLERS CLASS

The OrderHandlers class, shown in the following listing, defines the request handler methods that implement custom behavior, including API composition. The getOrder-Details() method, for example, performs API composition to retrieve information about an order. This class is injected with several proxy classes that make requests to backend services.

Listing 8.4   The OrderHandlers class implements custom request-handling logic.

```
public class OrderHandlers {

  private OrderService orderService;
  private KitchenService kitchenService;
  private DeliveryService deliveryService;
  private AccountingService accountingService;
```

```
    public OrderHandlers(OrderService orderService,
                         KitchenService kitchenService,
                         DeliveryService deliveryService,
                         AccountingService accountingService) {
      this.orderService = orderService;
      this.kitchenService = kitchenService;
      this.deliveryService = deliveryService;
      this.accountingService = accountingService;
    }

    public Mono<ServerResponse> getOrderDetails(ServerRequest serverRequest) {
      String orderId = serverRequest.pathVariable("orderId");

      Mono<OrderInfo> orderInfo = orderService.findOrderById(orderId);

      Mono<Optional<TicketInfo>> ticketInfo =
          kitchenService
              .findTicketByOrderId(orderId)
              .map(Optional::of)
              .onErrorReturn(Optional.empty());

      Mono<Optional<DeliveryInfo>> deliveryInfo =
          deliveryService
              .findDeliveryByOrderId(orderId)
              .map(Optional::of)
              .onErrorReturn(Optional.empty());

      Mono<Optional<BillInfo>> billInfo = accountingService
              .findBillByOrderId(orderId)
              .map(Optional::of)
              .onErrorReturn(Optional.empty());

      Mono<Tuple4<OrderInfo, Optional<TicketInfo>,
                Optional<DeliveryInfo>, Optional<BillInfo>>> combined =
              Mono.when(orderInfo, ticketInfo, deliveryInfo, billInfo);

      Mono<OrderDetails> orderDetails =
          combined.map(OrderDetails::makeOrderDetails);

      return orderDetails.flatMap(person -> ServerResponse.ok()
              .contentType(MediaType.APPLICATION_JSON)
              .body(fromObject(person)));
    }
  }
```

- **Transform a TicketInfo into an Optional<TicketInfo>.**
- **If the service invocation failed, return Optional.empty().**
- **Combine the four values into a single value, a Tuple4.**
- **Transform the Tuple4 into an OrderDetails.**
- **Transform the OrderDetails into a ServerResponse.**

The getOrderDetails() method implements API composition to fetch the order details. It's written in a scalable, reactive style using the Mono abstraction , which is provided by Project Reactor. A Mono, which is a richer kind of Java 8 CompletableFuture, contains the outcome of an asynchronous operation that's either a value or an exception. It has a rich API for transforming and combining the values returned by asynchronous operations. You can use Monos to write concurrent code in a style that's simple and easy to understand. In this example, the `getOrderDetails()` method invokes the four services in parallel and combines the results to create an `Order-Details` object.

The `getOrderDetails()` method takes a `ServerRequest`, which is the Spring Web-Flux representation of an HTTP request, as a parameter and does the following:

1. It extracts the `orderId` from the path.

2. It invokes the four services asynchronously via their proxies, which return `Monos`. In order to improve availability, `getOrderDetails()` treats the results of all services except the `OrderService` as optional. If a `Mono` returned by an optional service contains an exception, the call to `onErrorReturn()` transforms it into a `Mono` containing an empty `Optional`.

3. It combines the results asynchronously using `Mono.when()`, which returns a `Mono<Tuple4>` containing the four values.

4. It transforms the `Mono<Tuple4>` into a `Mono<OrderDetails>` by calling `Order-Details::makeOrderDetails`.

5. It transforms the `OrderDetails` into a `ServerResponse`, which is the Spring WebFlux representation of the JSON/HTTP response.

As you can see, because `getOrderDetails()` uses `Monos`, it concurrently invokes the services and combines the results without using messy, difficult-to-read callbacks. Let's take a look at one of the service proxies that return the results of a service API call wrapped in a `Mono`.

THE ORDERSERVICE CLASS

The `OrderService` class, shown in the following listing, is a remote proxy for the `Order Service`. It invokes the `Order Service` using a `WebClient`, which is the Spring Web-Flux reactive HTTP client.

> **Listing 8.5   `OrderService` class—a remote proxy for `Order Service`**

```
@Service
public class OrderService {

  private OrderDestinations orderDestinations;

  private WebClient client;

  public OrderService(OrderDestinations orderDestinations, WebClient client)
    {
    this.orderDestinations = orderDestinations;
    this.client = client;
  }

  public Mono<OrderInfo> findOrderById(String orderId) {
    Mono<ClientResponse> response = client
        .get()
```

Invoke the service.

```
        .uri(orderDestinations.orderServiceUrl + "/orders/{orderId}",
              orderId)
        .exchange();
      return response.flatMap(resp -> resp.bodyToMono(OrderInfo.class));  ←─┐
    }
                                                          **Convert the response**
  }                                                       **body to an OrderInfo.**
```

The `findOrder()` method retrieves the `OrderInfo` for an order. It uses the `WebClient` to make the HTTP request to the `Order Service` and deserializes the JSON response to an `OrderInfo`. `WebClient` has a reactive API, and the response is wrapped in a `Mono`. The `findOrder()` method uses `flatMap()` to transform the `Mono<ClientResponse>` into a `Mono<OrderInfo>`. As the name suggests, the `bodyToMono()` method returns the response body as a `Mono`.

THE APIGATEWAYAPPLICATION CLASS

The `ApiGatewayApplication` class, shown in the following listing, implements the API gateway's `main()` method. It's a standard Spring Boot main class.

Listing 8.6 The `main()` method for the API gateway

```
@SpringBootConfiguration
@EnableAutoConfiguration
@EnableGateway
@Import(OrdersConfiguration.class)
public class ApiGatewayApplication {

  public static void main(String[] args) {
    SpringApplication.run(ApiGatewayApplication.class, args);
  }
}
```

The `@EnableGateway` annotation imports the Spring configuration for the Spring Cloud Gateway framework.

Spring Cloud Gateway is an excellent framework for implementing an API gateway. It enables you to configure basic proxying using a simple, concise routing rules DSL. It's also straightforward to route requests to handler methods that perform API composition and protocol translation. Spring Cloud Gateway is built using the scalable, reactive Spring Framework 5 and Project Reactor frameworks. But there's another appealing option for developing your own API gateway: GraphQL, a framework that provides graph-based query language. Let's look at how that works.

8.3.3 *Implementing an API gateway using GraphQL*

Imagine that you're responsible for implementing the FTGO's API Gateway's GET `/orders/{orderId}` endpoint, which returns the order details. On the surface, implementing this endpoint might appear to be simple. But as described in section 8.1, this endpoint retrieves data from multiple services. Consequently, you need to use the

API composition pattern and write code that invokes the services and combines the results.

Another challenge, mentioned earlier, is that different clients need slightly different data. For example, unlike the mobile application, the desktop SPA application displays your rating for the order. One way to tailor the data returned by the endpoint, as described in chapter 3, is to give the client the ability to specify the data they need. An endpoint can, for example, support query parameters such as the `expand` parameter, which specifies the related resources to return, and the `field` parameter, which specifies the fields of each resource to return. The other option is to define multiple versions of this endpoint as part of applying the Backends for frontends pattern. This is a lot of work for just one of the many API endpoints that the FTGO's API Gateway needs to implement.

Implementing an API gateway with a REST API that supports a diverse set of clients well is time consuming. Consequently, you may want to consider using a graph-based API framework, such as GraphQL, that's designed to support efficient data fetching. The key idea with graph-based API frameworks is that, as figure 8.9 shows, the server's API consists of a graph-based schema. The graph-based schema defines a set of *nodes* (types), which have *properties* (fields) and relationships with other nodes. The client retrieves data by executing a query that specifies the required data in terms of the graph's nodes and their properties and relationships. As a result, a client can retrieve the data it needs in a single round-trip to the API gateway.

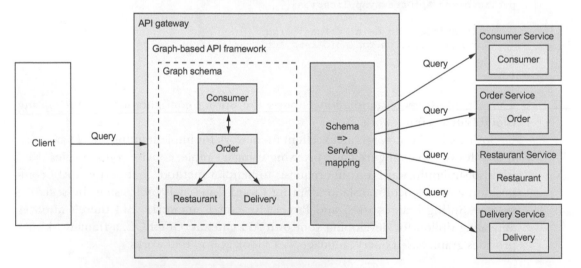

Figure 8.9   The API gateway's API consists of a graph-based schema that's mapped to the services. A client issues a query that retrieves multiple graph nodes. The graph-based API framework executes the query by retrieving data from one or more services.

Graph-based API technology has a couple of important benefits. It gives clients control over what data is returned. Consequently, developing a single API that's flexible enough to support diverse clients becomes feasible. Another benefit is that even though the API is much more flexible, this approach significantly reduces the development effort. That's because you write the server-side code using a query execution framework that's designed to support API composition and projections. It's as if, rather than force clients to retrieve data via stored procedures that you need to write and maintain, you let them execute queries against the underlying database.

Schema-driven API technologies

The two most popular graph-based API technologies are GraphQL (http://graphql.org) and Netflix Falcor (http://netflix.github.io/falcor/). Netflix Falcor models server-side data as a virtual JSON object graph. The Falcor client retrieves data from a Falcor server by executing a query that retrieves properties of that JSON object. The client can also update properties. In the Falcor server, the properties of the object graph are mapped to backend data sources, such as services with REST APIs. The server handles a request to set or get properties by invoking one or more backend data sources.

GraphQL, developed by Facebook and released in 2015, is another popular graph-based API technology. It models the server-side data as a graph of objects that have fields and references to other objects. The object graph is mapped to backend data sources. GraphQL clients can execute queries that retrieve data and mutations that create and update data. Unlike Netflix Falcor, which is an implementation, GraphQL is a standard, with clients and servers available for a variety of languages, including NodeJS, Java, and Scala.

Apollo GraphQL is a popular JavaScript/NodeJS implementation (www.apollographql .com). It's a platform that includes a GraphQL server and client. Apollo GraphQL implements some powerful extensions to the GraphQL specification, such as subscriptions that push changed data to the client.

This section talks about how to develop an API gateway using Apollo GraphQL. I'm only going to cover a few of the key features of GraphQL and Apollo GraphQL. For more information, you should consult the GraphQL and Apollo GraphQL documentation.

The GraphQL-based API gateway, shown in figure 8.10, is written in JavaScript using the NodeJS Express web framework and the Apollo GraphQL server. The key parts of the design are as follows:

- *GraphQL schema*—The GraphQL schema defines the server-side data model and the queries it supports.
- *Resolver functions*—The resolve functions map elements of the schema to the various backend services.
- *Proxy classes*—The proxy classes invoke the FTGO application's services.

There's also a small amount of glue code that integrates the GraphQL server with the Express web framework. Let's look at each part, starting with the GraphQL schema.

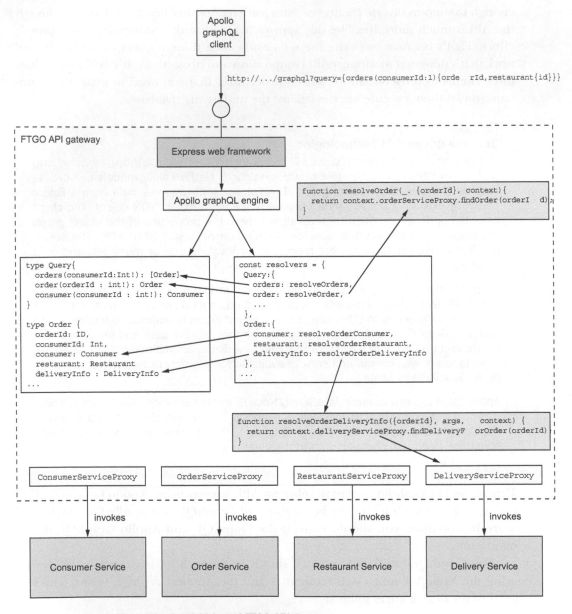

Figure 8.10 The design of the GraphQL-based FTGO API Gateway

DEFINING A GRAPHQL SCHEMA

A GraphQL API is centered around a *schema*, which consists of a collection of types that define the structure of the server-side data model and the operations, such as queries, that a client can perform. GraphQL has several different kinds of types. The example code in this section uses just two kinds of types: *object* types, which are the primary way of defining the data model, and *enums*, which are similar to Java enums. An object type has a name and a collection of typed, named fields. A *field* can be a scalar type, such as a number, string, or enum; a list of scalar types; a reference to another object type; or a collection of references to another object type. Despite resembling a field of a traditional object-oriented class, a GraphQL field is conceptually a function that returns a value. It can have arguments, which enable a GraphQL client to tailor the data the function returns.

GraphQL also uses fields to define the queries supported by the schema. You define the schema's queries by declaring an object type, which by convention is called Query. Each field of the Query object is a named query, which has an optional set of parameters, and a return type. I found this way of defining queries a little confusing when I first encountered it, but it helps to keep in mind that a GraphQL field is a function. It will become even clearer when we look at how fields are connected to the backend data sources.

The following listing shows part of the schema for the GraphQL-based FTGO API gateway. It defines several object types. Most of the object types correspond to the FTGO application's Consumer, Order, and Restaurant entities. It also has a Query object type that defines the schema's queries.

Listing 8.7 The GraphQL schema for the FTGO API gateway

```
type Query {
    orders(consumerId : Int!): [Order]          ◄─┐  Defines the queries
    order(orderId : Int!): Order                   │  that a client can
    consumer(consumerId : Int!): Consumer          │  execute
}

type Consumer {                    ┌ The unique ID
    id: ID                      ◄──┘  for a Consumer
    firstName: String
    lastName: String
    orders: [Order]            ◄─┐  A consumer has
}                                │  a list of orders.

type Order {
    orderId: ID,
    consumerId : Int,
    consumer: Consumer
    restaurant: Restaurant

    deliveryInfo : DeliveryInfo

    ...
}

type Restaurant {
    id: ID
    name: String
    ...
}
```

```
type DeliveryInfo {
  status : DeliveryStatus
  estimatedDeliveryTime : Int
  assignedCourier :String
}

enum DeliveryStatus {
  PREPARING
  READY_FOR_PICKUP
  PICKED_UP
  DELIVERED
}
```

Despite having a different syntax, the `Consumer`, `Order`, `Restaurant`, and `Delivery-Info` object types are structurally similar to the corresponding Java classes. One difference is the `ID` type, which represents a unique identifier.

This schema defines three queries:

- `orders()`—Returns the `Orders` for the specified `Consumer`
- `order()`—Returns the specified `Order`
- `consumer()`—Returns the specified `Consumer`

These queries may seem not different from the equivalent REST endpoints, but GraphQL gives the client tremendous control over the data that's returned. To understand why, let's look at how a client executes GraphQL queries.

EXECUTING GRAPHQL QUERIES

The principal benefit of using GraphQL is that its query language gives the client incredible control over the returned data. A client executes a query by making a request containing a query document to the server. In the simple case, a query document specifies the name of the query, the argument values, and the fields of the result object to return. Here's a simple query that retrieves `firstName` and `lastName` of the consumer with a particular ID:

```
query {
  consumer(consumerId:1)        ◁──── Specifies the query called consumer,
  {                                    which fetches a consumer
    firstName          ◁────
    lastName                  The fields of the
  }                           Consumer to return
}
```

This query returns those fields of the specified `Consumer`.

Here's a more elaborate query that returns a consumer, their orders, and the ID and name of each order's restaurant:

```
query {
    consumer(consumerId:1)   {
      id
      firstName
      lastName
```

```
      orders {
        orderId
        restaurant {
          id
          name
        }
        deliveryInfo {
          estimatedDeliveryTime
          name
        }
      }
    }
  }
}
```

This query tells the server to return more than just the fields of the Consumer. It retrieves the consumer's Orders and each Order's restaurant. As you can see, a GraphQL client can specify exactly the data to return, including the fields of transitively related objects.

The query language is more flexible than it might first appear. That's because a query is a field of the Query object, and a query document specifies which of those fields the server should return. These simple examples retrieve a single field, but a query document can execute multiple queries by specifying multiple fields. For each field, the query document supplies the field's arguments and specifies what fields of the result object it's interested in. Here's a query that retrieves two different consumers:

```
query {
  c1: consumer (consumerId:1)  { id, firstName, lastName}
  c2: consumer (consumerId:2)  { id, firstName, lastName}
}
```

In this query document, c1 and c2 are what GraphQL calls *aliases*. They're used to distinguish between the two Consumers in the result, which would otherwise both be called consumer. This example retrieves two objects of the same type, but a client could retrieve several objects of different types.

A GraphQL schema defines the shape of the data and the supported queries. To be useful, it has to be connected to the source of the data. Let's look at how to do that.

CONNECTING THE SCHEMA TO THE DATA

When the GraphQL server executes a query, it must retrieve the requested data from one or more data stores. In the case of the FTGO application, the GraphQL server must invoke the APIs of the services that own the data. You associate a GraphQL schema with the data sources by attaching resolver functions to the fields of the object types defined by the schema. The GraphQL server implements the API composition pattern by invoking resolver functions to retrieve the data, first for the top-level query, and then recursively for the fields of the result object or objects.

The details of how resolver functions are associated with the schema depend on which GraphQL server you are using. Listing 8.8 shows how to define the resolvers when using the Apollo GraphQL server. You create a doubly nested JavaScript object. Each top-level property corresponds to an object type, such as `Query` and `Order`. Each second-level property, such as `Order.consumer`, defines a field's resolver function.

Listing 8.8   Attaching the resolver functions to fields of the GraphQL schema

```
const resolvers = {
  Query: {
    orders: resolveOrders,                    The resolver for
    consumer: resolveConsumer,                the orders query
    order: resolveOrder
  },                                                    The resolver for
  Order: {                                              the consumer field
    consumer: resolveOrderConsumer,                     of an Order
    restaurant: resolveOrderRestaurant,
    deliveryInfo: resolveOrderDeliveryInfo
...
};
```

A resolver function has three parameters:

- *Object*—For a top-level query field, such as `resolveOrders`, `object` is a root object that's usually ignored by the resolver function. Otherwise, `object` is the value returned by the resolver for the parent object. For example, the resolver function for the `Order.consumer` field is passed the value returned by the `Order`'s resolver function.
- *Query arguments*—These are supplied by the query document.
- *Context*—Global state of the query execution that's accessible by all resolvers. It's used, for example, to pass user information and dependencies to the resolvers.

A resolver function might invoke a single service or it might implement the API composition pattern and retrieve data from multiple services. An Apollo GraphQL server resolver function returns a `Promise`, which is JavaScript's version of Java's `Completable-Future`. The promise contains the object (or a list of objects) that the resolver function retrieved from the data store. GraphQL engine includes the return value in the result object.

Let's look at a couple of examples. Here's the `resolveOrders()` function, which is the resolver for the orders query:

```
function resolveOrders(_, { consumerId }, context) {
  return context.orderServiceProxy.findOrders(consumerId);
}
```

This function obtains the `OrderServiceProxy` from the `context` and invokes it to fetch a consumer's orders. It ignores its first parameter. It passes the `consumerId` argument, provided by the query document, to `OrderServiceProxy.findOrders()`. The `findOrders()` method retrieves the consumer's orders from `OrderHistoryService`.

Here's the `resolveOrderRestaurant()` function, which is the resolver for the `Order.restaurant` field that retrieves an order's restaurant:

```
function resolveOrderRestaurant({restaurantId}, args, context) {
    return context.restaurantServiceProxy.findRestaurant(restaurantId);
}
```

Its first parameter is `Order`. It invokes `RestaurantServiceProxy.findRestaurant()` with the `Order`'s `restaurantId`, which was provided by `resolveOrders()`.

GraphQL uses a recursive algorithm to execute the resolver functions. First, it executes the resolver function for the top-level query specified by the Query document. Next, for each object returned by the query, it iterates through the fields specified in the Query document. If a field has a resolver, it invokes the resolver with the object and the arguments from the Query document. It then recurses on the object or objects returned by that resolver.

Figure 8.11 shows how this algorithm executes the query that retrieves a consumer's orders and each order's delivery information and restaurant. First, the GraphQL engine invokes `resolveConsumer()`, which retrieves `Consumer`. Next, it invokes `resolve-ConsumerOrders()`, which is the resolver for the `Consumer.orders` field that returns the consumer's orders. The GraphQL engine then iterates through `Orders`, invoking the resolvers for the `Order.restaurant` and `Order.deliveryInfo` fields.

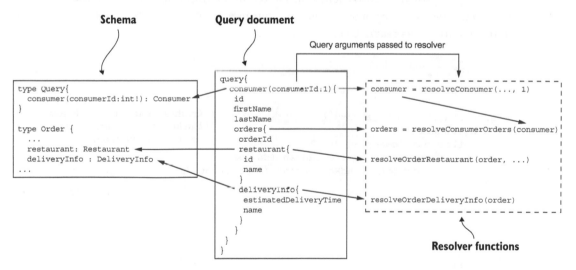

Figure 8.11 GraphQL executes a query by recursively invoking the resolver functions for the fields specified in the Query document. First, it executes the resolver for the query, and then it recursively invokes the resolvers for the fields in the result object hierarchy.

The result of executing the resolvers is a `Consumer` object populated with data retrieved from multiple services.

Let's now look at how to optimize the executing of resolvers by using batching and caching.

OPTIMIZING LOADING USING BATCHING AND CACHING

GraphQL can potentially execute a large number of resolvers when executing a query. Because the GraphQL server executes each resolver independently, there's a risk of poor performance due to excessive round-trips to the services. Consider, for example, a query that retrieves a consumer, their orders, and the orders' restaurants. If there are *N* orders, then a simplistic implementation would make one call to `Consumer Service`, one call to `Order History Service`, and then *N* calls to `Restaurant Service`. Even though the GraphQL engine will typically make the calls to `Restaurant Service` in parallel, there's a risk of poor performance. Fortunately, you can use a few techniques to improve performance.

One important optimization is to use a combination of server-side batching and caching. *Batching* turns *N* calls to a service, such as `Restaurant Service`, into a single call that retrieves a batch of *N* objects. *Caching* reuses the result of a previous fetch of the same object to avoid making an unnecessary duplicate call. The combination of batching and caching significantly reduces the number of round-trips to backend services.

A NodeJS-based GraphQL server can use the `DataLoader` module to implement batching and caching (https://github.com/facebook/dataloader). It coalesces loads that occur within a single execution of the event loop and calls a batch loading function that you provide. It also caches calls to eliminate duplicate loads. The following listing shows how `RestaurantServiceProxy` can use `DataLoader`. The `findRestaurant()` method loads a `Restaurant` via `DataLoader`.

> **Listing 8.9 Using a `DataLoader` to optimize calls to `Restaurant Service`**

```
const DataLoader = require('dataloader');

class RestaurantServiceProxy {
    constructor() {                                         Create a DataLoader, which uses
        this.dataLoader =                                   batchFindRestaurants() as the
            new DataLoader(restaurantIds =>                 batch loading functions.
              this.batchFindRestaurants(restaurantIds));
    }
                                                            Load the specified Restaurant
    findRestaurant(restaurantId) {                          via the DataLoader.
        return this.dataLoader.load(restaurantId);
    }
                                                            Load a batch of
    batchFindRestaurants(restaurantIds) {                   Restaurants.
        ...
    }
}
```

`RestaurantServiceProxy` and, hence, `DataLoader` are created for each request, so there's no possibility of `DataLoader` mixing together different users' data.

Let's now look at how to integrate the GraphQL engine with a web framework so that it can be invoked by clients.

INTEGRATING THE APOLLO GRAPHQL SERVER WITH EXPRESS

The Apollo GraphQL server executes GraphQL queries. In order for clients to invoke it, you need to integrate it with a web framework. Apollo GraphQL server supports several web frameworks, including Express, a popular NodeJS web framework.

Listing 8.10 shows how to use the Apollo GraphQL server in an Express application. The key function is `graphqlExpress`, which is provided by the `apollo-server-express` module. It builds an Express request handler that executes GraphQL queries against a schema. This example configures Express to route requests to the `GET /graphql` and `POST /graphql` endpoints of this GraphQL request handler. It also creates a GraphQL context containing the proxies, which makes them available to the resolvers.

Listing 8.10 Integrating the GraphQL server with the Express web framework

```
const {graphqlExpress} = require("apollo-server-express");

const typeDefs = gql`           ◁───┐  Define the GraphQL
  type Query {                       │  schema.
   orders: resolveOrders,
   ...
  }

  type Consumer {
   ...
                                Define the
const resolvers = {    ◁───┘   resolvers.
  Query: {
   ...
  }
}

const schema = makeExecutableSchema({ typeDefs, resolvers });   ◁───┘

const app = express();

function makeContextWithDependencies(req) {   ◁───┐
    const orderServiceProxy = new OrderServiceProxy();
    const consumerServiceProxy = new ConsumerServiceProxy();
    const restaurantServiceProxy = new RestaurantServiceProxy();
    ...
    return {orderServiceProxy, consumerServiceProxy,
            restaurantServiceProxy, ...};
}

function makeGraphQLHandler() {   ◁───┐
    return graphqlExpress(req => {
       return {schema: schema, context: makeContextWithDependencies(req)}
    });
}

app.post('/graphql', bodyParser.json(), makeGraphQLHandler());   ◁───

app.get('/graphql', makeGraphQLHandler());

app.listen(PORT);
```

Combine the schema with the resolvers to create an executable schema.

Inject repositories into the context so they're available to resolvers.

Make an express request handler that executes GraphQL queries against the executable schema.

Route POST /graphql and GET /graphql endpoints to the GraphQL server.

This example doesn't handle concerns such as security, but those would be straight-forward to implement. The API gateway could, for example, authenticate users using Passport, a NodeJS security framework described in chapter 11. The `makeContext-WithDependencies()` function would pass the user information to each repository's constructor so that they can propagate the user information to the services.

Let's now look at how a client can invoke this server to execute GraphQL queries.

WRITING A GRAPHQL CLIENT

There are a couple of different ways a client application can invoke the GraphQL server. Because the GraphQL server has an HTTP-based API, a client application could use an HTTP library to make requests, such as `GET http://localhost:3000/graphql?query={orders(consumerId:1){orderId,restaurant{id}}}'`. It's easier, though, to use a GraphQL client library, which takes care of properly formatting requests and typically provides features such as client-side caching.

The following listing shows the `FtgoGraphQLClient` class, which is a simple GraphQL-based client for the FTGO application. Its constructor instantiates `Apollo-Client`, which is provided by the Apollo GraphQL client library. The `FtgoGraphQL-Client` class defines a `findConsumer()` method that uses the client to retrieve the name of a consumer.

Listing 8.11   Using the Apollo GraphQL client to execute queries

```
class FtgoGraphQLClient {

    constructor(...) {
        this.client = new ApolloClient({ ... });
    }

    findConsumer(consumerId) {
        return this.client.query({
            variables: { cid: consumerId},        ◀── Supply the value of the $cid.
              query: gql`
               query foo($cid : Int!) {           ◀── Define $cid as a variable of type Int.
                 consumer(consumerId: $cid)  {     ◀── Set the value of query parameter consumerid to $cid.
                    id
                    firstName
                    lastName
                 }
               } `,
            })
    }

}
```

The `FtgoGraphQLClient` class can define a variety of query methods, such as `find-Consumer()`. Each one executes a query that retrieves exactly the data needed by the client.

This section has barely scratched the surface of GraphQL's capabilities. I hope I've demonstrated that GraphQL is a very appealing alternative to a more traditional, REST-based API gateway. It lets you implement an API that's flexible enough to support a diverse set of clients. Consequently, you should consider using GraphQL to implement your API gateway.

Summary

- Your application's external clients usually access the application's services via an API gateway. An API gateway provides each client with a custom API. It's responsible for request routing, API composition, protocol translation, and implementation of edge functions such as authentication.

- Your application can have a single API gateway or it can use the Backends for frontends pattern, which defines an API gateway for each type of client. The main advantage of the Backends for frontends pattern is that it gives the client teams greater autonomy, because they develop, deploy, and operate their own API gateway.

- There are numerous technologies you can use to implement an API gateway, including off-the-shelf API gateway products. Alternatively, you can develop your own API gateway using a framework.

- Spring Cloud Gateway is a good, easy-to-use framework for developing an API gateway. It routes requests using any request attribute, including the method and the path. Spring Cloud Gateway can route a request either directly to a backend service or to a custom handler method. It's built using the scalable, reactive Spring Framework 5 and Project Reactor frameworks. You can write your custom request handlers in a reactive style using, for example, Project Reactor's `Mono` abstraction.

- GraphQL, a framework that provides graph-based query language, is another excellent foundation for developing an API Gateway. You write a graph-oriented schema to describe the server-side data model and its supported queries. You then map that schema to your services by writing resolvers, which retrieve data. GraphQL-based clients execute queries against the schema that specify exactly the data that the server should return. As a result, a GraphQL-based API gateway can support diverse clients.

Testing microservices: Part 1

FTGO, like many organizations, had adopted a traditional approach to testing. *Testing* is primarily an activity that happens after development. The FTGO developers throw their code over a wall to the QA team, who verify that the software works as expected. What's more, most of their testing is done manually. Sadly, this approach to testing is broken—for two reasons:

- *Manual testing is extremely inefficient*—You should never ask a human to do what a machine can do better. Compared to machines, humans are slow and can't work 24/7. You won't be able to deliver software rapidly and safely if you rely on manual testing. It's essential that you write automated tests.
- *Testing is done far too late in the delivery process*—There certainly is a role for tests that critique an application after it's been written, but experience has shown that those tests are insufficient. A much better approach is for developers to

write automated tests as part of development. It improves their productivity because, for example, they'll have tests that provide immediate feedback while editing code.

In this regard, FTGO is a fairly typical organization. The Sauce Labs Testing Trends in 2018 report paints a fairly gloomy picture of the state of test automation (https://saucelabs.com/resources/white-papers/testing-trends-for-2018). It describes how only 26% of organizations are mostly automated, and a minuscule 3% are fully automated!

The reliance on manual testing isn't because of a lack of tooling and frameworks. For example, JUnit, a popular Java testing framework, was first released in 1998. The reason for the lack of automated tests is mostly cultural: "Testing is QA's job," "It's not the best use of a developers's time," and so on. It also doesn't help that developing a fast-running, yet effective, maintainable test suite is challenging. And, a typical large, monolithic application is extremely difficult to test.

One key motivation for using the microservice architecture is, as described in chapter 2, improving testability. Yet at the same time, the complexity of the microservice architecture demands that you write automated tests. Furthermore, some aspects of testing microservices are challenging. That's because we need to verify that services can interact correctly while minimizing the number of slow, complex, and unreliable end-to-end-tests that launch many services.

This chapter is the first of two chapters on testing. It's an introduction to testing. Chapter 10 covers more advanced testing concepts. The two chapters are long, but together they cover testing ideas and techniques that are essential to modern software development in general, and to the microservice architecture in particular.

I begin this chapter by describing effective testing strategies for a microservices-based application. These strategies enable you to be confident that your software works, while minimizing test complexity and execution time. After that, I describe how to write one particular kind of test for your services: unit tests. Chapter 10 covers the other kinds of tests: integration, component, and end-to-end.

Let's start by taking a look at testing strategies for microservices.

Why an introduction to testing?

You may be wondering why this chapter includes an introduction to basic testing concepts. If you're already familiar with concepts such as the test pyramid and the different types of tests, feel free to speed-read this chapter and move onto the next one, which focuses on microservices-specific testing topics. But based on my experiences consulting for and training clients all over the world, a fundamental weakness of many software development organizations is the lack of automated testing. That's because if you want to deliver software quickly and reliably, it's *absolutely essential* to do automated testing. It's the only way to have a short *lead time*, which is the time it takes to get committed code into production. Perhaps even more importantly, automated testing is essential because it forces you to develop a testable application. It's typically very difficult to introduce automating testing into an already large, complex application. In other words, the fast track to monolithic hell is to not write automated tests.

9.1   *Testing strategies for microservice architectures*

Let's say you've made a change to FTGO application's Order Service. Naturally, the next step is for you to run your code and verify that the change works correctly. One option is to test the change manually. First, you run Order Service and all its dependencies, which include infrastructure services such as a database and other application services. Then you "test" the service by either invoking its API or using the FTGO application's UI. The downside of this approach is that it's a slow, manual way to test your code.

A much better option is to have automated tests that you can run during development. Your development workflow should be: edit code, run tests (ideally with a single keystroke), repeat. The fast-running tests quickly tell you whether your changes work within a few seconds. But how do you write fast-running tests? And are they sufficient or do you need more comprehensive tests? These are the kind of questions I answer in this and other sections in this chapter.

I start this section with an overview of important automated testing concepts. We'll look at the purpose of testing and the structure of a typical test. I cover the different types of tests that you'll need to write. I also describe the test pyramid, which provides valuable guidance about where you should focus your testing efforts. After covering testing concepts, I discuss strategies for testing microservices. We'll look at the distinct challenges of testing applications that have a microservice architecture. I describe techniques you can use to write simpler and faster, yet still-effective, tests for your microservices.

Let's take a look at testing concepts.

9.1.1   *Overview of testing*

In this chapter, my focus is on automated testing, and I use the term *test* as shorthand for *automated test*. Wikipedia defines a *test case*, or test, as follows:

> *A test case is a set of test inputs, execution conditions, and expected results developed for a particular objective, such as to exercise a particular program path or to verify compliance with a specific requirement.*

> https://en.wikipedia.org/wiki/Test_case

In other words, the purpose of a test is, as figure 9.1 shows, to verify the behavior of the System Under Test (SUT). In this definition, *system* is a fancy term that means the software element being tested. It might be something as small as a class, as large as the entire application, or something in between, such as a cluster of classes or an individual service. A collection of related tests form a *test suite*.

Let's first look at the concept of an automated test. Then I discuss the different kinds of tests that you'll need to write. After that, I discuss the test pyramid, which describes the relative proportions of the different types of tests that you should write.

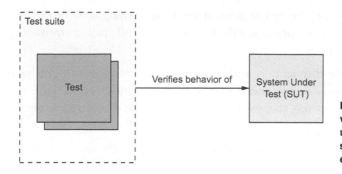

Figure 9.1 The goal of a test is to verify the behavior of the system under test. An SUT might be as small as a class or as large as an entire application.

WRITING AUTOMATED TESTS

Automated tests are usually written using a testing framework. JUnit, for example, is a popular Java testing framework. Figure 9.2 shows the structure of an automated test. Each test is implemented by a test method, which belongs to a test class.

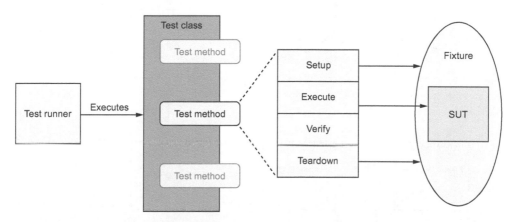

Figure 9.2 Each automated test is implemented by a test method, which belongs to a test class. A test consists of four phases: *setup*, which initializes the test fixture, which is everything required to run the test; *execute*, which invokes the SUT; *verify*, which verifies the outcome of the test; and *teardown*, which cleans up the test fixture.

An automated test typically consists of four phases (http://xunitpatterns.com/ Four%20Phase%20Test.html):

1 *Setup*—Initialize the test fixture, which consists of the SUT and its dependencies, to the desired initial state. For example, create the class under test and initialize it to the state required for it to exhibit the desired behavior.
2 *Exercise*—Invoke the SUT—for example, invoke a method on the class under test.
3 *Verify*—Make assertions about the invocation's outcome and the state of the SUT. For example, verify the method's return value and the new state of the class under test.

4   *Teardown*—Clean up the test fixture, if necessary. Many tests omit this phase, but some types of database test will, for example, roll back a transaction initiated by the setup phase.

In order to reduce code duplication and simplify tests, a test class might have setup methods that are run before a test method, and teardown methods that are run afterwards. A test *suite* is a set of test classes. The tests are executed by a *test runner*.

TESTING USING MOCKS AND STUBS

An SUT often has dependencies. The trouble with dependencies is that they can complicate and slow down tests. For example, the `OrderController` class invokes `Order-Service`, which ultimately depends on numerous other application services and infrastructure services. It wouldn't be practical to test the `OrderController` class by running a large portion of the system. We need a way to test an SUT in isolation.

The solution, as figure 9.3 shows, is to replace the SUT's dependencies with test doubles. A *test double* is an object that simulates the behavior of the dependency.

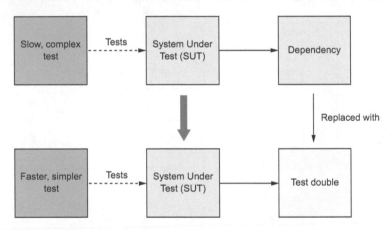

Figure 9.3   **Replacing a dependency with a test double enables the SUT to be tested in isolation. The test is simpler and faster.**

There are two types of test doubles: stubs and mocks. The terms *stubs* and *mocks* are often used interchangeably, although they have slightly different behavior. A *stub* is a test double that returns values to the SUT. A *mock* is a test double that a test uses to verify that the SUT correctly invokes a dependency. Also, a mock is often a stub.

Later on in this chapter, you'll see examples of test doubles in action. For example, section 9.2.5 shows how to test the `OrderController` class in isolation by using a test double for the `OrderService` class. In that example, the `OrderService` test double is implemented using Mockito, a popular mock object framework for Java. Chapter 10 shows how to test `Order Service` using test doubles for the other services that it invokes. Those test doubles respond to command messages sent by `Order Service`.

Let's now look at the different types of tests.

THE DIFFERENT TYPES OF TESTS

There are many different types of tests. Some tests, such as performance tests and usability tests, verify that the application satisfies its quality of service requirements. In this chapter, I focus on automated tests that verify the functional aspects of the application or service. I describe how to write four different types of tests:

- *Unit tests*—Test a small part of a service, such as a class.
- *Integration tests*—Verify that a service can interact with infrastructure services such as databases and other application services.
- *Component tests*—Acceptance tests for an individual service.
- *End-to-end tests*—Acceptance tests for the entire application.

They differ primarily in scope. At one end of the spectrum are unit tests, which verify behavior of the smallest meaningful program element. For an object-oriented language such as Java, that's a class. At the other end of the spectrum are end-to-end tests, which verify the behavior of an entire application. In the middle are component tests, which test individual services. Integration tests, as you'll see in the next chapter, have a relatively small scope, but they're more complex than pure unit tests. Scope is only one way of characterizing tests. Another way is to use the test quadrant.

Compile-time unit tests

Testing is an integral part of development. The modern development workflow is to edit code, then run tests. Moreover, if you're a Test-Driven Development (TDD) practitioner, you develop a new feature or fix a bug by first writing a failing test and then writing the code to make it pass. Even if you're not a TDD adherent, an excellent way to fix a bug is to write a test that reproduces the bug and then write the code that fixes it.

The tests that you run as part of this workflow are known as *compile-time* tests. In a modern IDE, such as IntelliJ IDEA or Eclipse, you typically don't compile your code as a separate step. Rather, you use a single keystroke to compile the code and run the tests. In order to stay in the flow, these tests need to execute quickly—ideally, no more than a few seconds.

USING THE TEST QUADRANT TO CATEGORIZE TESTS

A good way to categorize tests is Brian Marick's *test quadrant* (www.exampler.com/old-blog/2003/08/21/#agile-testing-project-1). The test quadrant, shown in figure 9.4, categorizes tests along two dimensions:

- *Whether the test is business facing or technology facing*—A business-facing test is described using the terminology of a domain expert, whereas a technology-facing test is described using the terminology of developers and the implementation.
- *Whether the goal of the test is to support programming or critique the application*—Developers use tests that support programming as part of their daily work. Tests that critique the application aim to identify areas that need improvement.

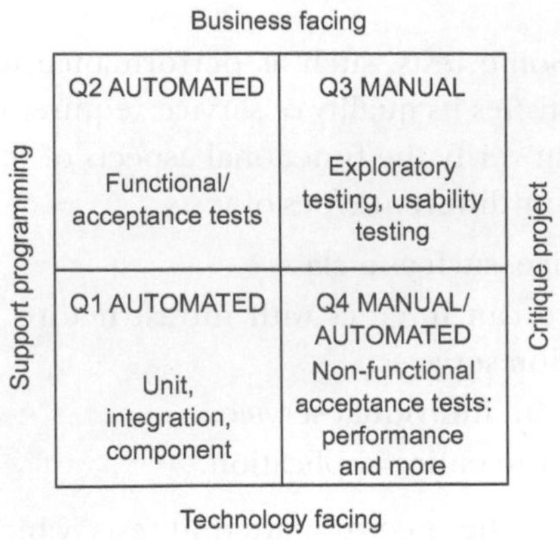

Figure 9.4 **The test quadrant categorizes tests along two dimensions. The first dimension is whether a test is business facing or technology facing. The second is whether the purpose of the test is to support programming or critique the application.**

The test quadrant defines four different categories of tests:

- *Q1*—Support programming/technology facing: unit and integration tests
- *Q2*—Support programming/business facing: component and end-to-end test
- *Q3*—Critique application/business facing: usability and exploratory testing
- *Q4*—Critique application/technology facing: nonfunctional acceptance tests such as performance tests

The test quadrant isn't the only way of organizing tests. There's also the test pyramid, which provides guidance on how many tests of each type to write.

USING THE TEST PYRAMID AS A GUIDE TO FOCUSING YOUR TESTING EFFORTS

We must write different kinds of tests in order to be confident that our application works. The challenge, though, is that the execution time and complexity of a test increase with its scope. Also, the larger the scope of a test and the more moving parts it has, the less reliable it becomes. Unreliable tests are almost as bad as no tests, because if you can't trust a test, you're likely to ignore failures.

On one end of the spectrum are unit tests for individual classes. They're fast to execute, easy to write, and reliable. At the other end of the spectrum are end-to-end tests for the entire application. These tend to be slow, difficult to write, and often unreliable because of their complexity. Because we don't have unlimited budget for development and testing, we want to focus on writing tests that have small scope without compromising the effectiveness of the test suite.

The test pyramid, shown in figure 9.5, is a good guide (https://martinfowler.com/bliki/TestPyramid.html). At the base of the pyramid are the fast, simple, and reliable unit tests. At the top of the pyramid are the slow, complex, and brittle end-to-end tests. Like the USDA food pyramid, although more useful and less controversial (https://en.wikipedia.org/wiki/History_of_USDA_nutrition_guides), the test pyramid describes the relative proportions of each type of test.

The key idea of the test pyramid is that as we move up the pyramid we should write fewer and fewer tests. We should write lots of unit tests and very few end-to-end tests.

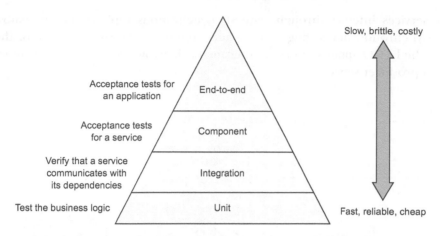

Figure 9.5   The test pyramid describes the relative proportions of each type of test that you need to write. As you move up the pyramid, you should write fewer and fewer tests.

As you'll see in this chapter, I describe a strategy that emphasizes testing the pieces of a service. It even minimizes the number of component tests, which test an entire service.

It's clear how to test individual microservices such as `Consumer Service`, which don't depend on any other services. But what about services such as `Order Service`, that do depend on numerous other services? And how can we be confident that the application as a whole works? This is the key challenge of testing applications that have a microservice architecture. The complexity of testing has moved from the individual services to the interactions between them. Let's look at how to tackle this problem.

9.1.2   The challenge of testing microservices

Interprocess communication plays a much more important role in a microservices-based application than in a monolithic application. A monolithic application might communicate with a few external clients and services. For example, the monolithic version of the FTGO application uses a few third-party web services, such as Stripe for payments, Twilio for messaging, and Amazon SES for email, which have stable APIs. Any interaction between the modules of the application is through programming language-based APIs. Interprocess communication is very much on the edge of the application.

In contrast, interprocess communication is central to microservice architecture. A microservices-based application is a distributed system. Teams are constantly developing their services and evolving their APIs. It's essential that developers of a service write tests that verify that their service interacts with its dependencies and clients.

As described in chapter 3, services communicate with each other using a variety of interaction styles and IPC mechanisms. Some services use request/response-style interaction that's implemented using a synchronous protocol, such as REST or gRPC.

Other services interact through request/asynchronous reply or publish/subscribe using asynchronous messaging. For instance, figure 9.6 shows how some of the services in the FTGO application communicate. Each arrow points from a consumer service to a producer service.

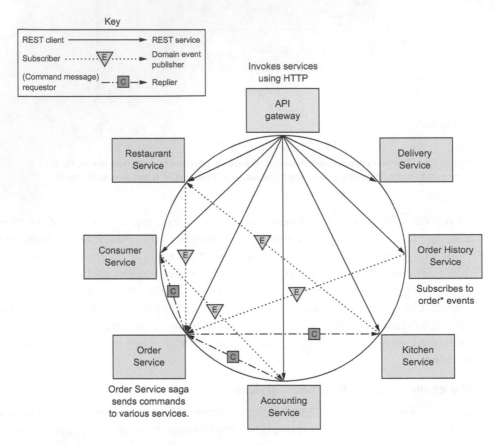

Figure 9.6   Some of the interservice communication in the FTGO application. Each arrow points from a consumer service to a producer service.

The arrow points in the direction of the dependency, from the consumer of the API to the provider of the API. The assumptions that a consumer makes about an API depend on the nature of the interaction:

- *REST client → service*—The API gateway routes requests to services and implements API composition.
- *Domain event consumer → publisher*—Order History Service consumes events published by Order Service.
- *Command message requestor → replier*—Order Service sends command messages to various services and consumes the replies.

Each interaction between a pair of services represents an agreement or contract between the two services. `Order History Service` and `Order Service` must, for example, agree on the event message structure and the channel that they're published to. Similarly, the API gateway and the services must agree on the REST API endpoints. And `Order Service` and each service that it invokes using asynchronous request/ response must agree on the command channel and the format of the command and reply messages.

As a developer of a service, you need to be confident that the services you consume have stable APIs. Similarly, you don't want to unintentionally make breaking changes to your service's API. For example, if you're working on `Order Service`, you want to be sure that the developers of your service's dependencies, such as `Consumer Service` and `Kitchen Service`, don't change their APIs in ways that are incompatible with your service. Similarly, you must ensure that you don't change the `Order Services`'s API in a way that breaks the `API Gateway` or `Order History Service`.

One way to verify that two services can interact is to run both services, invoke an API that triggers the communication, and verify that it has the expected outcome. This will certainly catch integration problems, but it's basically an end-to-end. The test likely would need to run numerous other transitive dependencies of those services. A test might also need to invoke complex, high-level functionality such as business logic, even if its goal is to test relatively low-level IPC. It's best to avoid writing end-to-end tests like these. Somehow, we need to write faster, simpler, and more reliable tests that ideally test services in isolation. The solution is to use what's known as *consumer-driven contract testing*.

CONSUMER-DRIVEN CONTRACT TESTING

Imagine that you're a member of the team developing `API Gateway`, described in chapter 8. The `API Gateway`'s `OrderServiceProxy` invokes various REST endpoints, including the `GET /orders/{orderId}` endpoint. It's essential that we write tests that verify that `API Gateway` and `Order Service` agree on an API. In the terminology of consumer contract testing, the two services participate in a *consumer-provider relationship*. `API Gateway` is a consumer, and `Order Service` is a provider. A consumer contract test is an integration test for a provider, such as `Order Service`, that verifies that its API matches the expectations of a consumer, such as `API Gateway`.

A consumer contract test focuses on verifying that the "shape" of a provider's API meets the consumer's expectations. For a REST endpoint, a contract test verifies that the provider implements an endpoint that

- Has the expected HTTP method and path
- Accepts the expected headers, if any
- Accepts a request body, if any
- Returns a response with the expected status code, headers, and body

It's important to remember that contract tests don't thoroughly test the provider's business logic. That's the job of unit tests. Later on, you'll see that consumer contract tests for a REST API are in fact mock controller tests.

The team that develops the consumer writes a contract test suite and adds it (for example, via a pull request) to the provider's test suite. The developers of other services that invoke `Order Service` also contribute a test suite, as shown in figure 9.7. Each test suite will test those aspects of `Order Service`'s API that are relevant to each consumer. The test suite for `Order History Service`, for example, verifies that `Order Service` publishes the expected events.

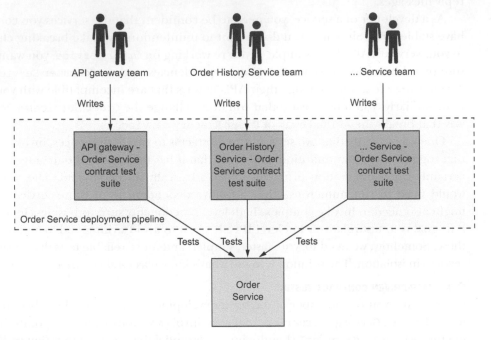

Figure 9.7 Each team that develops a service that consumes `Order Service`'s API contributes a contract test suite. The test suite verifies that the API matches the consumer's expectations. This test suite, along with those contributed by other teams, is run by `Order Service`'s deployment pipeline.

These test suites are executed by the deployment pipeline for `Order Service`. If a consumer contract test fails, that failure tells the producer team that they've made a breaking change to the API. They must either fix the API or talk to the consumer team.

> **Pattern: Consumer-driven contract test**
> Verify that a service meets the expectations of its clients See http://microservices.io/patterns/testing/service-integration-contract-test.html.

Consumer-driven contract tests typically use testing by example. The interaction between a consumer and provider is defined by a set of examples, known as contracts. Each *contract* consists of example messages that are exchanged during one interaction.

For instance, a contract for a REST API consists of an example HTTP request and response. On the surface, it may seem better to define the interaction using schemas written using, for example, OpenAPI or JSON schema. But it turns out schemas aren't that useful when writing tests. A test can validate the response using the schema but it still needs to invoke the provider with an example request.

What's more, consumer tests also need example responses. That's because even though the focus of consumer-driven contract testing is to test a provider, contracts are also used to verify that the consumer conforms to the contract. For instance, a consumer-side contract test for a REST client uses the contract to configure an HTTP stub service that verifies that the HTTP request matches the contract's request and sends back the contract's HTTP response. Testing both sides of interaction ensures that the consumer and provider agree on the API. Later on we'll look at examples of how to write this kind of testing, but first let's see how to write consumer contract tests using Spring Cloud Contract.

> **Pattern: Consumer-side contract test**
>
> Verify that the client of a service can communicate with the service. See https://microservices.io/patterns/testing/consumer-side-contract-test.html.

TESTING SERVICES USING SPRING CLOUD CONTRACT

Two popular contract testing frameworks are Spring Cloud Contract (https://cloud.spring.io/spring-cloud-contract/), which is a consumer contract testing framework for Spring applications, and the Pact family of frameworks (https://github.com/pact-foundation), which support a variety of languages. The FTGO application is a Spring framework-based application, so in this chapter I'm going to describe how to use Spring Cloud Contract. It provides a Groovy domain-specific language (DSL) for writing contracts. Each contract is a concrete example of an interaction between a consumer and a provider, such as an HTTP request and response. Spring Cloud Contract code generates contract tests for the provider. It also configures mocks, such as a mock HTTP server, for consumer integration tests.

Say, for example, you're working on API Gateway and want to write a consumer contract test for Order Service. Figure 9.8 shows the process, which requires you to collaborate with Order Service teams. You write contracts that define how API Gateway interacts with Order Service. The Order Service team uses these contracts to test Order Service, and you use them to test API Gateway. The sequence of steps is as follows:

1 You write one or more contracts, such as the one shown in listing 9.1. Each contract consists of an HTTP request that API Gateway might send to Order Service and an expected HTTP response. You give the contracts, perhaps via a Git pull request, to the Order Service team.

2 The Order Service team tests Order Service using consumer contract tests, which Spring Cloud Contract code generates from contracts.

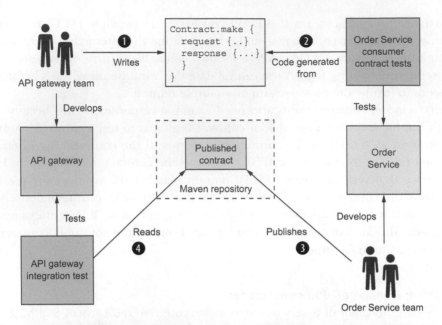

Figure 9.8 The API Gateway team writes the contracts. The Order Service team uses those contracts to test Order Service and publishes them to a repository. The API Gateway team uses the published contracts to test API Gateway.

3   The Order Service team publishes the contracts that tested Order Service to a Maven repository.

4   You use the published contracts to write tests for API Gateway.

Because you test API Gateway using the published contracts, you can be confident that it works with the deployed Order Service.

The contracts are the key part of this testing strategy. The following listing shows an example Spring Cloud Contract. It consists of an HTTP request and an HTTP response.

Listing 9.1   A contract that describes how API Gateway invokes Order Service

```
org.springframework.cloud.contract.spec.Contract.make {
    request {
        method 'GET'                              ◁──  The HTTP request's
        url '/orders/1223232'                          method and path
    }
    response {                     ◁──  The HTTP response's status
        status 200                      code, headers, and body
        headers {
            header('Content-Type': 'application/json;charset=UTF-8')
        }
        body("{ ... }")
    }
}
```

The request element is an HTTP request for the REST endpoint `GET /orders/ {orderId}`. The response element is an HTTP response that describes an `Order` expected by `API Gateway`. The Groovy contracts are part of the provider's code base. Each consumer team writes contracts that describe how their service interacts with the provider and gives them, perhaps via a Git pull request, to the provider team. The provider team is responsible for packaging the contracts as a JAR and publishing them to a Maven repository. The consumer-side tests download the JAR from the repository.

Each contract's request and response play dual roles of test data and the specification of expected behavior. In a consumer-side test, the contract is used to configure a stub, which is similar to a Mockito mock object and simulates the behavior of `Order Service`. It enables `API Gateway` to be tested without running `Order Service`. In the provider-side test, the generated test class invokes the provider with the contract's request and verifies that it returns a response that matches the contract's response. The next chapter discusses the details of how to use Spring Cloud Contract, but now we're going to look at how to use consumer contract testing for messaging APIs.

CONSUMER CONTRACT TESTS FOR MESSAGING APIS

A REST client isn't the only kind of consumer that has expectations of a provider's API. Services that subscribe to domain events and use asynchronous request/response-based communication are also consumers. They consume some other service's messaging API, and make assumptions about the nature of that API. We must also write consumer contract tests for these services.

Spring Cloud Contract also provides support for testing messaging-based interactions. The structure of a contract and how it's used by the tests depend on the type of interaction. A contract for domain event publishing consists of an example domain event. A provider test causes the provider to emit an event and verifies that it matches the contract's event. A consumer test verifies that the consumer can handle that event. In the next chapter, I describe an example test.

A contract for an asynchronous request/response interaction is similar to an HTTP contract. It consists of a request message and a response message. A provider test invokes the API with the contract's request message and verifies that the response matches the contract's response. A consumer test uses the contract to configure a stub subscriber, which listens for the contract's request message and replies with the specified response. The next chapter discusses an example test. But first we'll take a look at the deployment pipeline, which runs these and other tests.

9.1.3 *The deployment pipeline*

Every service has a deployment pipeline. Jez Humble's book, Continuous Delivery (Addison-Wesley, 2010) describes a *deployment pipeline* as the automated process of getting code from the developer's desktop into production. As figure 9.9 shows, it consists of a series of stages that execute test suites, followed by a stage that releases or deploys the service. Ideally, it's fully automated, but it might contain manual steps. A deployment pipeline is often implemented using a Continuous Integration (CI) server, such as Jenkins.

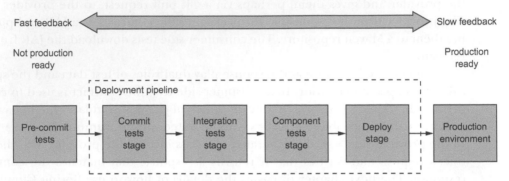

Figure 9.9   An example deployment pipeline for Order Service. **It consists of a series of stages. The pre-commit tests are run by the developer prior to committing their code. The remaining stages are executed by an automated tool, such as the Jenkins CI server.**

As code flows through the pipeline, the test suites subject it to increasingly more thorough testing in environments that are more production like. At the same time, the execution time of each test suite typically grows. The idea is to provide feedback about test failures as rapidly as possible.

The example deployment pipeline shown in figure 9.9 consists of the following stages:

- *Pre-commit tests stage*—Runs the unit tests. This is executed by the developer before committing their changes.
- *Commit tests stage*—Compiles the service, runs the unit tests, and performs static code analysis.
- *Integration tests stage*—Runs the integration tests.
- *Component tests stage*—Runs the component tests for the service.
- *Deploy stage*—Deploys the service into production.

The CI server runs the commit stage when a developer commits a change. It executes extremely quickly, so it provides rapid feedback about the commit. The later stages take longer to run, providing less immediate feedback. If all the tests pass, the final stage is when this pipeline deploys it into production.

In this example, the deployment pipeline is fully automated all the way from commit to deployment. There are, however, situations that require manual steps. For example, you might need a manual testing stage, such as a staging environment. In such a scenario, the code progresses to the next stage when a tester clicks a button to indicate that it was successful. Alternatively, a deployment pipeline for an on-premise product would release the new version of the service. Later on, the released services would be packaged into a product release and shipped to customers.

Now that we've looked at the organization of the deployment pipeline and when it executes the different types of tests, let's head to the bottom of the test pyramid and look at how to write unit tests for a service.

9.2   *Writing unit tests for a service*

Imagine that you want to write a test that verifies that the FTGO application's `Order Service` correctly calculates the subtotal of an `Order`. You could write tests that run `Order Service`, invoke its REST API to create an `Order`, and check that the HTTP response contains the expected values. The drawback of this approach is that not only is the test complex, it's also slow. If these tests were the compile-time tests for the `Order` class, you'd waste a lot of time waiting for it to finish. A much more productive approach is to write unit tests for the `Order` class.

As figure 9.10 shows, unit tests are the lowest level of the test pyramid. They're technology-facing tests that support development. A unit test verifies that a *unit*, which is a very small part of a service, works correctly. A unit is typically a class, so the goal of unit testing is to verify that it behaves as expected.

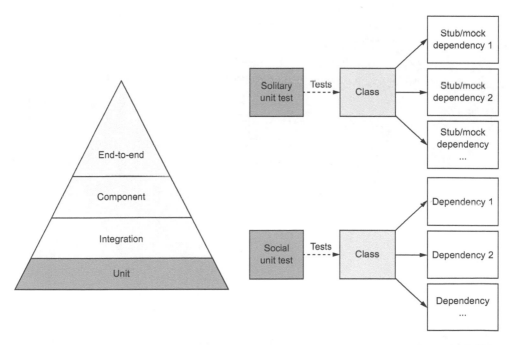

Figure 9.10   Unit tests are the base of the pyramid. They're fast running, easy to write, and reliable. A solitary unit test tests a class in isolation, using mocks or stubs for its dependencies. A sociable unit test tests a class and its dependencies.

There are two types of unit tests (https://martinfowler.com/bliki/UnitTest.html):

- *Solitary unit test*—Tests a class in isolation using mock objects for the class's dependencies
- *Sociable unit test*—Tests a class and its dependencies

The responsibilities of the class and its role in the architecture determine which type of test to use. Figure 9.11 shows the hexagonal architecture of a typical service and the type of unit test that you'll typically use for each kind of class. Controller and service classes are often tested using solitary unit tests. Domain objects, such as entities and value objects, are typically tested using sociable unit tests.

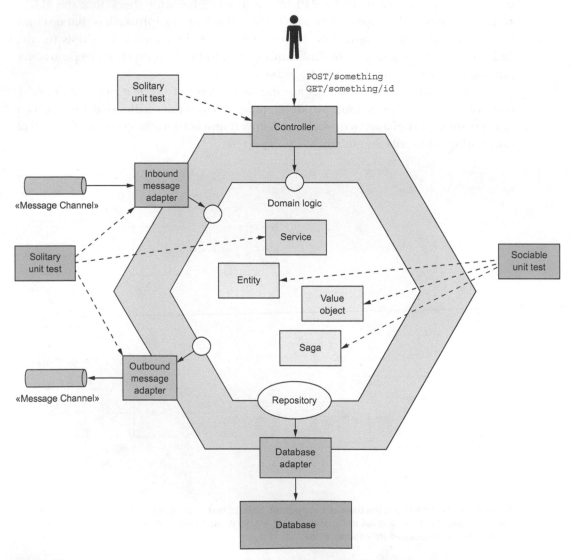

Figure 9.11   The responsibilities of a class determine whether to use a solitary or sociable unit test.

The typical testing strategy for each class is as follows:

- Entities, such as `Order`, which as described in chapter 5 are objects with persistent identity, are tested using sociable unit tests.
- Value objects, such as `Money`, which as described in chapter 5 are objects that are collections of values, are tested using sociable unit tests.
- Sagas, such as `CreateOrderSaga`, which as described in chapter 4 maintain data consistency across services, are tested using sociable unit tests.
- Domain services, such as `OrderService`, which as described in chapter 5 are classes that implement business logic that doesn't belong in entities or value objects, are tested using solitary unit tests.
- Controllers, such as `OrderController`, which handle HTTP requests, are tested using solitary unit tests.
- Inbound and outbound messaging gateways are tested using solitary unit tests.

Let's begin by looking at how to test entities.

9.2.1 Developing unit tests for entities

The following listing shows an excerpt of `OrderTest` class, which implements the unit tests for the `Order` entity. The class has an `@Before` `setUp()` method that creates an `Order` before running each test. Its `@Test` methods might further initialize `Order`, invoke one of its methods, and then make assertions about the return value and the state of `Order`.

> **Listing 9.2 A simple, fast-running unit test for the `Order` entity**

```
public class OrderTest {

  private ResultWithEvents<Order> createResult;
  private Order order;

  @Before
  public void setUp() throws Exception {
    createResult = Order.createOrder(CONSUMER_ID, AJANTA_ID, CHICKEN_VINDALOO
      _LINE_ITEMS);
    order = createResult.result;
  }

  @Test
  public void shouldCalculateTotal() {
    assertEquals(CHICKEN_VINDALOO_PRICE.multiply(CHICKEN_VINDALOO_QUANTITY),
      order.getOrderTotal());
  }

  ...

}
```

The `@Test` `shouldCalculateTotal()` method verifies that `Order.getOrderTotal()` returns the expected value. Unit tests thoroughly test the business logic. They are sociable unit tests for the `Order` class and its dependencies. You can use them as compile-time tests because they execute extremely quickly. The `Order` class relies on the `Money` value object, so it's important to test that class as well. Let's see how to do that.

9.2.2   *Writing unit tests for value objects*

Value objects are immutable, so they tend to be easy to test. You don't have to worry about side effects. A test for a value object typically creates a value object in a particular state, invokes one of its methods, and makes assertions about the return value. Listing 9.3 shows the tests for the `Money` value object, which is a simple class that represents a money value. These tests verify the behavior of the `Money` class's methods, including `add()`, which adds two `Money` objects, and `multiply()`, which multiplies a `Money` object by an integer. They are solitary tests because the `Money` class doesn't depend on any other application classes.

Listing 9.3   A simple, fast-running test for the `Money` value object

```
public class MoneyTest {

  private final int M1_AMOUNT = 10;
  private final int M2_AMOUNT = 15;

  private Money m1 = new Money(M1_AMOUNT);
  private Money m2 = new Money(M2_AMOUNT);                    Verify that two
                                                             Money objects can
                                                             be added together.
  @Test
  public void shouldAdd() {
     assertEquals(new Money(M1_AMOUNT + M2_AMOUNT), m1.add(m2));
  }
                                         Verify that a Money
  @Test                                  object can be multiplied
  public void shouldMultiply() {         by an integer.
    int multiplier = 12;
    assertEquals(new Money(M2_AMOUNT * multiplier), m2.multiply(multiplier));
  }

  ...
}
```

Entities and value objects are the building blocks of a service's business logic. But some business logic also resides in the service's sagas and services. Let's look at how to test those.

9.2.3   *Developing unit tests for sagas*

A saga, such as the `CreateOrderSaga` class, implements important business logic, so needs to be tested. It's a persistent object that sends command messages to saga participants and processes their replies. As described in chapter 4, `CreateOrderSaga` exchanges command/reply messages with several services, such as `Consumer Service` and `Kitchen Service`. A test for this class creates a saga and verifies that it sends the expected sequence of messages to the saga participants. One test you need to write is for the happy path. You must also write tests for the various scenarios where the saga rolls back because a saga participant sent back a failure message.

One approach would be to write tests that use a real database and message broker along with stubs to simulate the various saga participants. For example, a stub for `Consumer Service` would subscribe to the `consumerService` command channel and send back the desired reply message. But tests written using this approach would be quite slow. A much more effective approach is to write tests that mock those classes that interact with the database and message broker. That way, we can focus on testing the saga's core responsibility.

Listing 9.4 shows a test for `CreateOrderSaga`. It's a sociable unit test that tests the saga class and its dependencies. It's written using the Eventuate Tram Saga testing framework (https://github.com/eventuate-tram/eventuate-tram-sagas). This framework provides an easy-to-use DSL that abstracts away the details of interacting with sagas. With this DSL, you can create a saga and verify that it sends the correct command messages. Under the covers, the Saga testing framework configures the Saga framework with mocks for the database and messaging infrastructure.

Listing 9.4　A simple, fast-running unit test for `CreateOrderSaga`

```
public class CreateOrderSagaTest {

  @Test
  public void shouldCreateOrder() {
    given()
        .saga(new CreateOrderSaga(kitchenServiceProxy),
              new CreateOrderSagaState(ORDER_ID,
                  CHICKEN_VINDALOO_ORDER_DETAILS)).
    expect().
        command(new ValidateOrderByConsumer(CONSUMER_ID, ORDER_ID,
                CHICKEN_VINDALOO_ORDER_TOTAL)).
        to(ConsumerServiceChannels.consumerServiceChannel).
    andGiven().
        successReply().
      expect().
          command(new CreateTicket(AJANTA_ID, ORDER_ID, null)).
          to(KitchenServiceChannels.kitchenServiceChannel);
  }

  @Test
  public void shouldRejectOrderDueToConsumerVerificationFailed() {
    given()
        .saga(new CreateOrderSaga(kitchenServiceProxy),
              new CreateOrderSagaState(ORDER_ID,
                      CHICKEN_VINDALOO_ORDER_DETAILS)).
    expect().
        command(new ValidateOrderByConsumer(CONSUMER_ID, ORDER_ID,
                CHICKEN_VINDALOO_ORDER_TOTAL)).
        to(ConsumerServiceChannels.consumerServiceChannel).
    andGiven().
```

Create the saga.

Verify that it sends a ValidateOrderBy-Consumer message to Consumer Service.

Send a Success reply to that message.

Verify that it sends a CreateTicket message to Kitchen Service.

```
        failureReply().
    expect().
        command(new RejectOrderCommand(ORDER_ID)).
        to(OrderServiceChannels.orderServiceChannel);
  }

}
```

→ **Send a failure reply indicating that Consumer Service rejected Order.**

Verify that the saga sends a RejectOrderCommand message to Order Service.

The `@Test shouldCreateOrder()` method tests the happy path. The `@Test should-RejectOrderDueToConsumerVerificationFailed()` method tests the scenario where `Consumer Service` rejects the order. It verifies that `CreateOrderSaga` sends a `Reject-OrderCommand` to compensate for the consumer being rejected. The `CreateOrder-SagaTest` class has methods that test other failure scenarios.

Let's now look at how to test domain services.

9.2.4   *Writing unit tests for domain services*

The majority of a service's business logic is implemented by the entities, value objects, and sagas. Domain service classes, such as the `OrderService` class, implement the remainder. This class is a typical domain service class. Its methods invoke entities and repositories and publish domain events. An effective way to test this kind of class is to use a mostly solitary unit test, which mocks dependencies such as repositories and messaging classes.

Listing 9.5 shows the `OrderServiceTest` class, which tests `OrderService`. It defines solitary unit tests, which use Mockito mocks for the service's dependencies. Each test implements the test phases as follows:

1 *Setup*—Configures the mock objects for the service's dependencies
2 *Execute*—Invokes a service method
3 *Verify*—Verifies that the value returned by the service method is correct and that the dependencies have been invoked correctly

Listing 9.5   A simple, fast-running unit test for the `OrderService` class

```
public class OrderServiceTest {

  private OrderService orderService;
  private OrderRepository orderRepository;
  private DomainEventPublisher eventPublisher;
  private RestaurantRepository restaurantRepository;
  private SagaManager<CreateOrderSagaState> createOrderSagaManager;
  private SagaManager<CancelOrderSagaData> cancelOrderSagaManager;
  private SagaManager<ReviseOrderSagaData> reviseOrderSagaManager;

  @Before
  public void setup() {
    orderRepository = mock(OrderRepository.class);
    eventPublisher = mock(DomainEventPublisher.class);
    restaurantRepository = mock(RestaurantRepository.class);
```

→ **Create Mockito mocks for OrderService's dependencies.**

```
          createOrderSagaManager = mock(SagaManager.class);
          cancelOrderSagaManager = mock(SagaManager.class);
          reviseOrderSagaManager = mock(SagaManager.class);
          orderService = new OrderService(orderRepository, eventPublisher,    ⟵─┐
                  restaurantRepository, createOrderSagaManager,
                  cancelOrderSagaManager, reviseOrderSagaManager);
      }
```
Create an OrderService injected with mock dependencies.

```
      @Test
      public void shouldCreateOrder() {
        when(restaurantRepository                              ⟵
            .findById(AJANTA_ID)).thenReturn(Optional.of(AJANTA_RESTAURANT_));
        when(orderRepository.save(any(Order.class))).then(invocation -> {   ⟵
          Order order = (Order) invocation.getArguments()[0];
          order.setId(ORDER_ID);
          return order;
        });
```
Configure RestaurantRepository.findById() to return the Ajanta restaurant.

Configure OrderRepository.save() to set Order's ID.

Invoke OrderService .create().
```
      ┌─▷ Order order = orderService.createOrder(CONSUMER_ID,
      │             AJANTA_ID, CHICKEN_VINDALOO_MENU_ITEMS_AND_QUANTITIES);
```

```
          verify(orderRepository).save(same(order));              ⟵
```
Verify that OrderService saved the newly created Order in the database.

Verify that OrderService published an Order-CreatedEvent.
```
      ┌─▷ verify(eventPublisher).publish(Order.class, ORDER_ID,
      │             singletonList(
      │                 new OrderCreatedEvent(CHICKEN_VINDALOO_ORDER_DETAILS)));
```

```
          verify(createOrderSagaManager)                    ⟵
                  .create(new CreateOrderSagaState(ORDER_ID,
                      CHICKEN_VINDALOO_ORDER_DETAILS),
                  Order.class, ORDER_ID);
      }

    }
```
Verify that Order-Service created a CreateOrderSaga.

The `setUp()` method creates an `OrderService` injected with mock dependencies. The `@Test shouldCreateOrder()` method verifies that `OrderService.createOrder()` invokes `OrderRepository` to save the newly created `Order`, publishes an `OrderCreated-Event`, and creates a `CreateOrderSaga`.

Now that we've seen how to unit test the domain logic classes, let's look at how to unit test the adapters that interact with external systems.

9.2.5 *Developing unit tests for controllers*

Services, such as `Order Service`, typically have one or more controllers that handle HTTP requests from other services and the API gateway. A controller class consists of a set of request handler methods. Each method implements a REST API endpoint. A method's parameters represent values from the HTTP request, such as path variables. It typically invokes a domain service or a repository and returns a response object.

OrderController, for instance, invokes OrderService and OrderRepository. An effective testing strategy for controllers is solitary unit tests that mock the services and repositories.

You could write a test class similar to the OrderServiceTest class to instantiate a controller class and invoke its methods. But this approach doesn't test some important functionality, such as request routing. It's much more effective to use a mock MVC testing framework, such as Spring Mock Mvc, which is part of the Spring Framework, or Rest Assured Mock MVC, which builds on Spring Mock Mvc. Tests written using one of these frameworks make what appear to be HTTP requests and make assertions about HTTP responses. These frameworks enable you to test HTTP request routing and conversion of Java objects to and from JSON without having to make real network calls. Under the covers, Spring Mock Mvc instantiates just enough of the Spring MVC classes to make this possible.

Are these really unit tests?

Because these tests use the Spring Framework, you might argue that they're not unit tests. They're certainly more heavyweight than the unit tests I've described so far. The Spring Mock Mvc documentation refers to these as out-of-servlet-container integration tests (https://docs.spring.io/spring/docs/current/spring-framework-reference/testing.html#spring-mvc-test-vs-end-to-end-integration-tests). Yet Rest Assured Mock MVC describes these tests as unit tests (https://github.com/rest-assured/rest-assured/wiki/Usage#spring-mock-mvc-module). Regardless of the debate over terminology, these are important tests to write.

Listing 9.6 shows the OrderControllerTest class, which tests Order Service's Order-Controller. It defines solitary unit tests that use mocks for OrderController's dependencies. It's written using Rest Assured Mock MVC , which provides a simple DSL that abstracts away the details of interacting with controllers. Rest Assured makes it easy to send a mock HTTP request to a controller and verify the response. OrderController-Test creates a controller that's injected with Mockito mocks for OrderService and OrderRepository. Each test configures the mocks, makes an HTTP request, verifies that the response is correct, and possibly verifies that the controller invoked the mocks.

> **Listing 9.6   A simple, fast-running unit test for the OrderController class**

```
public class OrderControllerTest {

  private OrderService orderService;
  private OrderRepository orderRepository;

  @Before
  public void setUp() throws Exception {              Create mocks for
    orderService = mock(OrderService.class);     ◁── OrderController's
    orderRepository = mock(OrderRepository.class);     dependencies.
```

```
    orderController = new OrderController(orderService, orderRepository);
}


@Test
public void shouldFindOrder() {

    when(orderRepository.findById(1L))
        .thenReturn(Optional.of(CHICKEN_VINDALOO_ORDER_));    ◁─┘

    given().
        standaloneSetup(configureControllers(    ◁─
            new OrderController(orderService, orderRepository))).
    when().
        get("/orders/1").
    then().
        statusCode(200).    ◁─┘
        body("orderId",
            equalTo(new Long(OrderDetailsMother.ORDER_ID).intValue())).
        body("state",
            equalTo(OrderDetailsMother.CHICKEN_VINDALOO_ORDER_STATE.name())).
        body("orderTotal",
            equalTo(CHICKEN_VINDALOO_ORDER_TOTAL.asString()))
    ;
}


@Test
public void shouldFindNotOrder() { ... }

private StandaloneMockMvcBuilder controllers(Object... controllers) { ... }

}
```

Configure the mock OrderRepository to return an Order.

Configure OrderController.

Make an HTTP request.

Verify the response status code.

Verify elements of the JSON response body.

The shouldFindOrder() test method first configures the OrderRepository mock to return an Order. It then makes an HTTP request to retrieve the order. Finally, it checks that the request was successful and that the response body contains the expected data.

Controllers aren't the only adapters that handle requests from external systems. There are also event/message handlers, so let's talk about how to unit test those.

9.2.6 *Writing unit tests for event and message handlers*

Services often process messages sent by external systems. Order Service, for example, has OrderEventConsumer, which is a message adapter that handles domain events published by other services. Like controllers, message adapters tend to be simple classes that invoke domain services. Each of a message adapter's methods typically invokes a service method with data from the message or event.

We can unit test message adapters using an approach similar to the one we used for unit testing controllers. Each test instances the message adapter, sends a message to a channel, and verifies that the service mock was invoked correctly. Behind the scenes, though, the messaging infrastructure is stubbed, so no message broker is involved. Let's look at how to test the `OrderEventConsumer` class.

Listing 9.7 shows part of the `OrderEventConsumerTest` class, which tests `Order-EventConsumer`. It verifies that `OrderEventConsumer` routes each event to the appropriate handler method and correctly invokes `OrderService`. The test uses the Eventuate Tram Mock Messaging framework, which provides an easy-to-use DSL for writing mock messaging tests that uses the same given-when-then format as Rest Assured. Each test instantiates `OrderEventConsumer` injected with a mock `Order-Service`, publishes a domain event, and verifies that `OrderEventConsumer` correctly invokes the service mock.

Listing 9.7   A fast-running unit test for the `OrderEventConsumer` class

```
public class OrderEventConsumerTest {

  private OrderService orderService;
  private OrderEventConsumer orderEventConsumer;

  @Before                                                        ┐ Instantiate
  public void setUp() throws Exception {                         │ OrderEventConsumer with
    orderService = mock(OrderService.class);                     │ mocked dependencies.
    orderEventConsumer = new OrderEventConsumer(orderService);  ◄─┘
  }

  @Test                                                                  ┐ Configure
  public void shouldCreateMenu() {                                       │ OrderEventConsumer
                                                                         │ domain handlers.
    given().
            eventHandlers(orderEventConsumer.domainEventHandlers()).  ◄──┘
    when().
      aggregate("net.chrisrichardson.ftgo.restaurantservice.domain.Restaurant",
            AJANTA_ID).
      publishes(new RestaurantCreated(AJANTA_RESTAURANT_NAME,
                        RestaurantMother.AJANTA_RESTAURANT_MENU))
    then().
      verify(() -> {                          ◄─┐ Verify that OrderEventConsumer
        verify(orderService)                    │ invoked OrderService.createMenu().
              .createMenu(AJANTA_ID,
            new RestaurantMenu(RestaurantMother.AJANTA_RESTAURANT_MENU_ITEMS));
      })
    ;
  }

}
```

Publish a Restaurant-Created event points to the `publishes(new RestaurantCreated(...))` line.

The `setUp()` method creates an `OrderEventConsumer` injected with a mock `Order-Service`. The `shouldCreateMenu()` method publishes a `RestaurantCreated` event and verifies that `OrderEventConsumer` invoked `OrderService.createMenu()`. The `OrderEventConsumerTest` class and the other unit test classes execute extremely quickly. The unit tests run in just a few seconds.

But the unit tests don't verify that a service, such as `Order Service`, properly interacts with other services. For example, the unit tests don't verify that an `Order` can be persisted in MySQL. Nor do they verify that `CreateOrderSaga` sends command messages in the right format to the right message channel. And they don't verify that the `RestaurantCreated` event processed by `OrderEventConsumer` has the same structure as the event published by `Restaurant Service`. In order to verify that a service properly interacts with other services, we must write integration tests. We also need to write component tests that test an entire service in isolation. The next chapter discusses how to conduct those types of tests, as well as end-to-end tests.

Summary

- Automated testing is the key foundation of rapid, safe delivery of software. What's more, because of its inherent complexity, to fully benefit from the microservice architecture you *must* automate your tests.

- The purpose of a test is to verify the behavior of the system under test (SUT). In this definition, *system* is a fancy term that means the software element being tested. It might be something as small as a class, as large as the entire application, or something in between, such as a cluster of classes or an individual service. A collection of related tests form a test suite.

- A good way to simplify and speed up a test is to use test doubles. A test double is an object that simulates the behavior of a SUT's dependency. There are two types of test doubles: stubs and mocks. A stub is a test double that returns values to the SUT. A mock is a test double that a test uses to verify that the SUT correctly invokes a dependency.

- Use the test pyramid to determine where to focus your testing efforts for your services. The majority of your tests should be fast, reliable, and easy-to-write unit tests. You must minimize the number of end-to-end tests, because they're slow, brittle, and time consuming to write.

Testing microservices: Part 2

This chapter builds on the previous chapter, which introduced testing concepts, including the test pyramid. The *test pyramid* describes the relative proportions of the different types of tests that you should write. The previous chapter described how to write unit tests, which are at the base of the testing pyramid. In this chapter, we continue our ascent of the testing pyramid.

This chapter begins with how to write integration tests, which are the level above unit tests in the testing pyramid. *Integration tests* verify that a service can properly interact with infrastructure services, such as databases, and other application services. Next, I cover *component tests*, which are acceptance tests for services. A component test tests a service in isolation by using stubs for its dependencies. After that, I describe how to write end-to-end tests, which test a group of services or the entire application. End-to-end tests are at the top of the test pyramid and should, therefore, be used sparingly.

Let's start by taking a look at how to write integration tests.

10.1 *Writing integration tests*

Services typically interact with other services. For example, Order Service, as figure 10.1 shows, interacts with several services. Its REST API is consumed by API Gateway, and its domain events are consumed by services, including Order History Service. Order Service uses several other services. It persists Orders in MySQL. It also sends commands to and consumes replies from several other services, such as Kitchen Service.

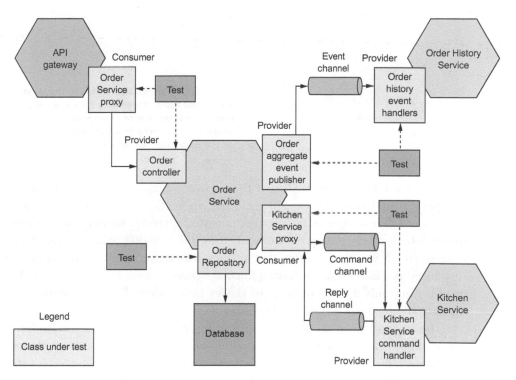

Figure 10.1 Integration tests must verify that a service can communicate with its clients and dependencies. But rather than testing whole services, the strategy is to test the individual adapter classes that implement the communication.

In order to be confident that a service such as Order Service works as expected, we must write tests that verify that the service can properly interact with infrastructure services and other application services. One approach is to launch all the services and test them through their APIs. This, however, is what's known as end-to-end testing, which is slow, brittle, and costly. As explained in section 10.3, there's a role for end-to-end testing sometimes, but it's at the top of the test pyramid, so you want to minimize the number of end-to-end tests.

A much more effective strategy is to write what are known as integration tests. As figure 10.2 shows, integration tests are the layer above unit tests in the testing pyramid. They verify that a service can properly interact with infrastructure services and other services. But unlike end-to-end tests, they don't launch services. Instead, we use a couple of strategies that significantly simplify the tests without impacting their effectiveness.

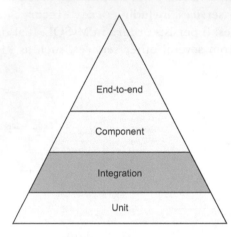

Figure 10.2   Integration tests are the layer above unit tests. They verify that a service can communicate with its dependencies, which includes infrastructure services, such as the database, and application services.

The first strategy is to test each of the service's adapters, along with, perhaps, the adapter's supporting classes. For example, in section 10.1.1 you'll see a JPA persistence test that verifies that Orders are persisted correctly. Rather than test persistence through Order Service's API, it directly tests the OrderRepository class. Similarly, in section 10.1.3 you'll see a test that verifies that Order Service publishes correctly structured domain events by testing the OrderDomainEventPublisher class. The benefit of testing only a small number of classes rather than the entire service is that the tests are significantly simpler and faster.

The second strategy for simplifying integration tests that verify interactions between application services is to use contracts, discussed in chapter 9. A *contract* is a concrete example of an interaction between a pair of services. As table 10.1 shows, the structure of a contract depends on the type of interaction between the services.

Table 10.1   The structure of a contract depends on the type of interaction between the services.

Interaction style	Consumer	Provider	Contract
REST-based, request/response	API Gateway	Order Service	HTTP request and response
Publish/subscribe	Order History Service	Order Service	Domain event
Asynchronous request/response	Order Service	Kitchen Service	Command message and reply message

A contract consists of either one message, in the case of publish/subscribe style interactions, or two messages, in the case of request/response and asynchronous request/response style interactions.

The contracts are used to test both the consumer and the provider, which ensures that they agree on the API. They're used in slightly different ways depending on whether you're testing the consumer or the provider:

- *Consumer-side tests*—These are tests for the consumer's adapter. They use the contracts to configure stubs that simulate the provider, enabling you to write integration tests for a consumer that don't require a running provider.
- *Provider-side tests*—These are tests for the provider's adapter. They use the contracts to test the adapters using mocks for the adapters's dependencies.

Later in this section, I describe examples of these types of tests—but first let's look at how to write persistence tests.

10.1.1 Persistence integration tests

Services typically store data in a database. For instance, `Order Service` persists aggregates, such as `Order`, in MySQL using JPA. Similarly, `Order History Service` maintains a CQRS view in AWS DynamoDB. The unit tests we wrote earlier only test in-memory objects. In order to be confident that a service works correctly, we must write persistence integration tests, which verify that a service's database access logic works as expected. In the case of `Order Service`, this means testing the JPA repositories, such as `OrderRepository`.

Each phase of a persistence integration test behaves as follows:

- *Setup*—Set up the database by creating the database schema and initializing it to a known state. It might also begin a database transaction.
- *Execute*—Perform a database operation.
- *Verify*—Make assertions about the state of the database and objects retrieved from the database.
- *Teardown*—An optional phase that might undo the changes made to the database by, for example, rolling back the transaction that was started by the setup phase.

Listing 10.1 shows a persistent integration test for the `Order` aggregate and `Order-Repository`. Apart from relying on JPA to create the database schema, the persistence integration tests don't make any assumption about the state of the database. Consequently, tests don't need to roll back the changes they make to the database, which avoids problems with the ORM caching data changes in memory.

> **Listing 10.1 An integration test that verifies that an `Order` can be persisted**

```
@RunWith(SpringRunner.class)
@SpringBootTest(classes = OrderJpaTestConfiguration.class)
public class OrderJpaTest {
```

```
@Autowired
private OrderRepository orderRepository;

@Autowired
private TransactionTemplate transactionTemplate;

@Test
public void shouldSaveAndLoadOrder() {

  Long orderId = transactionTemplate.execute((ts) -> {
    Order order =
            new Order(CONSUMER_ID, AJANTA_ID, CHICKEN_VINDALOO_LINE_ITEMS);
    orderRepository.save(order);
    return order.getId();
  });

  transactionTemplate.execute((ts) -> {
    Order order = orderRepository.findById(orderId).get();

    assertEquals(OrderState.APPROVAL_PENDING, order.getState());
    assertEquals(AJANTA_ID, order.getRestaurantId());
    assertEquals(CONSUMER_ID, order.getConsumerId().longValue());
    assertEquals(CHICKEN_VINDALOO_LINE_ITEMS, order.getLineItems());
    return null;
  });

}

}
```

The `shouldSaveAndLoadOrder()` test method executes two transactions. The first saves a newly created `Order` in the database. The second transaction loads the `Order` and verifies that its fields are properly initialized.

One problem you need to solve is how to provision the database that's used in persistence integration tests. An effective solution to run an instance of the database during testing is to use Docker. Section 10.2 describes how to use the Docker Compose Gradle plugin to automatically run services during component testing. You can use a similar approach to run MySQL, for example, during persistence integration testing.

The database is only one of the external services a service interacts with. Let's now look at how to write integration tests for interservice communication between application services, starting with REST.

10.1.2 *Integration testing REST-based request/response style interactions*

REST is a widely used interservice communication mechanism. The REST client and REST service must agree on the REST API, which includes the REST endpoints and the structure of the request and response bodies. The client must send an HTTP request to the correct endpoint, and the service must send back the response that the client expects.

For example, chapter 8 describes how the FTGO application's `API Gateway` makes REST API calls to numerous services, including `ConsumerService`, `Order Service`, and `Delivery Service`. The `OrderService`'s `GET /orders/{orderId}` endpoint is one of the endpoints invoked by the `API Gateway`. In order to be confident that `API Gateway` and `Order Service` can communicate without using an end-to-end test, we need to write integration tests.

As stated in the preceding chapter, a good integration testing strategy is to use consumer-driven contract tests. The interaction between `API Gateway` and `GET /orders/{orderId}` can be described using a set of HTTP-based contracts. Each contract consists of an HTTP request and an HTTP reply. The contracts are used to test `API Gateway` and `Order Service`.

Figure 10.3 shows how to use Spring Cloud Contract to test REST-based interactions. The consumer-side `API Gateway` integration tests use the contracts to configure an HTTP stub server that simulates the behavior of `Order Service`. A contract's request specifies an HTTP request from the API gateway, and the contract's response specifies the response that the stub sends back to the API gateway. Spring Cloud Contract uses the contracts to code-generate the provider-side `Order Service` integration tests, which test the controllers using Spring Mock MVC or Rest Assured Mock MVC. The contract's request specifies the HTTP request to make to the controller, and the contract's response specifies the controller's expected response.

The consumer-side `OrderServiceProxyTest` invokes `OrderServiceProxy`, which has been configured to make HTTP requests to WireMock. WireMock is a tool for efficiently mocking HTTP servers—in this test it simulates `Order Service`. Spring Cloud

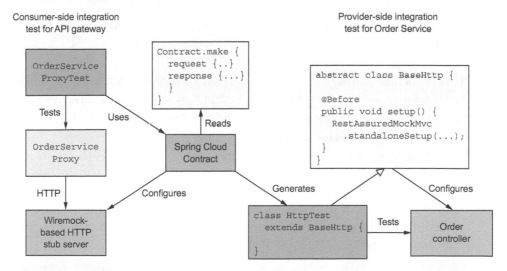

Figure 10.3   The contracts are used to verify that the adapter classes on both sides of the REST-based communication between `API Gateway` and `Order Service` conform to the contract. The consumer-side tests verify that `OrderServiceProxy` invokes `Order Service` correctly. The provider-side tests verify that `OrderController` implements the REST API endpoints correctly.

Contract manages WireMock and configures it to respond to the HTTP requests defined by the contracts.

On the provider side, Spring Cloud Contract generates a test class called `HttpTest`, which uses Rest Assured Mock MVC to test `Order Service`'s controllers. Test classes such as `HttpTest` must extend a handwritten base class. In this example, the base class `BaseHttp` instantiates `OrderController` injected with mock dependencies and calls `RestAssuredMockMvc.standaloneSetup()` to configure Spring MVC.

Let's take a closer look at how this works, starting with an example contract.

AN EXAMPLE CONTRACT FOR A REST API

A REST contract, such as the one shown in listing 10.2, specifies an HTTP request, which is sent by the REST client, and the HTTP response, which the client expects to get back from the REST server. A contract's request specifies the HTTP method, the path, and optional headers. A contract's response specifies the HTTP status code, optional headers, and, when appropriate, the expected body.

> **Listing 10.2   A contract that describes an HTTP-based request/response style interaction**

```
org.springframework.cloud.contract.spec.Contract.make {
    request {
        method 'GET'
        url '/orders/1223232'
    }
    response {
        status 200
        headers {
            header('Content-Type': 'application/json;charset=UTF-8')
        }
        body('''{"orderId" : "1223232", "state" : "APPROVAL_PENDING"}''')
    }
}
```

This particular contract describes a successful attempt by `API Gateway` to retrieve an `Order` from `Order Service`. Let's now look at how to use this contract to write integration tests, starting with the tests for `Order Service`.

CONSUMER-DRIVEN CONTRACT INTEGRATION TESTS FOR ORDER SERVICE

The consumer-driven contract integration tests for `Order Service` verify that its API meets its clients' expectations. Listing 10.3 shows `HttpBase`, which is the base class for the test class code-generated by Spring Cloud Contract. It's responsible for the setup phase of the test. It creates the controllers injected with mock dependencies and configures those mocks to return values that cause the controller to generate the expected response.

> **Listing 10.3   The abstract base class for the tests code-generated by Spring Cloud Contract**

```
public abstract class HttpBase {

  private StandaloneMockMvcBuilder controllers(Object... controllers) {

    ...
```

```
        return MockMvcBuilders.standaloneSetup(controllers)
                    .setMessageConverters(...);
    }
```

Create OrderRepository injected with mocks.

```
    @Before
    public void setup() {
      OrderService orderService = mock(OrderService.class);        ⟵
       OrderRepository orderRepository = mock(OrderRepository.class);
      OrderController orderController =
              new OrderController(orderService, orderRepository);

      when(orderRepository.findById(1223232L))                    ⟵
              .thenReturn(Optional.of(OrderDetailsMother.CHICKEN_VINDALOO_ORDER));
      ...
      RestAssuredMockMvc.standaloneSetup(controllers(orderController));  ⟵

    }                                             **Configure Spring MVC with**
}                                                     **OrderController.**
```

Configure OrderResponse to return an Order when findById() is invoked with the orderId specified in the contract.

The argument `1223232L` that's passed to the mock `OrderRepository`'s `findById()` method matches the `orderId` specified in the contract shown in listing 10.3. This test verifies that `Order Service` has a `GET /orders/{orderId}` endpoint that matches its client's expectations.

Let's take a look at the corresponding client test.

CONSUMER-SIDE INTEGRATION TEST FOR API GATEWAY'S ORDERSERVICEPROXY

API Gateway's `OrderServiceProxy` invokes the `GET /orders/{orderId}` endpoint. Listing 10.4 shows the `OrderServiceProxyIntegrationTest` test class, which verifies that it conforms to the contracts. This class is annotated with `@AutoConfigureStubRunner`, provided by Spring Cloud Contract. It tells Spring Cloud Contract to run the Wire-Mock server on a random port and configure it using the specified contracts. `Order-ServiceProxyIntegrationTest` configures `OrderServiceProxy` to make requests to the WireMock port.

> **Listing 10.4 A consumer-side integration test for `API Gateway`'s `OrderServiceProxy`**

Obtain the randomly assigned port that WireMock is running on.

Tell Spring Cloud Contract to configure WireMock with Order Service's contracts.

```
@RunWith(SpringRunner.class)
@SpringBootTest(classes=TestConfiguration.class,
        webEnvironment= SpringBootTest.WebEnvironment.NONE)
@AutoConfigureStubRunner(ids =                                    ⟵
        {"net.chrisrichardson.ftgo.contracts:ftgo-order-service-contracts"},
        workOffline = false)
@DirtiesContext
public class OrderServiceProxyIntegrationTest {

  @Value("${stubrunner.runningstubs.ftgo-order-service-contracts.port}")
```

```
    private int port;
    private OrderDestinations orderDestinations;
    private OrderServiceProxy orderService;

    @Before
    public void setUp() throws Exception {
      orderDestinations = new OrderDestinations();
      String orderServiceUrl = "http://localhost:" + port;
      orderDestinations.setOrderServiceUrl(orderServiceUrl);
      orderService = new OrderServiceProxy(orderDestinations,
                                     WebClient.create());
    }

    @Test
    public void shouldVerifyExistingCustomer() {
      OrderInfo result = orderService.findOrderById("1223232").block();
      assertEquals("1223232", result.getOrderId());
      assertEquals("APPROVAL_PENDING", result.getState());
    }

    @Test(expected = OrderNotFoundException.class)
    public void shouldFailToFindMissingOrder() {
      orderService.findOrderById("555").block();
    }

}
```

Create an OrderServiceProxy configured to make requests to WireMock.

Each test method invokes `OrderServiceProxy` and verifies that either it returns the correct values or throws the expected exception. The `shouldVerifyExisting-Customer()` test method verifies that `findOrderById()` returns values equal to those specified in the contract's response. The `shouldFailToFindMissingOrder()` attempts to retrieve a nonexistent `Order` and verifies that `OrderServiceProxy` throws an `Order-NotFoundException`. Testing both the REST client and the REST service using the same contracts ensures that they agree on the API.

Let's now look at how to do the same kind of testing for services that interact using messaging.

10.1.3 *Integration testing publish/subscribe-style interactions*

Services often publish domain events that are consumed by one or more other services. Integration testing must verify that the publisher and its consumers agree on the message channel and the structure of the domain events. `Order Service`, for example, publishes `Order*` events whenever it creates or updates an `Order` aggregate. `Order History Service` is one of the consumers of those events. We must, therefore, write tests that verify that these services can interact.

Figure 10.4 shows the approach to integration testing publish/subscribe interactions. Its quite similar to the approach used for testing REST interactions. As before, the interactions are defined by a set of contracts. What's different is that each contract specifies a domain event.

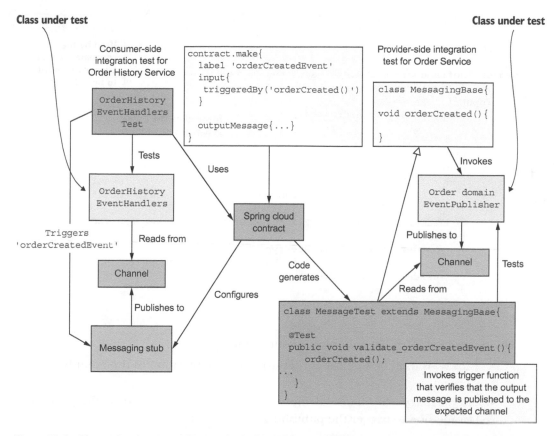

Figure 10.4 The contracts are used to test both sides of the publish/subscribe interaction. The provider-side tests verify that `OrderDomainEventPublisher` publishes events that confirm to the contract. The consumer-side tests verify that `OrderHistoryEventHandlers` consume the example events from the contract.

Each consumer-side test publishes the event specified by the contract and verifies that `OrderHistoryEventHandlers` invokes its mocked dependencies correctly.

On the provider side, Spring Cloud Contract code-generates test classes that extend `MessagingBase`, which is a hand-written abstract superclass. Each test method invokes a hook method defined by `MessagingBase`, which is expected to trigger the publication of an event by the service. In this example, each hook method invokes `OrderDomainEventPublisher`, which is responsible for publishing `Order` aggregate events. The test method then verifies that `OrderDomainEventPublisher` published the expected event. Let's look at the details of how these tests work, starting with the contract.

THE CONTRACT FOR PUBLISHING AN ORDERCREATED EVENT

Listing 10.5 shows the contract for an `OrderCreated` event. It specifies the event's channel, along with the expected body and message headers.

Listing 10.5   A contract for a publish/subscribe interaction style

```
package contracts;                                            Used by the
                                                              consumer test to
org.springframework.cloud.contract.spec.Contract.make {      trigger the event
    label 'orderCreatedEvent'                            ◄    to be published
    input {
        triggeredBy('orderCreated()')        ◄    Invoked by the code-
    }                                             generated provider test

    outputMessage {
        sentTo('net.chrisrichardson.ftgo.orderservice.domain.Order')
        body('''{"orderDetails":{"lineItems":[{"quantity":5,"menuItemId":"1",
                "name":"Chicken Vindaloo","price":"12.34","total":"61.70"}],
                "orderTotal":"61.70","restaurantId":1,
        "consumerId":1511300065921},"orderState":"APPROVAL_PENDING"}''')
        headers {
            header('event-aggregate-type',
                        'net.chrisrichardson.ftgo.orderservice.domain.Order')
            header('event-aggregate-id', '1')
        }
    }
}
```

An Order-Created domain event *(annotation pointing to the outputMessage block)*

The contract also has two other important elements:

- label—is used by a consumer test to trigger publication of the event by Spring Contact
- triggeredBy—the name of the superclass method invoked by the generated test method to trigger the publishing of the event

Let's look at how the contract is used, starting with the provider-side test for Order-Service.

CONSUMER-DRIVEN CONTRACT TESTS FOR ORDER SERVICE

The provider-side test for Order Service is another consumer-driven contract integration test. It verifies that OrderDomainEventPublisher, which is responsible for publishing Order aggregate domain events, publishes events that match its clients' expectations. Listing 10.6 shows MessagingBase, which is the base class for the test classes code-generated by Spring Cloud Contract. It's responsible for configuring the OrderDomainEventPublisher class to use in-memory messaging stubs. It also defines the methods, such as orderCreated(), which are invoked by the generated tests to trigger the publishing of the event.

Listing 10.6   The abstract base class for the Spring Cloud Contract provider-side tests

```
@RunWith(SpringRunner.class)
@SpringBootTest(classes = MessagingBase.TestConfiguration.class,
                webEnvironment = SpringBootTest.WebEnvironment.NONE)
@AutoConfigureMessageVerifier
public abstract class MessagingBase {
```

```
@Configuration
@EnableAutoConfiguration
@Import({EventuateContractVerifierConfiguration.class,
        TramEventsPublisherConfiguration.class,
        TramInMemoryConfiguration.class})
public static class TestConfiguration {

  @Bean
  public OrderDomainEventPublisher
        OrderDomainEventPublisher(DomainEventPublisher eventPublisher) {
    return new OrderDomainEventPublisher(eventPublisher);
  }
}
```

> orderCreated() is invoked by a
> code-generated test subclass
> to publish the event.

```
  @Autowired
  private OrderDomainEventPublisher OrderDomainEventPublisher;

  protected void orderCreated() {                              ◄─────
    OrderDomainEventPublisher.publish(CHICKEN_VINDALOO_ORDER,
        singletonList(new OrderCreatedEvent(CHICKEN_VINDALOO_ORDER_DETAILS)
    ));
  }

}
```

This test class configures OrderDomainEventPublisher with in-memory messaging stubs. orderCreated() is invoked by the test method generated from the contract shown earlier in listing 10.5. It invokes OrderDomainEventPublisher to publish an OrderCreated event. The test method attempts to receive this event and then verifies that it matches the event specified in the contract. Let's now look at the corresponding consumer-side tests.

CONSUMER-SIDE CONTRACT TEST FOR THE ORDER HISTORY SERVICE

Order History Service consumes events published by Order Service. As I described in chapter 7, the adapter class that handles these events is the OrderHistoryEvent-Handlers class. Its event handlers invoke OrderHistoryDao to update the CQRS view. Listing 10.7 shows the consumer-side integration test. It creates an OrderHistoryEvent-Handlers injected with a mock OrderHistoryDao. Each test method first invokes Spring Cloud to publish the event defined in the contract and then verifies that OrderHistory-EventHandlers invokes OrderHistoryDao correctly.

> **Listing 10.7 The consumer-side integration test for the** OrderHistoryEventHandlers **class**

```
@RunWith(SpringRunner.class)
@SpringBootTest(classes= OrderHistoryEventHandlersTest.TestConfiguration.class,
        webEnvironment= SpringBootTest.WebEnvironment.NONE)
@AutoConfigureStubRunner(ids =
        {"net.chrisrichardson.ftgo.contracts:ftgo-order-service-contracts"},
        workOffline = false)
```

```
@DirtiesContext
public class OrderHistoryEventHandlersTest {

  @Configuration
  @EnableAutoConfiguration
  @Import({OrderHistoryServiceMessagingConfiguration.class,
          TramCommandProducerConfiguration.class,
          TramInMemoryConfiguration.class,
          EventuateContractVerifierConfiguration.class})
  public static class TestConfiguration {

    @Bean
    public OrderHistoryDao orderHistoryDao() {
      return mock(OrderHistoryDao.class);        ◁——
    }
  }

  @Test
  public void shouldHandleOrderCreatedEvent() throws ... {
    stubFinder.trigger("orderCreatedEvent");     ◁——
    eventually(() -> {
      verify(orderHistoryDao).addOrder(any(Order.class), any(Optional.class));
    });
  }
}
```

Create a mock OrderHistoryDao to inject into OrderHistory-EventHandlers.

Trigger the orderCreatedEvent stub, which emits an OrderCreated event.

Verify that OrderHistoryEventHandlers invoked orderHistoryDao.addOrder().

The shouldHandleOrderCreatedEvent() test method tells Spring Cloud Contract to publish the OrderCreated event. It then verifies that OrderHistoryEventHandlers invoked orderHistoryDao.addOrder(). Testing both the domain event's publisher and consumer using the same contracts ensures that they agree on the API. Let's now look at how to do integration test services that interact using asynchronous request/response.

10.1.4 Integration contract tests for asynchronous request/response interactions

Publish/subscribe isn't the only kind of messaging-based interaction style. Services also interact using asynchronous request/response. For example, in chapter 4 we saw that Order Service implements sagas that send command messages to various services, such as Kitchen Service, and processes the reply messages.

The two parties in an asynchronous request/response interaction are the requestor, which is the service that sends the command, and the replier, which is the service that processes the command and sends back a reply. They must agree on the name of command message channel and the structure of the command and reply messages. Let's look at how to write integration tests for asynchronous request/response interactions.

Figure 10.5 shows how to test the interaction between Order Service and Kitchen Service. The approach to integration testing asynchronous request/response interactions is quite similar to the approach used for testing REST interactions. The interactions between the services are defined by a set of contracts. What's different is that a contract specifies an input message and an output message instead of an HTTP request and reply.

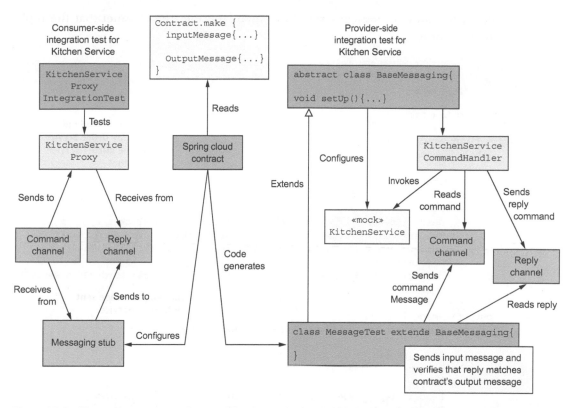

Figure 10.5 The contracts are used to test the adapter classes that implement each side of the asynchronous request/response interaction. The provider-side tests verify that `KitchenServiceCommandHandler` handles commands and sends back replies. The consumer-side tests verify `KitchenServiceProxy` sends commands that conform to the contract, and that it handles the example replies from the contract.

The consumer-side test verifies that the command message proxy class sends correctly structured command messages and correctly processes reply messages. In this example, `KitchenServiceProxyTest` tests `KitchenServiceProxy`. It uses Spring Cloud Contract to configure messaging stubs that verify that the command message matches a contract's input message and replies with the corresponding output message.

The provider-side tests are code-generated by Spring Cloud Contract. Each test method corresponds to a contract. It sends the contract's input message as a command message and verifies that the reply message matches the contract's output message. Let's look at the details, starting with the contract.

EXAMPLE ASYNCHRONOUS REQUEST/RESPONSE CONTRACT

Listing 10.8 shows the contract for one interaction. It consists of an input message and an output message. Both messages specify a message channel, message body, and message headers. The naming convention is from the provider's perspective. The input message's `messageFrom` element specifies the channel that the message is read from.

Similarly, the output message's `sentTo` element specifies the channel that the reply should be sent to.

Listing 10.8   Contract describing how `Order Service` asynchronously invokes `Kitchen Service`

```
package contracts;

org.springframework.cloud.contract.spec.Contract.make {
    label 'createTicket'
    input {
        messageFrom('kitchenService')
        messageBody('''{"orderId":1,"restaurantId":1,"ticketDetails":{...}}''')
        messageHeaders {
            header('command_type','net.chrisrichardson...CreateTicket')
            header('command_saga_type','net.chrisrichardson...CreateOrderSaga')
            header('command_saga_id',$(consumer(regex('[0-9a-f]{16}-[0-9a-f]
                {16}'))))
            header('command_reply_to','net.chrisrichardson...CreateOrderSaga-Reply')
        }
    }
    outputMessage {
        sentTo('net.chrisrichardson...CreateOrderSaga-reply')
        body([
                ticketId: 1
        ])
        headers {
            header('reply_type', 'net.chrisrichardson...CreateTicketReply')
            header('reply_outcome-type', 'SUCCESS')
        }
    }
}
```

> The command message sent by Order Service to the kitchenService channel

> The reply message sent by Kitchen Service

In this example contract, the input message is a `CreateTicket` command that's sent to the `kitchenService` channel. The output message is a successful reply that's sent to the `CreateOrderSaga`'s reply channel. Let's look at how to use this contract in tests, starting with the consumer-side tests for `Order Service`.

CONSUMER-SIDE CONTRACT INTEGRATION TEST FOR AN ASYNCHRONOUS REQUEST/RESPONSE INTERACTION

The strategy for writing a consumer-side integration test for an asynchronous request/response interaction is similar to testing a REST client. The test invokes the service's messaging proxy and verifies two aspects of its behavior. First, it verifies that the messaging proxy sends a command message that conforms to the contract. Second, it verifies that the proxy properly handles the reply message.

Listing 10.9 shows the consumer-side integration test for `KitchenServiceProxy`, which is the messaging proxy used by `Order Service` to invoke `Kitchen Service`. Each test sends a command message using `KitchenServiceProxy` and verifies that it returns the expected result. It uses Spring Cloud Contract to configure messaging stubs for

Kitchen Service that find the contract whose input message matches the command message and sends its output message as the reply. The tests use in-memory messaging for simplicity and speed.

Listing 10.9 The consumer-side contract integration test for Order Service

```
@RunWith(SpringRunner.class)
@SpringBootTest(classes=
    KitchenServiceProxyIntegrationTest.TestConfiguration.class,
       webEnvironment= SpringBootTest.WebEnvironment.NONE)
@AutoConfigureStubRunner(ids =
       {"net.chrisrichardson.ftgo.contracts:ftgo-kitchen-service-contracts"},
       workOffline = false)
@DirtiesContext
public class KitchenServiceProxyIntegrationTest {
```

Configure the stub
Kitchen Service to
respond to messages.

```
  @Configuration
  @EnableAutoConfiguration
  @Import({TramCommandProducerConfiguration.class,
         TramInMemoryConfiguration.class,
           EventuateContractVerifierConfiguration.class})
  public static class TestConfiguration { ... }

  @Autowired
  private SagaMessagingTestHelper sagaMessagingTestHelper;

  @Autowired
  private  KitchenServiceProxy kitchenServiceProxy;

  @Test
  public void shouldSuccessfullyCreateTicket() {
    CreateTicket command = new CreateTicket(AJANTA_ID,
         OrderDetailsMother.ORDER_ID,
      new TicketDetails(Collections.singletonList(
        new TicketLineItem(CHICKEN_VINDALOO_MENU_ITEM_ID,
                         CHICKEN_VINDALOO,
                         CHICKEN_VINDALOO_QUANTITY))));
```

Send the
command and
wait for a reply.

```
    String sagaType = CreateOrderSaga.class.getName();

    CreateTicketReply reply =
       sagaMessagingTestHelper
            .sendAndReceiveCommand(kitchenServiceProxy.create,
                             command,
                             CreateTicketReply.class, sagaType);
```

Verify the
reply.

```
    assertEquals(new CreateTicketReply(OrderDetailsMother.ORDER_ID), reply);

  }

}
```

The `shouldSuccessfullyCreateTicket()` test method sends a `CreateTicket` com-mand message and verifies that the reply contains the expected data. It uses `Saga-MessagingTestHelper`, which is a test helper class that synchronously sends and receives messages.

Let's now look at how to write provider-side integration tests.

WRITING PROVIDER-SIDE, CONSUMER-DRIVEN CONTRACT TESTS FOR ASYNCHRONOUS REQUEST/RESPONSE INTERACTIONS

A provider-side integration test must verify that the provider handles a command mes-sage by sending the correct reply. Spring Cloud Contract generates test classes that have a test method for each contract. Each test method sends the contract's input message and verifies that the reply matches the contract's output message.

The provider-side integration tests for Kitchen Service test `KitchenService-CommandHandler`. The `KitchenServiceCommandHandler` class handles a message by invoking `KitchenService`. The following listing shows the `AbstractKitchenService-ConsumerContractTest` class, which is the base class for the Spring Cloud Contract-generated tests. It creates a `KitchenServiceCommandHandler` injected with a mock `KitchenService`.

> Listing 10.10   **Superclass of provider-side, consumer-driven contract tests for** `Kitchen Service`

```
@RunWith(SpringRunner.class)
@SpringBootTest(classes =
    AbstractKitchenServiceConsumerContractTest.TestConfiguration.class,
             webEnvironment = SpringBootTest.WebEnvironment.NONE)
@AutoConfigureMessageVerifier
public abstract class AbstractKitchenServiceConsumerContractTest {

  @Configuration
  @Import(RestaurantMessageHandlersConfiguration.class)
  public static class TestConfiguration {
    ...
    @Bean
    public KitchenService kitchenService() {          ◁── Overrides the definition
      return mock(KitchenService.class);                  of the kitchenService
    }                                                      @Bean with a mock
  }

  @Autowired
  private KitchenService kitchenService;

  @Before
  public void setup() {
    reset(kitchenService);                             Configures the mock to
    when(kitchenService                                return the values that match
        .createTicket(eq(1L), eq(1L),     ◁──────────  a contract's output message
                      any(TicketDetails.class)))
        .thenReturn(new Ticket(1L, 1L,
```

```
                           new TicketDetails(Collections.emptyList())));
   }

}
```

`KitchenServiceCommandHandler` invokes `KitchenService` with arguments that are derived from a contract's input message and creates a reply message that's derived from the return value. The test class's `setup()` method configures the mock `Kitchen-Service` to return the values that match the contract's output message

Integration tests and unit tests verify the behavior of individual parts of a service. The integration tests verify that services can communicate with their clients and dependencies. The unit tests verify that a service's logic is correct. Neither type of test runs the entire service. In order to verify that a service as a whole works, we'll move up the pyramid and look at how to write component tests.

10.2 *Developing component tests*

So far, we've looked at how to test individual classes and clusters of classes. But imagine that we now want to verify that `Order Service` works as expected. In other words, we want to write the service's acceptance tests, which treat it as a black box and verify its behavior through its API. One approach is to write what are essentially end-to-end tests and deploy `Order Service` and all of its transitive dependencies. As you should know by now, that's a slow, brittle, and expensive way to test a service.

> **Pattern: Service component test**
>
> Test a service in isolation. See http://microservices.io/patterns/testing/service-component-test.html.

A much better way to write acceptance tests for a service is to use component testing. As figure 10.6 shows, *component tests* are sandwiched between integration tests and end-to-end tests. Component testing verifies the behavior of a service in isolation. It replaces a service's dependencies with stubs that simulate their behavior. It might even use in-memory versions of infrastructure services such as databases. As a result, component tests are much easier to write and faster to run.

I begin by briefly describing how to use a testing DSL called Gherkin to write acceptance tests for services, such as `Order Service`. After that I discuss various component testing design issues. I then show how to write acceptance tests for `Order Service`.

Let's look at writing acceptance tests using Gherkin.

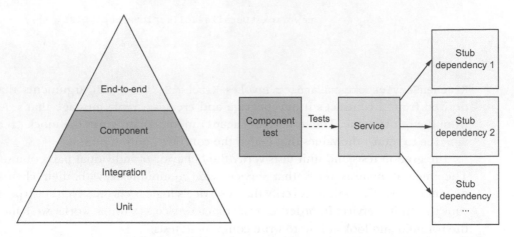

Figure 10.6 A component test tests a service in isolation. It typically uses stubs for the service's dependencies.

10.2.1 *Defining acceptance tests*

Acceptance tests are business-facing tests for a software component. They describe the desired externally visible behavior from the perspective of the component's clients rather than in terms of the internal implementation. These tests are derived from user stories or use cases. For example, one of the key stories for `Order Service` is the `Place Order` story:

```
As a consumer of the Order Service
I should be able to place an order
```

We can expand this story into scenarios such as the following:

```
Given a valid consumer
Given using a valid credit card
Given the restaurant is accepting orders
When I place an order for Chicken Vindaloo at Ajanta
Then the order should be APPROVED
And an OrderAuthorized event should be published
```

This scenario describes the desired behavior of `Order Service` in terms of its API.

Each scenario defines an acceptance test. The *givens* correspond to the test's setup phase, the *when* maps to the execute phase, and the *then* and the *and* to the verification phase. Later, you see a test for this scenario that does the following:

1 Creates an `Order` by invoking the `POST /orders` endpoint
2 Verifies the state of the `Order` by invoking the `GET /orders/{orderId}` endpoint
3 Verifies that the `Order Service` published an `OrderAuthorized` event by subscribing to the appropriate message channel

We could translate each scenario into Java code. An easier option, though, is to write the acceptance tests using a DSL such as Gherkin.

10.2.2 *Writing acceptance tests using Gherkin*

Writing acceptance tests in Java is challenging. There's a risk that the scenarios and the Java tests diverge. There's also a disconnect between the high-level scenarios and the Java tests, which consist of low-level implementation details. Also, there's a risk that a scenario lacks precision or is ambiguous and can't be translated into Java code. A much better approach is to eliminate the manual translation step and write executable scenarios.

Gherkin is a DSL for writing executable specifications. When using Gherkin, you define your acceptance tests using English-like scenarios, such as the one shown earlier. You then execute the specifications using Cucumber, a test automation framework for Gherkin. Gherkin and Cucumber eliminate the need to manually translate scenarios into runnable code.

The Gherkin specification for a service such as Order Service consists of a set of features. Each *feature* is described by a set of scenarios such as the one you saw earlier. A scenario has the given-when-then structure. The *givens* are the preconditions, the *when* is the action or event that occurs, and the *then/and* are the expected outcome.

For example, the desired behavior of Order Service is defined by several features, including Place Order, Cancel Order, and Revise Order. Listing 10.11 is an excerpt of the Place Order feature. This feature consists of several elements:

- *Name*—For this feature, the name is Place Order.
- *Specification brief*—This describes why the feature exists. For this feature, the specification brief is the user story.
- *Scenarios*—Order authorized and Order rejected due to expired credit card.

> **Listing 10.11 The Gherkin definition of the Place Order feature and some of its scenarios**

```
Feature: Place Order

  As a consumer of the Order Service
  I should be able to place an order

  Scenario: Order authorized
    Given a valid consumer
    Given using a valid credit card
    Given the restaurant is accepting orders
    When I place an order for Chicken Vindaloo at Ajanta
    Then the order should be APPROVED
    And an OrderAuthorized event should be published

  Scenario: Order rejected due to expired credit card
    Given a valid consumer
    Given using an expired credit card
    Given the restaurant is accepting orders
    When I place an order for Chicken Vindaloo at Ajanta
    Then the order should be REJECTED
    And an OrderRejected event should be published

  . . .
```

In both scenarios, a consumer attempts to place an order. In the first scenario, they succeed. In the second scenario, the order is rejected because the consumer's credit card has expired. For more information on Gherkin, see the book *Writing Great Specifications: Using Specification by Example and Gherkin* by Kamil Nicieja (Manning, 2017).

EXECUTING GHERKIN SPECIFICATIONS USING CUCUMBER

Cucumber is an automated testing framework that executes tests written in Gherkin. It's available in a variety of languages, including Java. When using Cucumber for Java, you write a step definition class, such as the one shown in listing 10.12. A *step definition class* consists of methods that define the meaning of each given-then-when step. Each step definition method is annotated with either @Given, @When, @Then, or @And. Each of these annotations has a value element that's a regular expression, which Cucumber matches against the steps.

> **Listing 10.12   The Java step definitions class makes the Gherkin scenarios executable.**

```
public class StepDefinitions ...  {

  ...

  @Given("A valid consumer")
  public void useConsumer() { ... }

  @Given("using a(.?) (.*) credit card")
  public void useCreditCard(String ignore, String creditCard) { ... }

  @When("I place an order for Chicken Vindaloo at Ajanta")
  public void placeOrder() { ... }

  @Then("the order should be (.*)")
  public void theOrderShouldBe(String desiredOrderState) { ... }

  @And("an (.*) event should be published")
  public void verifyEventPublished(String expectedEventClass)  { ... }

}
```

Each type of method is part of a particular phase of the test:

- @Given—The setup phase
- @When—The execute phase
- @Then *and* @And—The verification phase

Later in section 10.2.4, when I describe this class in more detail, you'll see that many of these methods make REST calls to Order Service. For example, the placeOrder() method creates Order by invoking the POST /orders REST endpoint. The theOrderShouldBe() method verifies the status of the order by invoking GET /orders/{orderId}.

But before getting into the details of how to write step classes, let's explore some design issues with component tests.

10.2.3 *Designing component tests*

Imagine you're implementing the component tests for Order Service. Section 10.2.2 shows how to specify the desired behavior using Gherkin and execute it using Cucumber. But before a component test can execute the Gherkin scenarios, it must first run Order Service and set up the service's dependencies. You need to test Order Service in isolation, so the component test must configure stubs for several services, including Kitchen Service. It also needs to set up a database and the messaging infrastructure. There are a few different options that trade off realism with speed and simplicity.

IN-PROCESS COMPONENT TESTS

One option is to write in-process component tests. An *in-process component test* runs the service with in-memory stubs and mocks for its dependencies. For example, you can write a component test for a Spring Boot-based service using the Spring Boot testing framework. A test class, which is annotated with @SpringBootTest, runs the service in the same JVM as the test. It uses dependency injection to configure the service to use mocks and stubs. For instance, a test for Order Service would configure it to use an in-memory JDBC database, such as H2, HSQLDB, or Derby, and in-memory stubs for Eventuate Tram. In-process tests are simpler to write and faster, but have the downside of not testing the deployable service.

OUT-OF-PROCESS COMPONENT TESTING

A more realistic approach is to package the service in a production-ready format and run it as a separate process. For example, chapter 12 explains that it's increasingly common to package services as Docker container images. An *out-of-process component test* uses real infrastructure services, such as databases and message brokers, but uses stubs for any dependencies that are application services. For example, an out-of-process component test for FTGO Order Service would use MySQL and Apache Kafka, and stubs for services including Consumer Service and Accounting Service. Because Order Service interacts with those services using messaging, these stubs would consume messages from Apache Kafka and send back reply messages.

A key benefit of out-of-process component testing is that it improves test coverage, because what's being tested is much closer to what's being deployed. The drawback is that this type of test is more complex to write, slower to execute, and potentially more brittle than an in-process component test. You also have to figure out how to stub the application services. Let's look at how to do that.

HOW TO STUB SERVICES IN OUT-OF-PROCESS COMPONENT TESTS

The service under test often invokes dependencies using interaction styles that involve sending back a response. Order Service, for example, uses asynchronous request/response and sends command messages to various services. API Gateway uses HTTP, which is a request/response interaction style. An out-of-process test must configure stubs for these kinds of dependencies, which handle requests and send back replies.

One option is to use Spring Cloud Contract, which we looked at earlier in section 10.1 when discussing integration tests. We could write contracts that configure stubs for component tests. One thing to consider, though, is that it's likely that these contracts, unlike those used for integration, would only be used by the component tests.

Another drawback of using Spring Cloud Contract for component testing is that because its focus is consumer contract testing, it takes a somewhat heavyweight approach. The JAR files containing the contracts must be deployed in a Maven repository rather than merely being on the classpath. Handling interactions involving dynamically generated values is also challenging. Consequently, a simpler option is to configure stubs from within the test itself.

A test can, for example, configure an HTTP stub using the WireMock stubbing DSL. Similarly, a test for a service that uses Eventuate Tram messaging can configure messaging stubs. Later in this section I show an easy-to-use Java library that does this.

Now that we've looked at how to design component tests, let's consider how to write component tests for the FTGO `Order Service`.

10.2.4 *Writing component tests for the FTGO Order Service*

As you saw earlier in this section, there are a few different ways to implement component tests. This section describes the component tests for `Order Service` that use the out-of-process strategy to test the service running as a Docker container. You'll see how the tests use a Gradle plugin to start and stop the Docker container. I discuss how to use Cucumber to execute the Gherkin-based scenarios that define the desired behavior for `Order Service`.

Figure 10.7 shows the design of the component tests for `Order Service`. `Order-ServiceComponentTest` is the test class that runs Cucumber:

```
@RunWith(Cucumber.class)
@CucumberOptions(features = "src/component-test/resources/features")
public class OrderServiceComponentTest {
}
```

It has an `@CucumberOptions` annotation that specifies where to find the Gherkin feature files. It's also annotated with `@RunWith(Cucumber.class)`, which tells JUNIT to use the Cucumber test runner. But unlike a typical JUNIT-based test class, it doesn't have any test methods. Instead, it defines the tests by reading the Gherkin features and uses the `OrderServiceComponentTestStepDefinitions` class to make them executable.

Using Cucumber with the Spring Boot testing framework requires a slightly unusual structure. Despite not being a test class, `OrderServiceComponentTestStepDefinitions` is still annotated with `@ContextConfiguration`, which is part of the Spring Testing framework. It creates Spring `ApplicationContext`, which defines the various Spring components, including messaging stubs. Let's look at the details of the step definitions.

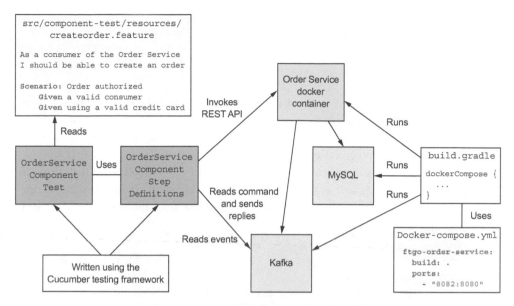

Figure 10.7 The component tests for `Order Service` **use the Cucumber testing framework to execute tests scenarios written using Gherkin acceptance testing DSL. The tests use Docker to run** `Order Service` **along with its infrastructure services, such as Apache Kafka and MySQL.**

THE ORDERSERVICECOMPONENTTESTSTEPDEFINITIONS CLASS

The `OrderServiceComponentTestStepDefinitions` class is the heart of the tests. This class defines the meaning of each step in `Order Service`'s component tests. The following listing shows the `usingCreditCard()` method, which defines the meaning of the `Given using ... credit card` step.

Listing 10.13   The `@GivenuseCreditCard()` method defines the meaning of the `Given using ... credit card` step.

```
@ContextConfiguration(classes =
      OrderServiceComponentTestStepDefinitions.TestConfiguration.class)
public class OrderServiceComponentTestStepDefinitions {

  ...

  @Autowired
  protected SagaParticipantStubManager sagaParticipantStubManager;

  @Given("using a(.?) (.*) credit card")
  public void useCreditCard(String ignore, String creditCard) {
    if (creditCard.equals("valid"))
      sagaParticipantStubManager                          Send a
          .forChannel("accountingService")                success reply.
          .when(AuthorizeCommand.class).replyWithSuccess();
    else if (creditCard.equals("invalid"))                Send a failure
      sagaParticipantStubManager                          reply.
```

```
        .forChannel("accountingService")
        .when(AuthorizeCommand.class).replyWithFailure();
    else
      fail("Don't know what to do with this credit card");
}
```

This method uses the `SagaParticipantStubManager` class, a test helper class that configures stubs for saga participants. The `useCreditCard()` method uses it to configure the `Accounting Service` stub to reply with either a success or a failure message, depending on the specified credit card.

The following listing shows the `placeOrder()` method, which defines the `When I place an order for Chicken Vindaloo at Ajanta` step. It invokes the `Order Service` REST API to create `Order` and saves the response for validation in a later step.

> **Listing 10.14   The `placeOrder()` method defines the `When I place an order for Chicken Vindaloo at Ajanta` step.**

```
@ContextConfiguration(classes =
    OrderServiceComponentTestStepDefinitions.TestConfiguration.class)
public class OrderServiceComponentTestStepDefinitions {

  private int port = 8082;
  private String host = System.getenv("DOCKER_HOST_IP");

  protected String baseUrl(String path) {
    return String.format("http://%s:%s%s", host, port, path);
  }

  private Response response;

  @When("I place an order for Chicken Vindaloo at Ajanta")
  public void placeOrder() {                          Invokes the Order
                                                      Service REST API
    response = given().                               to create Order
            body(new CreateOrderRequest(consumerId,
                RestaurantMother.AJANTA_ID, Collections.singletonList(
                  new CreateOrderRequest.LineItem(
                    RestaurantMother.CHICKEN_VINDALOO_MENU_ITEM_ID,
                    OrderDetailsMother.CHICKEN_VINDALOO_QUANTITY)))).
            contentType("application/json").
            when().
            post(baseUrl("/orders"));
  }
}
```

The `baseUrl()` help method returns the URL of the order service.

Listing 10.15 shows the `theOrderShouldBe()` method, which defines the meaning of the `Then the order should be …` step. It verifies that `Order` was successfully created and that it's in the expected state.

```
@ContextConfiguration(classes =
    OrderServiceComponentTestStepDefinitions.TestConfiguration.class)
public class OrderServiceComponentTestStepDefinitions {

  @Then("the order should be (.*)")
  public void theOrderShouldBe(String desiredOrderState) {

    Integer orderId =
            this.response. then(). statusCode(200).
                extract(). path("orderId");

    assertNotNull(orderId);

    eventually(() -> {
      String state = given().
              when().
              get(baseUrl("/orders/" + orderId)).
              then().
              statusCode(200)
              .extract().
                      path("state");
      assertEquals(desiredOrderState, state);
      });

  }
]
```

The text on the right side of the listing reads: "Verify that Order was created successfully." (pointing to the `Integer orderId = ... extract(). path("orderId");` block) and "Verify the state of Order." (pointing to the `assertEquals(desiredOrderState, state);` line).

The assertion of the expected state is wrapped in a call to eventually(), which repeatedly executes the assertion.

The following listing shows the verifyEventPublished() method, which defines the And an ... event should be published step. It verifies that the expected domain event was published.

```
@ContextConfiguration(classes =
    OrderServiceComponentTestStepDefinitions.TestConfiguration.class)
public class OrderServiceComponentTestStepDefinitions {

  @Autowired
  protected MessageTracker messageTracker;

  @And("an (.*) event should be published")
  public void verifyEventPublished(String expectedEventClass) throws ClassNot
    FoundException {
    messageTracker.assertDomainEventPublished("net.chrisrichardson.ftgo.order
    service.domain.Order",
```

```
            (Class<DomainEvent>)Class.forName("net.chrisrichardson.ftgo.order
        service.domain." + expectedEventClass));
    }
    ....
}
```

The verifyEventPublished() method uses the MessageTracker class, a test helper class that records the events that have been published during the test. This class and SagaParticipantStubManager are instantiated by the TestConfiguration @Configuration class.

Now that we've looked at the step definitions, let's look at how to run the component tests.

RUNNING THE COMPONENT TESTS

Because these tests are relatively slow, we don't want to run them as part of ./gradlew test. Instead, we'll put the test code in a separate src/component-test/java directory and run them using ./gradlew componentTest. Take a look at the ftgo-order-service/build.gradle file to see the Gradle configuration.

The tests use Docker to run Order Service and its dependencies. As described in chapter 12, a Docker container is a lightweight operating system virtualization mechanism that lets you deploy a service instance in an isolated sandbox. Docker Compose is an extremely useful tool with which you can define a set of containers and start and stop them as a unit. The FTGO application has a docker-compose file in the root directory that defines containers for all the services, and the infrastructure service.

We can use the Gradle Docker Compose plugin to run the containers before executing the tests and stop the containers once the tests complete:

```
apply plugin: 'docker-compose'

dockerCompose.isRequiredBy(componentTest)
componentTest.dependsOn(assemble)

dockerCompose {
    startedServices = [ 'ftgo-order-service']
}
```

The preceding snippet of Gradle configuration does two things. First, it configures the Gradle Docker Compose plugin to run before the component tests and start Order Service along with the infrastructure services that it's configured to depend on. Second, it configures componentTest to depend on assemble so that the JAR file required by the Docker image is built first. With that in place, we can run these component tests with the following commands:

```
./gradlew  :ftgo-order-service:componentTest
```

Those commands, which take a couple of minutes, perform the following actions:

1 Build `Order Service`.
2 Run the service and its infrastructure services.
3 Run the tests.
4 Stop the running services.

Now that we've looked at how to test a service in isolation, we'll see how to test the entire application.

10.3 Writing end-to-end tests

Component testing tests each service separately. End-to-end testing, though, tests the entire application. As figure 10.8 shows, end-to-end testing is the top of the test pyramid. That's because these kinds of tests are—say it with me now—slow, brittle, and time consuming to develop.

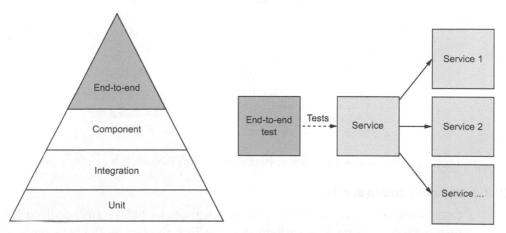

Figure 10.8   End-to-end tests are at the top of the test pyramid. They are slow, brittle, and time consuming to develop. You should minimize the number of end-to-end tests.

End-to-end tests have a large number of moving parts. You must deploy multiple services and their supporting infrastructure services. As a result, end-to-end tests are slow. Also, if your test needs to deploy a large number of services, there's a good chance one of them will fail to deploy, making the tests unreliable. Consequently, you should minimize the number of end-to-end tests.

10.3.1 Designing end-to-end tests

As I've explained, it's best to write as few of these as possible. A good strategy is to write user journey tests. A *user journey test* corresponds to a user's journey through the system. For example, rather than test create order, revise order, and cancel order separately, you can write a single test that does all three. This approach significantly reduces the number of tests you must write and shortens the test execution time.

10.3.2 *Writing end-to-end tests*

End-to-end tests are, like the acceptance tests covered in section 10.2, business-facing tests. It makes sense to write them in a high-level DSL that's understood by the business people. You can, for example, write the end-to-end tests using Gherkin and execute them using Cucumber. The following listing shows an example of such a test. It's similar to the acceptance tests we looked at earlier. The main difference is that rather than a single Then, this test has multiple actions.

Listing 10.17   A Gherkin-based specification of a user journey

```
Feature: Place Revise and Cancel

  As a consumer of the Order Service
  I should be able to place, revise, and cancel an order

  Scenario: Order created, revised, and cancelled
    Given a valid consumer
    Given using a valid credit card
    Given the restaurant is accepting orders            Create
    When I place an order for Chicken Vindaloo at Ajanta  ←┘ Order.
     Then the order should be APPROVED
    Then the order total should be 16.33                Revise
    And when I revise the order by adding 2 vegetable samosas ←┘ Order.
     Then the order total should be 20.97
    And when I cancel the order              Cancel
    Then the order should be CANCELLED   ←┘ Order.
```

This scenario places an order, revises it, and then cancels it. Let's look at how to run it.

10.3.3 *Running end-to-end tests*

End-to-end tests must run the entire application, including any required infrastructure services. As you saw in earlier in section 10.2, the Gradle Docker Compose plugin provides a convenient way to do this. Instead of running a single application service, though, the Docker Compose file runs all the application's services.

Now that we've looked at different aspects of designing and writing end-to-end tests, let's see an example end-to-end test.

The ftgo-end-to-end-test module implements the end-to-end tests for the FTGO application. The implementation of the end-to-end test is quite similar to the implementation of the component tests discussed earlier in section 10.2. These tests are written using Gherkin and executed using Cucumber. The Gradle Docker Compose plugin runs the containers before the tests run. It takes around four to five minutes to start the containers and run the tests.

That may not seem like a long time, but this is a relatively simple application with just a handful of containers and tests. Imagine if there were hundreds of containers and many more tests. The tests could take quite a long time. Consequently, it's best to focus on writing tests that are lower down the pyramid.

Summary

- Use contracts, which are example messages, to drive the testing of interactions between services. Rather than write slow-running tests that run both services and their transitive dependencies, write tests that verify that the adapters of both services conform to the contracts.

- Write component tests to verify the behavior of a service via its API. You should simplify and speed up component tests by testing a service in isolation, using stubs for its dependencies.

- Write user journey tests to minimize the number of end-to-end tests, which are slow, brittle, and time consuming. A user journey test simulates a user's journey through the application and verifies high-level behavior of a relatively large slice of the application's functionality. Because there are few tests, the amount of per-test overhead, such as test setup, is minimized, which speeds up the tests.

Developing
production-ready services

This chapter covers:

- Developing secure services
- Applying the Externalized configuration pattern
- Applying the observability patterns:
  - Health check API
  - Log aggregation
  - Distributed tracing
  - Exception tracking
  - Application metrics
  - Audit logging
- Simplifying the development of services by applying the Microservice chassis pattern

Mary and her team felt that they had mastered service decomposition, interservice communication, transaction management, querying and business logic design, and testing. They were confident that they could develop services that met their functional requirements. But in order for a service to be ready to be deployed into production, they needed to ensure that it would also satisfy three critically important quality attributes: security, configurability, and observability.

The first quality attribute is *application security*. It's essential to develop secure applications, unless you want your company to be in the headlines for a data breach. Fortunately, most aspects of security in a microservice architecture are not any different than in a monolithic application. The FTGO team knew that much of what they had learned over the years developing the monolith also applied to microservices. But the microservice architecture forces you to implement some aspects of application-level security differently. For example, you need to implement a mechanism to pass the identity of the user from one service to another.

The second quality attribute you must address is *service configurability*. A service typically uses one or more external services, such as message brokers and databases. The network location and credentials of each external service often depend on the environment that the service is running in. You can't hard-wire the configuration properties into the service. Instead, you must use an externalized configuration mechanism that provides a service with configuration properties at runtime.

The third quality attribute is *observability*. The FTGO team had implemented monitoring and logging for the existing application. But a microservice architecture is a distributed system, and that presents some additional challenges. Every request is handled by the API gateway and at least one service. Imagine, for example, that you're trying to determine which of six services is causing a latency issue. Or imagine trying to understand how a request is handled when the log entries are scattered across five different services. In order to make it easier to understand the behavior of your application and troubleshoot problems, you must implement several observability patterns.

I begin this chapter by describing how to implement security in a microservice architecture. Next, I discuss how to design services that are configurable. I cover a couple of different service configuration mechanisms. After that I talk about how to make your services easier to understand and troubleshoot by using the observability patterns. I end the chapter by showing how to simplify the implementation of these and other concerns by developing your services on top of a microservice chassis framework.

Let's first look at security.

11.1   *Developing secure services*

Cybersecurity has become a critical issue for every organization. Almost every day there are headlines about how hackers have stolen a company's data. In order to develop secure software and stay out of the headlines, an organization needs to tackle a diverse range of security issues, including physical security of the hardware, encryption of data in transit and at rest, authentication and authorization, and policies for patching software vulnerabilities. Most of these issues are the same regardless of whether you're using a monolithic or microservice architecture. This section focuses on how the microservice architecture impacts security at the application level.

An application developer is primarily responsible for implementing four different aspects of security:

- *Authentication*—Verifying the identity of the application or human (a.k.a. the *principal*) that's attempting to access the application. For example, an application typically verifies a principal's credentials, such as a user ID and password or an application's API key and secret.
- *Authorization*—Verifying that the principal is allowed to perform the requested operation on the specified data. Applications often use a combination of role-based security and access control lists (ACLs). Role-based security assigns each user one or more roles that grant them permission to invoke particular operations. ACLs grant users or roles permission to perform an operation on a particular business object, or aggregate.
- *Auditing*—Tracking the operations that a principal performs in order to detect security issues, help customer support, and enforce compliance.
- *Secure interprocess communication*—Ideally, all communication in and out of services should be over Transport Layer Security (TLS). Interservice communication may even need to use authentication.

I describe auditing in detail in section 11.3 and touch on securing interservice communication when discussing service meshes in section 11.4.1. This section focuses on implementing authentication and authorization.

I begin by first describing how security is implemented in the FTGO monolith application. I then describe the challenges with implementing security in a microservice architecture and how techniques that work well in a monolithic architecture can't be used in a microservice architecture. After that I cover how to implement security in a microservice architecture.

Let's start by reviewing how the monolithic FTGO application handles security.

11.1.1 *Overview of security in a traditional monolithic application*

The FTGO application has several kinds of human users, including consumers, couriers, and restaurant staff. They access the application using browser-based web applications and mobile applications. All FTGO users must log in to access the application. Figure 11.1 shows how the clients of the monolithic FTGO application authenticate and make requests.

When a user logs in with their user ID and password, the client makes a POST request containing the user's credentials to the FTGO application. The FTGO application verifies the credentials and returns a session token to the client. The client includes the session token in each subsequent request to the FTGO application.

Figure 11.2 shows a high-level view of how the FTGO application implements security. The FTGO application is written in Java and uses the Spring Security framework, but I'll describe the design using generic terms that are applicable to other frameworks, such as Passport for NodeJS.

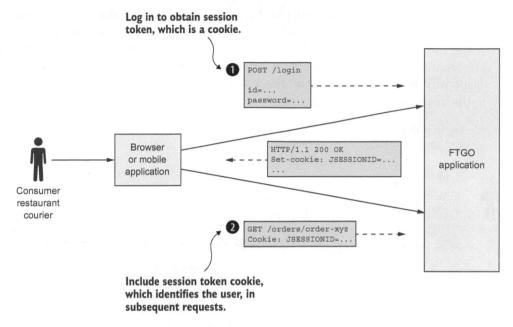

Figure 11.1 A client of the FTGO application first logs in to obtain a session token, which is often a cookie. The client includes the session token in each subsequent request it makes to the application.

Using a security framework

Implementing authentication and authorization correctly is challenging. It's best to use a proven security framework. Which framework to use depends on your application's technology stack. Some popular frameworks include the following:

- *Spring Security* (https://projects.spring.io/spring-security/)—A popular framework for Java applications. It's a sophisticated framework that handles authentication and authorization.
- *Apache Shiro* (https://shiro.apache.org)—Another Java framework.
- *Passport* (http://www.passportjs.org)—A popular security framework for NodeJS applications that's focused on authentication.

One key part of the security architecture is the session, which stores the principal's ID and roles. The FTGO application is a traditional Java EE application, so the session is an HttpSession in-memory session. A *session* is identified by a session token, which the client includes in each request. It's usually an opaque token such as a cryptographically strong random number. The FTGO application's session token is an HTTP cookie called JSESSIONID.

The other key part of the security implementation is the security *context*, which stores information about the user making the current request. The Spring Security framework uses the standard Java EE approach of storing the security context in a static, thread-local variable, which is readily accessible to any code that's invoked to handle the request. A request handler can call `SecurityContextHolder.getContext()` `.getAuthentication()` to obtain information about the current user, such as their identity and roles. In contrast, the Passport framework stores the security context as the `user` attribute of the `request`.

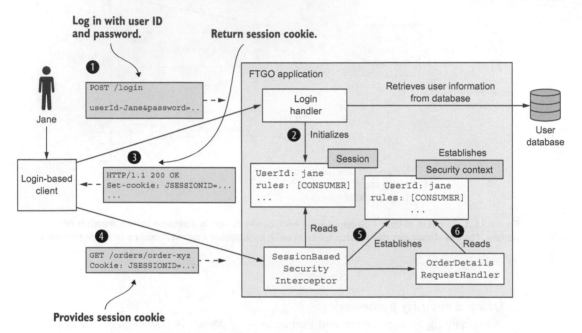

Figure 11.2   When a client of the FTGO application makes a login request, `Login Handler` authenticates the user, initializes the session user information, and returns a session token cookie, which securely identifies the session. Next, when the client makes a request containing the session token, `SessionBasedSecurity-` `Interceptor` retrieves the user information from the specified session and establishes the security context. Request handlers, such as `OrderDetailsRequestHandler`, retrieve the user information from the security context.

The sequence of events shown in Figure 11.2 is as follows:

1. The client makes a login request to the FTGO application.
2. The login request is handled by `LoginHandler`, which verifies the credentials, creates the session, and stores information about the principal in the session.
3. `Login Handler` returns a session token to the client.
4. The client includes the session token in requests that invoke operations.
5. These requests are first processed by `SessionBasedSecurityInterceptor`. The interceptor authenticates each request by verifying the session token and establishes a security context. The security context describes the principal and its roles.

6 A request handler uses the security context to determine whether to allow a user to perform the requested operation and obtain their identity.

The FTGO application uses *role-based* authorization. It defines several roles corresponding to the different kinds of users, including CONSUMER, RESTAURANT, COURIER, and ADMIN. It uses Spring Security's declarative security mechanism to restrict access to URLs and service methods to specific roles. Roles are also interwoven into the business logic. For example, a consumer can only access their orders, whereas an administrator can access all orders.

The security design used by the monolithic FTGO application is only one possible way to implement security. For example, one drawback of using an in-memory session is that it requires all requests for a particular session to be routed to the same application instance. This requirement complicates load balancing and operations. You must, for example, implement a session draining mechanism that waits for all sessions to expire before shutting down an application instance. An alternative approach, which avoids these problems, is to store the session in a database.

You can sometimes eliminate the server-side session entirely. For example, many applications have API clients that provide their credentials, such as an API key and secret, in every request. As a result, there's no need to maintain a server-side session. Alternatively, the application can store session state in the session token. Later in this section, I describe one way to use a session token to store the session state. But let's begin by looking at the challenges of implementing security in a microservice architecture.

11.1.2 *Implementing security in a microservice architecture*

A microservice architecture is a distributed architecture. Each external request is handled by the API gateway and at least one service. Consider, for example, the get-OrderDetails() query, discussed in chapter 8. The API gateway handles this query by invoking several services, including Order Service, Kitchen Service, and Accounting Service. Each service must implement some aspects of security. For instance, Order Service must only allow a consumer to see their orders, which requires a combination of authentication and authorization. In order to implement security in a microservice architecture we need to determine who is responsible for authenticating the user and who is responsible for authorization.

One challenge with implementing security in a microservices application is that we can't just copy the design from a monolithic application. That's because two aspects of the monolithic application's security architecture are nonstarters for a microservice architecture:

- *In-memory security context*—Using an in-memory security context, such as a thread-local, to pass around user identity. Services can't share memory, so they can't use an in-memory security context, such as a thread-local, to pass around the user identity. In a microservice architecture, we need a different mechanism for passing user identity from one service to another.

■ *Centralized session* —Because an in-memory security context doesn't make sense, neither does an in-memory session. In theory, multiple services could access a database-based session, except that it would violate the principle of loose coupling. We need a different session mechanism in a microservice architecture.

Let's begin our exploration of security in a microservice architecture by looking at how to handle authentication.

HANDLING AUTHENTICATION IN THE API GATEWAY

There are a couple of different ways to handle authentication. One option is for the individual services to authenticate the user. The problem with this approach is that it permits unauthenticated requests to enter the internal network. It relies on every development team correctly implementing security in all of their services. As a result, there's a significant risk of an application containing security vulnerabilities.

Another problem with implementing authentication in the services is that different clients authenticate in different ways. Pure API clients supply credentials with each request using, for example, basic authentication. Other clients might first log in and then supply a session token with each request. We want to avoid requiring services to handle a diverse set of authentication mechanisms.

A better approach is for the API gateway to authenticate a request before forwarding it to the services. Centralizing API authentication in the API gateway has the advantage that there's only one place to get right. As a result, there's a much smaller chance of a security vulnerability. Another benefit is that only the API gateway has to deal with the various different authentication mechanisms. It hides this complexity from the services.

Figure 11.3 shows how this approach works. Clients authenticate with the API gateway. API clients include credentials in each request. Login-based clients POST the user's credentials to the API gateway's authentication and receive a session token. Once the API gateway has authenticated a request, it invokes one or more services.

Pattern: Access token

The API gateway passes a token containing information about the user, such as their identity and their roles, to the services that it invokes. See http://microservices.io/patterns/security/access-token.html.

A service invoked by the API gateway needs to know the principal making the request. It must also verify that the request has been authenticated. The solution is for the API gateway to include a token in each service request. The service uses the token to validate the request and obtain information about the principal. The API gateway might also give the same token to session-oriented clients to use as the session token.

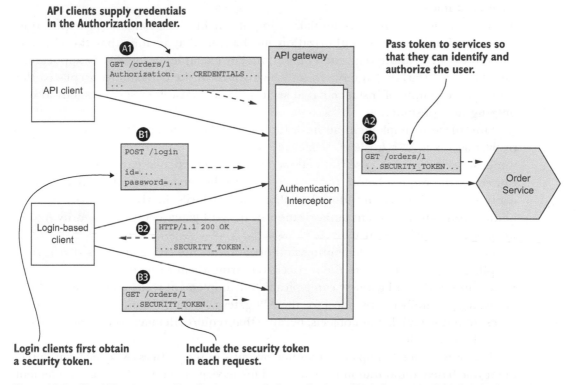

Figure 11.3 **The API gateway authenticates requests from clients and includes a security token in the requests it makes to services. The services use the token to obtain information about the principal. The API gateway can also use the security token as a session token.**

The sequence of events for API clients is as follows:

1 A client makes a request containing credentials.
2 The API gateway authenticates the credentials, creates a security token, and passes that to the service or services.

The sequence of events for login-based clients is as follows:

1 A client makes a login request containing credentials.
2 The API gateway returns a security token.
3 The client includes the security token in requests that invoke operations.
4 The API gateway validates the security token and forwards it to the service or services.

A little later in this chapter, I describe how to implement tokens, but let's first look at the other main aspect of security: authorization.

HANDLING AUTHORIZATION

Authenticating a client's credentials is important but insufficient. An application must also implement an authorization mechanism that verifies that the client is allowed to perform the requested operation. For example, in the FTGO application the `getOrderDetails()` query can only be invoked by the consumer who placed the `Order` (an example of instance-based security) and a customer service agent who is helping the consumer.

One place to implement authorization is the API gateway. It can, for example, restrict access to `GET /orders/{orderId}` to only users who are consumers and customer service agents. If a user isn't allowed to access a particular path, the API gateway can reject the request before forwarding it on to the service. As with authentication, centralizing authorization within the API gateway reduces the risk of security vulnerabilities. You can implement authorization in the API gateway using a security framework, such as Spring Security.

One drawback of implementing authorization in the API gateway is that it risks coupling the API gateway to the services, requiring them to be updated in lockstep. What's more, the API gateway can typically only implement role-based access to URL paths. It's generally not practical for the API gateway to implement ACLs that control access to individual domain objects, because that requires detailed knowledge of a service's domain logic.

The other place to implement authorization is in the services. A service can implement role-based authorization for URLs and for service methods. It can also implement ACLs to manage access to aggregates. `Order Service` can, for example, implement the role-based and ACL-based authorization mechanism for controlling access to orders. Other services in the FTGO application implement similar authorization logic.

USING JWTS TO PASS USER IDENTITY AND ROLES

When implementing security in a microservice architecture, you need to decide which type of token an API gateway should use to pass user information to the services. There are two types of tokens to choose from. One option is to use *opaque* tokens, which are typically UUIDs. The downside of opaque tokens is that they reduce performance and availability and increase latency. That's because the recipient of such a token must make a synchronous RPC call to a security service to validate the token and retrieve the user information.

An alternative approach, which eliminates the call to the security service, is to use a *transparent* token containing information about the user. One such popular standard for transparent tokens is the JSON Web Token (JWT). JWT is standard way to securely represent claims, such as user identity and roles, between two parties. A JWT has a payload, which is a JSON object that contains information about the user, such as their identity and roles, and other metadata, such as an expiration date. It's signed with a secret that's only known to the creator of the JWT, such as the API gateway and the recipient of the JWT, such as a service. The secret ensures that a malicious third party can't forge or tamper with a JWT.

One issue with JWT is that because a token is self-contained, it's irrevocable. By design, a service will perform the request operation after verifying the JWT's signature and expiration date. As a result, there's no practical way to revoke an individual JWT that has fallen into the hands of a malicious third party. The solution is to issue JWTs with short expiration times, because that limits what a malicious party could do. One drawback of short-lived JWTs, though, is that the application must somehow continually reissue JWTs to keep the session active. Fortunately, this is one of the many protocols that are solved by a security standard calling OAuth 2.0. Let's look at how that works.

USING OAUTH 2.0 IN A MICROSERVICE ARCHITECTURE

Let's say you want to implement a `User Service` for the FTGO application that manages a user database containing user information, such as credentials and roles. The API gateway calls the `User Service` to authenticate a client request and obtain a JWT. You could design a `User Service` API and implement it using your favorite web framework. But that's generic functionality that isn't specific to the FTGO application—developing such a service wouldn't be an efficient use of development resources.

Fortunately, you don't need to develop this kind of security infrastructure. You can use an off-the-shelf service or framework that implements a standard called OAuth 2.0. OAuth 2.0 is an authorization protocol that was originally designed to enable a user of a public cloud service, such as GitHub or Google, to grant a third-party application access to its information without revealing its password. For example, OAuth 2.0 is the mechanism that enables you to securely grant a third party cloud-based Continuous Integration (CI) service access to your GitHub repository.

Although the original focus of OAuth 2.0 was authorizing access to public cloud services, you can also use it for authentication and authorization in your application. Let's take a quick look at how a microservice architecture might use OAuth 2.0.

About OAuth 2.0

OAuth 2.0 is a complex topic. In this chapter, I can only provide a brief overview and describe how it can be used in a microservice architecture. For more information on OAuth 2.0, check out the online book *OAuth 2.0 Servers* by Aaron Parecki (www.oauth.com). Chapter 7 of *Spring Microservices in Action* (Manning, 2017) also covers this topic (https://livebook.manning.com/#!/book/spring-microservices-in-action/chapter-7/).

The key concepts in OAuth 2.0 are the following:

- `Authorization Server`—Provides an API for authenticating users and obtaining an access token and a refresh token. Spring OAuth is a great example of a framework for building an OAuth 2.0 authorization server.
- `Access Token`—A token that grants access to a `Resource Server`. The format of the access token is implementation dependent. But some implementations, such as Spring OAuth, use JWTs.

- Refresh Token—A long-lived yet revocable token that a `Client` uses to obtain a new `AccessToken`.
- Resource Server—A service that uses an access token to authorize access. In a microservice architecture, the services are resource servers.
- Client—A client that wants to access a `Resource Server`. In a microservice architecture, `API Gateway` is the OAuth 2.0 client.

Later in this section, I describe how to support login-based clients. But first, let's talk about how to authenticate API clients.

Figure 11.4 shows how the API gateway authenticates a request from an API client. The API gateway authenticate the API client by making a request to the OAuth 2.0 authorization server, which returns an access token. The API gateway then makes one or more requests containing the access token to the services.

The sequence of events shown in figure 11.4 is as follows:

1 The client makes a request, supplying its credentials using basic authentication.
2 The API gateway makes an OAuth 2.0 Password Grant request (www.oauth.com/oauth2-servers/access-tokens/password-grant/) to the OAuth 2.0 authentication server.

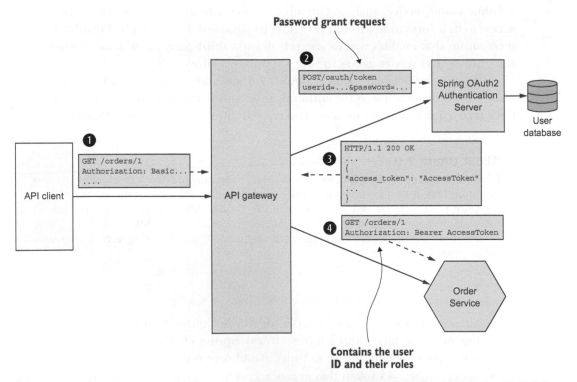

Figure 11.4   An API gateway authenticates an API client by making a Password Grant request to the OAuth 2.0 authentication server. The server returns an access token, which the API gateway passes to the services. A service verifies the token's signature and extracts information about the user, including their identity and roles.

3 The authentication server validates the API client's credentials and returns an access token and a refresh token.

4 The API gateway includes the access token in the requests it makes to the services. A service validates the access token and uses it to authorize the request.

An OAuth 2.0-based API gateway can authenticate session-oriented clients by using an OAuth 2.0 access token as a session token. What's more, when the access token expires, it can obtain a new access token using the refresh token. Figure 11.5 shows how an API gateway can use OAuth 2.0 to handle session-oriented clients. An API client initiates a session by POSTing its credentials to the API gateway's /login endpoint. The API gateway returns an access token and a refresh token to the client. The API client then supplies both tokens when it makes requests to the API gateway.

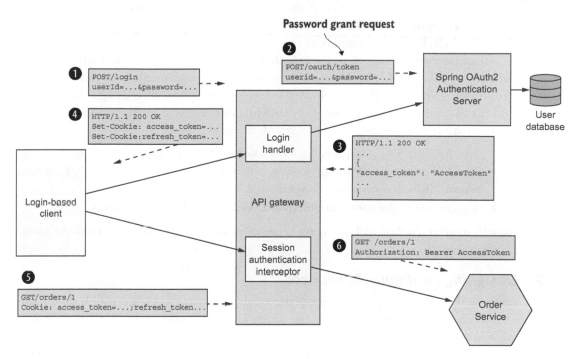

Figure 11.5 A client logs in by POSTing its credentials to the API gateway. The API gateway authenticates the credentials using the OAuth 2.0 authentication server and returns the access token and refresh token as cookies. A client includes these tokens in the requests it makes to the API gateway.

The sequence of events is as follows:

1 The login-based client POSTs its credentials to the API gateway.

2 The API gateway's Login Handler makes an OAuth 2.0 Password Grant request (www.oauth.com/oauth2-servers/access-tokens/password-grant/) to the OAuth 2.0 authentication server.

3 The authentication server validates the client's credentials and returns an access token and a refresh token.

4 The API gateway returns the access and refresh tokens to the client—as cookies, for example.

5 The client includes the access and refresh tokens in requests it makes to the API gateway.

6 The API gateway's `Session Authentication Interceptor` validates the access token and includes it in requests it makes to the services.

If the access token has expired or is about to expire, the API gateway obtains a new access token by making an OAuth 2.0 Refresh Grant request (www.oauth.com/oauth2-servers/access-tokens/refreshing-access-tokens/), which contains the refresh token, to the authorization server. If the refresh token hasn't expired or been revoked, the authorization server returns a new access token. `API Gateway` passes the new access token to the services and returns it to the client.

An important benefit of using OAuth 2.0 is that it's a proven security standard. Using an off-the-shelf OAuth 2.0 `Authentication Server` means you don't have to waste time reinventing the wheel or risk developing an insecure design. But OAuth 2.0 isn't the only way to implement security in a microservice architecture. Regardless of which approach you use, the three key ideas are as follows:

- The API gateway is responsible for authenticating clients.
- The API gateway and the services use a transparent token, such as a JWT, to pass around information about the principal.
- A service uses the token to obtain the principal's identity and roles.

Now that we've looked at how to make services secure, let's see how to make them configurable.

11.2 *Designing configurable services*

Imagine that you're responsible for `Order History Service`. As figure 11.6 shows, the service consumes events from Apache Kafka and reads and writes AWS DynamoDB table items. In order for this service to run, it needs various configuration properties, including the network location of Apache Kafka and the credentials and network location for AWS DynamoDB.

The values of these configuration properties depend on which environment the service is running in. For example, the developer and production environments will use different Apache Kafka brokers and different AWS credentials. It doesn't make sense to hard-wire a particular environment's configuration property values into the deployable service because that would require it to be rebuilt for each environment. Instead, a service should be built once by the deployment pipeline and deployed into multiple environments.

Nor does it make sense to hard-wire different sets of configuration properties into the source code and use, for example, the Spring Framework's profile mechanism to

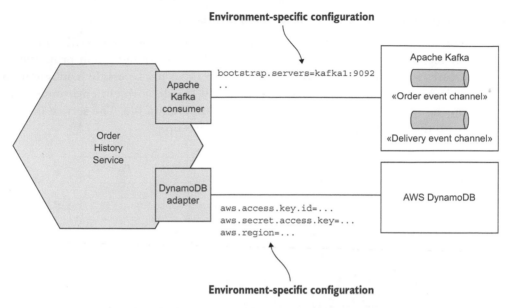

Figure 11.6 Order History Service uses Apache Kafka and AWS DynamoDB. It needs to be configured with each service's network location, credentials, and so on.

select the appropriate set at runtime. That's because doing so would introduce a security vulnerability and limit where it can be deployed. Additionally, sensitive data such as credentials should be stored securely using a secrets storage mechanism, such as Hashicorp Vault (www.vaultproject.io) or AWS Parameter Store (https://docs.aws .amazon.com/systems-manager/latest/userguide/systems-manager-paramstore.html). Instead, you should supply the appropriate configuration properties to the service at runtime by using the Externalized configuration pattern.

Pattern: Externalized configuration

Supply configuration property values, such as database credentials and network location, to a service at runtime. See http://microservices.io/patterns/externalized-configuration.html.

An externalized configuration mechanism provides the configuration property values to a service instance at runtime. There are two main approaches:

- *Push model*—The deployment infrastructure passes the configuration properties to the service instance using, for example, operating system environment variables or a configuration file.
- *Pull model*—The service instance reads its configuration properties from a configuration server.

We'll look at each approach, starting with the push model.

11.2.1 *Using push-based externalized configuration*

The push model relies on the collaboration of the deployment environment and the service. The deployment environment supplies the configuration properties when it creates a service instance. It might, as figure 11.7 shows, pass the configuration properties as environment variables. Alternatively, the deployment environment may supply the configuration properties using a configuration file. The service instance then reads the configuration properties when it starts up.

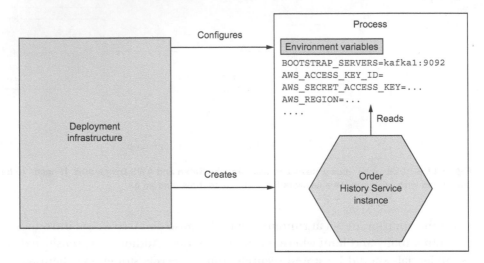

Figure 11.7   When the deployment infrastructure creates an instance of `Order History Service`**, it sets the environment variables containing the externalized configuration.** `Order History Service` **reads those environment variables.**

The deployment environment and the service must agree on how the configuration properties are supplied. The precise mechanism depends on the specific deployment environment. For example, chapter 12 describes how you can specify the environment variables of a Docker container.

Let's imagine that you've decided to supply externalized configuration property values using environment variables. Your application could call `System.getenv()` to obtain their values. But if you're a Java developer, it's likely that you're using a framework that provides a more convenient mechanism. The FTGO services are built using Spring Boot, which has an extremely flexible externalized configuration mechanism that retrieves configuration properties from a variety of sources with well-defined precedence rules (https://docs.spring.io/spring-boot/docs/current/reference/html/boot-features-external-config.html). Let's look at how it works.

Spring Boot reads properties from a variety of sources. I find the following sources useful in a microservice architecture:

1 Command-line arguments
2 `SPRING_APPLICATION_JSON`, an operating system environment variable or JVM system property that contains JSON
3 JVM System properties
4 Operating system environment variables
5 A configuration file in the current directory

A particular property value from a source earlier in this list overrides the same property from a source later in this list. For example, operating system environment variables override properties read from a configuration file.

Spring Boot makes these properties available to the Spring Framework's `ApplicationContext`. A service can, for example, obtain the value of a property using the `@Value` annotation:

```
public class OrderHistoryDynamoDBConfiguration {

  @Value("${aws.region}")
  private String awsRegion;
```

The Spring Framework initializes the `awsRegion` field to the value of the `aws.region` property. This property is read from one of the sources listed earlier, such as a configuration file or from the `AWS_REGION` environment variable.

The push model is an effective and widely used mechanism for configuring a service. One limitation, however, is that reconfiguring a running service might be challenging, if not impossible. The deployment infrastructure might not allow you to change the externalized configuration of a running service without restarting it. You can't, for example, change the environment variables of a running process. Another limitation is that there's a risk of the configuration property values being scattered throughout the definition of numerous services. As a result, you may want to consider using a pull-based model. Let's look at how it works.

11.2.2 Using pull-based externalized configuration

In the pull model, a service instance reads its configuration properties from a configuration server. Figure 11.8 shows how it works. On startup, a service instance queries the configuration service for its configuration. The configuration properties for accessing the configuration server, such as its network location, are provided to the service instance via a push-based configuration mechanism, such as environment variables.

There are a variety of ways to implement a configuration server, including the following:

- Version control system such as Git
- SQL and NoSQL databases
- Specialized configuration servers, such as Spring Cloud Config Server, Hashicorp Vault, which is a store for sensitive data such as credentials, and AWS Parameter Store

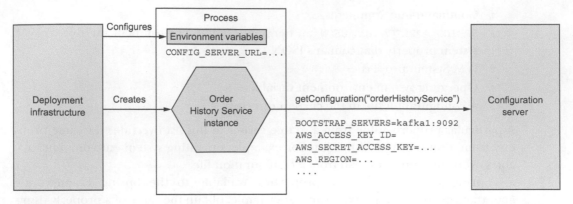

Figure 11.8   On startup, a service instance retrieves its configuration properties from a configuration server. The deployment infrastructure provides the configuration properties for accessing the configuration server.

The Spring Cloud Config project is a good example of a configuration server-based framework. It consists of a server and a client. The server supports a variety of backends for storing configuration properties, including version control systems, databases, and Hashicorp Vault. The client retrieves configuration properties from the server and injects them into the Spring `ApplicationContext`.

Using a configuration server has several benefits:

- *Centralized configuration*—All the configuration properties are stored in one place, which makes them easier to manage. What's more, in order to eliminate duplicate configuration properties, some implementations let you define global defaults, which can be overridden on a per-service basis.
- *Transparent decryption of sensitive data*—Encrypting sensitive data such as database credentials is a security best practice. One challenge of using encryption, though, is that usually the service instance needs to decrypt them, which means it needs the encryption keys. Some configuration server implementations automatically decrypt properties before returning them to the service.
- *Dynamic reconfiguration*—A service could potentially detect updated property values by, for example, polling, and reconfigure itself.

The primary drawback of using a configuration server is that unless it's provided by the infrastructure, it's yet another piece of infrastructure that needs to be set up and maintained. Fortunately, there are various open source frameworks, such as Spring Cloud Config, which make it easier to run a configuration server.

Now that we've looked at how to design configurable services, let's talk about how to design observable services.

11.3   *Designing observable services*

Let's say you've deployed the FTGO application into production. You probably want to know what the application is doing: requests per second, resource utilization, and so on. You also need to be alerted if there's a problem, such as a failed service instance or a disk filling up—ideally before it impacts a user. And, if there's a problem, you need to be able to troubleshoot and identify the root cause.

Many aspects of managing an application in production are outside the scope of the developer, such as monitoring hardware availability and utilization. These are clearly the responsibility of operations. But there are several patterns that you, as a service developer, must implement to make your service easier to manage and troubleshoot. These patterns, shown in figure 11.9, expose a service instance's behavior and health. They enable a monitoring system to track and visualize the state of a service and generate alerts when there's a problem. These patterns also make troubleshooting problems easier.

You can use the following patterns to design observable services:

- *Health check API*—Expose an endpoint that returns the health of the service.
- *Log aggregation*—Log service activity and write logs into a centralized logging server, which provides searching and alerting.

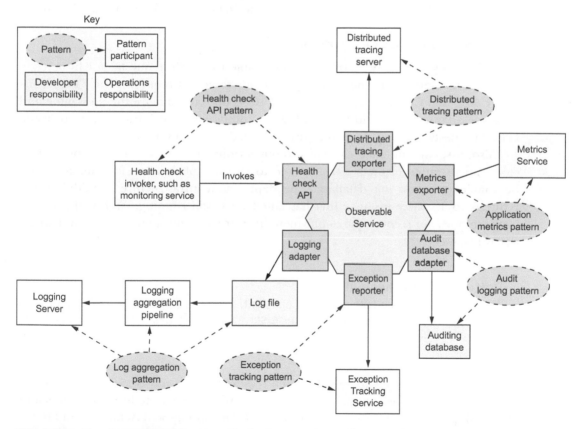

Figure 11.9 The observability patterns enable developers and operations to understand the behavior of an application and troubleshoot problems. Developers are responsible for ensuring that their services are observable. Operations are responsible for the infrastructure that collects the information exposed by the services.

- *Distributed tracing*—Assign each external request a unique ID and trace requests as they flow between services.
- *Exception tracking*—Report exceptions to an exception tracking service, which de-duplicates exceptions, alerts developers, and tracks the resolution of each exception.
- *Application metrics*—Services maintain metrics, such as counters and gauges, and expose them to a metrics server.
- *Audit logging*—Log user actions.

A distinctive feature of most of these patterns is that each pattern has a developer component and an operations component. Consider, for example, the Health check API pattern. The developer is responsible for ensuring that their service implements a health check endpoint. Operations is responsible for the monitoring system that periodically invokes the health check API. Similarly, for the Log aggregation pattern, a developer is responsible for ensuring that their services log useful information, whereas operations is responsible for log aggregation.

Let's take a look at each of these patterns, starting with the Health check API pattern.

11.3.1 *Using the Health check API pattern*

Sometimes a service may be running but unable to handle requests. For instance, a newly started service instance may not be ready to accept requests. The FTGO Consumer Service, for example, takes around 10 seconds to initialize the messaging and database adapters. It would be pointless for the deployment infrastructure to route HTTP requests to a service instance until it's ready to process them.

Also, a service instance can fail without terminating. For example, a bug might cause an instance of Consumer Service to run out of database connections and be unable to access the database. The deployment infrastructure shouldn't route requests to a service instance that has failed yet is still running. And, if the service instance does not recover, the deployment infrastructure must terminate it and create a new instance.

> **Pattern: Health check API**
>
> A service exposes a health check API endpoint, such as GET /health, which returns the health of the service. See http://microservices.io/patterns/observability/health-check-api.html.

A service instance needs to be able to tell the deployment infrastructure whether or not it's able to handle requests. A good solution is for a service to implement a health check endpoint, which is shown in figure 11.10. The Spring Boot Actuator Java library, for example, implements a GET /actuator/health endpoint, which returns 200 if and only if the service is healthy, and 503 otherwise. Similarly, the HealthChecks .NET library implements a GET /hc endpoint (https://docs.microsoft.com/en-us/dotnet/standard/microservices-architecture/implement-resilient-applications/monitor-app-health). The deployment infrastructure periodically invokes this endpoint to determine the health of the service instance and takes the appropriate action if it's unhealthy.

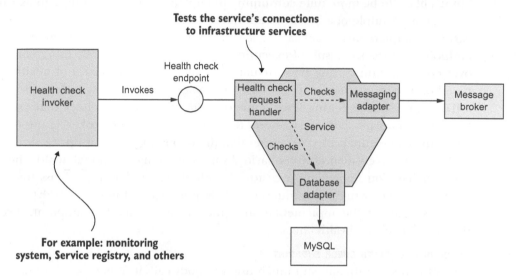

Figure 11.10   A service implements a health check endpoint, which is periodically invoked by the deployment infrastructure to determine the health of the service instance.

A Health Check Request Handler typically tests the service instance's connections to external services. It might, for example, execute a test query against a database. If all the tests succeed, Health Check Request Handler returns a healthy response, such as an HTTP 200 status code. If any of them fails, it returns an unhealthy response, such as an HTTP 500 status code.

Health Check Request Handler might simply return an empty HTTP response with the appropriate status code. Or it might return a detailed description of the health of each of the adapters. The detailed information is useful for troubleshooting. But because it may contain sensitive information, some frameworks, such as Spring Boot Actuator, let you configure the level of detail in the health endpoint response.

There are two issues you need to consider when using health checks. The first is the implementation of the endpoint, which must report back on the health of the service instance. The second issue is how to configure the deployment infrastructure to invoke the health check endpoint. Let's first look at how to implement the endpoint.

IMPLEMENTING THE HEALTH CHECK ENDPOINT

The code that implements the health check endpoint must somehow determine the health of the service instance. One simple approach is to verify that the service instance can access its external infrastructure services. How to do this depends on the infrastructure service. The health check code can, for example, verify that it's connected to an RDBMS by obtaining a database connection and executing a test query. A more elaborate approach is to execute a synthetic transaction that simulates the invocation of the service's API by a client. This kind of health check is more thorough, but it's likely to be more time consuming to implement and take longer to execute.

A great example of a health check library is Spring Boot Actuator. As mentioned earlier, it implements a `/actuator/health` endpoint. The code that implements this endpoint returns the result of executing a set of health checks. By using convention over configuration, Spring Boot Actuator implements a sensible set of health checks based on the infrastructure services used by the service. If, for example, a service uses a JDBC `DataSource`, Spring Boot Actuator configures a health check that executes a test query. Similarly, if the service uses the RabbitMQ message broker, it automatically configures a health check that verifies that the RabbitMQ server is up.

You can also customize this behavior by implementing additional health checks for your service. You implement a custom health check by defining a class that implements the `HealthIndicator` interface. This interface defines a `health()` method, which is called by the implementation of the `/actuator/health` endpoint. It returns the outcome of the health check.

INVOKING THE HEALTH CHECK ENDPOINT

A health check endpoint isn't much use if nobody calls it. When you deploy your service, you must configure the deployment infrastructure to invoke the endpoint. How you do that depends on the specific details of your deployment infrastructure. For example, as described in chapter 3, you can configure some service registries, such as Netflix Eureka, to invoke the health check endpoint in order to determine whether traffic should be routed to the service instance. Chapter 12 discusses how to configure Docker and Kubernetes to invoke a health check endpoint.

11.3.2 *Applying the Log aggregation pattern*

Logs are a valuable troubleshooting tool. If you want to know what's wrong with your application, a good place to start is the log files. But using logs in a microservice architecture is challenging. For example, imagine you're debugging a problem with the `getOrderDetails()` query. As described in chapter 8, the FTGO application implements this query using API composition. As a result, the log entries you need are scattered across the log files of the API gateway and several services, including `Order Service` and `Kitchen Service`.

> #### Pattern: Log aggregation
> Aggregate the logs of all services in a centralized database that supports searching and alerting. See http://microservices.io/patterns/observability/application-logging .html.

The solution is to use log aggregation. As figure 11.11 shows, the log aggregation pipeline sends the logs of all of the service instances to a centralized logging server. Once the logs are stored by the logging server, you can view, search, and analyze them. You can also configure alerts that are triggered when certain messages appear in the logs.

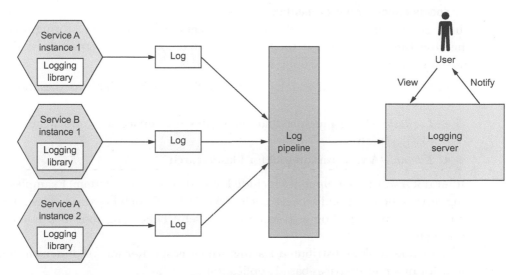

Figure 11.11 The log aggregation infrastructure ships the logs of each service instance to a centralized logging server. Users can view and search the logs. They can also set up alerts, which are triggered when log entries match search criteria.

The logging pipeline and server are usually the responsibility of operations. But service developers are responsible for writing services that generate useful logs. Let's first look at how a service generates a log.

HOW A SERVICE GENERATES A LOG

As a service developer, there are a couple of issues you need to consider. First you need to decide which logging library to use. The second issue is where to write the log entries. Let's first look at the logging library.

Most programming languages have one or more logging libraries that make it easy to generate correctly structured log entries. For example, three popular Java logging libraries are Logback, log4j, and JUL (java.util.logging). There's also SLF4J, which is a logging facade API for the various logging frameworks. Similarly, Log4JS is a popular logging framework for NodeJS. One reasonable way to use logging is to sprinkle calls to one of these logging libraries in your service's code. But if you have strict logging requirements that can't be enforced by the logging library, you may need to define your own logging API that wraps a logging library.

You also need to decide where to log. Traditionally, you would configure the logging framework to write to a log file in a well-known location in the filesystem. But with the more modern deployment technologies, such as containers and serverless, described in chapter 12, this is often not the best approach. In some environments, such as AWS Lambda, there isn't even a "permanent" filesystem to write the logs to! Instead, your service should log to `stdout`. The deployment infrastructure will then decide what to do with the output of your service.

THE LOGGING AGGREGATION INFRASTRUCTURE

The logging infrastructure is responsible for aggregating the logs, storing them, and enabling the user to search them. One popular logging infrastructure is the ELK stack. ELK consists of three open source products:

- *Elasticsearch*—A text search-oriented NoSQL database that's used as the logging server
- *Logstash*—A log pipeline that aggregates the service logs and writes them to Elasticsearch
- *Kibana*—A visualization tool for Elasticsearch

Other open source log pipelines include Fluentd and Apache Flume. Examples of logging servers include cloud services, such as AWS CloudWatch Logs, as well as numerous commercial offerings. Log aggregation is a useful debugging tool in a microservice architecture.

Let's now look at distributed tracing, which is another way of understanding the behavior of a microservices-based application.

11.3.3   *Using the Distributed tracing pattern*

Imagine you're a FTGO developer who is investigating why the `getOrderDetails()` query has slowed down. You've ruled out the problem being an external networking issue. The increased latency must be caused by either the API gateway or one of the services it has invoked. One option is to look at each service's average response time. The trouble with this option is that it's an average across requests rather than the timing breakdown for an individual request. Plus more complex scenarios might involve many nested service invocations. You may not even be familiar with all services. As a result, it can be challenging to troubleshoot and diagnose these kinds of performance problems in a microservice architecture.

Pattern: Distributed tracing

Assign each external request a unique ID and record how it flows through the system from one service to the next in a centralized server that provides visualization and analysis. See http://microservices.io/patterns/observability/distributed-tracing.html.

A good way to get insight into what your application is doing is to use distributed tracing. *Distributed tracing* is analogous to a performance profiler in a monolithic application. It records information (for example, start time and end time) about the tree of service calls that are made when handling a request. You can then see how the services interact during the handling of external requests, including a breakdown of where the time is spent.

Figure 11.12 shows an example of how a distributed tracing server displays what happens when the API gateway handles a request. It shows the inbound request to the API gateway and the request that the gateway makes to `Order Service`. For each request, the distributed tracing server shows the operation that's performed and the timing of the request.

Figure 11.12   **The Zipkin server shows how the FTGO application handles a request that's routed by the API gateway to `Order Service`. Each request is represented by a trace. A trace is a set of spans. Each span, which can contain child spans, is the invocation of a service. Depending on the level of detail collected, a span can also represent the invocation of an operation inside a service.**

Figure 11.12 shows what in distributed tracing terminology is called a *trace*. A trace represents an external request and consists of one or more spans. A *span* represents an operation, and its key attributes are an operation name, start timestamp, and end time. A span can have one or more child spans, which represent nested operations. For example, a top-level span might represent the invocation of the API gateway, as is the case in figure 11.12. Its child spans represent the invocations of services by the API gateway.

A valuable side effect of distributed tracing is that it assigns a unique ID to each external request. A service can include the request ID in its log entries. When combined with log aggregation, the request ID enables you to easily find all log entries for a particular external request. For example, here's an example log entry from `Order Service`:

```
2018-03-04 17:38:12.032 DEBUG [ftgo-order-
    service,8d8fdc37be104cc6,8d8fdc37be104cc6,false]
  7 --- [nio-8080-exec-6] org.hibernate.SQL                          :
  select order0_.id as id1_3_0_, order0_.consumer_id as consumer2_3_0_, order
    0_.city as city3_3_0_,
  order0_.delivery_state as delivery4_3_0_, order0_.street1 as street5_3_0_,
  order0_.street2 as street6_3_0_, order0_.zip as zip7_3_0_,
order0_.delivery_time as delivery8_3_0_, order0_.a
```

The [ftgo-order-service,8d8fdc37be104cc6,8d8fdc37be104cc6,false] part of the log entry (the SLF4J Mapped Diagnostic Context—see www.slf4j.org/manual.html) contains information from the distributed tracing infrastructure. It consists of four values:

- ftgo-order-service—The name of the application
- 8d8fdc37be104cc6—The traceId
- 8d8fdc37be104cc6—The spanId
- false—Indicates that this span wasn't exported to the distributed tracing server

If you search the logs for 8d8fdc37be104cc6, you'll find all log entries for that request.

Figure 11.13 shows how distributed tracing works. There are two parts to distributed tracing: an instrumentation library, which is used by each service, and a distributed tracing server. The instrumentation library manages the traces and spans. It also adds

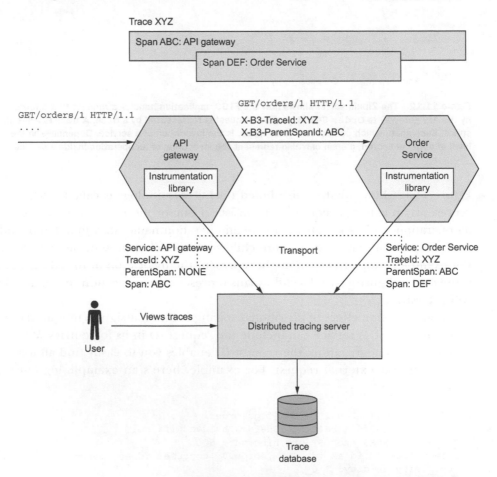

Figure 11.13   Each service (including the API gateway) uses an instrumentation library. The instrumentation library assigns an ID to each external request, propagates tracing state between services, and reports spans to the distributed tracing server.

tracing information, such as the current trace ID and the parent span ID, to outbound requests. For example, one common standard for propagating trace information is the B3 standard (https://github.com/openzipkin/b3-propagation), which uses headers such as X-B3-TraceId and X-B3-ParentSpanId. The instrumentation library also reports traces to the distributed tracing server. The distributed tracing server stores the traces and provides a UI for visualizing them.

Let's take a look at the instrumentation library and the distribution tracing server, beginning with the library.

USING AN INSTRUMENTATION LIBRARY

The instrumentation library builds the tree of spans and sends them to the distributed tracing server. The service code could call the instrumentation library directly, but that would intertwine the instrumentation logic with business and other logic. A cleaner approach is to use interceptors or aspect-oriented programming (AOP).

A great example of an AOP-based framework is Spring Cloud Sleuth. It uses the Spring Framework's AOP mechanism to automagically integrate distributed tracing into the service. As a result, you have to add Spring Cloud Sleuth as a project dependency. Your service doesn't need to call a distributed tracing API except in those cases that aren't handled by Spring Cloud Sleuth.

ABOUT THE DISTRIBUTED TRACING SERVER

The instrumentation library sends the spans to a distributed tracing server. The distributed tracing server stitches the spans together to form complete traces and stores them in a database. One popular distributed tracing server is Open Zipkin. Zipkin was originally developed by Twitter. Services can deliver spans to Zipkin using either HTTP or a message broker. Zipkin stores the traces in a storage backend, which is either a SQL or NoSQL database. It has a UI that displays traces, as shown earlier in figure 11.12. AWS X-ray is another example of a distributed tracing server.

11.3.4 Applying the Application metrics pattern

A key part of the production environment is monitoring and alerting. As figure 11.14 shows, the monitoring system gathers metrics, which provide critical information about the health of an application, from every part of the technology stack. Metrics range from infrastructure-level metrics, such as CPU, memory, and disk utilization, to application-level metrics, such as service request latency and number of requests executed. Order Service, for example, gathers metrics about the number of placed, approved, and rejected orders. The metrics are collected by a metrics service, which provides visualization and alerting.

> **Pattern: Application metrics**
> Services report metrics to a central server that provides aggregation, visualization, and alerting.

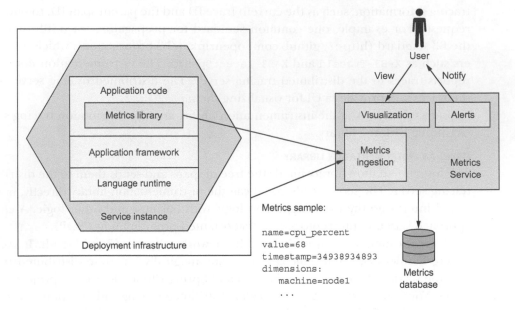

Figure 11.14   Metrics at every level of the stack are collected and stored in a metrics service, which provides visualization and alerting.

Metrics are sampled periodically. A metric sample has the following three properties:

- *Name*—The name of the metric, such as `jvm_memory_max_bytes` or `placed_orders`
- *Value*—A numeric value
- *Timestamp*—The time of the sample

In addition, some monitoring systems support the concept of *dimensions*, which are arbitrary name-value pairs. For example, `jvm_memory_max_bytes` is reported with dimensions such as `area="heap",id="PS Eden Space"` and `area="heap",id="PS Old Gen"`. Dimensions are often used to provide additional information, such as the machine name or service name, or a service instance identifier. A monitoring system typically *aggregates* (sums or averages) metric samples along one or more dimensions.

Many aspects of monitoring are the responsibility of operations. But a service developer is responsible for two aspects of metrics. First, they must instrument their service so that it collects metrics about its behavior. Second, they must expose those service metrics, along with metrics from the JVM and the application framework, to the metrics server.

Let's first look at how a service collects metrics.

COLLECTING SERVICE-LEVEL METRICS

How much work you need to do to collect metrics depends on the frameworks that your application uses and the metrics you want to collect. A Spring Boot-based service can, for example, gather (and expose) basic metrics, such as JVM metrics, by including the Micrometer Metrics library as a dependency and using a few lines of configuration. Spring Boot's autoconfiguration takes care of configuring the metrics library and exposing the metrics. A service only needs to use the Micrometer Metrics API directly if it gathers application-specific metrics.

The following listing shows how `OrderService` can collect metrics about the number of orders placed, approved, and rejected. It uses `MeterRegistry`, which is the interface-provided Micrometer Metrics, to gather custom metrics. Each method increments an appropriately named counter.

Listing 11.1 `OrderService` tracks the number of orders placed, approved, and rejected.

```
public class OrderService {

    @Autowired
    private MeterRegistry meterRegistry;          <── The Micrometer Metrics
                                                       library API for managing
                                                       application-specific meters

    public Order createOrder(...) {
        ...
        meterRegistry.counter("placed_orders").increment();   <── Increments the
        return order;                                              placedOrders counter
    }                                                              when an order has
                                                                   successfully been
                                                                   placed

    public void approveOrder(long orderId) {
        ...                                                    Increments the
        meterRegistry.counter("approved_orders").increment(); <── approvedOrders
    }                                                              counter when an
                                                                   order has been
                                                                   approved

    public void rejectOrder(long orderId) {
        ...                                                    Increments the
        meterRegistry.counter("rejected_orders").increment(); <── rejectedOrders
    }                                                              counter when an
                                                                   order has been
                                                                   rejected
```

DELIVERING METRICS TO THE METRICS SERVICE

A service delivers metrics to the Metrics Service in one of two ways: push or pull. With the *push* model, a service instance sends the metrics to the Metrics Service by invoking an API. AWS Cloudwatch metrics, for example, implements the push model.

With the *pull* model, the Metrics Service (or its agent running locally) invokes a service API to retrieve the metrics from the service instance. Prometheus, a popular open source monitoring and alerting system, uses the pull model.

The FTGO application's `Order Service` uses the `micrometer-registry-prometheus` library to integrate with Prometheus. Because this library is on the classpath, Spring Boot exposes a `GET /actuator/prometheus` endpoint, which returns metrics in the format that Prometheus expects. The custom metrics from `OrderService` are reported as follows:

```
$ curl -v http://localhost:8080/actuator/prometheus | grep _orders
# HELP placed_orders_total
# TYPE placed_orders_total counter
```

```
placed_orders_total{service="ftgo-order-service",} 1.0
# HELP approved_orders_total
# TYPE approved_orders_total counter
approved_orders_total{service="ftgo-order-service",} 1.0
```

The `placed_orders` counter is, for example, reported as a metric of type `counter`.

The Prometheus server periodically polls this endpoint to retrieve metrics. Once the metrics are in Prometheus, you can view them using Grafana, a data visualization tool (https://grafana.com). You can also set up alerts for these metrics, such as when the rate of change for `placed_orders_total` falls below some threshold.

Application metrics provide valuable insights into your application's behavior. Alerts triggered by metrics enable you to quickly respond to a production issue, perhaps before it impacts users. Let's now look at how to observe and respond to another source of alerts: exceptions.

11.3.5   *Using the Exception tracking pattern*

A service should rarely log an exception, and when it does, it's important that you identify the root cause. The exception might be a symptom of a failure or a programming bug. The traditional way to view exceptions is to look in the logs. You might even configure the logging server to alert you if an exception appears in the log file. There are, however, several problems with this approach:

- Log files are oriented around single-line log entries, whereas exceptions consist of multiple lines.
- There's no mechanism to track the resolution of exceptions that occur in log files. You would have to manually copy/paste the exception into an issue tracker.
- There are likely to be duplicate exceptions, but there's no automatic mechanism to treat them as one.

> **Pattern: Exception tracking**
> Services report exceptions to a central service that de-duplicates exceptions, generates alerts, and manages the resolution of exceptions. See http://microservices.io/patterns/observability/audit-logging.html.

A better approach is to use an exception tracking service. As figure 11.15 shows, you configure your service to report exceptions to an exception tracking service via, for example, a REST API. The exception tracking service de-duplicates exceptions, generates alerts, and manages the resolution of exceptions.

There are a couple of ways to integrate the exception tracking service into your application. Your service could invoke the exception tracking service's API directly. A better approach is to use a client library provided by the exception tracking service. For example, HoneyBadger's client library provides several easy-to-use integration mechanisms, including a Servlet Filter that catches and reports exceptions.

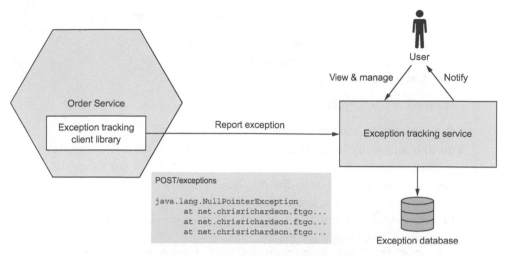

Figure 11.15 A service reports exceptions to an exception tracking service, which de-duplicates exceptions and alerts developers. It has a UI for viewing and managing exceptions.

Exception tracking services

There are several exception tracking services. Some, such as Honeybadger (www .honeybadger.io), are purely cloud-based. Others, such as Sentry.io (https://sentry.io/ welcome/), also have an open source version that you can deploy on your own infrastructure. These services receive exceptions from your application and generate alerts. They provide a console for viewing exceptions and managing their resolution. An exception tracking service typically provides client libraries in a variety of languages.

The Exception tracking pattern is a useful way to quickly identify and respond to production issues.

It's also important to track user behavior. Let's look at how to do that.

11.3.6 *Applying the Audit logging pattern*

The purpose of audit logging is to record each user's actions. An audit log is typically used to help customer support, ensure compliance, and detect suspicious behavior. Each audit log entry records the identity of the user, the action they performed, and the business object(s). An application usually stores the audit log in a database table.

Pattern: Audit logging

Record user actions in a database in order to help customer support, ensure compliance, and detect suspicious behavior. See http://microservices.io/patterns/ observability/audit-logging.html.

There are a few different ways to implement audit logging:

- Add audit logging code to the business logic.
- Use aspect-oriented programming (AOP).
- Use event sourcing.

Let's look at each option.

ADD AUDIT LOGGING CODE TO THE BUSINESS LOGIC

The first and most straightforward option is to sprinkle audit logging code throughout your service's business logic. Each service method, for example, can create an audit log entry and save it in the database. The drawback with this approach is that it intertwines auditing logging code and business logic, which reduces maintainability. The other drawback is that it's potentially error prone, because it relies on the developer writing audit logging code.

USE ASPECT-ORIENTED PROGRAMMING

The second option is to use AOP. You can use an AOP framework, such as Spring AOP, to define advice that automatically intercepts each service method call and persists an audit log entry. This is a much more reliable approach, because it automatically records every service method invocation. The main drawback of using AOP is that the advice only has access to the method name and its arguments, so it might be challenging to determine the business object being acted upon and generate a business-oriented audit log entry.

USE EVENT SOURCING

The third and final option is to implement your business logic using event sourcing. As mentioned in chapter 6, *event sourcing* automatically provides an audit log for create and update operations. You need to record the identity of the user in each event. One limitation with using event sourcing, though, is that it doesn't record queries. If your service must create log entries for queries, then you'll have to use one of the other options as well.

11.4 Developing services using the Microservice chassis pattern

This chapter has described numerous concerns that a service must implement, including metrics, reporting exceptions to an exception tracker, logging and health checks, externalized configuration, and security. Moreover, as described in chapter 3, a service may also need to handle service discovery and implement circuit breakers. That's not something you'd want to set up from scratch each time you implement a new service. If you did, it would potentially be days, if not weeks, before you wrote your first line of business logic.

> **Pattern: Microservice chassis**
>
> Build services on a framework or collection of frameworks that handle cross-cutting concerns, such as exception tracking, logging, health checks, externalized configuration, and distributed tracing. See http://microservices.io/patterns/microservice-chassis.html.

A much faster way to develop services is to build your services upon a microservices chassis. As figure 11.16 shows, a *microservice chassis* is a framework or set of frameworks that handle these concerns. When using a microservice chassis, you write little, if any, code to handle these concerns.

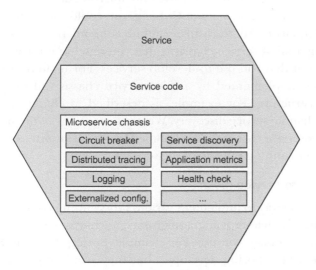

Figure 11.16 **A microservice chassis is a framework that handles numerous concerns, such as exception tracking, logging, health checks, externalized configuration, and distributed tracing.**

In this section, I first describe the concept of a microservice chassis and suggest some excellent microservice chassis frameworks. After that I introduce the concept of a service mesh, which at the time of writing is emerging as an intriguing alternative to using frameworks and libraries.

Let's first look at the idea of a microservice chassis.

11.4.1 *Using a microservice chassis*

A microservices chassis is a framework or set of frameworks that handle numerous concerns including the following:

- Externalized configuration
- Health checks
- Application metrics
- Service discovery

- Circuit breakers
- Distributed tracing

It significantly reduces the amount of code you need to write. You may not even need to write any code. Instead, you configure the microservice chassis to fit your requirements. A microservice chassis enables you to focus on developing your service's business logic.

The FTGO application uses Spring Boot and Spring Cloud as the microservice chassis. Spring Boot provides functions such as externalized configuration. Spring Cloud provides functions such as circuit breakers. It also implements client-side service discovery, although the FTGO application relies on the infrastructure for service discovery. Spring Boot and Spring Cloud aren't the only microservice chassis frameworks. If, for example, you're writing services in GoLang, you could use either Go Kit (https://github.com/go-kit/kit) or Micro (https://github.com/micro/micro).

One drawback of using a microservice chassis is that you need one for every language/platform combination that you use to develop services. Fortunately, it's likely that many of the functions implemented by a microservice chassis will instead be implemented by the infrastructure. For example, as described in chapter 3, many deployment environments handle service discovery. What's more, many of the network-related functions of a microservice chassis will be handled by what's known as a service mesh, an infrastructure layer running outside of the services.

11.4.2 *From microservice chassis to service mesh*

A microservice chassis is a good way to implement various cross-cutting concerns, such as circuit breakers. But one obstacle to using a microservice chassis is that you need one for each programming language you use. For example, Spring Boot and Spring Cloud are useful if you're a Java/Spring developer, but they aren't any help if you want to write a NodeJS-based service.

> **Pattern: Service mesh**
>
> Route all network traffic in and out of services through a networking layer that implements various concerns, including circuit breakers, distributed tracing, service discovery, load balancing, and rule-based traffic routing. See http://microservices.io/patterns/deployment/service-mesh.html.

An emerging alternative that avoids this problem is to implement some of this functionality outside of the service in what's known as a service mesh. A *service mesh* is networking infrastructure that mediates the communication between a service and other services and external applications. As figure 11.17 shows, all network traffic in and out of a service goes through the service mesh. It implements various concerns including circuit breakers, distributed tracing, service discovery, load balancing, and rule-based traffic routing. A service mesh can also secure interprocess communication by using

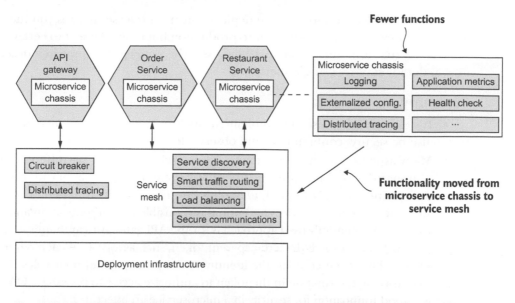

Figure 11.17 All network traffic in and out of a service flows through the service mesh. The service mesh implements various functions including circuit breakers, distributed tracing, service discovery, and load balancing. Fewer functions are implemented by the microservice chassis. It also secures interprocess communication by using TLS-based IPC between services.

TLS-based IPC between services. As a result, you no longer need to implement these particular concerns in the services.

When using a service mesh, the microservice chassis is much simpler. It only needs to implement concerns that are tightly integrated with the application code, such as externalized configuration and health checks. The microservice chassis must support distributed tracing by propagating distributed tracing information, such as the B3 standard headers I discussed earlier in section 11.3.3.

The current state of service mesh implementations

There are various service mesh implementations, including the following:

- Istio (https://istio.io)
- Linkerd (https://linkerd.io)
- Conduit (https://conduit.io)

As of the time of writing, Linkerd is the most mature, with Istio and Conduit still under active development. For more information about this exciting new technology, take a look at each product's documentation.

The service mesh concept is an extremely promising idea. It frees the developer from having to deal with various cross-cutting concerns. Also, the ability of a service mesh to route traffic enables you to separate deployment from release. It gives you the ability to deploy a new version of a service into production but only release it to certain users, such as internal test users. Chapter 12 discusses this concept further when describing how to deploy services using Kubernetes.

Summary

- It's essential that a service implements its functional requirements, but it must also be secure, configurable, and observable.
- Many aspects of security in a microservice architecture are no different than in a monolithic architecture. But there are some aspects of application security that are necessarily different, including how user identity is passed between the API gateway and the services and who is responsible for authentication and authorization. A commonly used approach is for the API gateway to authenticate clients. The API gateway includes a transparent token, such as a JWT, in each request to a service. The token contains the identity of the principal and their roles. The services use the information in the token to authorize access to resources. OAuth 2.0 is a good foundation for security in a microservice architecture.
- A service typically uses one or more external services, such as message brokers and databases. The network location and credentials of each external service often depend on the environment that the service is running in. You must apply the Externalized configuration pattern and implement a mechanism that provides a service with configuration properties at runtime. One commonly used approach is for the deployment infrastructure to supply those properties via operating system environment variables or a properties file when it creates a service instance. Another option is for a service instance to retrieve its configuration from a configuration properties server.
- Operations and developers share responsibility for implementing the observability patterns. Operations is responsible for the observability infrastructure, such as servers that handle log aggregation, metrics, exception tracking, and distributed tracing. Developers are responsible for ensuring that their services are observable. Services must have health check API endpoints, generate log entries, collect and expose metrics, report exceptions to an exception tracking service, and implement distributed tracing.
- In order to simplify and accelerate development, you should develop services on top of a microservices chassis. A microservices chassis is framework or set of frameworks that handle various cross-cutting concerns, including those described in this chapter. Over time, though, it's likely that many of the networking-related functions of a microservice chassis will migrate into a service mesh, a layer of infrastructure software through which all of a service's network traffic flows.

Deploying microservices

12

This chapter covers

- The four key deployment patterns, how they work, and their benefits and drawbacks:
  - Language-specific packaging format
  - Deploying a service as a VM
  - Deploying a service as a container
  - Serverless deployment
- Deploying services with Kubernetes
- Using a service mesh to separate deployment from release
- Deploying services with AWS Lambda
- Picking a deployment pattern

Mary and her team at FTGO are almost finished writing their first service. Although it's not yet feature complete, it's running on developer laptops and the Jenkins CI server. But that's not good enough. Software has no value to FTGO until it's running in production and available to users. FTGO needs to deploy their service into production.

Deployment is a combination of two interrelated concepts: process and architecture. The deployment process consists of the steps that must be performed by people—developers and operations—in order to get software into production. The deployment architecture defines the structure of the environment in which that software runs. Both aspects of deployment have changed radically since I first started developing Enterprise Java applications in the late 1990s. The manual process of developers throwing code over the wall to production has become highly automated. As figure 12.1 shows, physical production environments have been replaced by increasingly lightweight and ephemeral computing infrastructure.

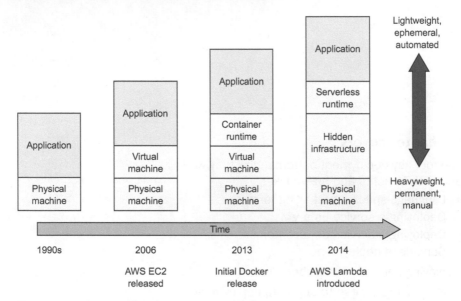

Figure 12.1 Heavyweight and long-lived physical machines have been abstracted away by increasingly lightweight and ephemeral technologies.

Back in the 1990s, if you wanted to deploy an application into production, the first step was to throw your application along with a set of operating instructions over the wall to operations. You might, for example, file a trouble ticket asking operations to deploy the application. Whatever happened next was entirely the responsibility of operations, unless they encountered a problem they needed your help to fix. Typically, operations bought and installed expensive and heavyweight application servers such as WebLogic or WebSphere. Then they would log in to the application server console and deploy your applications. They would lovingly care for those machines, as if they were pets, installing patches and updating the software.

In the mid 2000s, the expensive application servers were replaced with open source, lightweight web containers such as Apache Tomcat and Jetty. You could still run multiple applications on each web container, but having one application per web container became feasible. Also, virtual machines started to replace physical machines.

But machines were still treated as beloved pets, and deployment was still a fundamentally manual process.

Today, the deployment process is radically different. Instead of handing off code to a separate production team, the adoption of DevOps means that the development team is also responsible for deploying their application or services. In some organizations, operations provides developers with a console for deploying their code. Or, better yet, once the tests pass, the deployment pipeline automatically deploys the code into production.

The computing resources used in a production environment have also changed radically with physical machines being abstracted away. Virtual machines running on a highly automated cloud, such as AWS, have replaced the long-lived, pet-like physical and virtual machines. Today's virtual machines are immutable. They're treated as disposable cattle instead of pets and are discarded and recreated rather than being reconfigured. *Containers,* an even more lightweight abstraction layer of top of virtual machines, are an increasingly popular way of deploying applications. You can also use an even more lightweight *serverless* deployment platform, such as AWS Lambda, for many use cases.

It's no coincidence that the evolution of deployment processes and architectures has coincided with the growing adoption of the microservice architecture. An application might have tens or hundreds of services written in a variety of languages and frameworks. Because each service is a small application, that means you have tens or hundreds of applications in production. It's no longer practical, for example, for system administrators to hand configure servers and services. If you want to deploy microservices at scale, you need a highly automated deployment process and infrastructure.

Figure 12.2 shows a high-level view of a production environment. The production environment enables developers to configure and manage their services, the deployment

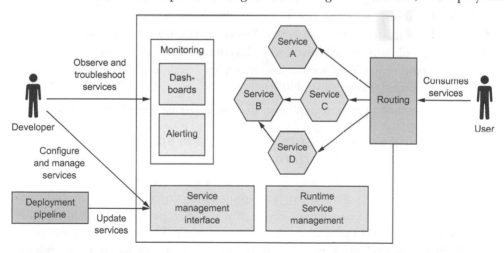

Figure 12.2   A simplified view of the production environment. It provides four main capabilities: service management enables developers to deploy and manage their services, runtime management ensures that the services are running, monitoring visualizes service behavior and generates alerts, and request routing routes requests from users to the services.

pipeline to deploy new versions of services, and users to access functionality implemented by those services.

A production environment must implement four key capabilities:

- *Service management interface*—Enables developers to create, update, and configure services. Ideally, this interface is a REST API invoked by command-line and GUI deployment tools.
- *Runtime service management*—Attempts to ensure that the desired number of service instances is running at all times. If a service instance crashes or is somehow unable to handle requests, the production environment must restart it. If a machine crashes, the production environment must restart those service instances on a different machine.
- *Monitoring*—Provides developers with insight into what their services are doing, including log files and metrics. If there are problems, the production environment must alert the developers. Chapter 11 describes monitoring, also called *observability*.
- *Request routing*—Routes requests from users to the services.

In this chapter I discuss the four main deployment options:

- Deploying services as language-specific packages, such as Java JAR or WAR files. It's worthwhile exploring this option, because even though I recommend using one of the other options, its drawbacks motivate the other options.
- Deploying services as virtual machines, which simplifies deployment by packaging a service as a virtual machine image that encapsulate the service's technology stack.
- Deploying services as containers, which are more lightweight than virtual machines. I show how to deploy the FTGO application's `Restaurant Service` using Kubernetes, a popular Docker orchestration framework.
- Deploying services using serverless deployment, which is even more modern than containers. We'll look at how to deploy `Restaurant Service` using AWS Lambda, a popular serverless platform.

Let's first look at how to deploy services as language-specific packages.

12.1   Deploying services using the Language-specific packaging format pattern

Let's imagine that you want to deploy the FTGO application's `Restaurant Service`, which is a Spring Boot-based Java application. One way to deploy this service is by using the Service as a language-specific package pattern. When using this pattern, what's deployed in production and what's managed by the service runtime is a service in its language-specific package. In the case of `Restaurant Service`, that's either the executable JAR file or a WAR file. For other languages, such as NodeJS, a service is a directory of source code and modules. For some languages, such as GoLang, a service is an operating system-specific executable.

Pattern: Language-specific packaging format
Deploy a language-specific package into production. See http://microservices.io/patterns/deployment/language-specific-packaging.html.

To deploy Restaurant Service on a machine, you would first install the necessary runtime, which in this case is the JDK. If it's a WAR file, you also need to install a web container such as Apache Tomcat. Once you've configured the machine, you copy the package to the machine and start the service. Each service instance runs as a JVM process.

Ideally, you've set up your deployment pipeline to automatically deploy the service to production, as shown in figure 12.3. The deployment pipeline builds an executable JAR file or WAR file. It then invokes the production environment's service management interface to deploy the new version.

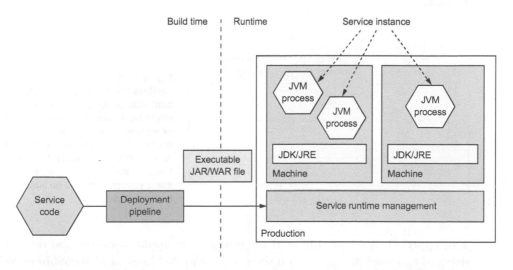

Figure 12.3 The deployment pipeline builds an executable JAR file and deploys it into production. In production, each service instance is a JVM running on a machine that has the JDK or JRE installed.

A service instance is typically a single process but sometimes may be a group of processes. A Java service instance, for example, is a process running the JVM. A NodeJS service might spawn multiple worker processes in order to process requests concurrently. Some languages support deploying multiple service instances within the same process.

Sometimes you might deploy a single service instance on a machine, while retaining the option to deploy multiple service instances on the same machine. For example, as figure 12.4 shows, you could run multiple JVMs on a single machine. Each JVM runs a single service instance.

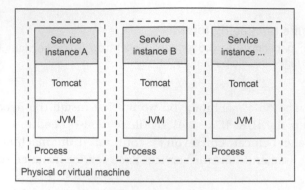

Figure 12.4   **Deploying multiple service instances on the same machine. They might be instances of the same service or instances of different services. The overhead of the OS is shared among the service instances. Each service instance is a separate process, so there's some isolation between them.**

Some languages also let you run multiple services instances in a single process. For example, as figure 12.5 shows, you can run multiple Java services on a single Apache Tomcat.

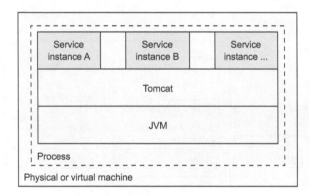

Figure 12.5   **Deploying multiple services instances on the same web container or application server. They might be instances of the same service or instances of different services. The overhead of the OS and runtime is shared among all the service instances. But because the service instances are in the same process, there's no isolation between them.**

This approach is commonly used when deploying applications on traditional expensive and heavyweight application servers, such as WebLogic and WebSphere. You can also package services as OSGI bundles and run multiple service instances in each OSGI container.

The Service as a language-specific package pattern has both benefits and drawbacks. Let's first look at the benefits.

12.1.1 *Benefits of the Service as a language-specific package pattern*

The Service as a language-specific package pattern has a few benefits:

- Fast deployment
- Efficient resource utilization, especially when running multiple instances on the same machine or within the same process

Let's look at each one.

FAST DEPLOYMENT

One major benefit of this pattern is that deploying a service instance is relatively fast: you copy the service to a host and start it. If the service is written in Java, you copy a JAR or WAR file. For other languages, such as NodeJS or Ruby, you copy the source code. In either case, the number of bytes copied over the network is relatively small.

Also, starting a service is rarely time consuming. If the service is its own process, you start it. Otherwise, if the service is one of several instances running in the same container process, you either dynamically deploy it into the container or restart the container. Because of the lack of overhead, starting a service is usually fast.

EFFICIENT RESOURCE UTILIZATION

Another major benefit of this pattern is that it uses resources relatively efficiently. Multiple service instances share the machine and its operating system. It's even more efficient if multiple service instances run within the same process. For example, multiple web applications could share the same Apache Tomcat server and JVM.

12.1.2 Drawbacks of the Service as a language-specific package pattern

Despite its appeal, the Service as a language-specific package pattern has several significant drawbacks:

- Lack of encapsulation of the technology stack.
- No ability to constrain the resources consumed by a service instance.
- Lack of isolation when running multiple service instances on the same machine.
- Automatically determining where to place service instances is challenging.

Let's look at each drawback.

LACK OF ENCAPSULATION OF THE TECHNOLOGY STACK

The operation team must know the specific details of how to deploy each and every service. Each service needs a particular version of the runtime. A Java web application, for example, needs particular versions of Apache Tomcat and the JDK. Operations must install the correct version of each required software package.

To make matters worse, services can be written in a variety of languages and frameworks. They might also be written in multiple versions of those languages and frameworks. Consequently, the development team must share lots of details with operations. This complexity increases the risk of errors during deployment. A machine might, for example, have the wrong version of the language runtime.

NO ABILITY TO CONSTRAIN THE RESOURCES CONSUMED BY A SERVICE INSTANCE

Another drawback is that you can't constrain the resources consumed by a service instance. A process can potentially consume all of a machine's CPU or memory, starving other service instances and operating systems of resources. This might happen, for example, because of a bug.

LACK OF ISOLATION WHEN RUNNING MULTIPLE SERVICE INSTANCES ON THE SAME MACHINE

The problem is even worse when running multiple instances on the same machine. The lack of isolation means that a misbehaving service instance can impact other service instances. As a result, the application risks being unreliable, especially when running multiple service instances on the same machine.

AUTOMATICALLY DETERMINING WHERE TO PLACE SERVICE INSTANCES IS CHALLENGING

Another challenge with running multiple service instances on the same machine is determining the placement of service instances. Each machine has a fixed set of resources, CPU, memory, and so on, and each service instance needs some amount of resources. It's important to assign service instances to machines in a way that uses the machines efficiently without overloading them. As I explain shortly, VM-based clouds and container orchestration frameworks handle this automatically. When deploying services natively, it's likely that you'll need to manually decide the placement.

As you can see, despite its familiarity, the Service as a language-specific package pattern has some significant drawbacks. You should rarely use this approach, except perhaps when efficiency outweighs all other concerns.

Let's now look at modern ways of deploying services that avoid these problems.

12.2 Deploying services using the Service as a virtual machine pattern

Once again, imagine you want to deploy the FTGO `Restaurant Service`, except this time it's on AWS EC2. One option would be to create and configure an EC2 instance and copy onto it the executable or WAR file. Although you would get some benefit from using the cloud, this approach suffers from the drawbacks described in the preceding section. A better, more modern approach is to package the service as an Amazon Machine Image (AMI), as shown in figure 12.6. Each service instance is an EC2 instance created from that AMI. The EC2 instances would typically be managed by an AWS Auto Scaling group, which attempts to ensure that the desired number of healthy instances is always running.

> **Pattern: Deploy a service as a VM**
> Deploy services packaged as VM images into production. Each service instance is a VM. See http://microservices.io/patterns/deployment/service-per-vm.html.

The virtual machine image is built by the service's deployment pipeline. The deployment pipeline, as figure 12.6 shows, runs a VM image builder to create a VM image that contains the service's code and whatever software is required to run it. For example, the VM builder for a FTGO service installs the JDK and the service's executable JAR. The VM image builder configures the VM image machine to run the application when the VM boots, using Linux's `init` system, such as upstart.

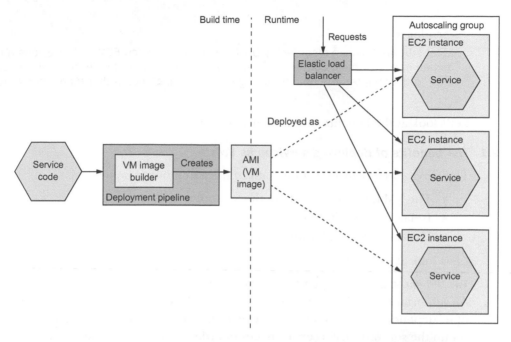

Figure 12.6 The deployment pipeline packages a service as a virtual machine image, such as an EC2 AMI, containing everything required to run the service, including the language runtime. At runtime, each service instance is a VM, such as an EC2 instance, instantiated from that image. An EC2 Elastic Load Balancer routes requests to the instances.

There are a variety of tools that your deployment pipeline can use to build VM images. One early tool for creating EC2 AMIs is Aminator, created by Netflix, which used it to deploy its video-streaming service on AWS (https://github.com/Netflix/aminator). A more modern VM image builder is Packer, which unlike Aminator supports a variety of virtualization technologies, including EC2, Digital Ocean, Virtual Box, and VMware (www.packer.io). To use Packer to create an AMI, you write a configuration file that specifies the base image and a set of provisioners that install software and configure the AMI.

About Elastic Beanstalk

Elastic Beanstalk, which is provided by AWS, is an easy way to deploy your services using VMs. You upload your code, such as a WAR file, and Elastic Beanstalk deploys it as one or more load-balanced and managed EC2 instances. Elastic Beanstalk is perhaps not quite as fashionable as, say, Kubernetes, but it's an easy way to deploy a microservices-based application on EC2.

Interestingly, Elastic Beanstalk combines elements of the three deployment patterns described in this chapter. It supports several packaging formats for several languages, including Java, Ruby, and .NET. It deploys the application as VMs, but rather than building an AMI, it uses a base image that installs the application on startup.

> **(continued)**
>
> Elastic Beanstalk can also deploy Docker containers. Each EC2 instance runs a collection of one or more containers. Unlike a Docker orchestration framework, covered later in the chapter, the unit of scaling is the EC2 instance rather than a container.

Let's look at the benefits and drawbacks of using this approach.

12.2.1 *The benefits of deploying services as VMs*

The Service as a virtual machine pattern has a number of benefits:

- The VM image encapsulates the technology stack.
- Isolated service instances.
- Uses mature cloud infrastructure.

Let's look at each one.

THE VM IMAGE ENCAPSULATES THE TECHNOLOGY STACK

An important benefit of this pattern is that the VM image contains the service and all of its dependencies. It eliminates the error-prone requirement to correctly install and set up the software that a service needs in order to run. Once a service has been packaged as a virtual machine, it becomes a black box that encapsulates your service's technology stack. The VM image can be deployed anywhere without modification. The API for deploying the service becomes the VM management API. Deployment becomes much simpler and more reliable.

SERVICE INSTANCES ARE ISOLATED

A major benefit of virtual machines is that each service instance runs in complete isolation. That, after all, is one of the main goals of virtual machine technology. Each virtual machine has a fixed amount of CPU and memory and can't steal resources from other services.

USES MATURE CLOUD INFRASTRUCTURE

Another benefit of deploying your microservices as virtual machines is that you can leverage mature, highly automated cloud infrastructure. Public clouds such as AWS attempt to schedule VMs on physical machines in a way that avoids overloading the machine. They also provide valuable features such as load balancing of traffic across VMs and autoscaling.

12.2.2 *The drawbacks of deploying services as VMs*

The Service as a VM pattern also has some drawbacks:

- Less-efficient resource utilization
- Relatively slow deployments
- System administration overhead

Let's look at each drawback in turn.

LESS-EFFICIENT RESOURCE UTILIZATION

Each service instance has the overhead of an entire virtual machine, including its operating system. Moreover, a typical public IaaS virtual machine offers a limited set of VM sizes, so the VM will probably be underutilized. This is less likely to be a problem for Java-based services because they're relatively heavyweight. But this pattern might be an inefficient way of deploying lightweight NodeJS and GoLang services.

RELATIVELY SLOW DEPLOYMENTS

Building a VM image typically takes some number of minutes because of the size of the VM. There are lots of bits to be moved over the network. Also, instantiating a VM from a VM image is time consuming because of, once again, the amount of data that must be moved over the network. The operating system running inside the VM also takes some time to boot, though *slow* is a relative term. This process, which perhaps takes minutes, is much faster than the traditional deployment process. But it's much slower than the more lightweight deployment patterns you'll read about soon.

SYSTEM ADMINISTRATION OVERHEAD

You're responsible for patching the operation system and runtime. System administration may seem inevitable when deploying software, but later in section 12.5, I describe serverless deployment, which eliminates this kind of system administration.

Let's now look at an alternative way to deploy microservices that's more lightweight, yet still has many of the benefits of virtual machines.

12.3 Deploying services using the Service as a container pattern

Containers are a more modern and lightweight deployment mechanism. They're an operating-system-level virtualization mechanism. A container, as figure 12.7 shows, consists of usually one but sometimes multiple processes running in a sandbox, which isolates it from other containers. A container running a Java service, for example, would typically consist of the JVM process.

From the perspective of a process running in a container, it's as if it's running on its own machine. It typically has its own IP address, which eliminates port conflicts. All Java processes can, for example, listen on port 8080. Each container also has its own root filesystem. The container runtime uses operating system mechanisms to isolate the containers from each other. The most popular example of a container runtime is Docker, although there are others, such as Solaris Zones.

Pattern: Deploy a service as a container

Deploy services packaged as container images into production. Each service instance is a container. See http://microservices.io/patterns/deployment/service-per-container .html.

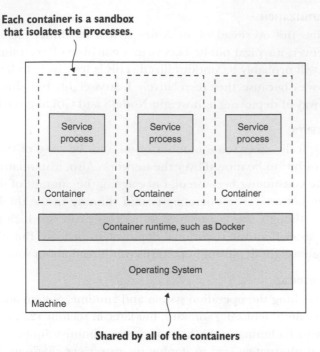

Figure 12.7   A container consists of one or more processes running in an isolated sandbox. Multiple containers usually run on a single machine. The containers share the operating system.

When you create a container, you can specify its CPU, memory resources, and, depending on the container implementation, perhaps the I/O resources. The container runtime enforces these limits and prevents a container from hogging the resources of its machine. When using a Docker orchestration framework such as Kubernetes, it's especially important to specify a container's resources. That's because the orchestration framework uses a container's requested resources to select the machine to run the container and thereby ensure that machines aren't overloaded.

Figure 12.8 shows the process of deploying a service as a container. At build-time, the deployment pipeline uses a container image-building tool, which reads the service's code and a description of the image, to create the container image and stores it in a registry. At runtime, the container image is pulled from the registry and used to create containers.

Let's take a look at build-time and runtime steps in more detail.

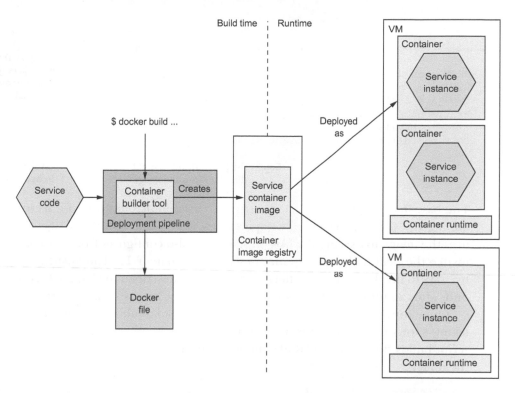

Figure 12.8 A service is packaged as a container image, which is stored in a registry. At runtime the service consists of multiple containers instantiated from that image. Containers typically run on virtual machines. A single VM will usually run multiple containers.

12.3.1 *Deploying services using Docker*

To deploy a service as a container, you must package it as a container image. A *container image* is a filesystem image consisting of the application and any software required to run the service. It's often a complete Linux root filesystem, although more lightweight images are also used. For example, to deploy a Spring Boot-based service, you build a container image containing the service's executable JAR and the correct version of the JDK. Similarly, to deploy a Java web application, you would build a container image containing the WAR file, Apache Tomcat, and the JDK.

BUILDING A DOCKER IMAGE

The first step in building an image is to create a Dockerfile. A *Dockerfile* describes how to build a Docker container image. It specifies the base container image, a series of instructions for installing software and configuring the container, and the shell command to run when the container is created. Listing 12.1 shows the Dockerfile used to build an image for `Restaurant Service`. It builds a container image containing the service's executable JAR file. It configures the container to run the `java -jar` command on startup.

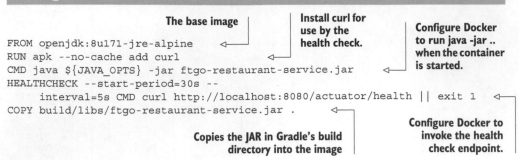

Listing 12.1   The `Dockerfile` used to build `Restaurant Service`

The base image

Install curl for use by the health check.

Configure Docker to run java -jar .. when the container is started.

```
FROM openjdk:8u171-jre-alpine
RUN apk --no-cache add curl
CMD java ${JAVA_OPTS} -jar ftgo-restaurant-service.jar
HEALTHCHECK --start-period=30s --
        interval=5s CMD curl http://localhost:8080/actuator/health || exit 1
COPY build/libs/ftgo-restaurant-service.jar .
```

Copies the JAR in Gradle's build directory into the image

Configure Docker to invoke the health check endpoint.

The base image `openjdk:8u171-jre-alpine` is a minimal footprint Linux image containing the JRE. The Dockerfile copies the service's JAR into the image and configures the image to execute the JAR on startup. It also configures Docker to periodically invoke the health check endpoint, described in chapter 11. The `HEALTHCHECK` directive says to invoke the health check endpoint API, described in chapter 11, every 5 seconds after an initial 30-second delay, which gives the service time to start.

Once you've written the `Dockerfile`, you can then build the image. The following listing shows the shell commands to build the image for `Restaurant Service`. The script builds the service's JAR file and executes the `docker build` command to create the image.

Listing 12.2   The shell commands used to build the container image for Restaurant Service

Change to the service's directory.

Build the service's JAR.

```
cd ftgo-restaurant-service
../gradlew assemble
docker build -t ftgo-restaurant-service .
```

Build the image.

The `docker build` command has two arguments: the `-t` argument specifies the name of the image, and the `.` specifies what Docker calls the context. The *context*, which in this example is the current directory, consists of `Dockerfile` and the files used to build the image. The `docker build` command uploads the context to the Docker daemon, which builds the image.

PUSHING A DOCKER IMAGE TO A REGISTRY

The final step of the build process is to push the newly built Docker image to what is known as a registry. A Docker *registry* is the equivalent of a Java Maven repository for Java libraries, or a NodeJS npm registry for NodeJS packages. Docker hub is an example of a public Docker registry and is equivalent to Maven Central or NpmJS.org. But for your applications you'll probably want to use a private registry provided by services, such as Docker Cloud registry or AWS EC2 Container Registry.

You must use two Docker commands to push an image to a registry. First, you use the `docker tag` command to give the image a name that's prefixed with the hostname and optional port of the registry. The image name is also suffixed with the version, which will be important when you make a new release of the service. For example, if the hostname of the registry is `registry.acme.com`, you would use this command to tag the image:

```
docker tag ftgo-restaurant-service registry.acme.com/ftgo-restaurant-
    service:1.0.0.RELEASE
```

Next you use the `docker push` command to upload that tagged image to the registry:

```
docker push registry.acme.com/ftgo-restaurant-service:1.0.0.RELEASE
```

This command often takes much less time than you might expect. That's because a Docker image has what's known as a *layered file system,* which enables Docker to only transfer part of the image over the network. An image's operating system, Java runtime, and the application are in separate layers. Docker only needs to transfer those layers that don't exist in the destination. As a result, transferring an image over a network is quite fast when Docker only has to move the application's layers, which are a small fraction of the image.

Now that we've pushed the image to a registry, let's look at how to create a container.

RUNNING A DOCKER CONTAINER

Once you've packaged your service as a container image, you can then create one or more containers. The container infrastructure will pull the image from the registry onto a production server. It will then create one or more containers from that image. Each container is an instance of your service.

As you might expect, Docker provides a `docker run` command that creates and starts a container. Listing 12.3 shows how to use this command to run `Restaurant Service`. The `docker run` command has several arguments, including the container image and a specification of environment variables to set in the runtime container. These are used to pass an externalized configuration, such as the database's network location and more.

Listing 12.3 Using `docker run` to run a containerized service

```
docker run \
  -d \                                  Runs it as a background daemon
  --name ftgo-restaurant-service \      The name of the container
  -p 8082:8080 \                        Binds port 8080 of the container to port 8082 of the host machine
  -e SPRING_DATASOURCE_URL=... -e SPRING_DATASOURCE_USERNAME=... \    Environment variables
  -e SPRING_DATASOURCE_PASSWORD=... \
  registry.acme.com/ftgo-restaurant-service:1.0.0.RELEASE            Image to run
```

The `docker run` command pulls the image from the registry if necessary. It then creates and starts the container, which runs the `java -jar` command specified in the Dockerfile.

Using the `docker run` command may seem simple, but there are a couple of problems. One is that `docker run` isn't a reliable way to deploy a service, because it creates a container running on a single machine. The Docker engine provides some basic management features, such as automatically restarting containers if they crash or if the machine is rebooted. But it doesn't handle machine crashes.

Another problem is that services typically don't exist in isolation. They depend on other services, such as databases and message brokers. It would be nice to deploy or undeploy a service and its dependencies as a unit.

A better approach that's especially useful during development is to use Docker Compose. Docker Compose is a tool that lets you declaratively define a set of containers using a YAML file, and then start and stop those containers as a group. What's more, the YAML file is a convenient way to specify numerous externalized configuration properties. To learn more about Docker Compose, I recommend reading *Docker in Action* by Jeff Nickoloff (Manning, 2016) and looking at the docker-compose.yml file in the example code.

The problem with Docker Compose, though, is that it's limited to a single machine. To deploy services reliably, you must use a Docker orchestration framework, such as Kubernetes, which turns a set of machines into a pool of resources. I describe how to use Kubernetes later, in section 12.4. First, let's review the benefits and drawbacks of using containers.

12.3.2 *Benefits of deploying services as containers*

Deploying services as containers has several benefits. First, containers have many of the benefits of virtual machines:

- Encapsulation of the technology stack in which the API for managing your services becomes the container API.
- Service instances are isolated.
- Service instances's resources are constrained.

But unlike virtual machines, containers are a lightweight technology. Container images are typically fast to build. For example, on my laptop it takes as little as five seconds to package a Spring Boot application as a container image. Moving a container image over the network, such as to and from the container registry, is also relatively fast, primarily because only a subset of an image's layers need to be transferred. Containers also start very quickly, because there's no lengthy OS boot process. When a container starts, all that runs is the service.

12.3.3 *Drawbacks of deploying services as containers*

One significant drawback of containers is that you're responsible for the undifferentiated heavy lifting of administering the container images. You must patch the operating system and runtime. Also, unless you're using a hosted container solution such as Google Container Engine or AWS ECS, you must administer the container infrastructure and possibly the VM infrastructure it runs on.

12.4 *Deploying the FTGO application with Kubernetes*

Now that we've looked at containers and their trade-offs, let's look at how to deploy the FTGO application's `Restaurant Service` using Kubernetes. Docker Compose, described in section 12.3.1, is great for development and testing. But to reliably run containerized services in production, you need to use a much more sophisticated container runtime, such as Kubernetes. Kubernetes is a Docker orchestration framework, a layer of software on top of Docker that turns a set of machines into a single pool of resources for running services. It endeavors to keep the desired number of instances of each service running at all times, even when service instances or machines crash. The agility of containers combined with the sophistication of Kubernetes is a compelling way to deploy services.

In this section, I first give an overview of Kubernetes, its functionality, and its architecture. After that, I show how to deploy a service using Kubernetes. Kubernetes is a complex topic, and covering it exhaustively is beyond the scope of this book, so I only show how to use Kubernetes from the perspective of a developer. For more information, I recommend *Kubernetes in Action* by Marko Luksa (Manning, 2018).

12.4.1 *Overview of Kubernetes*

Kubernetes is a Docker orchestration framework. A *Docker orchestration framework* treats a set of machines running Docker as a pool of resources. You tell the Docker orchestration framework to run *N* instances of your service, and it handles the rest. Figure 12.9 shows the architecture of a Docker orchestration framework.

A Docker orchestration framework, such as Kubernetes , has three main functions:

- *Resource management*—Treats a cluster of machines as a pool of CPU, memory, and storage volumes, turning the collection of machines into a single machine.
- *Scheduling*—Selects the machine to run your container. By default, scheduling considers the resource requirements of the container and each node's available resources. It might also implement *affinity*, which colocates containers on the same node, and *anti-affinity*, which places containers on different nodes.
- *Service management*—Implements the concept of named and versioned services that map directly to services in the microservice architecture. The orchestration framework ensures that the desired number of healthy instances is running at all times. It load balances requests across them. The orchestration framework performs rolling upgrades of services and lets you roll back to an old version.

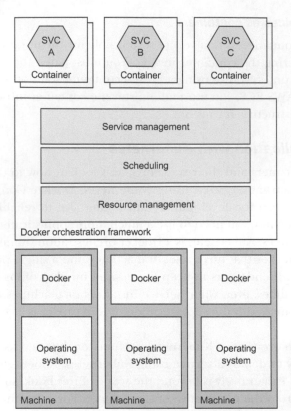

Figure 12.9 A Docker orchestration framework turns a set of machines running Docker into a cluster of resources. It assigns containers to machines. The framework attempts to keep the desired number of healthy containers running at all times.

Docker orchestration frameworks are an increasingly popular way to deploy applications. Docker Swarm is part of the Docker engine, so is easy to set up and use. Kubernetes is much more complex to set up and administer, but it's much more sophisticated. At the time of writing, Kubernetes has tremendous momentum, with a massive open source community. Let's take a closer look at how it works.

KUBERNETES ARCHITECTURE

Kubernetes runs on a cluster of machines. Figure 12.10 shows the architecture of a Kubernetes cluster. Each machine in a Kubernetes cluster is either a master or a node. A typical cluster has a small number of masters—perhaps just one—and many nodes. A *master* machine is responsible for managing the cluster. A *node* is a worker than runs one or more pods. A *pod* is Kubernetes's unit of deployment and consists of a set of containers.

A master runs several components, including the following:

- *API server*—The REST API for deploying and managing services, used by the `kubectl` command-line interface, for example.
- *Etcd*—A key-value NoSQL database that stores the cluster data.

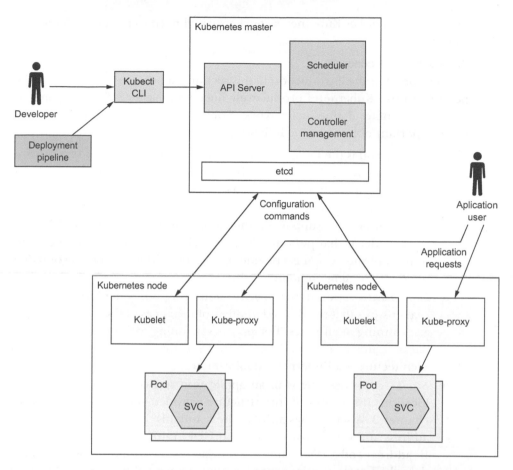

Figure 12.10 A Kubernetes cluster consists of a master, which manages the cluster, and nodes, which run the services. Developers and the deployment pipeline interact with Kubernetes through the API server, which along with other cluster-management software runs on the master. Application containers run on nodes. Each node runs a Kubelet, which manages the application container, and a kube-proxy, which routes application requests to the pods, either directly as a proxy or indirectly by configuring iptables routing rules built into the Linux kernel.

- *Scheduler*—Selects a node to run a pod.
- *Controller manager*—Runs the controllers, which ensure that the state of the cluster matches the intended state. For example, one type of controller known as a *replication* controller ensures that the desired number of instances of a service are running by starting and terminating instances.

A node runs several components, including the following:

- *Kubelet*—Creates and manages the pods running on the node
- *Kube-proxy*—Manages networking, including load balancing across pods
- *Pods*—The application services

Let's now look at key Kubernetes concepts you'll need to master to deploy services on Kubernetes.

KEY KUBERNETES CONCEPTS

As mentioned in the introduction to this section, Kubernetes is quite complex. But it's possible to use Kubernetes productively once you master a few key concepts, called *objects*. Kubernetes defines many types of objects. From a developer's perspective, the most important objects are the following:

- *Pod*—A pod is the basic unit of deployment in Kubernetes. It consists of one or more containers that share an IP address and storage volumes. The pod for a service instance often consists of a single container, such as a container running the JVM. But in some scenarios a pod contains one or more *sidecar* containers, which implement supporting functions. For example, an NGINX server could have a sidecar that periodically does a `git pull` to download the latest version of the website. A pod is ephemeral, because either the pod's containers or the node it's running on might crash.

- *Deployment*—A declarative specification of a pod. A deployment is a controller that ensures that the desired number of instances of the pod (service instances) are running at all times. It supports versioning with rolling upgrades and roll-backs. Later in section 12.4.2, you'll see that each service in a microservice architecture is a Kubernetes deployment.

- *Service*—Provides clients of an application service with a static/stable network location. It's a form of infrastructure-provided service discovery, described in chapter 3. A service has an IP address and a DNS name that resolves to that IP address and load balances TCP and UDP traffic across one or more pods. The IP address and a DNS name are only accessible within the Kubernetes. Later, I describe how to configure services that are accessible from outside the cluster.

- *ConfigMap*—A named collection of name-value pairs that defines the external-ized configuration for one or more application services (see chapter 11 for an overview of externalized configuration). The definition of a pod's container can reference a ConfigMap to define the container's environment variables. It can also use a ConfigMap to create configuration files inside the container. You can store sensitive information, such as passwords, in a form of ConfigMap called a Secret.

Now that we've reviewed the key Kubernetes concepts, let's see them in action by looking at how to deploy an application service on Kubernetes.

12.4.2 *Deploying the Restaurant service on Kubernetes*

As mentioned earlier, to deploy a service on Kubernetes, you need to define a deploy-ment. The easiest way to create a Kubernetes object such as a deployment is by writing a YAML file. Listing 12.4 is a YAML file defining a deployment for `Restaurant Service`. This deployment specifies running two replicas of a pod. The pod has just one container.

The container definition specifies the Docker image running along with other attributes, such as the values of environment variables. The container's environment variables are the service's externalized configuration. They are read by Spring Boot and made available as properties in the application context.

Listing 12.4   Kubernetes `Deployment` for `ftgo-restaurant-service`

```
apiVersion: extensions/v1beta1                    Specifies that this is an
kind: Deployment                          ◁────    object of type Deployment
metadata:
 name: ftgo-restaurant-service           ◁────    The name of the deployment
spec:
 replicas: 2        ◁────    Number of pod replicas
  template:
   metadata:                                      Gives each pod a label
    labels:                                       called app whose value is
      app: ftgo-restaurant-service      ◁────    ftgo-restaurant-service
   spec:                                   ◁──
    containers:                                    The specification of
    - name: ftgo-restaurant-service                the pod, which defines
      image: msapatterns/ftgo-restaurant-service:latest   just one container
      imagePullPolicy: Always
      ports:
      - containerPort: 8080              ◁────    The container's port
        name: httpport
      env:                                  ◁──
       - name: JAVA_OPTS                            The container's environment
         value: "-Dsun.net.inetaddr.ttl=30"         variables, which are read by
       - name: SPRING_DATASOURCE_URL                Spring Boot
         value: jdbc:mysql://ftgo-mysql/eventuate
       name: SPRING_DATASOURCE_USERNAME
         valueFrom:
           secretKeyRef:
             name: ftgo-db-secret
             key: username
       - name: SPRING_DATASOURCE_PASSWORD          Sensitive values that
         valueFrom:                                are retrieved from the
           secretKeyRef:                           Kubernetes Secret
             name: ftgo-db-secret                  called ftgo-db-secret
             key: password              ◁──
       - name: SPRING_DATASOURCE_DRIVER_CLASS_NAME
         value: com.mysql.jdbc.Driver
       - name: EVENTUATELOCAL_KAFKA_BOOTSTRAP_SERVERS
         value: ftgo-kafka:9092
       - name: EVENTUATELOCAL_ZOOKEEPER_CONNECTION_STRING
         value: ftgo-zookeeper:2181
      livenessProbe:                      ◁──
        httpGet:                                  Configure Kubernetes
          path: /actuator/health                  to invoke the health
          port: 8080                              check endpoint.
        initialDelaySeconds: 60
        periodSeconds: 20
      readinessProbe:
```

```
httpGet:
  path: /actuator/health
  port: 8080
initialDelaySeconds: 60
periodSeconds: 20
```

This deployment definition configures Kubernetes to invoke `Restaurant Service`'s health check endpoint. As described in chapter 11, a health check endpoint enables Kubernetes to determine the health of the service instance. Kubernetes implements two different checks. The first check is `readinessProbe`, which it uses to determine whether it should route traffic to a service instance. In this example, Kubernetes invokes the `/actuator/health` HTTP endpoint every 20 seconds after an initial 30-second delay, which gives it a chance to initialize. If some number (default is 1) of consecutive `readinessProbe`s succeeds, Kubernetes considers the service to be ready, whereas if some number (default, 3) of consecutive `readinessProbe`s fail, it's considered not to be ready. Kubernetes will only route traffic to the service instance when the `readinessProbe` indicates that it's ready.

The second health check is the `livenessProbe`. It's configured the same way as the `readinessProbe`. But rather than determine whether traffic should be routed to a service instance, the `livenessProbe` determines whether Kubernetes should terminate and restart the service instance. If some number (default, 3) of consecutive `liveness-Probe`s fail in a row, Kubernetes will terminate and restart the service.

Once you've written the YAML file, you can create or update the deployment by using the `kubectl apply` command:

```
kubectl apply -f ftgo-restaurant-service/src/deployment/kubernetes/ftgo-
    restaurant-service.yml
```

This command makes a request to the Kubernetes API server that results in the creation of the deployment and the pods.

To create this deployment, you must first create the Kubernetes Secret called `ftgo-db-secret`. One quick and insecure way to do that is as follows:

```
kubectl create secret generic ftgo-db-secret \
  --from-literal=username=mysqluser --from-literal=password=mysqlpw
```

This command creates a secret containing the database user ID and password specified on the command line. See the Kubernetes documentation (https://kubernetes .io/docs/concepts/configuration/secret/#creating-your-own-secrets) for more secure ways to create secrets.

CREATING A KUBERNETES SERVICE

At this point the pods are running, and the Kubernetes deployment will do its best to keep them running. The problem is that the pods have dynamically assigned IP addresses and, as such, aren't that useful to a client that wants to make an HTTP request. As described in chapter 3, the solution is to use a service discovery mechanism.

One approach is to use a client-side discovery mechanism and install a service registry, such as Netflix OSS Eureka. Fortunately, we can avoid doing that by using the service discovery mechanism built in to Kubernetes and define a Kubernetes service.

A *service* is a Kubernetes object that provides the clients of one or more pods with a stable endpoint. It has an IP address and a DNS name that resolves that IP address. The service load balances traffic to that IP address across the pods. Listing 12.5 shows the Kubernetes service for `Restaurant Service`. This service routes traffic from `http://ftgo-restaurant-service:8080` to the pods defined by the deployment shown in the listing.

> **Listing 12.5 The YAML definition of the Kubernetes service for `ftgo-restaurant-service`**

```
apiVersion: v1
kind: Service
metadata:
  name: ftgo-restaurant-service        ← The name of the service,
                                          also the DNS name
spec:
  ports:
  - port: 8080            ← The exposed port
    targetPort: 8080      ← The container port to route traffic to
  selector:
    app: ftgo-restaurant-service    ← Selects the containers to route traffic to
---
```

The key part of the service definition is `selector`, which selects the target pods. It selects those pods that have a label named `app` with the value `ftgo-restaurant-service`. If you look closely, you'll see that the container defined in listing 12.4 has such a label.

Once you've written the YAML file, you can create the service using this command:

```
kubectl apply -f ftgo-restaurant-service-service.yml
```

Now that we've created the Kubernetes service, any clients of `Restaurant Service` that are running inside the Kubernetes cluster can access its REST API via `http://ftgo-restaurant-service:8080`. Later, I discuss how to upgrade running services, but first let's take a look at how to make the services accessible from outside the Kubernetes cluster.

12.4.3 *Deploying the API gateway*

The Kubernetes service for `Restaurant Service`, shown in listing 12.5, is only accessible from within the cluster. That's not a problem for `Restaurant Service`, but what about `API Gateway`? Its role is to route traffic from the outside world to the service. It therefore needs to be accessible from outside the cluster. Fortunately, a Kubernetes service supports this use case as well. The service we looked at earlier is a `ClusterIP` service, which is the default, but there are, however, two other types of services: `NodePort` and `LoadBalancer`.

A `NodePort` service is accessible via a cluster-wide port on all the nodes in the cluster. Any traffic to that port on any cluster node is load balanced to the backend pods. You must select an available port in the range of 30000–32767. For example, listing 12.6 shows a service that routes traffic to port 30000 of `Consumer Service`.

> **Listing 12.6   The YAML definition of a `NodePort` service that routes traffic to port 8082 of `Consumer Service`**

```
apiVersion: v1
kind: Service
metadata:
  name: ftgo-api-gateway
spec:                              Specifies a type
  type: NodePort      <──┘        of NodePort
  ports:
  - nodePort: 30000    <──          The cluster-
      port: 80              ┘       wide port
    targetPort: 8080
  selector:
    app: ftgo-api-gateway
---
```

API Gateway is within the cluster using the URL `http://ftgo-api-gateway` and outside the URL `http://<node-ip-address>:3000/`, where `node-ip-address` is the IP address of one of the nodes. After configuring a `NodePort` service you can, for example, configure an AWS Elastic Load Balancer (ELB) to load balance requests from the internet across the nodes. A key benefit of this approach is that the ELB is entirely under your control. You have complete flexibility when configuring it.

A `NodePort` type service isn't the only option, though. You can also use a `Load-Balancer` service, which automatically configures a cloud-specific load balancer. The load balancer will be an ELB if Kubernetes is running on AWS. One benefit of this type of service is that you no longer have to configure your own load balancer. The drawback, however, is that although Kubernetes does give a few options for configuring the ELB, such the SSL certificate, you have a lot less control over its configuration.

12.4.4 *Zero-downtime deployments*

Imagine you've updated `Restaurant Service` and want to deploy those changes into production. Updating a running service is a simple three-step process when using Kubernetes:

1 Build a new container image and push it to the registry using the same process described earlier. The only difference is that the image will be tagged with a different version tag—for example, `ftgo-restaurant-service:1.1.0.RELEASE`.
2 Edit the YAML file for the service's deployment so that it references the new image.
3 Update the deployment using the `kubectl apply -f` command.

Kubernetes will then perform a rolling upgrade of the pods. It will incrementally create pods running version `1.1.0.RELEASE` and terminate the pods running version

1.0.0.RELEASE. What's great about how Kubernetes does this is that it doesn't terminate old pods until their replacements are ready to handle requests. It uses the readinessProbe mechanism, a health check mechanism described earlier in this section, to determine whether a pod is ready. As a result, there will always be pods available to handle requests. Eventually, assuming the new pods start successfully, all the deployment's pods will be running the new version.

But what if there's a problem and the version 1.1.0.RELEASE pods don't start? Perhaps there's a bug, such as a misspelled container image name or a missing environment variable for a new configuration property. If the pods fail to start, the deployment will become stuck. At that point, you have two options. One option is to fix the YAML file and rerun kubectl apply -f to update the deployment. The other option is to roll back the deployment.

A deployment maintains the history of what are termed *rollouts*. Each time you update the deployment, it creates a new rollout. As a result, you can easily roll back a deployment to a previous version by executing the following command:

```
kubectl rollout undo deployment ftgo-restaurant-service
```

Kubernetes will then replace the pods running version 1.1.0.RELEASE with pods running the older version, 1.0.0.RELEASE.

A Kubernetes deployment is a good way to deploy a service without downtime. But what if a bug only appears after the pod is ready and receiving production traffic? In that situation, Kubernetes will continue to roll out new versions, so a growing number of users will be impacted. Though your monitoring system will hopefully detect the issue and quickly roll back the deployment, you won't avoid impacting at least some users. To address this issue and make rolling out a new version of a service more reliable, we need to separate *deploying*, which means getting the service running in production, from *releasing* the service, which means making it available to handle production traffic. Let's look at how to accomplish that using a service mesh.

12.4.5 *Using a service mesh to separate deployment from release*

The traditional way to roll out a new version of a service is to first test it in a staging environment. Then, once it's passed the test in staging, you deploy in production by doing a rolling upgrade that replaces old instances of the service with new service instances. On one hand, as you just saw, Kubernetes deployments make doing a rolling upgrade very straightforward. On the other hand, this approach assumes that once a service version has passed the tests in the staging environment, it will work in production. Sadly, this is not always the case.

One reason is because staging is unlikely to be an exact clone, if for no other reason than the production environment is likely to be much larger and handle much more traffic. It's also time consuming to keep the two environments synchronized. As a result of discrepancies, it's likely that some bugs will only show up in production. And even it were an exact clone, you can't guarantee that testing will catch all bugs.

A much more reliable way to roll out a new version is to separate deployment from release:

- *Deployment*—Running in the production environment
- *Releasing a service*—Making it available to end users

You then deploy a service into production using the following steps:

1 Deploy the new version into production without routing any end-user requests to it.
2 Test it in production.
3 Release it to a small number of end users.
4 Incrementally release it to an increasingly larger number of users until it's handling all the production traffic.
5 If at any point there's an issue, revert back to the old version—otherwise, once you're confident the new version is working correctly, delete the old version.

Ideally, those steps will be performed by a fully automated deployment pipeline that carefully monitors the newly deployed service for errors.

Traditionally, separating deployments and releases in this way has been challenging because it requires a lot of work to implement it. But one of the benefits of using a service mesh is that using this style of deployment is a lot easier. A *service mesh* is, as described in chapter 11, networking infrastructure that mediates all communication between a service and other services and external applications. In addition to taking on some of the responsibilities of the microservice chassis framework, a service mesh provides rule-based load balancing and traffic routing that lets you safely run multiple versions of your services simultaneously. Later in this section, you'll see that you can route test users to one version of a service and end-users to a different version, for example.

As described in chapter 11, there are several service meshes to choose from. In this section, I show you how to use Istio, a popular, open source service mesh originally developed by Google, IBM, and Lyft. I begin by providing a brief overview of Istio and a few of its many features. Next I describe how to deploy an application using Istio. After that, I show how to use its traffic-routing capabilities to deploy and release an upgrade to a service.

OVERVIEW OF THE ISTIO SERVICE MESH

The Istio website describes Istio as an "An open platform to connect, manage, and secure microservices" (https://istio.io). It's a networking layer through which all of your services' network traffic flows. Istio has a rich set of features organized into four main categories:

- *Traffic management*—Includes service discovery, load balancing, routing rules, and circuit breakers
- *Security*—Secures interservice communication using Transport Layer Security (TLS)

- *Telemetry*—Captures metrics about network traffic and implements distributed tracing
- *Policy enforcement*—Enforces quotas and rate limits

This section focuses on Istio's traffic-management capabilities.

Figure 12.11 shows Istio's architecture. It consists of a control plane and a data plane. The control plane implements management functions, including configuring the data plane to route traffic. The data plane consists of Envoy proxies, one per service instance.

The two main components of the control plane are the Pilot and the Mixer. The *Pilot* extracts information about deployed services from the underlying infrastructure. When running on Kubernetes, for example, the Pilot retrieves the services and healthy pods. It configures the Envoy proxies to route traffic according to the defined routing rules. The *Mixer* collects telemetry from the Envoy proxies and enforces policies.

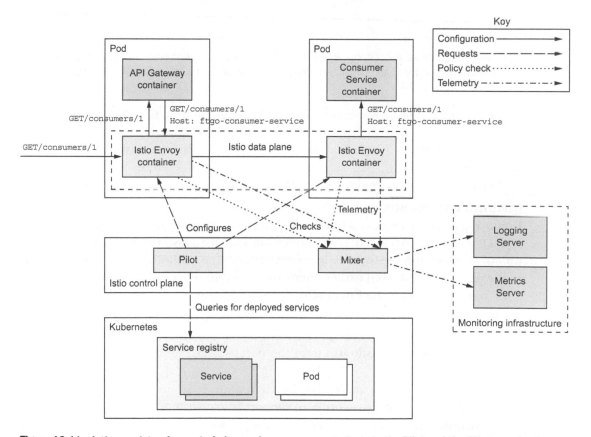

Figure 12.11 Istio consists of a control plane, whose components include the Pilot and the Mixer, and a data plane, which consists of Envoy proxy servers. The Pilot extracts information about deployed services from the underlying infrastructure and configures the data plane. The Mixer enforces policies such as quotas and gathers telemetry, reporting it to the monitoring infrastructure servers. The Envoy proxy servers route traffic in and out of services. There's one Envoy proxy server per service instance.

The Istio Envoy proxy is a modified version of Envoy (www.envoyproxy.io). It's a high-performance proxy that supports a variety of protocols, including TCP, low-level protocols such as HTTP and HTTPS, and higher-level protocols. It also understands MongoDB, Redis, and DynamoDB protocols. Envoy also supports robust interservice communication with features such as circuit breakers, rate limiting, and automatic retries. It can secure communication within the application by using TLS for inter-Envoy communication.

Istio uses Envoy as a sidecar, a process or container that runs alongside the service instance and implements cross-cutting concerns. When running on Kubernetes, the Envoy proxy is a container within the service's pod. In other environments that don't have the pod concept, Envoy runs in the same container as the service. All traffic to and from a service flows through its Envoy proxy, which routes traffic according to the routing rules given to it by the control plane. For example, direct Service → Service communication becomes Service → Source Envoy → Destination Envoy → Service.

> **Pattern: Sidecar**
> Implement cross-cutting concerns in a sidecar process or container that runs alongside the service instance. See http://microservices.io/patterns/deployment/sidecar.html.

Istio is configured using Kubernetes-style YAML configuration files. It has a command-line tool called `istioctl` that's similar to `kubectl`. You use `istioctl` for creating, updating, and deleting rules and policies. When using Istio on Kubernetes, you can also use `kubectl`.

Let's look at how to deploy a service with Istio.

DEPLOYING A SERVICE WITH ISTIO

Deploying a service on Istio is quite straightforward. You define a Kubernetes `Service` and a `Deployment` for each of your application's services. Listing 12.7 shows the definition of `Service` and `Deployment` for `Consumer Service`. Although it's almost identical to the definitions I showed earlier, there are a few differences. That's because Istio has a few requirements for the Kubernetes services and pods:

- A Kubernetes service port must use the Istio naming convention of `<protocol>[-<suffix>]`, where protocol is `http`, `http2`, `grpc`, `mongo`, or `redis`. If the port is unnamed, Istio will treat the port as a TCP port and won't apply rule-based routing.
- A pod should have an `app` label such as `app: ftgo-consumer-service`, which identifies the service, in order to support Istio distributed tracing.
- In order to run multiple versions of a service simultaneously, the name of a Kubernetes deployment must include the version, such as `ftgo-consumer-service-v1`, `ftgo-consumer-service-v2`, and so on. A deployment's pods should have a `version` label, such as `version: v1`, which specifies the version, so that Istio can route to a specific version.

Listing 12.7   Deploying Consumer Service with Istio

```
apiVersion: v1
kind: Service
metadata:
  name: ftgo-consumer-service
spec:
  ports:
  - name: http          ←┘  Named port
    port: 8080
    targetPort: 8080
  selector:
    app: ftgo-consumer-service
---
apiVersion: extensions/v1beta1
kind: Deployment
metadata:                            Versioned
 name: ftgo-consumer-service-v2   ←┘ deployment
 spec:
 replicas: 1
 template:
   metadata:
     labels:                        Recommended
       app: ftgo-consumer-service ←┘ labels
       version: v2
     spec:                                     Image
       containers:                             version
       - image: image: ftgo-consumer-service:v2 ←┘
  ...
```

By now, you may be wondering how to run the Envoy proxy container in the service's pod. Fortunately, Istio makes that remarkably easy by automating modifying the pod definition to include the Envoy proxy. There are two ways to do that. The first is to use *manual sidecar injection* and run the `istioctl kube-inject` command:

```
istioctl kube-inject -f ftgo-consumer-service/src/deployment/kubernetes/ftgo-
    consumer-service.yml | kubectl apply -f -
```

This command reads a Kubernetes YAML file and outputs the modified configuration containing the Envoy proxy. The modified configuration is then piped into `kubectl apply`.

The second way to add the Envoy sidecar to the pod is to use *automatic sidecar injection*. When this feature is enabled, you deploy a service using `kubectl apply`. Kubernetes automatically invokes Istio to modify the pod definition to include the Envoy proxy.

If you describe your service's pod, you'll see that it consists of more than your service's container:

```
$ kubectl describe po ftgo-consumer-service-7db65b6f97-q9jpr

Name:          ftgo-consumer-service-7db65b6f97-q9jpr
Namespace:     default
   ...
```

```
Init Containers:
  istio-init:                    ◁────  Initializes the pod
    Image:            docker.io/istio/proxy_init:0.8.0
    ....
Containers:                                              The service
  ftgo-consumer-service:                            ◁──  container
    Image:            msapatterns/ftgo-consumer-service:latest
    ...
  istio-proxy:                                       The Envoy
    Image:            docker.io/istio/proxyv2:0.8.0  ◁──  container
  ...
```

Now that we've deployed the service, let's look at how to define routing rules.

CREATE ROUTING RULES TO ROUTE TO THE V1 VERSION

Let's imagine that you deployed the `ftgo-consumer-service-v2` deployment. In the absence of routing rules, Istio load balances requests across all versions of a service. It would, therefore, load balance across versions 1 and 2 of `ftgo-consumer-service`, which defeats the purpose of using Istio. In order to safely roll out a new version, you must define a routing rule that routes all traffic to the current v1 version.

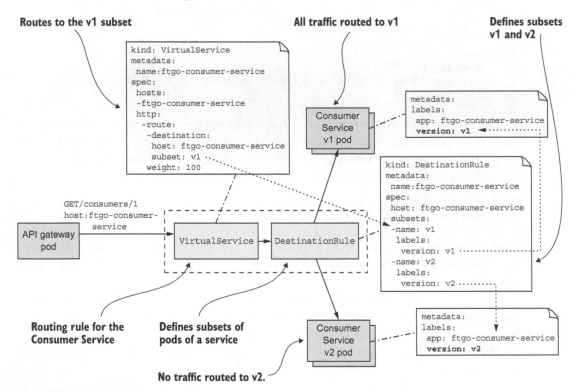

Figure 12.12   The routing rule for `Consumer Service`, which routes all traffic to the v1 pods. It consists of a `VirtualService`, which routes its traffic to the v1 subset, and a `DestinationRule`, which defines the v1 subset as the pods labeled with `version: v1`. Once you've defined this rule, you can safely deploy a new version without routing any traffic to it initially.

Figure 12.12 shows the routing rule for Consumer Service that routes all traffic to v1. It consists of two Istio objects: a VirtualService and a DestinationRule.

A VirtualService defines how to route requests for one or more hostnames. In this example, VirtualService defines the routes for a single hostname: ftgo-consumer-service. Here's the definition of VirtualService for Consumer Service:

```
apiVersion: networking.istio.io/v1alpha3
kind: VirtualService
metadata:
  name: ftgo-consumer-service
spec:
  hosts:                                    Applies to the
  - ftgo-consumer-service                   Consumer Service
  http:
    - route:                                Routes to
      - destination:                        Consumer Service
          host: ftgo-consumer-service
          subset: v1                        The v1 subset
```

It routes all requests for the v1 subset of the pods of Consumer Service. Later, I show more complex examples that route based on HTTP requests and load balance across multiple weighted destinations.

In addition to VirtualService, you must also define a DestinationRule, which defines one or more subsets of pods for a service. A subset of pods is typically a service version. A DestinationRule can also define traffic policies, such as the load-balancing algorithm. Here's the DestinationRule for Consumer Service:

```
apiVersion: networking.istio.io/v1alpha3
kind: DestinationRule
metadata:
  name: ftgo-consumer-service
spec:
  host: ftgo-consumer-service
  subsets:                                  The name of
  - name: v1                                the subset
    labels:
      version: v1                           The pod selector
  - name: v2                                for the subset
    labels:
      version: v2
```

This DestinationRule defines two subsets of pods: v1 and v2. The v1 subset selects pods with the label version: v1. The v2 subset selects pods with the label version: v2.

Once you've defined these rules, Istio will only route traffic pods labeled version: v1. It's now safe to deploy v2.

DEPLOYING VERSION 2 OF CONSUMER SERVICE

Here's an excerpt of the version 2 `Deployment` for Consumer Service:

```
apiVersion: extensions/v1beta1
kind: Deployment
metadata:
  name: ftgo-consumer-service-v2          ⟵——— Version 2
spec:
 replicas: 1
 template:
   metadata:
     labels:
        app: ftgo-consumer-service       ┐ Pod is labeled
        version: v2                      ⟵┘ with the version
 ...
```

This deployment is called `ftgo-consumer-service-v2`. It labels its pods with `version:` `v2`. After creating this deployment, both versions of the `ftgo-consumer-service` will be running. But because of the routing rules, Istio won't route any traffic to `v2`. You're now ready to route some test traffic to `v2`.

ROUTING TEST TRAFFIC TO VERSION 2

Once you've deployed a new version of a service, the next step is to test it. Let's suppose that requests from test users have a `testuser` header . We can enhance the `ftgo-consumer-service` `VirtualService` to route requests with this header to `v2` instances by making the following change:

```
apiVersion: networking.istio.io/v1alpha3
kind: VirtualService
metadata:
  name: ftgo-consumer-service
spec:
  hosts:
  - ftgo-consumer-service
  http:
    - match:
      - headers:
          testuser:
            regex: "^.+$"       ┐ Matches a nonblank
                                ⟵┘ testuser header
      route:
      - destination:
          host: ftgo-consumer-service   ┐ Routes test
          subset: v2                    ⟵┘ users to v2
     - route:
       - destination:
          host: ftgo-consumer-service   ┐ Routes everyone
          subset: v1                    ⟵┘ else to v1
```

In addition to the original default route, `VirtualService` has a routing rule that routes requests with the `testuser` header to the `v2` subset. After you've updated the rules, you can now test `Consumer Service`. Then, once you feel confident that the v2 is working, you can route some production traffic to it. Let's look at how to do that.

ROUTING PRODUCTION TRAFFIC TO VERSION 2

After you've tested a newly deployed service, the next step is to start routing production traffic to it. A good strategy is to initially only route a small amount of traffic. Here, for example, is a rule that routes 95% of traffic to v1 and 5% to v2:

```
apiVersion: networking.istio.io/v1alpha3
kind: VirtualService
metadata:
  name: ftgo-consumer-service
spec:
  hosts:
  - ftgo-consumer-service
  http:
    - route:
      - destination:
          host: ftgo-consumer-service
          subset: v1
        weight: 95
      - destination:
          host: ftgo-consumer-service
          subset: v2
        weight: 5
```

As you gain confidence that the service can handle production traffic, you can incrementally increase the amount of traffic going to the version 2 pods until it reaches 100%. At that point, Istio isn't routing any traffic to the v1 pods. You could leave them running for a little while longer before deleting the version 1 `Deployment`.

By letting you easily separate deployment from release, Istio makes rolling out a new version of a service much more reliable. Yet I've barely scratched the surface of Istio's capabilities. As of the time of writing, the current version of Istio is 0.8. I'm excited to watch it and the other service meshes mature and become a standard part of a production environment.

12.5 Deploying services using the Serverless deployment pattern

The Language-specific packaging (section 12.1), Service as a VM (section 12.2), and Service as a container (section 12.3) patterns are all quite different, but they share some common characteristics. The first is that with all three patterns you must preprovision some computing resources—either physical machines, virtual machines, or containers. Some deployment platforms implement autoscaling, which dynamically adjusts the number of VMs or containers based on the load. But you'll always need to pay for some VMs or containers, even if they're idle.

Another common characteristic is that you're responsible for system administration. If you're running any kind of machine, you must patch the operating system. In the case of physical machines, this also includes racking and stacking. You're also responsible for administering the language runtime. This is an example of what Amazon called "undifferentiated heavy lifting." Since the early days of computing, system administration has been one of those things you need to do. As it turns out, though, there's a solution: serverless.

12.5.1 *Overview of serverless deployment with AWS Lambda*

At AWS Re:Invent 2014, Werner Vogels, the CTO of Amazon, introduced AWS Lambda with the amazing phrase "magic happens at the intersection of functions, events, and data." As this phrase suggests, AWS Lambda was initially for deploying event-driven services. It's "magic" because, as you'll see, AWS Lambda is an example of serverless deployment technology.

Serverless deployment technologies

The main public clouds all provide a serverless deployment option, although AWS Lambda is the most advanced. Google Cloud has Google Cloud functions, which as of the time writing is in beta (https://cloud.google.com/functions/). Microsoft Azure has Azure functions (https://azure.microsoft.com/en-us/services/functions).

There are also open source serverless frameworks, such as Apache Openwhisk (https://openwhisk.apache.org) and Fission for Kubernetes (https://fission.io), that you can run on your own infrastructure. But I'm not entirely convinced of their value. You need to manage the infrastructure that runs the serverless framework—which doesn't exactly sound like *serverless*. Moreover, as you'll see later in this section, serverless provides a constrained programming model in exchange for minimal system administration. If you need to manage infrastructure, then you have the constraints without the benefit.

AWS Lambda supports Java, NodeJS, C#, GoLang, and Python. A *lambda* function is a stateless service. It typically handles requests by invoking AWS services. For example, a lambda function that's invoked when an image is uploaded to an S3 bucket could insert an item into a DynamoDB IMAGES table and publish a message to Kinesis to trigger image processing. A lambda function can also invoke third-party web services.

To deploy a service, you package your application as a ZIP file or JAR file, upload it to AWS Lambda, and specify the name of the function to invoke to handle a request (also called an *event*). AWS Lambda automatically runs enough instances of your microservice to handle incoming requests. You're billed for each request based on the time taken and the memory consumed. Of course, the devil is in the details, and later you'll see that AWS Lambda has limitations. But the notion that neither you as a developer nor anyone in your organization need worry about any aspect of servers, virtual machines, or containers is incredibly powerful.

Pattern: Serverless deployment

Deploy services using a serverless deployment mechanism provided by a public cloud. See http://microservices.io/patterns/deployment/serverless-deployment.html.

12.5.2 *Developing a lambda function*

Unlike when using the other three patterns, you must use a different programming model for your lambda functions. A lambda function's code and the packaging depend on the programming language. A Java lambda function is a class that implements the generic interface `RequestHandler`, which is defined by the AWS Lambda Java core library and shown in the following listing. This interface takes two type parameters: `I`, which is the input type, and `O`, which is the output type. The type of `I` and `O` depend on the specific kind of request that the lambda handles.

> **Listing 12.8 A Java lambda function is a class that implements the `RequestHandler` interface.**

```
public interface RequestHandler<I, O> {
    public O handleRequest(I input, Context context);
}
```

The `RequestHandler` interface defines a single `handleRequest()` method. This method has two parameters, an input object and a context, which provide access to the lambda execution environment, such as the request ID. The `handleRequest()` method returns an output object. For lambda functions that handle HTTP requests that are proxied by an AWS API Gateway, `I` and `O` are `APIGatewayProxyRequestEvent` and `APIGatewayProxyResponseEvent`, respectively. As you'll soon see, the handler functions are quite similar to old-style Java EE servlets.

A Java lambda is packaged as either a ZIP file or a JAR file. A JAR file is an uber JAR (or fat JAR) created by, for example, the Maven Shade plugin. A ZIP file has the classes in the root directory and JAR dependencies in the `lib` directory. Later, I show how a Gradle project can create a ZIP file. But first, let's look at the different ways of invoking lambda function.

12.5.3 *Invoking lambda functions*

There are four ways to invoke a lambda function:

- HTTP requests
- Events generated by AWS services
- Scheduled invocations
- Directly using an API call

Let's look at each one.

HANDLING **HTTP** REQUESTS

One way to invoke a lambda function is to configure an AWS API Gateway to route HTTP requests to your lambda. The API gateway exposes your lambda function as an HTTPS endpoint. It functions as an HTTP proxy, invokes the lambda function with an HTTP request object, and expects the lambda function to return an HTTP response object. By using the API gateway with AWS Lambda you can, for example, deploy RESTful services as lambda functions.

HANDLING EVENTS GENERATED BY AWS SERVICES

The second way to invoke a lambda function is to configure your lambda function to handle events generated by an AWS service. Examples of events that can trigger a lambda function include the following:

- An object is created in an S3 bucket.
- An item is created, updated, or deleted in a DynamoDB table.
- A message is available to read from a Kinesis stream.
- An email is received via the Simple email service.

Because of this integration with other AWS services, AWS Lambda is useful for a wide range of tasks.

DEFINING SCHEDULED LAMBDA FUNCTIONS

Another way to invoke a lambda function is to use a Linux cron-like schedule. You can configure your lambda function to be invoked periodically—for example, every minute, 3 hours, or 7 days. Alternatively, you can use a cron expression to specify when AWS should invoke your lambda. cron expressions give you tremendous flexibility. For example, you can configure a lambda to be invoked at 2:15 p.m. Monday through Friday.

INVOKING A LAMBDA FUNCTION USING A WEB SERVICE REQUEST

The fourth way to invoke a lambda function is for your application to invoke it using a web service request. The web service request specifies the name of the lambda function and the input event data. Your application can invoke a lambda function synchronously or asynchronously. If your application invokes the lambda function synchronously, the web service's HTTP response contains the response of the lambda function. Otherwise, if it invokes the lambda function asynchronously, the web service response indicates whether the execution of the lambda was successfully initiated.

12.5.4 *Benefits of using lambda functions*

Deploying services using lambda functions has several benefits:

- *Integrated with many AWS services*—It's remarkably straightforward to write lambdas that consume events generated by AWS services, such as DynamoDB and Kinesis, and handle HTTP requests via the AWS API Gateway.
- *Eliminates many system administration tasks*—You're no longer responsible for low-level system administration. There are no operating systems or runtimes to patch. As a result, you can focus on developing your application.
- *Elasticity*—AWS Lambda runs as many instances of your application as are needed to handle the load. You don't have the challenge of predicting needed capacity or run the risk of underprovisioning or overprovisioning VMs or containers.
- *Usage-based pricing*—Unlike a typical IaaS cloud, which charges by the minute or hour for a VM or container even when it's idle, AWS Lambda only charges you for the resources that are consumed while processing each request.

12.5.5 Drawbacks of using lambda functions

As you can see, AWS Lambda is an extremely convenient way to deploy services, but there are some significant drawbacks and limitations:

- *Long-tail latency*—Because AWS Lambda dynamically runs your code, some requests have high latency because of the time it takes for AWS to provision an instance of your application and for the application to start. This is particularly challenging when running Java-based services because they typically take at least several seconds to start. For instance, the example lambda function described in the next section takes a while to start up. Consequently, AWS Lambda may not be suited for latency-sensitive services.
- *Limited event/request-based programming model*—AWS Lambda isn't intended to be used to deploy long-running services, such as a service that consumes messages from a third-party message broker.

Because of these drawbacks and limitations, AWS Lambda isn't a good fit for all services. But when choosing a deployment pattern, I recommend first evaluating whether serverless deployment supports your service's requirements before considering alternatives.

12.6 Deploying a RESTful service using AWS Lambda and AWS Gateway

Let's take a look at how to deploy `Restaurant Service` using AWS Lambda. It's a service that has a REST API for creating and managing restaurants. It doesn't have long-lived connections to Apache Kafka, for example, so it's a good fit for AWS lambda. Figure 12.13 shows the deployment architecture for this service. The service consists of several lambda functions, one for each REST endpoint. An AWS API Gateway is responsible for routing HTTP requests to the lambda functions.

Each lambda function has a request handler class. The `ftgo-create-restaurant` lambda function invokes the `CreateRestaurantRequestHandler` class, and the `ftgo-find-restaurant` lambda function invokes `FindRestaurantRequestHandler`. Because these request handler classes implement closely related aspects of the same service, they're packaged together in the same ZIP file, `restaurant-service-aws-lambda.zip`. Let's look at the design of the service, including those handler classes.

12.6.1 The design of the AWS Lambda version of Restaurant Service

The architecture of the service, shown in figure 12.14, is quite similar to that of a traditional service. The main difference is that Spring MVC controllers have been replaced by AWS Lambda request handler classes. The rest of the business logic is unchanged.

The service consists of a presentation tier consisting of the request handlers, which are invoked by AWS Lambda to handle the HTTP requests, and a traditional business

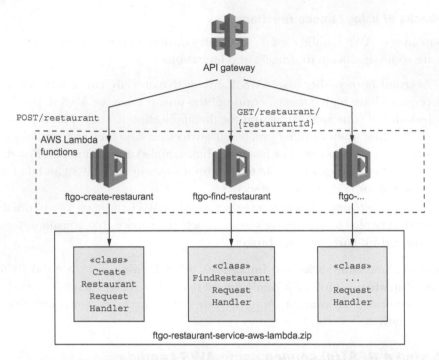

Figure 12.13   Deploying `Restaurant Service` as AWS Lambda functions. The AWS API Gateway routes HTTP requests to the AWS Lambda functions, which are implemented by request handler classes defined by `Restaurant Service`.

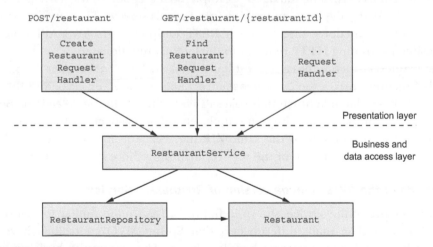

Figure 12.14   The design of the AWS Lambda-based `Restaurant Service`. The presentation layer consists of request handler classes, which implement the lambda functions. They invoke the business tier, which is written in a traditional style consisting of a service class, an entity, and a repository.

tier. The business tier consists of `RestaurantService`, the `Restaurant` JPA entity, and `RestaurantRepository`, which encapsulates the database.

Let's take a look at the `FindRestaurantRequestHandler` class.

THE FINDRESTAURANTREQUESTHANDLER CLASS

The `FindRestaurantRequestHandler` class implements the `GET /restaurant/ {restaurantId}` endpoint. This class along with the other request handler classes are the leaves of the class hierarchy shown in figure 12.15. The root of the hierarchy is `RequestHandler`, which is part of the AWS SDK. Its abstract subclasses handle errors and inject dependencies.

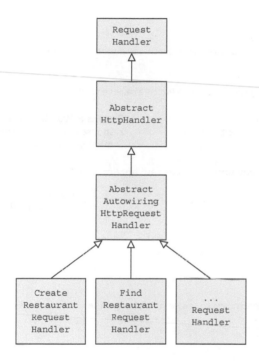

Figure 12.15 The design of the request handler classes. The abstract superclasses implement dependency injection and error handling.

The `AbstractHttpHandler` class is the abstract base class for HTTP request handlers. It catches unhandled exceptions thrown during request handling and returns a `500 - internal server error` response. The `AbstractAutowiringHttpRequestHandler` class implements dependency injection for request handlers. I'll describe these abstract superclasses shortly, but first let's look at the code for `FindRestaurantRequestHandler`.

Listing 12.9 shows the code for the `FindRestaurantRequestHandler` class. The `FindRestaurantRequestHandler` class has a `handleHttpRequest()` method, which takes an `APIGatewayProxyRequestEvent` representing an HTTP request as a parameter. It invokes `RestaurantService` to find the restaurant and returns an `APIGateway-ProxyResponseEvent` describing the HTTP response.

Listing 12.9 The handler class for `GET /restaurant/{restaurantId}`

```
public class FindRestaurantRequestHandler
    extends AbstractAutowiringHttpRequestHandler {

  @Autowired
  private RestaurantService restaurantService;

  @Override
  protected Class<?> getApplicationContextClass() {        The Spring Java
    return CreateRestaurantRequestHandler.class;      ◄─── configuration class to use
  }                                                        for the application context

  @Override
  protected APIGatewayProxyResponseEvent
      handleHttpRequest(APIGatewayProxyRequestEvent request, Context context) {
    long restaurantId;
    try {
      restaurantId = Long.parseLong(request.getPathParameters()
              .get("restaurantId"));
    } catch (NumberFormatException e) {              Returns a 400 - bad request
      return makeBadRequestResponse(context);   ◄─── response if the restaurantId
    }                                                is missing or invalid

    Optional<Restaurant> possibleRestaurant = restaurantService.findById(restaur
      antId);
                                                        Returns either the
    return possibleRestaurant                      ◄─── restaurant or a 404 -
            .map(this::makeGetRestaurantResponse)       not found response
          .orElseGet(() -> makeRestaurantNotFoundResponse(context,
                              restaurantId));

  }

  private APIGatewayProxyResponseEvent makeBadRequestResponse(Context context) {
    ...
  }

  private APIGatewayProxyResponseEvent
      makeRestaurantNotFoundResponse(Context context, long restaurantId) { ... }

  private  APIGatewayProxyResponseEvent
                      makeGetRestaurantResponse(Restaurant restaurant) { ... }
}
```

As you can see, it's quite similar to a servlet, except that instead of a `service()` method, which takes an `HttpServletRequest` and returns `HttpServletResponse`, it has a `handleHttpRequest()`, which takes an `APIGatewayProxyRequestEvent` and returns `APIGatewayProxyResponseEvent`.

Let's now take a look at its superclass, which implements dependency injection.

DEPENDENCY INJECTION USING THE ABSTRACTAUTOWIRINGHTTPREQUESTHANDLER CLASS

An AWS Lambda function is neither a web application nor an application with a `main()` method. But it would be a shame to not be able to use the features of Spring Boot that we've been accustomed to. The `AbstractAutowiringHttpRequestHandler` class, shown in the following listing, implements dependency injection for request handlers. It creates an `ApplicationContext` using `SpringApplication.run()` and autowires dependencies prior to handling the first request. Subclasses such as `FindRestaurant-RequestHandler` must implement the `getApplicationContextClass()` method.

Listing 12.10 An abstract `RequestHandler` that implements dependency injection

```java
public abstract class AbstractAutowiringHttpRequestHandler
    extends AbstractHttpHandler {

  private static ConfigurableApplicationContext ctx;
  private ReentrantReadWriteLock ctxLock = new ReentrantReadWriteLock();
  private boolean autowired = false;

  protected synchronized ApplicationContext getAppCtx() {       // Creates the Spring
    ctxLock.writeLock().lock();                                 // Boot application
    try {                                                       // context just once
      if (ctx == null) {
        ctx =  SpringApplication.run(getApplicationContextClass());
      }
      return ctx;
    } finally {
      ctxLock.writeLock().unlock();
    }
  }

  @Override
  protected void
      beforeHandling(APIGatewayProxyRequestEvent request, Context context) {
    super.beforeHandling(request, context);
    if (!autowired) {
      getAppCtx().getAutowireCapableBeanFactory().autowireBean(this);  // Injects dependencies into the request handler using autowiring before handling the first request
      autowired = true;
    }
  }

  protected abstract Class<?> getApplicationContextClass();    // Returns the @Configuration class used to create ApplicationContext
}
```

This class overrides the `beforeHandling()` method defined by `AbstractHttpHandler`. Its `beforeHandling()` method injects dependencies using autowiring before handling the first request.

THE ABSTRACTHTTPHANDLER CLASS

The request handlers for Restaurant Service ultimately extend `AbstractHttpHandler`, shown in listing 12.11. This class implements `RequestHandler<APIGatewayProxy-RequestEvent and APIGatewayProxyResponseEvent>`. Its key responsibility is to catch exceptions thrown when handling a request and throw a 500 error code.

```
public abstract class AbstractHttpHandler implements
    RequestHandler<APIGatewayProxyRequestEvent, APIGatewayProxyResponseEvent> {

  private Logger log = LoggerFactory.getLogger(this.getClass());

  @Override
  public APIGatewayProxyResponseEvent handleRequest(
      APIGatewayProxyRequestEvent input, Context context) {
    log.debug("Got request: {}", input);
    try {
      beforeHandling(input, context);
      return handleHttpRequest(input, context);
    } catch (Exception e) {
      log.error("Error handling request id: {}", context.getAwsRequestId(), e);
      return buildErrorResponse(new AwsLambdaError(
              "Internal Server Error",
              "500",
              context.getAwsRequestId(),
              "Error handling request: " + context.getAwsRequestId() + " "
      + input.toString()));
    }
  }

  protected void beforeHandling(APIGatewayProxyRequestEvent request,
      Context context) {
    // do nothing
  }

  protected abstract APIGatewayProxyResponseEvent handleHttpRequest(
      APIGatewayProxyRequestEvent request, Context context);
}
```

12.6.2 Packaging the service as ZIP file

Before the service can be deployed, we must package it as a ZIP file. We can easily build the ZIP file using the following Gradle task:

```
task buildZip(type: Zip) {
    from compileJava
    from processResources
    into('lib') {
        from configurations.runtime
    }
}
```

This task builds a ZIP with the classes and resources at the top level and the JAR dependencies in the lib directory.

Now that we've built the ZIP file, let's look at how to deploy the lambda function.

12.6.3 *Deploying lambda functions using the Serverless framework*

Using the tools provided by AWS to deploy lambda functions and configure the API gateway is quite tedious. Fortunately, the Serverless open source project makes using lambda functions a lot easier. When using Serverless, you write a simple `server-less.yml` file that defines your lambda functions and their RESTful endpoints. Serverless then deploys the lambda functions and creates and configures an API gateway that routes requests to them.

The following listing is an excerpt of the `serverless.yml` that deploys `Restaurant Service` as a lambda.

> **Listing 12.12 The `serverless.yml` deploys `Restaurant Service`.**

```
service: ftgo-application-lambda

provider:                                   Tells serverless to
  name: aws                    ←┘           deploy on AWS
  runtime: java8
  timeout: 35                               Supplies the service's
  region: ${env:AWS_REGION}                 externalized configuration
  stage: dev                                via environment variables
  environment:                 ←┘
    SPRING_DATASOURCE_DRIVER_CLASS_NAME: com.mysql.jdbc.Driver
    SPRING_DATASOURCE_URL: ...
    SPRING_DATASOURCE_USERNAME: ...         The ZIP file
    SPRING_DATASOURCE_PASSWORD: ...         containing the
                                            lambda functions
package:                       ←┘
    artifact: ftgo-restaurant-service-aws-lambda/build/distributions/
      ftgo-restaurant-service-aws-lambda.zip

                                            Lambda function definitions
                                            consisting of the handler
functions:                     ←────────┘   function and HTTP endpoint
  create-restaurant:
    handler: net.chrisrichardson.ftgo.restaurantservice.lambda
     .CreateRestaurantRequestHandler
    events:
      - http:
          path: restaurants
          method: post
  find-restaurant:
    handler: net.chrisrichardson.ftgo.restaurantservice.lambda
     .FindRestaurantRequestHandler
    events:
      - http:
          path: restaurants/{restaurantId}
          method: get
```

You can then use the `serverless deploy` command, which reads the `serverless.yml` file, deploys the lambda functions, and configures the AWS API Gateway. After a short wait, your service will be accessible via the API gateway's endpoint URL. AWS Lambda will provision as many instances of each `Restaurant Service` lambda function that are needed to support the load. If you change the code, you can easily update the lambda by rebuilding the ZIP file and rerunning `serverless deploy`. No servers involved!

The evolution of infrastructure is remarkable. Not that long ago, we manually deployed applications on physical machines. Today, highly automated public clouds provide a range of virtual deployment options. One option is to deploy services as virtual machines. Or better yet, we can package services as containers and deploy them using sophisticated Docker orchestration frameworks such as Kubernetes. Sometimes we even avoid thinking about infrastructure entirely and deploy services as lightweight, ephemeral lambda functions.

Summary

- You should choose the most lightweight deployment pattern that supports your service's requirements. Evaluate the options in the following order: serverless, containers, virtual machines, and language-specific packages.
- A serverless deployment isn't a good fit for every service, because of long-tail latencies and the requirement to use an event/request-based programming model. When it is a good fit, though, serverless deployment is an extremely compelling option because it eliminates the need to administer operating systems and runtimes and provides automated elastic provisioning and request-based pricing.
- Docker containers, which are a lightweight, OS-level virtualization technology, are more flexible than serverless deployment and have more predictable latency. It's best to use a Docker orchestration framework such as Kubernetes, which manages containers on a cluster of machines. The drawback of using containers is that you must administer the operating systems and runtimes and most likely the Docker orchestration framework and the VMs that it runs on.
- The third deployment option is to deploy your service as a virtual machine. On one hand, virtual machines are a heavyweight deployment option, so deployment is slower and it will most likely use more resources than the second option. On the other hand, modern clouds such as Amazon EC2 are highly automated and provide a rich set of features. Consequently, it may sometimes be easier to deploy a small, simple application using virtual machines than to set up a Docker orchestration framework.
- Deploying your services as language-specific packages is generally best avoided unless you only have a small number of services. For example, as described in chapter 13, when starting on your journey to microservices you'll probably deploy the services using the same mechanism you use for your monolithic application, which is most likely this option. You should only consider setting

up a sophisticated deployment infrastructure such as Kubernetes once you've developed some services.

- One of the many benefits of using a service mesh—a networking layer that mediates all network traffic in and out of services—is that it enables you to deploy a service in production, test it, and only then route production traffic to it. Separating deployment from release improves the reliability of rolling out new versions of services.

Refactoring to microservices

13

This chapter covers

- When to migrate a monolithic application to a microservice architecture
- Why using an incremental approach is essential when refactoring a monolithic application to microservices
- Implementing new features as services
- Extracting services from the monolith
- Integrating a service and the monolith

I hope that this book has given you a good understanding of the microservice architecture, its benefits and drawbacks, and when to use it. There is, however, a fairly good chance you're working on a large, complex monolithic application. Your daily experience of developing and deploying your application is slow and painful. Microservices, which appear like a good fit for your application, seem like distant nirvana. Like Mary and the rest of the FTGO development team, you're wondering how on earth you can adopt the microservice architecture?

Fortunately, there are strategies you can use to escape from monolithic hell without having to rewrite your application from scratch. You incrementally convert your monolith into microservices by developing what's known as a strangler application. The idea of a strangler application comes from strangler vines, which grow in rain forests by enveloping and sometimes killing trees. A *strangler application* is a new application consisting of microservices that you develop by implementing new functionality as services and extracting services from the monolith. Over time, as the strangler application implements more and more functionality, it shrinks and ultimately kills the monolith. An important benefit of developing a strangler application is that, unlike a big bang rewrite, it delivers value to the business early and often.

I begin this chapter by describing the motivations for refactoring a monolith to a microservice architecture. I then describe how to develop the strangler application by implementing new functionality as services and extracting services from the monolith. Next, I cover various design topics, including how to integrate the monolith and services, how to maintain database consistency across the monolith and services, and how to handle security. I end the chapter by describing a couple of example services. One service is `Delayed Order Service`, which implements brand new functionality. The other service is `Delivery Service`, which is extracted from the monolith. Let's start by taking a look at the concept of refactoring to a microservice architecture.

13.1 Overview of refactoring to microservices

Put yourself in Mary's shoes. You're responsible for the FTGO application, a large and old monolithic application. The business is extremely frustrated with engineering's inability to deliver features rapidly and reliably. FTGO appears to be suffering from a classic case of monolithic hell. Microservices seem, at least on the surface, to be the answer. Should you propose diverting development resources away from feature development to migrating to a microservice architecture?

I start this section by discussing why you should consider refactoring to microservices. I also discuss why it's important to be sure that your software development problems are because you're in monolithic hell rather than in, for example, a poor software development process. I then describe strategies for incrementally refactoring your monolith to a microservice architecture. Next, I discuss the importance of delivering improvements earlier and often in order to maintain the support of the business. I then describe why you should avoid investing in a sophisticated deployment infrastructure until you've developed a few services. Finally, I describe the various strategies you can use to introduce services into your architecture, including implementing new features as services and extracting services from the monolith.

13.1.1 Why refactor a monolith?

The microservice architecture has, as described in chapter 1, numerous benefits. It has much better maintainability, testability, and deployability, so it accelerates development. The microservice architecture is more scalable and improves fault isolation. It's also much easier to evolve your technology stack. But refactoring a monolith to microservices is a significant undertaking. It will divert resources away from new feature development. As a result, it's likely that the business will only support the adoption of microservices if it solves a significant business problem.

If you're in monolithic hell, it's likely that you already have at least one business problem. Here are some examples of business problems caused by monolithic hell:

- *Slow delivery*—The application is difficult to understand, maintain, and test, so developer productivity is low. As a result, the organization is unable to compete effectively and risks being overtaken by competitors.
- *Buggy software releases*—The lack of testability means that software releases are often buggy. This makes customers unhappy, which results in losing customers and reduced revenue.
- *Poor scalability*—Scaling a monolithic application is difficult because it combines modules with very different resource requirements into one executable component. The lack of scalability means that it's either impossible or prohibitively expensive to scale the application beyond a certain point. As a result, the application can't support the current or predicted needs of the business.

It's important to be sure that these problems are there because you've outgrown your architecture. A common reason for slow delivery and buggy releases is a poor software development process. For example, if you're still relying on manual testing, then adopting automated testing alone can significantly increase development velocity. Similarly, you can sometimes solve scalability problems without changing your architecture. You should first try simpler solutions. If, and only if, you still have software delivery problems should you then migrate to the microservice architecture. Let's look at how to do that.

13.1.2 *Strangling the monolith*

The process of transforming a monolithic application into microservices is a form of application modernization (https://en.wikipedia.org/wiki/Software_modernization). *Application modernization* is the process of converting a legacy application to one having a modern architecture and technology stack. Developers have been modernizing applications for decades. As a result, there is wisdom accumulated through experience we can use when refactoring an application into a microservice architecture. The most important lesson learned over the years is to not do a big bang rewrite.

A *big bang rewrite* is when you develop a new application—in this case, a microservices-based application—from scratch. Although starting from scratch and leaving the legacy code base behind sounds appealing, it's extremely risky and will likely end in failure. You will spend months, possibly years, duplicating the existing functionality, and only then can you implement the features that the business needs today! Also, you'll need to develop the legacy application anyway, which diverts effort away from the rewrite and means that you have a constantly moving target. What's more, it's possible that you'll waste time reimplementing features that are no longer needed. As Martin Fowler reportedly said, "the only thing a Big Bang rewrite guarantees is a Big Bang!" (www.randyshoup.com/evolutionary-architecture).

Instead of doing a big bang rewrite, you should, as figure 13.1 shows, incrementally refactor your monolithic application. You gradually build a new application, which is called a strangler application. It consists of microservices that runs in conjunction with your monolithic application. Over time, the amount of functionality implemented by the monolithic application shrinks until either it disappears entirely or it becomes just another microservice. This strategy is akin to servicing your car while driving down the highway at 70 mph. It's challenging, but is far less risky that attempting a big bang rewrite.

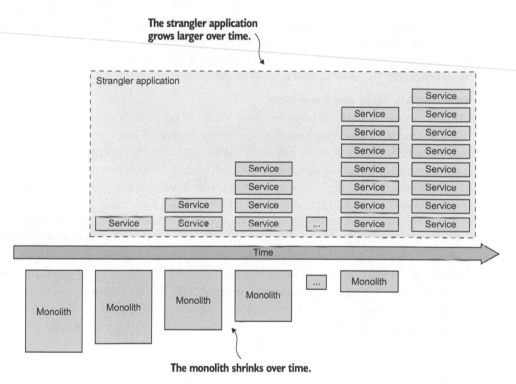

Figure 13.1   The monolith is incrementally replaced by a strangler application comprised of services. Eventually, the monolith is replaced entirely by the strangler application or becomes another microservice.

Martin Fowler refers to this application modernization strategy as the Strangler application pattern (www.martinfowler.com/bliki/StranglerApplication.html). The name comes from the strangler vine (or strangler fig—see https://en.wikipedia.org/wiki/Strangler_fig) that is found in rain forests. A strangler vine grows around a tree in order to reach the sunlight above the forest canopy. Often the tree dies, because either it's killed by the vine or it dies of old age, leaving a tree-shaped vine.

> ### Pattern: Strangler application
> Modernize an application by incrementally developing a new (strangler) application around the legacy application. See http://microservices.io/patterns/refactoring/strangler-application.html.

The refactoring process typically takes months, or years. For example, according to Steve Yegge (https://plus.google.com/+RipRowan/posts/eVeouesvaVX) it took Amazon.com a couple of years to refactor its monolith. In the case of a very large system, you may never complete the process. You could, for example, get to a point where you have tasks that are more important than breaking up the monolith, such as implementing revenue-generating features. If the monolith isn't an obstacle to ongoing development, you may as well leave it alone.

DEMONSTRATE VALUE EARLY AND OFTEN
An important benefit of incrementally refactoring to a microservice architecture is that you get an immediate return on your investment. That's very different than a big bang rewrite, which doesn't deliver any benefit until it's complete. When incrementally refactoring the monolith, you can develop each new service using a new technology stack and a modern, high-velocity, DevOps-style development and delivery process. As a result, your team's delivery velocity steadily increases over time.

What's more, you can migrate the high-value areas of your application to microservices first. For instance, imagine you're working on the FTGO application. The business might, for example, decide that the delivery scheduling algorithm is a key competitive advantage. It's likely that delivery management will be an area of constant, ongoing development. By extracting delivery management into a standalone service, the delivery management team will be able to work independently of the rest of the FTGO developers and significantly increase their development velocity. They'll be able to frequently deploy new versions of the algorithm and evaluate their effectiveness.

Another benefit of being able to deliver value earlier is that it helps maintain the business's support for the migration effort. Their ongoing support is essential, because the refactoring effort will mean that less time is spent on developing features. Some organizations have difficulty eliminating technical debt because past attempts were too ambitious and didn't provide much benefit. As a result, the business becomes reluctant to invest in further cleanup efforts. The incremental nature of refactoring to microservices means that the development team is able to demonstrate value early and often.

MINIMIZE CHANGES TO THE MONOLITH
A recurring theme in this chapter is that you should avoid making widespread changes to the monolith when migrating to a microservice architecture. It's inevitable

that you'll need to make some changes in order to support migration to services. Section 13.3.2 talks about how the monolith often needs to be modified so that it can participate in sagas that maintain data consistency across the monolith and services. The problem with making widespread changes to the monolith is that it's time consuming, costly, and risky. After all, that's probably why you want to migrate to microservices in the first place.

Fortunately, there are strategies you can use for reducing the scope of the changes you need to make. For example, in section 13.2.3, I describe the strategy of replicating data from an extracted service back to the monolith's database. And in section 13.3.2, I show how you can carefully sequence the extraction of services to reduce the impact on the monolith. By applying these strategies, you can reduce the amount of work required to refactor the monolith.

TECHNICAL DEPLOYMENT INFRASTRUCTURE: YOU DON'T NEED ALL OF IT YET

Throughout this book I've discussed a lot of shiny new technology, including deployment platforms such as Kubernetes and AWS Lambda and service discovery mechanisms. You might be tempted to begin your migrating to microservices by selecting technologies and building out that infrastructure. You might even feel pressure from the business people and from your friendly PaaS vendor to start spending money on this kind of infrastructure.

As tempting as it seems to build out this infrastructure up front, I recommend only making a minimal up-front investment in developing it. The only thing you can't live without is a deployment pipeline that performs automating testing. For example, if you only have a handful of services, you don't need a sophisticated deployment and observability infrastructure. Initially, you can even get away with just using a hard-coded configuration file for service discovery. I suggest deferring any decisions about technical infrastructure that involve significant investment until you've gained real experience with the microservice architecture. It's only once you have a few services running that you'll have the experience to pick technologies.

Let's now look at the strategies you can use for migrating to a microservice architecture.

13.2 Strategies for refactoring a monolith to microservices

There are three main strategies for strangling the monolith and incrementally replacing it with microservices:

1 Implement new features as services.
2 Separate the presentation tier and backend.
3 Break up the monolith by extracting functionality into services.

The first strategy stops the monolith from growing. It's typically a quick way to demonstrate the value of microservices, helping build support for the migration effort. The other two strategies break apart the monolith. When refactoring your monolith, you might sometimes use the second strategy, but you'll definitely use the third strategy, because it's how functionality is migrated from the monolith into the strangler application.

Let's take a look at each of these strategies, starting with implementing new features as services.

13.2.1 *Implement new features as services*

The Law of Holes states that "if you find yourself in a hole, stop digging" (https://en.m.wikipedia.org/wiki/Law_of_holes). This is great advice to follow when your monolithic application has become unmanageable. In other words, if you have a large, complex monolithic application, don't implement new features by adding code to the monolith. That will make your monolith even larger and more unmanageable. Instead, you should implement new features as services.

This is a great way to begin migrating your monolithic application to a microservice architecture. It reduces the growth rate of the monolith. It accelerates the development of the new features, because you're doing development in a brand new code base. It also quickly demonstrates the value of adopting the microservice architecture.

INTEGRATING THE NEW SERVICE WITH THE MONOLITH

Figure 13.2 shows the application's architecture after implementing a new feature as a service. Besides the new service and monolith, the architecture includes two other elements that integrate the service into the application:

- *API gateway*—Routes requests for new functionality to the new service and routes legacy requests to the monolith.
- *Integration glue code*—Integrates the service with the monolith. It enables the service to access data owned by the monolith and to invoke functionality implemented by the monolith.

The integration glue code isn't a standalone component. Instead, it consists of adapters in the monolith and the service that use one or more interprocess communication mechanisms. For example, integration glue for `Delayed Delivery Service`, described in section 13.4.1, uses both REST and domain events. The service retrieves customer contract information from the monolith by invoking a REST API. The monolith publishes `Order` domain events so that `Delayed Delivery Service` can track the state of `Orders` and respond to orders that won't be delivered on time. Section 13.3.1 describes the integration glue code in more detail.

WHEN TO IMPLEMENT A NEW FEATURE AS A SERVICE

Ideally, you should implement every new feature in the strangler application rather than in the monolith. You'll implement a new feature as either a new service or as part of an existing service. This way you'll avoid ever having to touch the monolith code base. Unfortunately, though, not every new feature can be implemented as a service.

That's because the essence of a microservice architecture is a set of loosely coupled services that are organized around business capabilities. A feature might, for instance, be too small to be a meaningful service. You might, for example, just need to add a

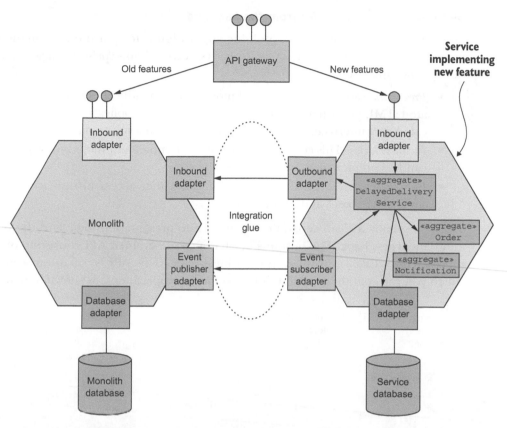

Figure 13.2 A new feature is implemented as a service that's part of the strangler application. The integration glue integrates the service with the monolith and consists of adapters that implement synchronous and asynchronous APIs. An API gateway routes requests that invoke new functionality to the service.

few fields and methods to an existing class. Or the new feature might be too tightly coupled to the code in the monolith. If you attempted to implement this kind of feature as a service you would typically find that performance would suffer because of excessive interprocess communication. You might also have problems maintaining data consistency. If a new feature can't be implemented as a service, the solution is often to initially implement the new feature in the monolith. Later on, you can then extract that feature along with other related features into their own service.

Implementing new features as services accelerates the development of those features. It's a good way to quickly demonstrate the value of the microservice architecture. It also reduces the monolith's growth rate. But ultimately, you need to break apart the monolith using the two other strategies. You need to migrate functionality to the strangler application by extracting functionality from the monolith into services. You might also be able to improve development velocity by splitting the monolith horizontally. Let's look at how to do that.

13.2.2   *Separate presentation tier from the backend*

One strategy for shrinking a monolithic application is to split the presentation layer from the business logic and data access layers. A typical enterprise application consists of the following layers:

- *Presentation logic*—This consists of modules that handle HTTP requests and generate HTML pages that implement a web UI. In an application that has a sophisticated user interface, the presentation tier is often a substantial body of code.
- *Business logic*—This consists of modules that implement the business rules, which can be complex in an enterprise application.
- *Data access logic*—This consists of modules that access infrastructure services such as databases and message brokers.

There is usually a clean separation between the presentation logic and the business and data access logic. The business tier has a coarse-grained API consisting of one or more facades that encapsulate the business logic. This API is a natural seam along which you can split the monolith into two smaller applications, as shown in figure 13.3.

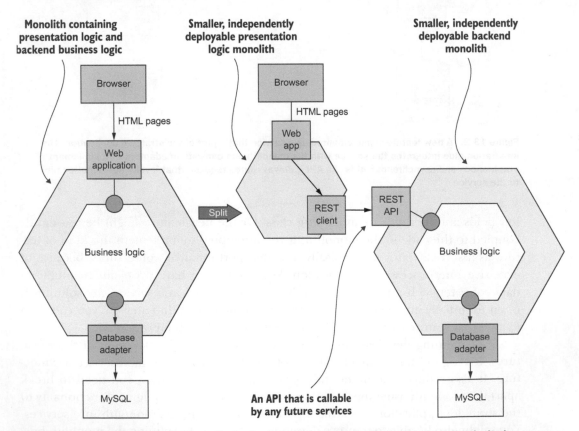

Figure 13.3   Splitting the frontend from the backend enables each to be deployed independently. It also exposes an API for services to invoke.

One application contains the presentation layer, and the other contains the business and data access logic. After the split, the presentation logic application makes remote calls to the business logic application.

Splitting the monolith in this way has two main benefits. It enables you to develop, deploy, and scale the two applications independently of one another. In particular, it allows the presentation layer developers to rapidly iterate on the user interface and easily perform A/B testing, for example, without having to deploy the backend. Another benefit of this approach is that it exposes a remote API that can be called by the microservices you develop later.

But this strategy is only a partial solution. It's very likely that at least one or both of the resulting applications will still be an unmanageable monolith. You need to use the third strategy to replace the monolith with services.

13.2.3 *Extract business capabilities into services*

Implementing new features as services and splitting the frontend web application from the backend will only get you so far. You'll still end up doing a lot of development in the monolithic code base. If you want to significantly improve your application's architecture and increase your development velocity, you need to break apart the monolith by incrementally migrating business capabilities from the monolith to services. For example, section 13.5 describes how to extract delivery management from the FTGO monolith into a new `Delivery Service`. When you use this strategy, over time the number of business capabilities implemented by the services grows, and the monolith gradually shrinks.

The functionality you want extract into a service is a vertical slice through the monolith. The slice consists of the following:

- Inbound adapters that implement API endpoints
- Domain logic
- Outbound adapters such as database access logic
- The monolith's database schema

As figure 13.4 shows, this code is extracted from the monolith and moved into a standalone service. An API gateway routes requests that invoke the extracted business capability to the service and routes the other requests to the monolith. The monolith and the service collaborate via the integration glue code. As described in section 13.3.1, the integration glue consists of adapters in the service and monolith that use one or more interprocess communication (IPC) mechanisms.

Extracting services is challenging. You need to determine how to split the monolith's domain model into two separate domain models, one of which becomes the service's domain model. You need to break dependencies such as object references. You might even need to split classes in order to move functionality into the service. You also need to refactor the database.

Extracting a service is often time consuming, especially because the monolith's code base is likely to be messy. Consequently, you need to carefully think about which

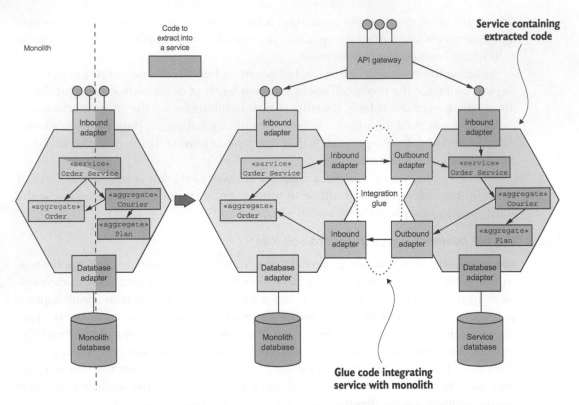

Figure 13.4   Break apart the monolith by extracting services. You identify a slice of functionality, which consists of business logic and adapters, to extract into a service. You move that code into the service. The newly extracted service and the monolith collaborate via the APIs provided by the integration glue.

services to extract. It's important to focus on refactoring those parts of the application that provide a lot of value. Before extracting a service, ask yourself what the benefit is of doing that.

For example, it's worthwhile to extract a service that implements functionality that's critical to the business and constantly evolving. It's not valuable to invest effort in extracting services when there's not much benefit from doing so. Later in this section I describe some strategies for determining what to extract and when. But first, let's look in more detail at some of the challenges you'll face when extracting a service and how to address them.

You'll encounter a couple of challenges when extracting a service:

- Splitting the domain model
- Refactoring the database

Let's look at each one, starting with splitting the domain model.

SPLITTING THE DOMAIN MODEL

In order to extract a service, you need to extract its domain model out of the monolith's domain model. You'll need to perform major surgery to split the domain models. One challenge you'll encounter is eliminating object references that would otherwise span service boundaries. It's possible that classes that remain in the monolith will reference classes that have been moved to the service or vice versa. For example, imagine that, as figure 13.5 shows, you extract `Order Service`, and as a result its `Order` class references the monolith's `Restaurant` class. Because a service instance is typically a process, it doesn't make sense to have object references that cross service boundaries. Somehow you need to eliminate these types of object reference.

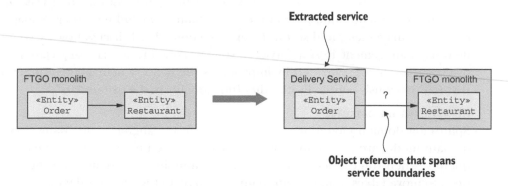

Figure 13.5 The `Order` domain class has a reference to a `Restaurant` class. If we extract `Order` into a separate service, we need to do something about its reference to `Restaurant`, because object references between processes don't make sense.

One good way to solve this problem is to think in terms of DDD aggregates, described in chapter 5. *Aggregates* reference each other using primary keys rather than object references. You would, therefore, think of the `Order` and `Restaurant` classes as aggregates and, as figure 13.6 shows, replace the reference to `Restaurant` in the `Order` class with a `restaurantId` field that stores the primary key value.

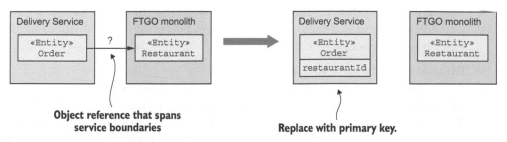

Figure 13.6 The `Order` class's reference to `Restaurant` is replaced with the `Restaurant`'s primary key in order to eliminate an object that would span process boundaries.

One issue with replacing object references with primary keys is that although this is a minor change to the class, it can potentially have a large impact on the clients of the class, which expect an object reference. Later in this section, I describe how to reduce the scope of the change by replicating data between the service and monolith. `Delivery Service`, for example, could define a `Restaurant` class that's a replica of the monolith's `Restaurant` class.

Extracting a service is often much more involved than moving entire classes into a service. An even greater challenge with splitting a domain model is extracting functionality that's embedded in a class that has other responsibilities. This problem often occurs in god classes, described in chapter 2, that have an excessive number of responsibilities. For example, the `Order` class is one of the god classes in the FTGO application. It implements multiple business capabilities, including order management, delivery management, and so on. Later in section 13.5, I discuss how extracting the delivery management into a service involves extracting a `Delivery` class from the `Order` class. The `Delivery` entity implements the delivery management functionality that was previously bundled with other functionality in the `Order` class.

REFACTORING THE DATABASE

Splitting a domain model involves more than just changing code. Many classes in a domain model are persistent. Their fields are mapped to a database schema. Consequently, when you extract a service from the monolith, you're also moving data. You need to move tables from the monolith's database to the service's database.

Also, when you split an entity you need to split the corresponding database table and move the new table to the service. For example, when extracting delivery management into a service, you split the `Order` entity and extract a `Delivery` entity. At the database level, you split the `ORDERS` table and define a new `DELIVERY` table. You then move the `DELIVERY` table to the service.

The book *Refactoring Databases* by Scott W. Ambler and Pramod J. Sadalage (Addison-Wesley, 2011) describes a set of refactorings for a database schema. For example, it describes the *Split Table* refactoring, which splits a table into two or more tables. Many of the technique in that book are useful when extracting services from the monolith. One such technique is the idea of replicating data in order to allow you to incrementally update clients of the database to use the new schema. We can adapt that idea to reduce the scope of the changes you must make to the monolith when extracting a service.

REPLICATE DATA TO AVOID WIDESPREAD CHANGES

As mentioned, extracting a service requires you to change to the monolith's domain model. For example, you replace object references with primary keys and split classes. These types of changes can ripple through the code base and require you to make widespread changes to the monolith. For example, if you split the `Order` entity and extract a `Delivery` entity, you'll have to change every place in the code that references the fields that have been moved. Making these kinds of changes can be extremely time consuming and can become a huge barrier to breaking up the monolith.

A great way to delay and possibly avoid making these kinds of expensive changes is to use an approach that's similar to the one described in *Refactoring Databases*. A major obstacle to refactoring a database is changing all the clients of that database to use the new schema. The solution proposed in the book is to preserve the original schema for a transition period and use triggers to synchronize the original and new schemas. You then migrate clients from the old schema to the new schema over time.

We can use a similar approach when extracting services from the monolith. For example, when extracting the `Delivery` entity, we leave the `Order` entity mostly unchanged for a transition period. As figure 13.7 shows, we make the delivery-related fields read-only and keep them up-to-date by replicating data from `Delivery Service` back to the monolith. As a result, we only need to find the places in the monolith's code that update those fields and change them to invoke the new `Delivery Service`.

Preserving the structure of the `Order` entity by replicating data from `Delivery Service` significantly reduces the amount of work we need to do immediately. Over time, we can migrate code that uses the delivery-related `Order` entity fields or `ORDERS` table columns to `Delivery Service`. What's more, it's possible that we never need to

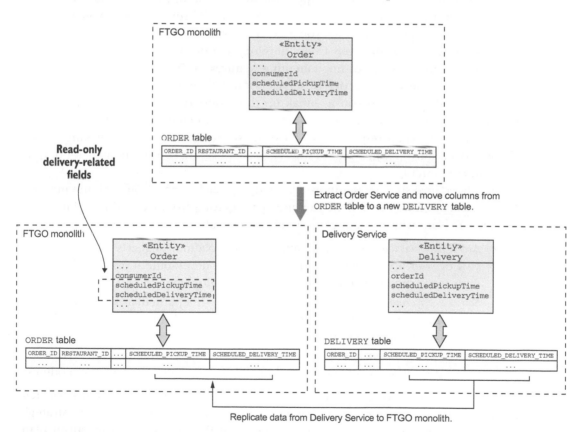

Figure 13.7 Minimize the scope of the changes to the FTGO monolith by replicating delivery-related data from the newly extracted `Delivery Service` back to the monolith's database.

make that change in the monolith. If that code is subsequently extracted into a service, then the service can access `Delivery Service`.

WHAT SERVICES TO EXTRACT AND WHEN

As I mentioned, breaking apart the monolith is time consuming. It diverts effort away from implementing features. As a result, you must carefully decide the sequence in which you extract services. You need to focus on extracting services that give the largest benefit. What's more, you want to continually demonstrate to the business that there's value in migrating to a microservice architecture.

On any journey, it's essential to know where you're going. A good way to start the migration to microservices is with a time-boxed architecture definition effort. You should spend a short amount of time, such as a couple of weeks, brainstorming your ideal architecture and defining a set of services. This gives you a destination to aim for. It's important, though, to remember that this architecture isn't set in stone. As you break apart the monolith and gain experience, you should revise the architecture to take into account what you've learned.

Once you've determined the approximate destination, the next step is to start breaking apart the monolith. There are a couple of different strategies you can use to determine the sequence in which you extract services.

One strategy is to effectively freeze development of the monolith and extract services on demand. Instead of implementing features or fixing bugs in the monolith, you extract the necessary service or service(s) and change those. One benefit of this approach is that it forces you to break up the monolith. One drawback is that the extraction of services is driven by short-term requirements rather than long-term needs. For instance, it requires you to extract services even if you're making a small change to a relatively stable part of the system. As a result, you risk doing a lot of work for minimal benefit.

An alternative strategy is a more planned approach, where you rank the modules of an application by the benefit you anticipate getting from extracting them. There are a few reasons why extracting a service is beneficial:

- *Accelerates development*—If your application's roadmap suggests that a particular part of your application will undergo a lot of development over the next year, then converting it to a service accelerates development.
- *Solves a performance, scaling, or reliability problem*—If a particular part of your application has a performance or scalability problem or is unreliable, then it's valuable to convert it to a service.
- *Enables the extraction of some other services*—Sometimes extracting one service simplifies the extraction of another service, due to dependencies between modules.

You can use these criteria to add refactoring tasks to your application's backlog, ranked by expected benefit. The benefit of this approach is that it's more strategic and much more closely aligned with the needs of the business. During sprint planning, you decide whether it's more valuable to implement features or extract services.

13.3 Designing how the service and the monolith collaborate

A service is rarely standalone. It usually needs to collaborate with the monolith. Sometimes a service needs to access data owned by the monolith or invoke its operations. For example, `Delayed Delivery Service`, described in detail in section 13.4.1, requires access to the monolith's orders and customer contact info. The monolith might also need to access data owned by the service or invoke its operations. For example, later in section 13.5, when discussing how to extract delivery management into a service, I describe how the monolith needs to invoke `Delivery Service`.

One important concern is maintaining data consistency between the service and monolith. In particular, when you extract a service from the monolith, you invariably split what were originally ACID transactions. You must be careful to ensure that data consistency is still maintained. As described later in this section, sometimes you use sagas to maintain data consistency.

The interaction between a service and the monolith is, as described earlier, facilitated by integration glue code. Figure 13.8 shows the structure of the integration glue. It consists of adapters in the service and monolith that communicate using some kind of IPC mechanism. Depending on the requirements, the service and monolith might interact over REST or they might use messaging. They might even communicate using multiple IPC mechanisms.

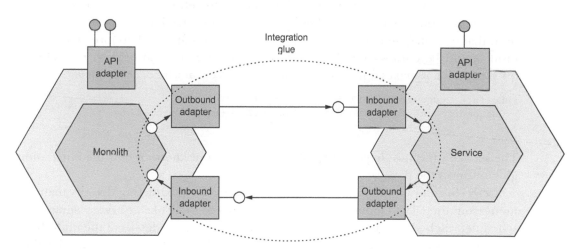

Figure 13.8 When migrating a monolith to microservices, the services and monolith often need to access each other's data. This interaction is facilitated by the integration glue, which consists of adapters that implement APIs. Some APIs are messaging based. Other APIs are RPI based.

For example, `Delayed Delivery Service` uses both REST and domain events. It retrieves customer contact info from the monolith using REST. It tracks the state of `Orders` by subscribing to domain events published by the monolith.

In this section, I first describe the design of the integration glue. I talk about the problems it solves and the different implementation options. After that I describe transaction management strategies, including the use of sagas. I discuss how sometimes the requirement to maintain data consistency changes the order in which you extract services.

Let's first look at the design of the integration glue.

13.3.1 *Designing the integration glue*

When implementing a feature as a service or extracting a service from the monolith, you must develop the integration glue that enables a service to collaborate with the monolith. It consists of code in both the service and monolith that uses some kind of IPC mechanism. The structure of the integration glue depends on the type of IPC mechanism that is used. If, for example, the service invokes the monolith using REST, then the integration glue consists of a REST client in the service and web controllers in the monolith. Alternatively, if the monolith subscribes to domain events published by the service, then the integration glue consists of an event-publishing adapter in the service and event handlers in the monolith.

DESIGNING THE INTEGRATION GLUE API

The first step in designing the integration glue is to decide what APIs it provides to the domain logic. There are a couple of different styles of interface to choose from, depending on whether you're querying data or updating data. Let's say you're working on `Delayed Delivery Service`, which needs to retrieve customer contact info from the monolith. The service's business logic doesn't need to know the IPC mechanism that the integration glue uses to retrieve the information. Therefore, that mechanism should be encapsulated by an interface. Because `Delayed Delivery Service` is querying data, it makes sense to define a `CustomerContactInfoRepository`:

```
interface CustomerContactInfoRepository {
  CustomerContactInfo findCustomerContactInfo(long customerId)
}
```

The service's business logic can invoke this API without knowing how the integration glue retrieves the data.

Let's consider a different service. Imagine that you're extracting delivery management from the FTGO monolith. The monolith needs to invoke `Delivery Service` to schedule, reschedule, and cancel deliveries. Once again, the details of the underlying IPC mechanism aren't important to the business logic and should be encapsulated by an interface. In this scenario, the monolith must invoke a service operation, so using a repository doesn't make sense. A better approach is to define a service interface, such as the following:

```
interface DeliveryService {
  void scheduleDelivery(...);
  void rescheduleDelivery(...);
  void cancelDelivery(...);
}
```

The monolith's business logic invokes this API without knowing how it's implemented by the integration glue.

Now that we've seen interface design, let's look at interaction styles and IPC mechanisms.

PICKING AN INTERACTION STYLE AND IPC MECHANISM

An important design decision you must make when designing the integration glue is selecting the interaction styles and IPC mechanisms that enable the service and the monolith to collaborate. As described in chapter 3, there are several interaction styles and IPC mechanisms to choose from. Which one you should use depends on what one *party*—the service or monolith—needs in order to query or update the other party.

If one party needs to query data owned by the other party, there are several options. One option is, as figure 13.9 shows, for the adapter that implements the repository interface to invoke an API of the data provider. This API will typically use a request/response interaction style, such as REST or gRPC. For example, `Delayed Delivery Service` might retrieve the customer contact info by invoking a REST API implemented by the FTGO monolith.

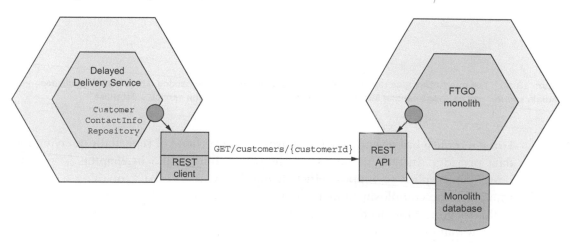

Figure 13.9   The adapter that implements the `CustomerContactInfoRepository` interface invokes the monolith's REST API to retrieve the customer information.

In this example, the `Delayed Delivery Service`'s domain logic retrieves the customer contact info by invoking the `CustomerContactInfoRepository` interface. The implementation of this interface invokes the monolith's REST API.

An important benefit of querying data by invoking a query API is its simplicity. The main drawback is that it's potentially inefficient. A consumer might need to make a large number of requests. A provider might return a large amount of data. Another drawback is that it reduces availability because it's synchronous IPC. As a result, it might not be practical to use a query API.

An alternative approach is for the data consumer to maintain a replica of the data, as shown in figure 13.10. The replica is essentially a CQRS view. The data consumer keeps the replica up-to-date by subscribing to domain events published by the data provider.

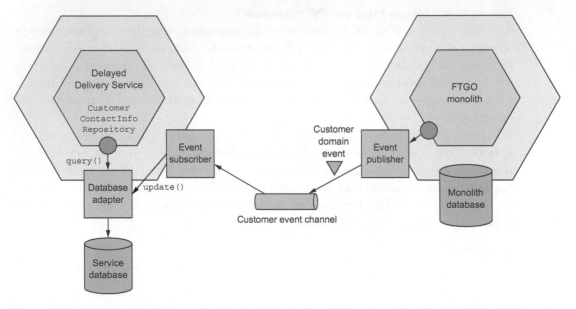

Figure 13.10 **The integration glue replicates data from the monolith to the service. The monolith publishes domain events, and an event handler implemented by the service updates the service's database.**

Using a replica has several benefits. It avoids the overhead of repeatedly querying the data provider. Instead, as discussed when describing CQRS in chapter 7, you can design the replica to support efficient queries. One drawback of using a replica, though, is the complexity of maintaining it. A potential challenge, as described later in this section, is the need to modify the monolith to publish domain events.

Now that we've discussed how to do queries, let's consider how to do updates. One challenge with performing updates is the need to maintain data consistency across the service and monolith. The party making the update request (the requestor) has updated or needs to update its database. So it's essential that both updates happen. The solution is for the service and monolith to communicate using transactional messaging implemented by a framework, such as Eventuate Tram. In simple scenarios, the requestor can send a notification message or publish an event to trigger an update. In more complex scenarios, the requestor must use a saga to maintain data consistency. Section 13.3.2 discusses the implications of using sagas.

IMPLEMENTING AN ANTI-CORRUPTION LAYER
Imagine you're implementing a new feature as a brand new service. You're not constrained by the monolith's code base, so you can use modern development techniques

such as DDD and develop a pristine new domain model. Also, because the FTGO monolith's domain is poorly defined and somewhat out-of-date, you'll probably model concepts differently. As a result, your service's domain model will have different class names, field names, and field values. For example, `Delayed Delivery Service` has a `Delivery` entity with narrowly focused responsibilities, whereas the FTGO monolith has an `Order` entity with an excessive number of responsibilities. Because the two domain models are different, you must implement what DDD calls an *anti-corruption layer* (ACL) in order for the service to communicate with the monolith.

> ## Pattern: Anti-corruption layer
> A software layer that translates between two different domain models in order to prevent concepts from one model polluting another. See https://microservices.io/patterns/refactoring/anti-corruption-layer.html.

The goal of an ACL is to prevent a legacy monolith's domain model from polluting a service's domain model. It's a layer of code that translates between the different domain models. For example, as figure 13.11 shows, `Delayed Delivery Service` has a `CustomerContactInfoRepository` interface, which defines a `findCustomerContact-Info()` method that returns `CustomerContactInfo`. The class that implements the `CustomerContactInfoRepository` interface must translate between the ubiquitous language of `Delayed Delivery Service` and that of the FTGO monolith.

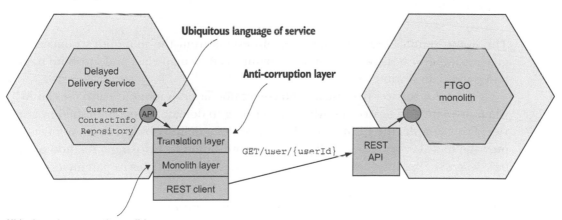

Figure 13.11 A service adapter that invokes the monolith must translate between the service's domain model and the monolith's domain model.

The implementation of `findCustomerContactInfo()` invokes the FTGO monolith to retrieve the customer information and translates the response to `CustomerContact-Info`. In this example, the translation is quite simple, but in other scenarios it could be quite complex and involve, for example, mapping values such as status codes.

An event subscriber, which consumes domain events, also has an ACL. Domain events are part of the publisher's domain model. An event handler must translate domain events to the subscriber's domain model. For example, as figure 13.12 shows, the FTGO monolith publishes `Order` domain events. `Delivery Service` has an event handler that subscribes to those events.

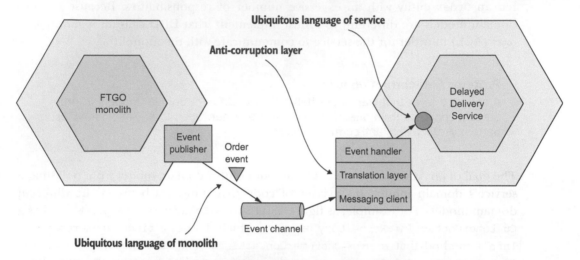

Figure 13.12   An event handler must translate from the event publisher's domain model to the subscriber's domain model.

The event handler must translate domain events from the monolith's domain language to that of `Delivery Service`. It might need to map class and attribute names and potentially attribute values.

It's not just services that use an anti-corruption layer. A monolith also uses an ACL when invoking the service and when subscribing to domain events published by a service. For example, the FTGO monolith schedules a delivery by sending a notification message to `Delivery Service`. It sends the notification by invoking a method on the `DeliveryService` interface. The implementation class translates its parameters into a message that `Delivery Service` understands.

HOW THE MONOLITH PUBLISHES AND SUBSCRIBES TO DOMAIN EVENTS

Domain events are an important collaboration mechanism. It's straightforward for a newly developed service to publish and consume events. It can use one of the mechanisms described in chapter 3, such as the Eventuate Tram framework. A service might even publish events using event sourcing, described in chapter 6. It's potentially challenging, though, to change the monolith to publish and consume events. Let's look at why.

There are a couple of different ways that a monolith can publish domain events. One approach is to use the same domain event publishing mechanism used by the services. You find all the places in the code that change a particular entity and insert a call to an event publishing API. The problem with this approach is that changing a monolith isn't always easy. It might be time consuming and error prone to locate all the places and insert calls to publish events. To make matters worse, some of the monolith's business logic might consist of stored procedures that can't easily publish domain events.

Another approach is to publish domain events at the database level. You can, for example, use either transaction logic tailing or polling, described in chapter 3. A key benefit of using transaction tailing is that you don't have to change the monolith. The main drawback of publishing events at the database level is that it's often difficult to identify the reason for the update and publish the appropriate high-level business event. As a result, the service will typically publish events representing changes to tables rather than business entities.

Fortunately, it's usually easier for the monolith to subscribe to domain events published as services. Quite often, you can write event handlers using a framework, such as Eventuate Tram. But sometimes it's even challenging for the monolith to subscribe to events. For example, the monolith might be written in a language that doesn't have a message broker client. In that situation, you need to write a small "helper" application that subscribes to events and updates the monolith's database directly.

Now that we've looked at how to design the integration glue that enables a service and the monolith to collaborate, let's look at another challenge you might face when migrating to microservices: maintaining data consistency across a service and a monolith.

13.3.2 *Maintaining data consistency across a service and a monolith*

When you develop a service, you might find it challenging to maintain data consistency across the service and the monolith. A service operation might need to update data in the monolith, or a monolith operation might need to update data in the service. For example, imagine you extracted Kitchen Service from the monolith. You would need to change the monolith's order-management operations, such as create-Order() and cancelOrder(), to use sagas in order to keep the Ticket consistent with the Order.

The problem with using sagas, however, is that the monolith might not be a willing participant. As described in chapter 4, sagas must use compensating transactions to undo changes. Create Order Saga, for example, includes a compensating transaction that marks an Order as rejected if it's rejected by Kitchen Service. The problem with compensating transactions in the monolith is that you might need to make numerous and time-consuming changes to the monolith in order to support them. The monolith might also need to implement countermeasures to handle the lack of isolation between sagas. The cost of these code changes can be a huge obstacle to extracting a service.

Key saga terminology

I cover sagas in chapter 4. Here are some key terms:

- *Saga*—A sequence of local transactions coordinated through asynchronous messaging.
- *Compensating transaction*—A transaction that undoes the updates made by a local transaction.
- *Countermeasure*—A design technique used to handle the lack of isolation between sagas.
- *Semantic lock*—A countermeasure that sets a flag in a record that is being updated by a saga.
- *Compensatable transaction*—A transaction that needs a compensating transaction because one of the transactions that follows it in the saga can fail.
- *Pivot transaction*—A transaction that is the saga's go/no-go point. If it succeeds, then the saga will run to completion.
- *Retriable transaction*—A transaction that follows the pivot transaction and is guaranteed to succeed.

Fortunately, many sagas are straightforward to implement. As covered in chapter 4, if the monolith's transactions are either *pivot transactions* or *retriable transactions*, then implementing sagas should be straightforward. You may even be able to simplify implementation by carefully ordering the sequence of service extractions so that the monolith's transactions never need to be compensatable. Or it may be relatively difficult to change the monolith to support compensating transactions. To understand why implementing compensating transactions in the monolith is sometimes challenging, let's look at some examples, beginning with a particularly troublesome one.

THE CHALLENGE OF CHANGING THE MONOLITH TO SUPPORT COMPENSATABLE TRANSACTIONS

Let's dig into the problem of compensating transactions that you'll need to solve when extracting `Kitchen Service` from the monolith. This refactoring involves splitting the `Order` entity and creating a `Ticket` entity in `Kitchen Service`. It impacts numerous commands implemented by the monolith, including `createOrder()`.

The monolith implements the `createOrder()` command as a single ACID transaction consisting of the following steps:

1. Validate order details.
2. Verify that the consumer can place an order.
3. Authorize consumer's credit card.
4. Create an `Order`.

You need to replace this ACID transaction with a saga consisting of the following steps:

1. In the monolith
   - Create an `Order` in an `APPROVAL_PENDING` state.
   - Verify that the consumer can place an order.

2 In the Kitchen Service
  − Validate order details.
  − Create a Ticket in the CREATE_PENDING state.
3 In the monolith
  − Authorize consumer's credit card.
  − Change state of Order to APPROVED.
4 In Kitchen Service
  − Change the state of the Ticket to AWAITING_ACCEPTANCE.

This saga is similar to CreateOrderSaga described in chapter 4. It consists of four local transactions, two in the monolith and two in Kitchen Service. The first transaction creates an Order in the APPROVAL_PENDING state. The second transaction creates a Ticket in the CREATE_PENDING state. The third transaction authorizes the Consumer credit card and changes the state of the order to APPROVED. The fourth and final transaction changes the state of the Ticket to AWAITING_ACCEPTANCE.

The challenge with implementing this saga is that the first step, which creates the Order, must be compensatable. That's because the second local transaction, which occurs in Kitchen Service, might fail and require the monolith to undo the updates performed by the first local transaction. As a result, the Order entity needs to have an APPROVAL_PENDING, a semantic lock countermeasure, described in chapter 4, that indicates an Order is in the process of being created.

The problem with introducing a new Order entity state is that it potentially requires widespread changes to the monolith. You might need to change every place in the code that touches an Order entity. Making these kinds of widespread changes to the monolith is time consuming and not the best investment of development resources. It's also potentially risky, because the monolith is often difficult to test.

SAGAS DON'T ALWAYS REQUIRE THE MONOLITH TO SUPPORT COMPENSATABLE TRANSACTIONS
Sagas are highly domain-specific. Some, such as the one we just looked at, require the monolith to support compensating transactions. But it's quite possible that when you extract a service, you may be able to design sagas that don't require the monolith to implement compensating transactions. That's because a monolith only needs to support compensating transactions if the transactions that follow the monolith's transaction can fail. If each of the monolith's transactions is either a pivot transaction or a retriable transaction, then the monolith never needs to execute a compensating transaction. As a result, you only need to make minimal changes to the monolith to support sagas.

For example, imagine that instead of extracting Kitchen Service, you extract Order Service. This refactoring involves splitting the Order entity and creating a slimmed-down Order entity in Order Service. It also impacts numerous commands, including createOrder(), which is moved from the monolith to Order Service. In order to extract Order Service, you need to change the createOrder() command to use a saga, using the following steps:

1 `Order Service`
   - Create an `Order` in an `APPROVAL_PENDING` state.
2 Monolith
   - Verify that the consumer can place an order.
   - Validate order details and create a `Ticket`.
   - Authorize consumer's credit card.
3 `Order Service`
   - Change state of `Order` to `APPROVED`.

This saga consists of three local transactions, one in the monolith and two in `Order Service`. The first transaction, which is in `Order Service`, creates an `Order` in the `APPROVAL_PENDING` state. The second transaction, which is in the monolith, verifies that the consumer can place orders, authorizes their credit card, and creates a `Ticket`. The third transaction, which is in `Order Service`, changes the state of the `Order` to `APPROVED`.

The monolith's transaction is the saga's pivot transaction—the point of no return for the saga. If the monolith's transaction completes, then the saga will run until completion. Only the first and second steps of this saga can fail. The third transaction can't fail, so the second transaction in the monolith never needs to be rolled back. As a result, all the complexity of supporting compensatable transactions is in `Order Service`, which is much more testable than the monolith.

If all the sagas that you need to write when extracting a service have this structure, you'll need to make far fewer changes to the monolith. What's more, it's possible to carefully sequence the extraction of services to ensure that the monolith's transactions are either pivot transactions or retriable transactions. Let's look at how to do that.

SEQUENCING THE EXTRACTION OF SERVICES TO AVOID IMPLEMENTING COMPENSATING TRANSACTIONS IN THE MONOLITH

As we just saw, extracting `Kitchen Service` requires the monolith to implement compensating transactions, whereas extracting `Order Service` doesn't. This suggests that the order in which you extract services matters. By carefully ordering the extraction of services, you can potentially avoid having to make widespread modifications to the monolith to support compensatable transactions. We can ensure that the monolith's transactions are either pivot transactions or retriable transactions. For example, if we first extract `Order Service` from the FTGO monolith and then extract `Consumer Service`, extracting `Kitchen Service` will be straightforward. Let's take a closer look at how to do that.

Once we have extracted `Consumer Service`, the `createOrder()` command uses the following saga:

1 `Order Service`: create an `Order` in an `APPROVAL_PENDING` state.
2 `Consumer Service`: verify that the consumer can place an order.

3 Monolith
- Validate order details and create a `Ticket`.
- Authorize consumer's credit card.
4 `Order Service`: change state of `Order` to APPROVED.

In this saga, the monolith's transaction is the pivot transaction. `Order Service` implements the compensatable transaction.

Now that we've extracted `Consumer Service`, we can extract `Kitchen Service`. If we extract this service, the `createOrder()` command uses the following saga:

1 `Order Service`: create an `Order` in an APPROVAL_PENDING state.
2 `Consumer Service`: verify that the consumer can place an order.
3 `Kitchen Service`: validate order details and create a PENDING `Ticket`.
4 Monolith: authorize consumer's credit card.
5 `Kitchen Service`: change state of `Ticket` to APPROVED.
6 `Order Service`: change state of `Order` to APPROVED.

In this saga, the monolith's transaction is still the pivot transaction. `Order Service` and `Kitchen Service` implement the compensatable transactions.

We can even continue to refactor the monolith by extracting `Accounting Service`. If we extract this service, the `createOrder()` command uses the following saga:

1 `Order Service`: create an `Order` in an APPROVAL_PENDING state.
2 `Consumer Service`: verify that the consumer can place an order.
3 `Kitchen Service`: validate order details and create a PENDING `Ticket`.
4 `Accounting Service`: authorize consumer's credit card.
5 `Kitchen Service`: change state of `Ticket` to APPROVED.
6 `Order Service`: change state of `Order` to APPROVED.

As you can see, by carefully sequencing the extractions, you can avoid using sagas that require making complex changes to the monolith. Let's now look at how to handle security when migrating to a microservice architecture.

13.3.3 *Handling authentication and authorization*

Another design issue you need to tackle when refactoring a monolithic application to a microservice architecture is adapting the monolith's security mechanism to support the services. Chapter 11 describes how to handle security in a microservice architecture. A microservices-based application uses tokens, such as JSON Web tokens (JWT), to pass around user identity. That's quite different than a typical traditional, monolithic application that uses in-memory session state and passes around the user identity using a thread local. The challenge when transforming a monolithic application to a microservice architecture is that you need to support both the monolithic and JWT-based security mechanisms simultaneously.

Fortunately, there's a straightforward way to solve this problem that only requires you to make one small change to the monolith's login request handler. Figure 13.13

shows how this works. The login handler returns an additional cookie, which in this example I call USERINFO, that contains user information, such as the user ID and roles. The browser includes that cookie in every request. The API gateway extracts the information from the cookie and includes it in the HTTP requests that it makes to a service. As a result, each service has access to the needed user information.

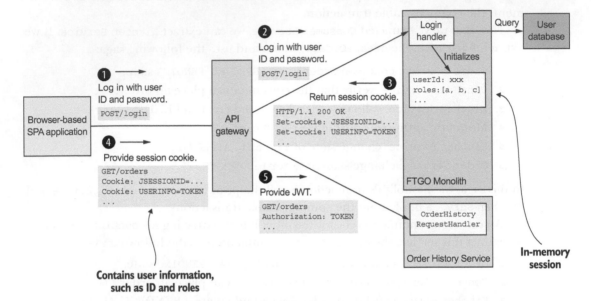

Figure 13.13   The login handler is enhanced to set a USERINFO **cookie, which is a JWT containing user information.** API Gateway **transfers the** USERINFO **cookie to an authorization header when it invokes a service.**

The sequence of events is as follows:

1   The client makes a login request containing the user's credentials.
2   API Gateway routes the login request to the FTGO monolith.
3   The monolith returns a response containing the JSESSIONID session cookie and the USERINFO cookie, which contains the user information, such as ID and roles.
4   The client makes a request, which includes the USERINFO cookie, in order to invoke an operation.
5   API Gateway validates the USERINFO cookie and includes it in the Authorization header of the request that it makes to the service. The service validates the USERINFO token and extracts the user information.

Let's look at LoginHandler and API Gateway in more detail.

THE MONOLITH'S LOGINHANDLER SETS THE USERINFO COOKIE
LoginHandler processes the POST of the user's credentials. It authenticates the user and stores information about the user in the session. It's often implemented by a

security framework, such as Spring Security or Passport for NodeJS. If the application is configured to use the default in-memory session, the HTTP response sets a session cookie, such as JSESSIONID. In order to support the migration to microservices, LoginHandler must also set the USERINFO cookie containing the JWT that describes the user.

THE API GATEWAY MAPS THE USERINFO COOKIE TO THE AUTHORIZATION HEADER

The API gateway, as described in chapter 8, is responsible for request routing and API composition. It handles each request by making one or more requests to the monolith and the services. When the API gateway invokes a service, it validates the USERINFO cookie and passes it to the service in the HTTP request's Authorization header. By mapping the cookie to the Authorization header, the API gateway ensures that it passes the user identity to the service in a standard way that's independent of the type of client.

Eventually, we'll most likely extract login and user management into services. But as you can see, by only making one small change to the monolith's login handler, it's now possible for services to access user information. This enables you focus on developing services that provide the greatest value to the business and delay extracting less valuable services, such as user management.

Now that we've looked at how to handle security when refactoring to microservices, let's see an example of implementing a new feature as a service.

13.4 *Implementing a new feature as a service: handling misdelivered orders*

Let's say you've been tasked with improving how FTGO handles misdelivered orders. A growing number of customers have been complaining about how customer service handles orders not being delivered. The majority of orders are delivered on time, but from time to time orders are either delivered late or not at all. For example, the courier gets delayed by unexpectedly bad traffic, so the order is picked up and delivered late. Or perhaps by the time the courier arrives at the restaurant, it's closed, and the delivery can't be made. To make matters worse, the first time customer service hears about the misdelivery is when they receive an angry email from an unhappy customer.

A true story: My missing ice cream

One Saturday night I was feeling lazy and placed an order using a well-known food delivery app to have ice cream delivered from Smitten. It never showed up. The only communication from the company was an email the next morning saying my order had been canceled. I also got a voicemail from a very confused customer service agent who clearly didn't know what she was calling about. Perhaps the call was prompted by one of my tweets describing what happened. Clearly, the delivery company had not established any mechanisms for properly handling inevitable mistakes.

The root cause for many of these delivery problems is the primitive delivery scheduling algorithm used by the FTGO application. A more sophisticated scheduler is under development but won't be finished for a few months. The interim solution is for FTGO to proactively handle delayed or canceled orders by apologizing to the customer, and in some cases offering compensation before the customer complains.

Your job is to implement a new feature that will do the following:

1 Notify the customer when their order won't be delivered on time.
2 Notify the customer when their order can't be delivered because it can't be picked up before the restaurant closes.
3 Notify customer service when an order can't be delivered on time so that they can proactively rectify the situation by compensating the customer.
4 Track delivery statistics.

This new feature is fairly simple. The new code must track the state of each `Order`, and if an `Order` can't be delivered as promised, the code must notify the customer and customer support, by, for example, sending an email.

But how—or perhaps more precisely, *where*—should you implement this new feature? One approach is to implement a new module in the monolith. The problem there is that developing and testing this code will be difficult. What's more, this approach increases the size of the monolith and thereby makes monolith hell even worse. Remember the Law of Holes from earlier: when you're in a hole, it's best to stop digging. Rather than make the monolith larger, a much better approach is to implement these new features as a service.

13.4.1 *The design of Delayed Delivery Service*

We'll implement this feature as a service called `Delayed Order Service`. Figure 13.14 shows the FTGO application's architecture after implementing this service. The application consists of the FTGO monolith, the new `Delayed Delivery Service`, and an `API Gateway`. `Delayed Delivery Service` has an API that defines a single query operation called `getDelayedOrders()`, which returns the currently delayed or undeliverable orders. `API Gateway` routes the `getDelayedOrders()` request to the service and all other requests to the monolith. The integration glue provides `Delayed Order Service` with access to the monolith's data.

The `Delayed Order Service`'s domain model consists of various entities, including `DelayedOrderNotification`, `Order`, and `Restaurant`. The core logic is implemented by the `DelayedOrderService` class. It's periodically invoked by a timer to find orders that won't be delivered on time. It does that by querying `Orders` and `Restaurants`. If an `Order` can't be delivered on time, `DelayedOrderService` notifies the consumer and customer service.

`Delayed Order Service` doesn't own the `Order` and `Restaurant` entities. Instead, this data is replicated from the FTGO monolith. What's more, the service doesn't store the customer contact information, but instead retrieves it from the monolith.

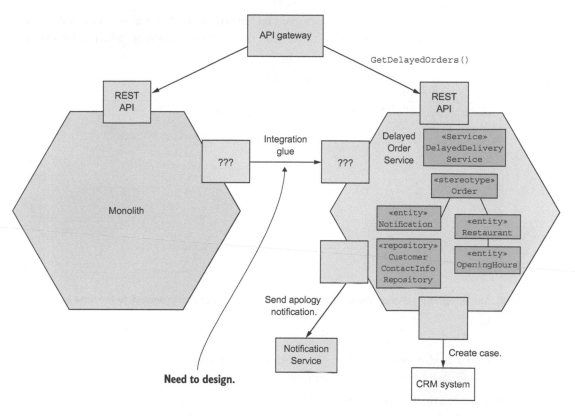

Figure 13.14 The design of `Delayed Delivery Service`. The integration glue provides `Delayed Delivery Service` access to data owned by the monolith, such as the `Order` and `Restaurant` entities, and the customer contact information.

Let's look at the design of the integration glue that provides `Delayed Order Service` access to the monolith's data.

13.4.2 Designing the integration glue for Delayed Delivery Service

Even though a service that implements a new feature defines its own entity classes, it usually accesses data that's owned by the monolith. `Delayed Delivery Service` is no exception. It has a `DelayedOrderNotification` entity, which represents a notification that it has sent to the consumer. But as I just mentioned, its `Order` and `Restaurant` entities replicate data from the FTGO monolith. It also needs to query user contact information in order to notify the user. Consequently, we need to implement integration glue that enables `Delivery Service` to access the monolith's data.

Figure 13.15 shows the design of the integration glue. The FTGO monolith publishes `Order` and `Restaurant` domain events. `Delivery Service` consumes these events and updates its replicas of those entities. The FTGO monolith implements a REST endpoint for querying the customer contact information. `Delivery Service` calls this endpoint when it needs to notify a user that their order cannot be delivered on time.

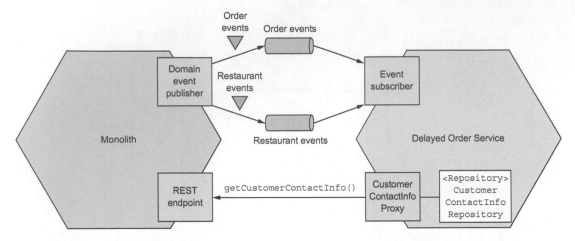

Figure 13.15   The integration glue provides `Delayed Delivery Service` with access to the data owned by the monolith.

Let's look at the design of each part of the integration, starting with the REST API for retrieving customer contact information.

Querying customer contact information using CustomerContactInfoRepository

As described in section 13.3.1, there are a couple of different ways that a service such as `Delayed Delivery Service` could read the monolith's data. The simplest option is for `Delayed Order Service` to retrieve data using the monolith's query API. This approach makes sense when retrieving the `User` contact information. There aren't any latency or performance, issues because `Delayed Delivery Service` rarely needs to retrieve a user's contact information, and the amount of data is quite small.

`CustomerContactInfoRepository` is an interface that enables `Delayed Delivery Service` to retrieve a consumer's contact info. It's implemented by a `CustomerContactInfoProxy`, which retrieves the user information by invoking the monolith's `getCustomerContactInfo()` REST endpoint.

Publishing and consuming Order and Restaurant domain events

Unfortunately, it isn't practical for `Delayed Delivery Service` to query the monolith for the state of all open `Orders` and `Restaurant` hours. That's because it's inefficient to repeatedly transfer a large amount of data over the network. Consequently, `Delayed Delivery Service` must use the second, more complex option and maintain a replica of `Orders` and `Restaurants` by subscribing to events published by the monolith. It's important to remember that the replica isn't a complete copy of the data from the monolith—it just stores a small subset of the attributes of `Order` and `Restaurant` entities.

As described earlier in section 13.3.1, there are a couple of different ways that we can change the FTGO monolith so that it publishes `Order` and `Restaurant` domain events. One option is to modify all the places in the monolith that update `Orders` and `Restaurants` to publish high-level domain events. The second option is to tail the transaction log to replicate the changes as events. In this particular scenario, we need to synchronize the two databases. We don't require the FTGO monolith to publish high-level domain events, so either approach is fine.

`Delayed Order Service` implements event handlers that subscribe to events from the monolith and update its `Order` and `Restaurant` entities. The details of the event handlers depend on whether the monolith publishes specific high-level events or low-level change events. In either case, you can think of an event handler as translating an event in the monolith's bounded context to the update of an entity in the service's bounded context.

An important benefit of using a replica is that it enables `Delayed Order Service` to efficiently query the orders and the restaurant opening hours. One drawback, however, is that it's more complex. Another drawback is that it requires the monolith to publish the necessary `Order` and `Restaurant` events. Fortunately, because `Delayed Delivery Service` only needs what's essentially a subset of the columns of the `ORDERS` and `RESTAURANT` tables, we shouldn't encounter the problems described in section 13.3.1.

Implementing a new feature such as delayed order management as a standalone service accelerates its development, testing, and deployment. What's more, it enables you to implement the feature using a brand new technology stack instead of the monolith's older one. It also stops the monolith from growing. Delayed order management is just one of many new features planned for the FTGO application. The FTGO team can implement many of these features as separate services.

Unfortunately, you can't implement all changes as new services. Quite often you must make extensive changes to the monolith to implement new features or change existing features. Any development involving the monolith will mostly likely be slow and painful. If you want to accelerate the delivery of these features, you must break up the monolith by migrating functionality from the monolith into services. Let's look at how to do that.

13.5 Breaking apart the monolith: extracting delivery management

To accelerate the delivery of features that are implemented by a monolith, you need to break up the monolith into services. For example, let's imagine that you want to enhance FTGO delivery management by implementing a new routing algorithm. A major obstacle to developing delivery management is that it's entangled with order management and is part of the monolithic code base. Developing, testing, and deploying delivery management is likely to be slow. In order to accelerate its development, you need to extract delivery management into a `Delivery Service`.

I start this section by describing delivery management and how it's currently embedded within the monolith. Next I discuss the design of the new, standalone `Delivery Service` and its API. I then describe how `Delivery Service` and the FTGO monolith collaborate. Finally I talk about some of the changes we need to make to the monolith to support `Delivery Service`.

Let's begin by reviewing the existing design.

13.5.1   *Overview of existing delivery management functionality*

Delivery management is responsible for scheduling the couriers that pick up orders at restaurants and deliver them to consumers. Each courier has a plan that is a schedule of pickup and deliver actions. A *pickup* action tells the `Courier` to pick up an order from a restaurant at a particular time. A *deliver* action tells the `Courier` to deliver an order to a consumer. The plans are revised whenever orders are placed, canceled, or revised, and as the location and availability of couriers changes.

Delivery management is one of the oldest parts of the FTGO application. As figure 13.16 shows, it's embedded within order management. Much of the code for managing deliveries is in `OrderService`. What's more, there's no explicit representation of a `Delivery`. It's embedded within the `Order` entity, which has various delivery-related fields, such as `scheduledPickupTime` and `scheduledDeliveryTime`.

Numerous commands implemented by the monolith invoke delivery management, including the following:

- `acceptOrder()`—Invoked when a restaurant accepts an order and commits to preparing it by a certain time. This operation invokes delivery management to schedule a delivery.
- `cancelOrder()`—Invoked when a consumer cancels an order. If necessary, it cancels the delivery.
- `noteCourierLocationUpdated()`—Invoked by the courier's mobile application to update the courier's location. It triggers the rescheduling of deliveries.
- `noteCourierAvailabilityChanged()`—Invoked by the courier's mobile application to update the courier's availability. It triggers the rescheduling of deliveries.

Also, various queries retrieve data maintained by delivery management, including the following:

- `getCourierPlan()`—Invoked by the courier's mobile application and returns the courier's plan
- `getOrderStatus()`—Returns the order's status, which includes delivery-related information such as the assigned courier and the ETA
- `getOrderHistory()`—Returns similar information as `getOrderStatus()` except about multiple orders

Quite often what's extracted into a service is, as mentioned in section 13.2.3, an entire vertical slice, with controllers at the top and database tables at the bottom. We could

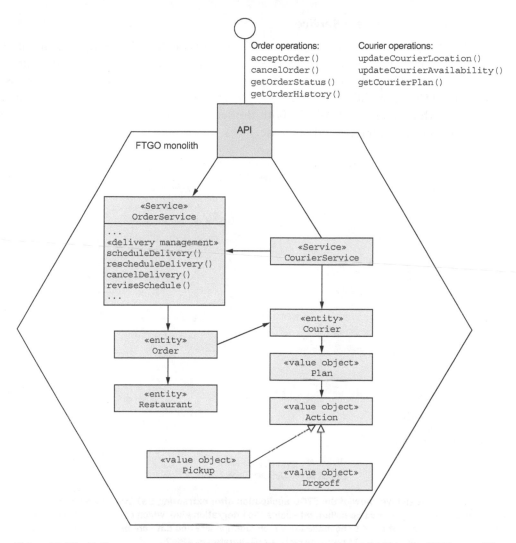

Figure 13.16 Delivery management is entangled with order management within the FTGO monolith.

consider the Courier-related commands and queries to be part of delivery management. After all, delivery management creates the courier plans and is the primary consumer of the Courier location and availability information. But in order to minimize the development effort, we'll leave those operations in the monolith and just extract the core of the algorithm. Consequently, the first iteration of Delivery Service won't expose a publicly accessible API. Instead, it will only be invoked by the monolith. Next, let's explore the design of Delivery Service.

13.5.2 *Overview of Delivery Service*

The proposed new `Delivery Service` is responsible for scheduling, rescheduling, and canceling deliveries. Figure 13.17 shows a high-level view of the architecture of the FTGO application after extracting `Delivery Service`. The architecture consists of the FTGO monolith and `Delivery Service`. They collaborate using the integration glue, which consists of APIs in both the service and monolith. `Delivery Service` has its own domain model and database.

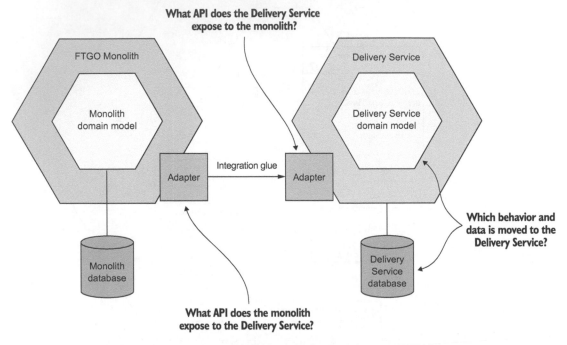

Figure 13.17　The high-level view of the FTGO application after extracting `Delivery Service`. The FTGO monolith and `Delivery Service` collaborate using the integration glue, which consists of APIs in each of them. The two key decisions that need to be made are which functionality and data are moved to `Delivery Service` and how do the monolith and `Delivery Service` collaborate via APIs?

In order to flesh out this architecture and determine the service's domain model, we need to answer the following questions:

- Which behavior and data are moved to `Delivery Service`?
- What API does `Delivery Service` expose to the monolith?
- What API does the monolith expose to `Delivery Service`?

These issues are interrelated because the distribution of responsibilities between the monolith and the service affects the APIs. For instance, `Delivery Service` will need to invoke an API provided by the monolith to access the data in the monolith's database and vice versa. Later, I'll describe the design of the integration glue that enables

Delivery Service and the FTGO monolith to collaborate. But first, let's look at the design of Delivery Service's domain model.

13.5.3 *Designing the Delivery Service domain model*

To be able to extract delivery management, we first need to identify the classes that implement it. Once we've done that, we can decide which classes to move to Delivery Service to form its domain logic. In some cases, we'll need to split classes. We'll also need to decide which data to replicate between the service and the monolith.

Let's start by identifying the classes that implement delivery management.

IDENTIFYING WHICH ENTITIES AND THEIR FIELDS ARE PART OF DELIVERY MANAGEMENT

The first step in the process of designing Delivery Service is to carefully review the delivery management code and identify the participating entities and their fields. Figure 13.18 shows the entities and fields that are part of delivery management. Some fields are inputs to the delivery-scheduling algorithm, and others are the outputs. The figure shows which of those fields are also used by other functionality implemented by the monolith.

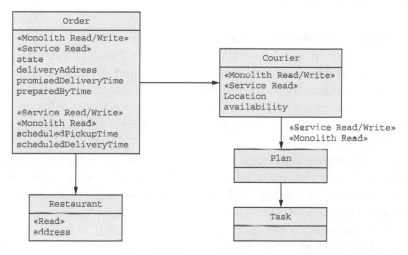

Figure 13.18   The entities and fields that are accessed by delivery management and other functionality implemented by the monolith. A field can be read or written or both. It can be accessed by delivery management, the monolith, or both.

The delivery scheduling algorithm reads various attributes including the Order's restaurant, promisedDeliveryTime, and deliveryAddress, and the Courier's location, availability, and current plans. It updates the Courier's plans, the Order's scheduled-PickupTime, and scheduledDeliveryTime. As you can see, the fields used by delivery management are also used by the monolith.

DECIDING WHICH DATA TO MIGRATE TO DELIVERY SERVICE

Now that we've identified which entities and fields participate in delivery management, the next step is to decide which of them we should move to the service. In an ideal scenario, the data accessed by the service is used exclusively by the service, so we could simply move that data to the service and be done. Sadly, it's rarely that simple, and this situation is no exception. All the entities and fields used by the delivery management are also used by other functionality implemented by the monolith.

As a result, when determining which data to move to the service, we need to keep in mind two issues. The first is: how does the service access the data that remains in the monolith? The second is: how does the monolith access data that's moved to the service? Also, as described earlier in section 13.3, we need to carefully consider how to maintain data consistency between the service and the monolith.

The essential responsibility of `Delivery Service` is managing courier plans and updating the `Order`'s `scheduledPickupTime` and `scheduledDeliveryTime` fields. It makes sense, therefore, for it to own those fields. We could also move the `Courier.location` and `Courier.availability` fields to `Delivery Service`. But because we're trying to make the smallest possible change, we'll leave those fields in the monolith for now.

THE DESIGN OF THE DELIVERY SERVICE DOMAIN LOGIC

Figure 13.19 shows the design of the `Delivery Service`'s domain model. The core of the service consists of domain classes such as `Delivery` and `Courier`. The `Delivery-ServiceImpl` class is the entry point into the delivery management business logic. It implements the `DeliveryService` and `CourierService` interfaces, which are invoked by `DeliveryServiceEventsHandler` and `DeliveryServiceNotificationsHandlers`, described later in this section.

The delivery management business logic is mostly code copied from the monolith. For example, we'll copy the `Order` entity from the monolith to `Delivery Service`, rename it to `Delivery`, and delete all fields except those used by delivery management. We'll also copy the `Courier` entity and delete most of its fields. In order to develop the domain logic for `Delivery Service`, we will need to untangle the code from the monolith. We'll need to break numerous dependencies, which is likely to be time consuming. Once again, it's a lot easier to refactor code when using a statically typed language, because the compiler will be your friend.

`Delivery Service` is not a standalone service. Let's look at the design of the integration glue that enables `Delivery Service` and the FTGO monolith to collaborate.

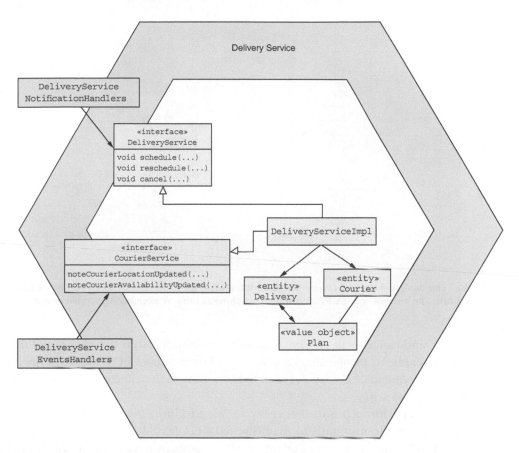

Figure 13.19   The design of the `Delivery Service`**'s domain model**

13.5.4 *The design of the Delivery Service integration glue*

The FTGO monolith needs to invoke `Delivery Service` to manage deliveries. The monolith also needs to exchange data with `Delivery Service`. This collaboration is enabled by the integration glue. Figure 13.20 shows the design of the `Delivery Service` integration glue. `Delivery Service` has a delivery management API. It also publishes `Delivery` and `Courier` domain events. The FTGO monolith publishes `Courier` domain events.

Let's look at the design of each part of the integration glue, starting with `Delivery Service`'s API for managing deliveries.

THE DESIGN OF THE DELIVERY SERVICE API

`Delivery Service` must provide an API that enables the monolith to schedule, revise, and cancel deliveries. As you've seen throughout this book, the preferred approach is to use asynchronous messaging, because it promotes loose coupling and increases availability. One approach is for `Delivery Service` to subscribe to `Order` domain events published by the monolith. Depending on the type of the event, it creates,

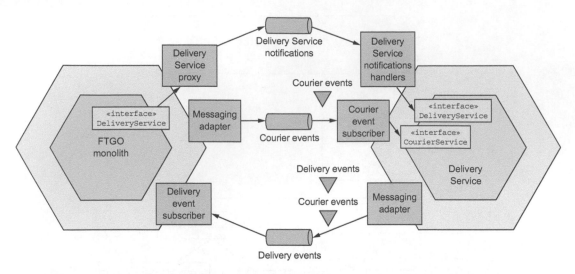

Figure 13.20   The design of the `Delivery Service` integration glue. `Delivery Service` has a delivery management API. The service and the FTGO monolith synchronize data by exchanging domain events.

revises, and cancels a `Delivery`. A benefit of this approach is that the monolith doesn't need to explicitly invoke `Delivery Service`. The drawback of relying on domain events is that it requires `Delivery Service` to know how each `Order` event impacts the corresponding `Delivery`.

A better approach is for `Delivery Service` to implement a notification-based API that enables the monolith to explicitly tell `Delivery Service` to create, revise, and cancel deliveries. `Delivery Service`'s API consists of a message notification channel and three message types: `ScheduleDelivery`, `ReviseDelivery`, or `CancelDelivery`. A notification message contains `Order` information needed by `Delivery Service`. For example, a `ScheduleDelivery` notification contains the pickup time and location and the delivery time and location. An important benefit of this approach is that `Delivery Service` doesn't have detailed knowledge of the `Order` lifecycle. It's entirely focused on managing deliveries and has no knowledge of orders.

This API isn't the only way that `Delivery Service` and the FTGO monolith collaborate. They also need to exchange data.

HOW THE DELIVERY SERVICE ACCESSES THE FTGO MONOLITH'S DATA

`Delivery Service` needs to access the `Courier` location and availability data, which is owned by the monolith. Because that's potentially a large amount of data, it's not practical for the service to repeatedly query the monolith. Instead, a better approach is for the monolith to replicate the data to `Delivery Service` by publishing `Courier` domain events, `CourierLocationUpdated` and `CourierAvailabilityUpdated`. `Delivery Service` has a `CourierEventSubscriber` that subscribes to the domain events and updates its version of the `Courier`. It might also trigger the rescheduling of deliveries.

How the FTGO monolith accesses the Delivery Service data

The FTGO monolith needs to read the data that's been moved to `Delivery Service`, such as the `Courier` plans. In theory, the monolith could query the service, but that requires extensive changes to the monolith. For the time being, it's easier to leave the monolith's domain model and database schema unchanged and replicate data from the service back to the monolith.

The easiest way to accomplish that is for `Delivery Service` to publish `Courier` and `Delivery` domain events. The service publishes a `CourierPlanUpdated` event when it updates a `Courier`'s plan, and a `DeliveryScheduleUpdate` event when it updates a `Delivery`. The monolith consumes these domain events and updates its database.

Now that we've looked at how the FTGO monolith and `Delivery Service` interact, let's see how to change the monolith.

13.5.5 *Changing the FTGO monolith to interact with Delivery Service*

In many ways, implementing `Delivery Service` is the easier part of the extraction process. Modifying the FTGO monolith is much more difficult. Fortunately, replicating data from the service back to the monolith reduces the size of the change. But we still need to change the monolith to manage deliveries by invoking `Delivery Service`. Let's look at how to do that.

Defining a DeliveryService interface

The first step is to encapsulate the delivery management code with a Java interface corresponding to the messaging-based API defined earlier. This interface, shown in figure 13.21, defines methods for scheduling, rescheduling, and canceling deliveries.

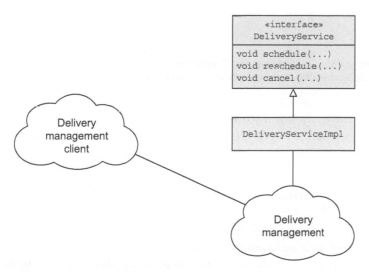

Figure 13.21 The first step is to define `DeliveryService`, which is a coarse-grained, remotable API for invoking the delivery management logic.

Eventually, we'll implement this interface with a proxy that sends messages to the delivery service. But initially, we'll implement this API with a class that calls the delivery management code.

The `DeliveryService` interface is a coarse-grained interface that's well suited to being implemented by an IPC mechanism. It defines `schedule()`, `reschedule()`, and `cancel()` methods, which correspond to the notification message types defined earlier.

REFACTORING THE MONOLITH TO CALL THE DELIVERYSERVICE INTERFACE

Next, as figure 13.22 shows, we need to identify all the places in the FTGO monolith that invoke delivery management and change them to use the `DeliveryService` interface. This may take some time and is one of the most challenging aspects of extracting a service from the monolith.

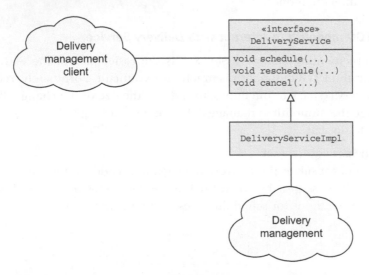

Figure 13.22   The second step is to change the FTGO monolith to invoke delivery management via the `DeliveryService` interface.

It certainly helps if the monolith is written in a statically typed language, such as Java, because the tools do a better job of identifying dependencies. If not, then hopefully you have some automated tests with sufficient coverage of the parts of the code that need to be changed.

IMPLEMENTING THE DELIVERYSERVICE INTERFACE

The final step is to replace the `DeliveryServiceImpl` class with a proxy that sends notification messages to the standalone `Delivery Service`. But rather than discard the existing implementation right away, we'll use a design, shown in figure 13.23, that enables the monolith to dynamically switch between the existing implementation and `Delivery Service`. We'll implement the `DeliveryService` interface with a class that uses a dynamic feature toggle to determine whether to invoke the existing implementation or `Delivery Service`.

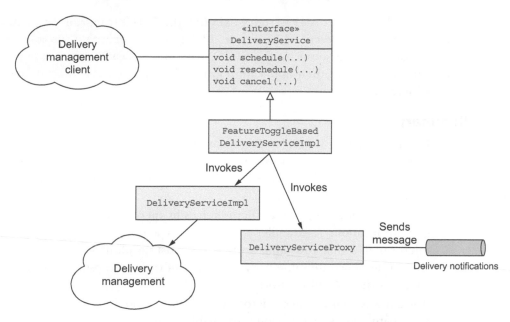

Figure 13.23 **The final step is to implement** `DeliveryService` **with a proxy class that sends messages** `Delivery Service`. **A feature toggle controls whether the FTGO monolith uses the old implementation or the new** `Delivery Service`.

Using a feature toggle significantly reduces the risk of rolling out `Delivery Service`. We can deploy `Delivery Service` and test it. And then, once we're sure it works, we can flip the toggle to route traffic to it. If we then discover that `Delivery Service` isn't working as expected, we can switch back to the old implementation.

About feature toggles

Feature toggles, or *feature flags*, let you deploy code changes without necessarily releasing them to users. They also enable you to dynamically change the behavior of the application by deploying new code. This article by Martin Fowler provides an excellent overview of the topic: https://martinfowler.com/articles/feature-toggles .html.

Once we're sure that `Delivery Service` is working as expected, we can then remove the delivery management code from the monolith.

`Delivery Service` and `Delayed Order Service` are examples of the services that the FTGO team will develop during their journey to the microservice architecture. Where they go next after implementing these services depends on the priorities of the business. One possible path is to extract `Order History Service`, described in chapter 7. Extracting this service partially eliminates the need for `Delivery Service` to replicate data back to the monolith.

After implementing `Order History Service`, the FTGO team can then extract the services in the order described in section 13.3.2: `Order Service`, `Consumer Service`, `Kitchen Service`, and so on. As the FTGO team extracts each service, the maintainability and testability of their application gradually improves, and their development velocity increases.

Summary

- Before migrating to a microservice architecture, it's important to be sure that your software delivery problems are a result of having outgrown your monolithic architecture. You might be able to accelerate delivery by improving your software development process.

- It's important to migrate to microservices by incrementally developing a strangler application. A strangler application is a new application consisting of microservices that you build around the existing monolithic application. You should demonstrate value early and often in order to ensure that the business supports the migration effort.

- A great way to introduce microservices into your architecture is to implement new features as services. Doing so enables you to quickly and easily develop a feature using a modern technology and development process. It's a good way to quickly demonstrate the value of migrating to microservices.

- One way to break up the monolith is to separate the presentation tier from the backend, which results in two smaller monoliths. Although it's not a huge improvement, it does mean that you can deploy each monolith independently. This allows, for example, the UI team to iterate more easily on the UI design without impacting the backend.

- The main way to break up the monolith is by incrementally migrating functionality from the monolith into services. It's important to focus on extracting the services that provide the most benefit. For example, you'll accelerate development if you extract a service that implements functionality that's being actively developed.

- Newly developed services almost always have to interact with the monolith. A service often needs to access a monolith's data and invoke its functionality. The monolith sometimes needs to access a service's data and invoke its functionality. To implement this collaboration, develop integration glue, which consists of inbound and outbound adapters in the monolith.

- To prevent the monolith's domain model from polluting the service's domain model, the integration glue should use an anti-corruption layer, which is a layer of software that translates between domain models.

- One way to minimize the impact on the monolith of extracting a service is to replicate the data that was moved to the service back to the monolith's database. Because the monolith's schema is left unchanged, this eliminates the need to make potentially widespread changes to the monolith code base.

- Developing a service often requires you to implement sagas that involve the monolith. But it can be challenging to implement a compensatable transaction that requires making widespread changes to the monolith. Consequently, you sometimes need to carefully sequence the extraction of services to avoid implementing compensatable transactions in the monolith.
- When refactoring to a microservice architecture, you need to simultaneously support the monolithic application's existing security mechanism, which is often based on an in-memory session, and the token-based security mechanism used by the services. Fortunately, a simple solution is to modify the monolith's login handler to generate a cookie containing a security token, which is then forwarded to the services by the API gateway.

index